Ambivalent
Neighbors

Ambivalent
<u>Neighbors</u>

The EU, NATO, and the Price of Membership

Anatol Lieven and Dmitri Trenin, Editors

CARNEGIE ENDOWMENT FOR INTERNATIONAL PEACE
Washington, D.C.

9021264

Carnegie Endowment for International Peace
1779 Massachusetts Avenue, N.W., Washington, D.C. 20036
202-483-7600   www.ceip.org

*The Carnegie Endowment normally does not take institutional positions on public policy issues;
the views and recommendations presented in this publication do not necessarily represent the views
of the Carnegie Endowment, its officers, staff, or trustees.*

To order, contact Carnegie's distributor:
The Brookings Institution Press
Department 029, Washington, D.C. 20042-0029, USA
1-800-275-1447 or 1-202-797-6258

Composition by Oakland Street Publishing. Text set in ITC Berkeley.
Printed by Malloy Lithographing, Inc., on acid-free paper (85% recycled content).

Library of Congress Cataloging-in-Publication Data

Ambivalent neighbors : the EU, NATO and the price of membership / Anatol Lieven
and Dmitri Trenin, editors.
    p. cm.
   ISBN 0-87003-199-6 (pbk : alk. paper) -- ISBN 0-87003-200-3 (cloth)
   1. European Union--Europe, Eastern. 2. North Atlantic Treaty Organization--
Membership. 3. National security--Europe. 4. Europe--Economic integration.
I. Lieven, Anatol. II. Trenin, Dmitriæi. III. Title.
   HC240.25.E852 A43 2002
   341.242'2--dc21

                                                              2002013915

09 08 07 06 05 04   5 4 3 2 1   1st Printing 2003

Contents

Foreword

Almost fifteen years after the end of the cold war, the process of creating a "Europe whole and free" is anything but complete and is unlikely to be so for the foreseeable future. This volume of essays examines the complex and interrelated processes of NATO and European Union enlargement in the context of the changed global situation since the terrorist attacks of September 11, 2001.

The intention in commissioning these essays was to view enlargement not only from the perspective of the west, but also from the point of view of those knocking at the door: the former communist countries themselves. This approach reflects the editors' conviction that the eastward movement of NATO and the EU should not be regarded simply as western-led processes to which the eastern states must adapt as best they can. If an enlarged NATO and EU are to be stable and successful in the long run, they must take due account not only of the wishes and interests of their would-be new members, but also of those European states which will not for the foreseeable future be admitted to NATO, the EU, or both.

The essays in this volume therefore were commissioned from a highly distinguished groups of contributors from both east and west. They do not treat the dual enlargements as unquestionably positive, but also try to bring out some of their more ambiguous and even negative aspects. They explain why—for different reasons—enlargement has provoked fear and hostility in some of the affected countries. They also try to explain why, in the case of the EU, this hostility has appeared extensively even in countries like Poland which have been seen for many years as deeply committed to westernization. They pay attention to the interests and concerns of elderly Polish farmers and small traders in Kaliningrad as well as to those of governments.

While none of these essays deals directly with the consequences of the September 11 attacks, most have inevitably been influenced by them. As of 2002, it seems that despite their dreadful nature, the impact of the attacks on international affairs has not been wholly bad. Despite fears that NATO enlargement would lead to a breakdown in relations with Russia, 2001–2002 in fact saw a very significant U.S.–Russian rapprochement; and a key reason for this was a new perception of shared interest in fighting terrorism.

There now seems a real possibility of fruitful NATO–Russian cooperation, embodied in a new council in which Russia has the right of consultation on a range of issues. However, it must also be said that this comes at a time when the future of NATO itself, and NATO's role in the war against terrorism, are far from clear. There is a danger that the new members are joining NATO just as the Alliance itself is becoming less significant as an organization, due in part to a certain preference on the part of the Bush administration for the creation of ad hoc groupings in which it is not necessary to seek unanimous agreement for any U.S. action.

The enlargement of the EU has proved vastly more difficult than that of NATO; as of early 2003, the EU had not in fact succeeded in admitting a single member from the former communist bloc. Moreover, the EU itself has been racked by endless and agonizing internal disputes about the changes it must make in order to admit new members from eastern and central Europe—especially as regards the Common Agricultural Policy and EU collective decision making. As several of the authors of this volume explain, this long-drawn-out process risks creating a dangerous mood of disillusionment and bitterness among applicants for EU membership.

And as this volume also brings out, beyond the question of how and when the EU will be able to admit Poland and the other front-ranking applicants looms the even more complicated question of long-term relations with countries that cannot become EU members in the foreseeable future: Romania, Ukraine, Russia, and probably Turkey. At present, all too many EU policies on trade and immigration are tending not to unite the whole of Europe but to draw a new wall down the middle of the continent.

If the integration of Europe is to proceed, this will require not just major changes in the presently excluded countries, but also real vision and generosity on the part of the west. A generation has now grown up in eastern Europe that hardly remembers communism at all. Unfortunately, it has also grown up with a strong awareness of continuing deep socioeconomic differences between the former communist states and those of the west. As the essays in this volume argue, these differences must be dramatically reduced before we can truly speak of a united Europe.

We are very grateful to the Carnegie Corporation of New York, the Charles Stewart Mott Foundation, and the Starr Foundation for their support of the Carnegie Moscow Center and the Endowment's Russian and Eurasian Program, which has made this book possible.

Jessica T. Mathews
President
Carnegie Endowment for International Peace

Acknowledgments

This volume was a collaborative effort, in which thanks are due to many people. First of all, of course, we would like to thank the authors of these essays both for their contributions and for their patience and helpfulness in the process of editing and updating—a process made much longer than expected by the crisis in international affairs brought on by the tragic events of September 11, 2001.

We would like to express our gratitude to our colleagues at the Carnegie Endowment in Washington and the Carnegie Moscow Center for all their help and support. Thanks are due to Tom Carothers, who was then vice president for studies, Andrew Kuchins, director of the Russian and Eurasian Program, and also Stephen Holmes of New York University for their support for the whole project, and for reading the manuscript and making numerous valuable suggestions.

The Carnegie publications team, Trish Reynolds and Sherry Pettie, conducted the whole publications process with exemplary professionalism and smoothness. Copy editor Alfred Imhoff did a quite outstanding job of not only correcting but improving the text. Ann Stecker was an indispensable figure in the organization of the entire project. And Marat Umerov and Zhanara Nauruzbayeva were of great help both with research and with tracking down errant citations.

Anatol Lieven
Dmitri Trenin

Ambivalent
Neighbors

1

Introduction: The Grand Redesign

Dmitri Trenin

It took the dust raised by the fall of the Berlin wall a rather long time to set-tle—for good reasons. The end of communism as a system of oppressive government and a powerful ideology; the demise of its standard bearer, the Soviet Union, resulting in the collapse of its global glacis, of its outer empire in eastern Europe, and then of the historical Russian *derzhava*; and last but not least, the end of the cold war, a 40-year-long military standoff, the most intense in history, coupled with the collapse of Soviet and Russian military might—all of these events had come so unexpectedly that, by definition, no one could have been prepared for them. In response to these dramatic changes, the principal western European military and political institutions, the North Atlantic Treaty Organization (NATO) and the European Union, took a generally cautious line, which could be explained by the predilections of multilateral bureaucracies. The western governments, for their part (with the natural exception of the former German Democratic Republic), shied away from resolute steps toward the liberated east and focused instead on reforming the winning west.

There was nothing like what had followed the end of World War II in Europe. No Marshall Plan was immediately proposed and no integration of former adversaries occurred; but no major crises erupted, and those which did, as in the Balkans, were very nasty but also rather peripheral, so that they could be contained. The cold war was succeeded not by a new era but by a

1

historical pause, an interlude characteristically named the post–cold war, because people on both sides of the former divide were not sure what they were stepping into. The Berlin wall was quietly dismantled, but much of the military and mental infrastructure of the confrontation which had led to its construction essentially survived. Bold wise people were nowhere to be seen. Instead, caution became the watchword in the west; at times, it was interpreted as egotism and indecisiveness by those who aspired to join western institutions, and as a proof of ulterior motives by those who held no such aspirations.

Now, a dozen years later, the interlude may finally be over. The beginning of the first decade of the new century is witnessing the deepening of the EU integration process, as evidenced by both the surprisingly smooth introduction of the euro and the efforts to develop a common foreign and defense policy twinned with a European security and defense identity. The EU is working on its constitution in order to be able to take in the first batch of members from central and eastern Europe by the mid-2000s. NATO, which was in fact enlarged in 1999, is formally preparing for a second and much bigger intake of former Warsaw Pact–Baltic countries. At the same time, however, as Anatol Lieven describes in the concluding chapter, NATO is seriously questioning its own future in a profoundly altered strategic environment.

On the face of it, Europe has already become EU-centric economically, and in the field of security, NATO-centric. The former Warsaw Pact–Council for Mutual Economic Assistance member countries are being absorbed into the new system, while others, including Russia and Ukraine, are looking for ways and means to associate themselves with it. The real importance of the September 2001 decision by Russian president Vladimir Putin to side with the United States and the west in the fight against international terrorism has been Moscow's unilateral withdrawal from competition with Washington in the fields of geopolitics and nuclear weapons. Based on a correct reading by Putin of Russia's domestic needs, this decision is backed by compelling and powerful economic interests and is unlikely to be reversed by Putin or his successors. There may be ups and downs in U.S.–Russian relations, but the rivalry is finally over.

There was no grand conference following the end of the cold war. Yet a settlement of sorts has been achieved. The "new west" is enthusiastically joining the old one, which reluctantly welcomes it—on certain conditions. A greater, or at least wider, Europe is emerging, consisting of EU and NATO members and their associates or partners. Yet these gains for prosperity and security can only be consolidated and made permanent through a fundamental redesign of both premier European and transatlantic institutions and the establishment of solid relations between these institutions and the countries in the geographical Europe that are unlikely, for the foreseeable future, to become part of the integrated unit. A failure to undertake either one of these tasks could halt the positive trends and release some of the demons of Europe's past.

This book treats the enlargement of European and Atlantic institutions as an equivalent of the postconfrontational settlement. It addresses the implications of the dual enlargement of the EU and NATO for all those concerned: the candidates, the core members, and the countries left out. The authors of the chapters come from all three groups of countries and offer their insights into the current Europewide processes from very different angles. The focus is very much on the EU and NATO. Although a more inclusive forum, whose membership has also been expanding since the fall of the iron curtain—namely, the Council of Europe—is mentioned only in passing, its role as the norm-setting and monitoring organization promoting European values is not negligible, as Russia's experience in Chechnya demonstrates.

The book, as its title suggests, focuses on a major part of this agenda, with the notable exception of the challenges related to the Balkans and Turkey. Dealing with the Albanian question and encouraging Serbia's progressive transformation will be anything but easy. "Fitting Turkey in" is only slightly less complicated than performing a similar feat with regard to Russia. Similarly, the book does not tackle the Mediterranean dimension, although Cyprus and Turkey bring the EU into direct proximity to the Middle East. The southern Caucasus and central Asia are just over the horizon, despite their new importance linked to the fight against international terrorism and the yearnings of at least one country, Georgia, to join both NATO and the EU. Even then, however, the subject of the present study is vast by any measure.

Great Expectations, Great Fears

It may now look as if the great expectations of 1989 and 1990 are at long last being realized. When the Yalta system was cheerfully dumped into the sea off the coast of Malta by George H. W. Bush and Mikhail Gorbachev, the vision of a "Europe whole and free" first moved within reach. Various politicians gave it different names, from the European confederation to a European peace order to a common European home. To all of them, however, the end of history prophesied by Francis Fukuyama seemed near. Freedom, democracy, and the market were deemed destined to prevail, releasing the energies which, it was believed, would soon make the former communist-ruled countries both liberal and prosperous. In many cases, these visions turned out to be mirages created by the flying dust of the Berlin wall.

The great expectations were mixed with great fears, of course. Once left alone by Moscow to fend for themselves, the eastern European communist regimes were giving way easily. Only in Romania was there significant bloodletting. Beyond the outer ring of the Soviet sphere of dominance, however, real trouble was looming. Empires had rarely left the historical scene without a battle, and what usually emerged in their wake was the chaos of ethnic strife. At the turn of the 1990s, the pitch of ethnic tension had been rising in both Yugoslavia and the Soviet Union itself, and violent conflicts were already erupting. The Balkan imbroglio was serious enough, but most people at the time viewed it as a preview for what could happen in the USSR. Never before had a nuclear superpower gone down, and its approaching breakup into independent and potentially hostile parts was being watched with great anxiety, even awe. And until virtually the eleventh hour—which was probably November 1991—no one could guarantee the ratification by the Soviet military, which had suddenly found itself without a master, of what to so many outsiders was already a verdict of history.

The immediate fears were only partially borne out by actual developments. There were violent conflicts and immense dislocations, but no civil war erupted. The Soviet communist elite, mellowed by the corruptible stagnation of the Brezhnevite era, was content, as the Russian quip at the time went, to "swap power for property." The military top brass, out of spite for Gorbachev, switched their allegiance to his rival Boris Yeltsin, in return for the promise of a free hand *within* the defense establishment. The liberal advisors to Yeltsin, who worshipped the invisible hand of the market and dreamed of "rejoining the west," were only glad to let go those republics which wished to go and to push away those which were still undecided. The deal rested on the inviolability of the existing, and often totally arbitrarily drawn, inter-republican borders, which at the same time were left fully transparent, creating the fiction of a continuing "common space" and thus successfully cushioning the populace from the shock of separation. The unity of command of the nuclear forces was successfully maintained, as was the security of the weapons themselves, and Washington and Moscow together leaned on the republics hard enough to ensure that no nuclear proliferation occurred.

Yugoslavia, of course, fared far worse. It is a sad irony indeed that only a decade before the country had been considered a potential candidate for membership in the European Economic Community. Where the Russians were the tired imperialists, the Serbs saw themselves as the aggrieved party and became violently aggressive. In Croatia, unlike in Ukraine, the presence of ethnic minorities fueled nationalism instead of inspiring moderation. The tragedy of Bosnia finally awakened Europe and the United States to the challenges of post–cold war settlement, but the immediate concern of the west was to contain the crisis so as to avoid its spillover beyond the former Yugoslavia. The European Union soon found itself unready and unwilling to get fully involved on the ground. It preferred to wait until the United States finally decided to enter the fray and impose peace on the warring parties. Still, the image of Sarajevo being slowly and methodically destroyed made the picture of jubilation atop the Berlin wall look dated and distant. Fukuyama was out, and Samuel Huntington was in.

Self-Selection

Actually, the first former communist state to join with the west was East Germany. With the prospect of Soviet military intervention removed by Gorbachev, the jubilant people of East Berlin, Leipzig, and Dresden soon replaced the slogan *wir sind das Volk* with *wir sind ein Volk*. Such was the overwhelming will of the people in the east that it helped set the agenda, and the timetable, in Bonn. There was little that the Four Powers could do other than ratify the will of the German nation. The German Democratic Republic's lightning-like absorption into the German Federal Republic in October 1990 was actually the first case of EU and NATO enlargement across the iron curtain.

Once the curtain was opened, the differences among the former communist-ruled countries became stark. Cold war Eastern Europe was suddenly no more, replaced by central Europe (Poland, the Czech Republic, Hungary, Slovenia, Slovakia), the Baltic states, southeastern Europe (Romania, Bulgaria, Moldova, Albania, and the states of the former Yugoslavia), and finally the new eastern Europe (Ukraine, Belarus, and Russia). The countries of the southern Caucasus were barely visible on the far edge of that picture, and the republics of central Asia, dismissively and half-derogatorily referred to as the "stans," were decidedly beyond it. The defining criterion was not so much per capita gross domestic product or standard of living as it was the political, economic, and societal culture—a culture that, as Alexander Motyl puts it in chapter 2 to follow, promised very different roads leading out of communism.

Even the East German *Länder*, a special case by all counts, found it hard to deal with the legacy of different varieties of totalitarian rule preceded by a long stretch of authoritarian rule. The rehabilitation of the former German Democratic Republic, which has been costing German taxpayers about $50 billion a year since reunification, should serve as both a test case and a warning for all three groups of countries that emerged after the collapse of the Soviet system.

The first group, once known as the Visegrad countries, quickly went beyond the option of forming a community *next to* the west, in the form of a NATO-bis or a central European economic unit. Instead, their elites set the goal of integration *into* the west, quickly achieved a domestic consensus, and started to work towards the goal. The second group ostensibly proclaimed the same goal, but was distracted and held back by their own demons of the past, ranging from ethnic hatred to political parochialism, and essentially marked time. The third group first had to seriously tackle their Soviet (and in Russia's case, imperial) legacy before they could secure any lasting results.

This self-differentiation had a major effect on the policies of the western countries. The first group, aided by its lobbyists within the western community, worked hard to make the west open up its institutions to the new arrivals. They zeroed in on NATO as the essential western club of the cold war (which was still very much on their minds), and the one where obtaining membership required mainly political action, not the much more difficult economic transformation. This was the right calculation, even though not all first-group countries were admitted to NATO in the first wave of candidates. The admission to NATO of Poland, Hungary, and the Czech Republic was the first breach that the former easterners succeeded in making in the walls of the western fortress. A new eastern march has emerged.

The second group tried to make the west pay attention by highlighting their problems. They pointed to the example of Yugoslavia, arguing that the best way to ensure that other countries did not follow that path would be to include them within the western community. The west listened with sympathy; but as William Wallace and Heather Grabbe point out in chapters 3 and 4, respectively, it was essentially unimpressed by these pleas, demanding real domestic progress in the applicant countries. Yet NATO and the EU had to get involved directly in the Balkans, in particular by assuming responsibility for Bosnia-Herzegovina and Kosovo, which have become de facto western protectorates. Even the nominally sovereign nations of Macedonia and Serbia-Montenegro are actually leaning on the EU as its client states. Thus a glacis or, better, an area of long-term responsibility is being formed by and for the west in the Balkans. At best, this is Europe's new frontier, a kind of wild southeast to be pacified and helped along towards prosperity; at worst, it is a buffer zone between the "civilized world" and its restive southeastern neighbors.

The third group exhibited the widest range of difficulties in the process of postcommunist transformation. Apart from the economic, political, and economic problems, all more fundamental than in either of the two previous groups, there came up the issue of identity. As Leonid Zaiko demonstrates in chapter 5, the Belarusians were faced with the challenge of building a national identity in a society which was perhaps the least nationalistic anywhere in the former Soviet empire. By the late 1990s, they ended up with an identity built around the figure of a neo-Soviet populist dictator who made this former "assembly line of USSR industry" into a place *very* different from all neighboring countries—east, west, north, or south. The Ukrainians, endowed with a strong nationalistic current, by contrast, faced up to the need to keep their country from breaking into several parts. In chapter 6, James Sherr depicts the sophisticated and so far successful balancing act being played by Kiev, for which "the east" and "the west" are both foreign *and* domestic policy notions.

The Russians spent much of the 1990s exiting from their empire. Though this departure is by no means over, they have gone through a number of stages, getting ever closer to the reality of their country's new position. Gone is the hope of becoming a fellow democratic superpower alongside the United States. Also gone is the attempt to fashion Russia as a first-order pole in a multipolar world, which would constrain American power. Finally, Russia the European country enters. This latest self-image is likely to stay. But the question is, What does it actually mean? Will this "Europeanness" resemble the picture of a prerevolutionary Russia, a continental empire with an arguably western facade, or will it mean modernity coupled with genuine western values? The former would mean Russia's further alienation from Europe; the latter, Russia fundamentally transforming itself.

So far, Russia has been, at best, *drifting* towards Europe. Over time, it has become much more aware of the intricacies of the EU. In 1994, it concluded a Partnership and Cooperation Agreement with the Union, aimed at creating a free-trade area. In 2001, an idea of a European economic space that would *include* Russia was first floated. In more practical terms, an energy partnership is being actively promoted. As a result of the EU's enlargement, the share of Europe in Russia's foreign trade will rise from the current 40 to about 50 percent. The Kremlin's public relations team has promoted a new slogan, "Russia—to Europe, together with Ukraine and Belarus." As Alexander Sergounin argues in chapter 7, the more immediate and compelling problem, however, is how to prevent the Kaliningrad Region from becoming a disaster area for Russia and a "black hole" inside the EU territory. Even though this "exclave" (or enclave) is a natural place for launching various EU–Russian cooperative projects, the immediate focus is the more contentious issues of communications and visas.

Before Kaliningrad demonstrated that EU enlargement can actually bite, Moscow had been considering the expanding EU as an alternative to NATO's extension to the east. Russia's post-1991 relations with NATO had been largely contentious. From the start, Moscow demanded exclusiveness and status to compensate for its growing weakness.

Unlike the former Warsaw Pact countries and ex-Soviet republics, Russia raised the problem of how to treat a former adversary. Immediately after the breakup of the USSR, some viewed this problem in terms of an alternative between "doing another Versailles" and proposing a new Marshall Plan. In fact, neither had a chance of becoming a reality. On the one hand, Russia of course was treated far more generously than post-1919 Germany. On the other hand, it was neither militarily defeated nor occupied by foreign forces, as Germany had been after 1945 to ensure a clean slate and enable a deep transformation. And there was no immediate common threat from a third party of a caliber which would have united the former cold war adversaries. The fight against international terrorism forms too narrow a basis for security integration. The new NATO–Russia Council, inaugurated in 2002, faces a difficult task to promote inclusivity and participation. Having ceased to be a threat to the west, Russia to this day has not become a place of opportunity.

Changes at the Core

It was the first post–cold war enlargement of the west—that is, the reunifi-cation of Germany in the fall of 1990—that pushed the process of European integration. The 1992 Treaty of Maastricht with its promise of a common currency, realized ten years later, had its roots in the perceived need to embed a united Germany within a more integrated Europe. The challenge of taking in new members from the traditionally poor, for decades com-munist-ruled part of Europe was also different, in both scale and kind, from the previous cases of European Community and European Union expan-sion. Thus, a slogan was born: "Deepen before you widen." Thus the promises of accession made in 1998–2000 to the 12 nations of central and eastern Europe and Turkey stimulated the internal reform of the EU; for it was felt, correctly, that the current structure and modus operandi could not be sustained when EU membership grew to 27 or 28.

The commitment to expansion made the EU *as a unit* come to grips with relations with the EU's "near abroad," that is, the left-outs—from the Balkans to the Commonwealth of Independent States to north Africa. The drafting of EU policy papers on Russia (1999) and Ukraine (2000) was a reflection of the Union's expanding field of vision as it prepared for its forthcoming geographical enlargement. This need to act as a Union rather than as a group of sovereign nation-states has also strengthened the incentive for a common EU foreign, security, and defense policy.

NATO started changing, timidly at first, after its 1990 London declara-tion. The founding of the North Atlantic Cooperation Council in 1991, which coincided with the formal dissolution of the USSR, became a step towards a politicization of the hitherto essentially military Alliance. The 1994 offer of a Partnership for Peace expanded that role through a range of programs promoting defense reform in the two dozen eastern partner coun-tries. The decision to invite the central European countries to join did not involve serious changes within NATO, but it clearly underlined the fact that the Alliance's mission had changed.

While political caution and bureaucratic conservatism still formally kept NATO wedded to its traditional collective defense function, this func-tion was becoming less and less relevant. NATO leaders recognized this reality in approving the Combined Joint Task Force project, which allowed for non-NATO participation. NATO-led peace operations in Bosnia, Kosovo, and Macedonia involved military contingents from a number of countries which aspired to NATO membership, but also from those which did not.

The NATO applicant queue is long, and expanding to, say, 30 members will have serious implications, which are not only related to decision-making arrangements, military capabilities, and compatibility. A much wider NATO would be less a defense bloc than a collective security mechanism. The accession of Romania and a new joint forum with Russia are highly indicative of NATO's evolution. At the same time, the rise of the far right in western Europe makes the old NATO function of preventing a renationalization of defense and security much more relevant than at the height of the cold war.

In the 1990s, NATO was enlarged in another way as well. The European Union singularly failed as the principal provider of security in the Balkans. After initial U.S. hesitation, NATO went beyond its former region and also beyond defense. It first became a peace enforcer in Bosnia, and then it waged an air campaign against Yugoslavia over Kosovo, where it continued as a security force on the ground. It also intervened in Macedonia to stave off the crisis there. This expansion of NATO's mission and region of operation, codified in its 1999 Strategic Concept, has given it a prime responsibility as a crisis manager in the loosely defined Euro-Atlantic area.

Both the deepening of the western institutions and their widening have contributed to differentiation within the EU and NATO. At some level, within the EU there is a hard core consisting essentially of Germany, France, and the Benelux countries, with concentric circles around it: the western partial opt-outs, like the United Kingdom, Denmark, and Sweden, with Italy on the borderline between the core and the first circle; the poorer southern European countries; the new arrivals from central Europe; the candidates; and the more distant associates like Ukraine and Russia. At another level, there is a dynamic balance between the nation-state and the supranational union, with the former not necessarily continuing to surrender its powers to the latter.

Essentially, the EU's core needs to decide what it wants to be internally (in terms of the Union's constitution) and internationally (what kind of a global player it wants to be). What is the right balance between the supranational and the national? How much of a single player will the EU be, and how much an assembly of individual and still partially sovereign players? Very important, in the post–September 11 situation, is the big question of the availability of the political will to make much-needed, if painful, changes.

The Demise of the Alternatives

Between them, the European Union and NATO are so preeminent in economic, political, security, and defense matters as to exclude any alternatives. Few nations considered investing in the Organization for Security and Cooperation in Europe (OSCE) as the overarching European security institution. No United Nations–type European security council came into being. Finally, Russia, as the chief promoter of the idea, lost faith in the organization as a result of its criticism of the Chechen war. The OSCE, whose membership includes the whole of Europe as well as central Asia and the Caucasus, must look for a different, and smaller, niche. It can successfully function as a continentwide assembly, a human rights monitor, and a facilitator of democracy.

Nor did any credible alternative emerge at the regional level. The short-lived idea of a central European grouping has already been mentioned. The Baltic states, curiously, refuse to be counted as a group, with the Estonians, as Zaneta Ozolina points out, calling themselves Nordic, and the Lithuanians, central European. Further to the east, the post-Soviet Commonwealth of Independent States has remained a loose post-imperial arrangement rather than becoming an integrationist organization. Whether in the economic area (the Customs Union and the Eurasian Economic Community) or in the field of security (the Collective Security Treaty), its record has been less than impressive. However, the rival groupings such as GUUAM (Georgia, Ukraine, Uzbekistan, Azerbaijan, and Moldova) and the regional forums, such as the Central Asian Union, are even less viable, with interaction there being skin-deep.

Within the traditional west, neutrality is definitely passé. The accession of Austria, Sweden, and Finland to the European Union in 1995 makes them subject to a common foreign, security, and defense policy. It is not unthinkable that some of these countries may join NATO before 2010. Within the same time frame, Norway (a founding member of NATO) may overcome its lingering doubts and finally decide to accede to the EU. This would leave Switzerland as the only surviving neutral country on the continent, but the 2002 Swiss vote to apply for United Nations membership demonstrates the general trend.

As a result, not only does the west enlarge, but the east gradually disappears—*as an alternative*. There are many divisions and fault lines, to be sure, but no competition between "the west and the rest" within Europe. This development is of historical importance. The former center is now "east of the west"—its moving frontier—and "the rest" is essentially a periphery.

Politically, the postcommunist, and especially post-Soviet regimes, are often imitations of democracy, but they all are aware of the implications of being placed too close to the west. Serbia's Slobodan Milosevic lost power as the electorate became emboldened by the promise of a better—"European"—future. Belarus's Alexander Lukashenko feels exposed due to a common border with a NATO country. Actually, Lukashenko is hardly the worst post-Soviet dictator; his chief problem is that Belarus is located in eastern Europe, not central Asia.

It is interesting that it is the EU portion of Europe that is being seen by ethnic Russians in the Baltic states and part of the population of Kaliningrad as the prime vehicle for the positive change to which they aspire. The future "Eurorussians" in Estonia and Latvia in particular expect the EU to work as a great equalizer, allowing them to improve their chances vis-à-vis the dominant majorities. This hope may have been one of the factors which so far have guaranteed the remarkably nonviolent interethnic relations in the Baltic countries. The positive effect may not be exhausted with the inclusion of Estonia, Latvia, and Lithuania in the EU.

The demonstration effect of Baltic EU membership on Russia—and to some extent on Belarus—should not be underestimated. To the extent that they are successful, the hundreds of thousands of Eurorussians will act as another powerful argument for a deeper economic transformation of Russia itself. In more general terms, the gap between central Europe and the Baltic states on the one hand and the new eastern Europe of Belarus, Ukraine, and Russia on the other can cut both ways. It is likely to stimulate the feeling of exclusion, and lead to alienation, despair, and the rise of anti-western attitudes among both elites and publics. At the same time, the success of the former inmates of the same "socialist camp" could increase pressure for reform and modernization.

Common Space, Uneven Terrain

All this raises the need to rethink the concept of "the west," which in its present form is a product of the cold war confrontation between communism and the free world. As a result of the east drawing closer to the west, something like "the north" is slowly emerging, which is a more relevant concept in the context of the early twenty-first century. This new large space will include North America and the whole of Europe (i.e., with Russia). This community is only partly institutionalized (NATO, the EU, the North American Free Trade Agreement) and is not to be confused with the anti-terrorist coalition. The issue of Russian membership in NATO, discussed in chapter 8 by Karl-Heinz Kamp, is not and will not be the order of the day. Rather, the salient feature of the new arrangement could be the absence of traditional great-power competition among its informal members. This in turn can serve as a basis for creating a zone of stable peace spanning the northern third or quarter of the globe.

The new space of the north, however, is highly uneven. The authors of this volume analyze the many problems of the candidates for NATO and EU membership, and the implications of the western enlargement for the left-outs. The rise of parochial economic interests in many of the candidate countries and the resultant political backlash against modernization and globalization, are all too evident—but natural—as Christopher Bobinski and Charles King demonstrate in chapters 10 and 11, respectively. Even in the new NATO armies, certain Warsaw Pact habits die hard. To deal successfully with these issues will be a leadership test for the new elites in the "new west."

The enormity of the task of reforming Russia—and Ukraine, for that matter—is daunting. Russia's medium-term objective should be to achieve compatibility with the European Union. On the issue of entry into the World Trade Organization, those who regard themselves as competitive are pitted against sure losers, and the battle is real and hard-fought. In chapter 12, Vladimir Baranovsky describes the changing Russian attitudes towards both the EU and NATO. The more forward-looking Russian leaders boast of having read Ludwig Ehrhardt's books, but few even among them give enough thought to the fact that without Konrad Adenauer's Westbindung there would not have been Ehrhardt's Wirtschaftswunder. At the other end of the spectrum, even as the Russian president is withdrawing from geo-political and strategic competition with the west, the Russian Orthodox Church is fighting fierce battles against "encroachments" by the Vatican into its "canonical territory," Ukraine, Belarus, and Russia proper. In this fight, the Moscow patriarchate is using its enhanced influence in the councils of the Russian state.

This is, however, not the whole story. The opening to the east and south-east heightens tension which is already there within the mature western countries. Fear of immigrants—who will compete for jobs, drive wages down, and eventually bring their families and thus change the very complexion of European societies—is very powerful. As Joerg Haider in Austria, Jean-Marie Le Pen in France, and others across the continent have demonstrated, this fear can strike at the very foundation of the European Union. The backlash reaches beyond "fortress Europe"; unless checked, it could send things back to the kind of divisions and tensions which prevailed before 1945. This counterattack probably will not succeed, but the notion that "history is not bunk" applies to the affluent west as much as to the destitute east.

The real problem is the unwillingness to tackle the difficult issues. The near-paralysis of political will in western Europe, which contrasts so starkly with America's post–September 11 strong resolve, is not only hindering the EU from exercising a more active international role; it may have consequences closer to home. In this day and age, most of these difficult issues revolve around attitudes towards the Muslim world—both on Europe's fringes and within the EU itself. It should be made clear that what is needed is big-picture thinking. Yet much of the political discussion in the "old west" is still dominated by the parochial issues of pensions and welfare benefits. The opening to the east will not "save" western Europe, to be sure. But it could at least make it think big.

2

Ukraine, Europe, and Russia: Exclusion or Dependence?

Alexander J. Motyl

Although the European Union will probably expand into east-central Europe at least by 2010, it will almost certainly not incorporate Ukraine at any time in the foreseeable future—say, by 2030. What, then, are the likely consequences of EU enlargement for Ukraine? Continued exclusion from Europe need not directly result in Ukraine's increasing dependence on Russia, but it will facilitate such an outcome. Moreover, Ukraine's isolation from Europe—especially in conjunction with isolation from globalization— is likely to reinforce already existing tendencies in both Ukraine and Russia towards political authoritarianism and away from economic liberalism. Isolated and authoritarian, Ukraine and Russia will be inclined either to join in an unequal partnership against the west or to enter into a conflictual relationship with each other. In either case, Russia will probably dominate Ukraine.

EU Enlargement

The odds are very good that the European Union will incorporate some east-central European states in the first decade of the twenty-first century. Although the issue has been on the table since the collapse of communism in 1989–1991, it was only in 1997, with the formulation of its *Agenda 2000*, that the EU first spelled out an explicit commitment to a "stronger and larger Union."[1] The December 1999 summit in Helsinki went significantly further, dividing potential entrants into three categories, according to their degree of readiness for admission. The first included Poland, the Czech Republic, Hungary, Estonia, Slovenia, and Cyprus; the second, Slovakia, Latvia, Lithuania, Romania, Bulgaria, and Malta; and the third, only Turkey.[2] Most important perhaps, the EU summit in Nice in December 2000 effectively accepted the ineluctability of enlargement by proposing a far-reaching reform of EU voting procedures with an eye to the impact on such a reform of new members with additional votes.[3] The commitment to enlargement was strengthened further by the Gothenburg summit of June 2001. Individual policy makers—those from Germany and Sweden in particular—reinforced EU declarations with their own statements of support. The most-favored east-central Europeans, for their part, adopted intensive measures to bring their political, social, economic, and legal systems in line with those of the EU.

By 2002, therefore, the formal declarations and policy initiatives of EU agencies, of leading European political and economic figures, and of east-central European policy makers had produced a ramified policy discourse that defines the future vitality and viability of the EU in terms of, on the one hand, the emergence of an imagined ethical-cultural community called "Europe" and, on the other hand, this new Europe's capacity to expand the zone of democracy, markets, and human rights eastwards. As Vaclav Havel has put it, "Enlargement to the east may be the most important goal of European history."[4] While a new and different redefinition of Europe is not inconceivable for further in the future, it could be undertaken only under conditions of crisis or breakdown. In particular, the vision of Europe as a unique metahistorical entity that represents the culmination of democratic development and transcends the evils of modern European history would have to be abandoned and the abject failure of fifty years of European teleology would have to be admitted. The real Europe's capacity to grow has therefore become a test of the imagined Europe's capacity to survive. It is not surprising that European policy makers have generally reacted to Ireland's rejection of the Nice Treaty in a June 2001 referendum as a temporary embarrassment and stumbling block that will perforce be overcome.[5]

If, therefore, both western and eastern Europe remain more or less stable, nonenlargement will be, for all practical purposes, discursively impossible. And in the EU, where words acquire enormous weight as a result of the fact that continual negotiation and renegotiation are at the core of the European experiment, a discursive imperative is virtually tantamount to a policy imperative.[6] The dynamic is not unlike that at the heart of NATO expansion. Although the merits and demerits of enlarging NATO had hardly been discussed by the time the decision on this was made, the case for expansion had become so entrenched in the political discourse as to preclude and/or marginalize all criticism.[7]

How far the European Union will expand is another question. Poland's joining the EU is perhaps least in doubt, largely because Germany (along with those European states fearful of a unified Germany) is committed to such an outcome on the grounds that it must be nested in and surrounded by stable European states. Hungary, the Czech Republic, Estonia, and Slovenia are small and relatively advanced, and thus would not put an unmanageable burden on the EU's budget and governance procedures. No other east-central European country is as geopolitically important to the EU and Germany as Poland or as small and advanced as the other four. After the first wave of enlargement takes place, the EU will have no pressing reason to continue the process, except perhaps as regards the other two Baltic states, Latvia and Lithuania.

More important, the EU will have every reason to take a breather, as it attempts to cope with the potentially destabilizing consequences of broadening and deepening. Even after they are admitted, the east-central European front-runners will still have some way to go before their polities, societies, and economies are fully compatible with the increasingly stringent requirements of EU membership.[8] Poland, for instance, has an enormous, as well as an enormously inefficient, agricultural sector. Modernizing is a precondition for membership, but moving one-fifth of the population from the countryside to the cities is no easy task in the best of circumstances, and it is an especially arduous one when Poland must also modernize its grossly inefficient heavy industry. The Czech Republic has an equally inefficient heavy industrial sector and thoroughly corrupt banks. Slovenia, Estonia, and Hungary may become integrated into the EU more easily, but they also lag substantially behind many EU norms and still evince excessively high levels of corruption.[9]

In turn, the European Union—even with the best of intentions and the least of frictions—will need time to adjust to the medium- and long-term impact of enlargement. The EU's current budget could not sustain the agricultural and developmental subsidies that would have to be apportioned to a wave of poorer members.[10] No less problematic is the fact that, as of 2001, the EU still had to address and resolve the question of labor migration within an enlarged Europe. According to a study by the Ifo-Institut in Munich, for example, Germany alone would, within fifteen years of admission of new members from east-central Europe, be the recipient of approximately 4 million labor migrants. Because almost half of that number is expected to be Poles, Germany has insisted on a moratorium on Polish labor migration even after Poland's accession to the EU.[11]

Equally important is the impact that new members would have on the EU's contentiously interpreted governance procedures—a problem that the Nice summit highlighted but failed adequately to solve.[12] Last but not least, the Europeans have to clarify just what kind of political values Europe stands for before another wave of postcommunist states with especially complex histories and checkered legacies join. The Joerg Haider affair in Austria nicely illustrated the dilemmas that growing political and economic integration will produce. It suggested, worrisomely, that European leaders might be willing to disregard democratic procedures if they produced results that were deemed incompatible with what the vision of Europe ostensibly represents.[13] The response to Haider also suggested that European actions rested on a double standard of moral severity vis-à-vis small states with xenophobic problems and moral lassitude vis-à-vis big states—such as France, Germany, and most recently Silvio Berlusconi's Italy—with far more vociferous and violent homegrown racists.[14]

Ukraine Outside the EU

Enlarging the EU thus represents an enormous challenge for the east-central European states, which must adapt a whole range of diverse institutions to EU norms within a short period of time—a process that is not unlike revolution from above—and an equally difficult challenge for the European Union, which must not only absorb new members, but also transform its governance procedures, all at the same time. Only after these exceedingly complex issues were fully resolved could the practical mechanics of Ukraine's joining the European Union be possible to contemplate seriously. Ukraine is so far behind Poland, Hungary, and the Czech Republic, and the EU is so unprepared to absorb an impoverished state of 49 million people, that the question of Ukraine's membership in the EU is at present only of normative interest.

Freedom House's Nations in Transit rankings provide a good sense of the distance—with respect to democracy, civil society, independent media, governance and public administration, rule of law, corruption, and free-market economy—between Ukraine, the east-central European front runners, and the EU. While the EU in general would deserve a Freedom House cumulative score of at least 64, and Poland, Hungary, the Czech Republic, and Slovenia have scores in the 50s, Ukraine's score is a mere 29.[15]

There are many reasons for Ukraine's failure to move significantly towards meeting EU standards—the one on which I shall place most emphasis later in this chapter involves institutional legacies—but suffice it to say that some combination of unfavorable initial conditions (Ukraine's noncompetitive heavy industry, demoralized peasantry, energy dependence, east–west regional divide, and elite incompetence), ineffective government, poorly designed reforms, widespread corruption, and popular apathy has been more than enough to do the trick. Worse, these factors have, over time, coalesced to form a logically coherent system prone to stagnation and resistant to change.

If Ukraine's eventual membership in the EU were considered normatively desirable and essentially a matter of time by both Ukraine and the EU, then two behavioral consequences should follow. One would expect Ukraine to do exactly what it has done—make hortatory declarations about its "European choice"[16]—and the EU to do exactly what the Helsinki summit chose *not* to do—create a fourth and even fifth category of potential EU entrants, of which Ukraine would have been one. In light of the extreme unlikelihood that Turkey, the sole country in the third category, will be admitted into the EU anytime soon, the creation of two more categories would have obligated the EU to do absolutely nothing while having the salutary effect of rhetorically acknowledging that the vision of Europe will not be complete without the countries excluded from the first three categories.

Indeed, if political and economic backwardness were the only obstacle to EU membership for Ukraine, there might be good reason for long-term optimism. After all, Ukraine just might, like Poland and the other east-central European front-runners, eventually succeed in putting its domestic house in order. Thereafter, once the EU had successfully absorbed the first three waves of entrants, its turn for membership also could come. Reform plus time would therefore equal a guarantee of membership.

The 1998 Partnership and Cooperation Agreement (PCA) and a number of other accords between the EU and Ukraine do seem to go some way towards making such a cost-free commitment. Although the EU endorsed "the emergence of a democratic, stable, open, and economically successful Ukraine as a prominent actor in the new Europe"[17] at the December 1999 Helsinki summit, the singular significance of the PCA lies in the fact that it is premised on Ukraine's exclusion from—and, thus, capacity *only* for partnership with—the European Union. In this sense, the PCA is not unlike the Partnership for Peace, which represents a way of regulating and institutionalizing relations between NATO members and nonmembers and not a procedure, however drawn out, for transforming nonmembers into members. The European Union's stance towards Ukraine thus consists of two mutually exclusive dimensions—rhetorically supporting Ukraine's European choice, while practically excluding Ukraine from any real prospect of EU membership.[18]

Openly rejecting Ukraine—or, for that matter, Russia—is a discursive faux pas in an age that claims the primacy, not of old-fashioned geopolitical interests—such as embedding a resurgent Germany in a stable network of democratic European states—but of human rights, integration, democracy, and the like. The only discursively permissible case for Ukraine's exclusion must therefore, like Russia's, be framed in cultural terms, on the grounds that Ukraine and Russia are not fit for membership because their civilizational values are alien to those embodied by the concept of Europe. Although EU bureaucrats have to eschew the language of civilizational incompatibility in their official statements, leading individual Europeans do not. According to Helmut Schmidt, Ukraine has radically different cultural traditions that, *eo ipso*, disqualify it from integration into Europe: Ukraine, like Russia, is simply too different.[19] The French historian Jacques Le Goff claims that Russia "is a problem" for Europe, both because it may "perhaps want to remain Russian"—or *more* Russian than European—and because it is so "enormous."[20] Underlying both arguments is Samuel Huntington's unfortunate thesis of the "clash of civilizations" as applied to the Catholic and Christian west and the Orthodox east.[21]

Claims of civilizational incompatibility, besides being both inherently vague and implicitly supercilious, are also misapplied in the case of both Ukraine and Russia. Ukraine's intermediate position between east and west—where "east" has been made to stand for, above all, Russia and "west" for Europe—means that Ukraine has as many justified claims on a European identity as do many countries within the European Union. Despite the quasi-mystical overtones that the name has acquired in EU discourse, "Europe" is not a homogeneous region that experienced the same exact processes of Christianization, Enlightenment, industrialization, modernization, and the like. Quite the contrary, both the real Europe and the imaginary Europe are products of centuries of violence and bloodshed.[22] Because the EU's current and future members share no coherent set of identical cultural, political, and social characteristics, it is relatively easy to show that Ukraine (indeed, even Russia) shares as many of these historical features, at least to some degree, as most "bona fide" European states.

In reality, the case for excluding Ukraine from the EU in principle can only be premised on fairly straightforward geopolitical considerations. Seen in this light, the case for expanding the EU to include Poland, the Czech Republic, and Hungary is primarily, though by no means exclusively, a function of the perceived geopolitical need to embed a powerful unified Germany in the center of Europe. That same logic was at the core of the argument for NATO expansion.

By the same token, the case for not including Ukraine—even theoretically, in some fourth or fifth class of potential entrants—is also driven by strategic considerations related to the fear of alienating Russia by meddling in its "sphere of influence."[23] The possibility of Ukrainian membership in either the EU or NATO terrifies European elites justifiably wary of alienating Russia. As Semyon Appatov puts it, "The EU continues to view Ukraine as outside Europe and in Eurasia. This is exemplified by the EU's continued focus on the identity question: "Does Ukraine see itself as closer to Europe or to the Slavs in the East?"[24] It is, alas, just not true that "no-one is disqualified by geography or history from joining the EU or NATO."[25]

Unfortunately, exclusion from the European Union is not just about exclusion from the quasi-mystical entity known as Europe. Rather, it is about exclusion from a whole set of institutional arrangements. After all, EU enlargement is part and parcel of a process also involving NATO enlargement and leading, in the final analysis, to the construction of a new institutional entity. Just as the EU is constantly deepening, NATO also is redefining itself as both a security alliance and a promoter of democracy, human rights, and stability.[26] Increasingly, the EU and NATO may become, as their supporters hope, complementary parts of a new Europe, with both claiming to be different institutional expressions of the same countries and the same kind of countries: more or less prosperous and more or less stable industrial democracies that define themselves, and only themselves, as European in culture and spirit.

With Europe in the process of constructing an interlocking set of highly sophisticated institutions related to democracy, rule of law, civil society, and the market, the expansion of both the EU and NATO into east-central Europe is nothing less than the extension of already formidable European institutional boundaries eastwards.[27] And unlike the transparent boundaries between and among the post-Soviet states, those between Europe and its eastern neighbors will be opaque. Seen in this light, the Schengen Agreement of 1995, which discontinued passport and border controls within Europe while creating legal barriers to the movement of non-EU populations into or through Europe, only formalized the EU's already impassable institutional barriers.[28] Poland's foreign minister, Radek Sikorski, has described the problem in the following terms: "We are under a contradictory directive. On the one hand, we are told to keep good relations with the Russians; on the other hand, to impose visas on them."[29] Sikorski could just as easily have been speaking of Ukraine.

The following example illustrates the logic of the emerging situation. Until 1998, Ukraine and Poland enjoyed unusually close political and economic relations. In particular, Ukrainian laborers and traders could cross into Poland with few restrictions. Not surprisingly, the Polish–Ukrainian border also became a conduit for migrants, refugees, and criminals seeking to enter the European Union.[30] With Poland on the verge of membership in the EU, however, Brussels insisted in 1998 that its border controls be brought in line with Schengen. Warsaw, in turn, informed Kiev that continued access to Poland for Ukrainians would be contingent on Ukraine's establishing Schengen-like controls on its border with Russia.

That Ukraine will fail to establish such controls goes without saying. The boundary is transparent, the cross-border ties are too many and too dense, a Russian-Ukrainian population straddles the border, and the Ukrainian state is too weak to impose such controls or to risk alienating the superpower next door. Once it becomes clear that Ukraine has failed, Poland will have no choice but to comply fully with Schengen and cordon itself off from Ukraine.[31] Bratislava, significantly, abolished visa-free travel to Slovakia for Ukrainians *after* Vladimir Meciar had been deposed and its chances of EU membership had grown accordingly.[32] And Slovakia was only following in the footsteps of the Czech Republic, which imposed a new visa regime in early 2000.[33]

But Schengen represents far more than a boundary between two sets of states. At the same time as the European states are transforming their own relations both quantitatively and qualitatively, most of the postcommunist states outside central Europe and the Baltic are making at best very slow and incremental progress towards meeting the membership criteria of the EU and NATO. As western Europeans develop exponentially, most of the countries outside the first category of potential EU members are developing arithmetically, with very low positive slopes at best. Some, especially in Central Asia, are actually moving in the opposite direction. Worse, there is good reason to think that this gap will not diminish in the foreseeable future.

For most of the 1990s, the 27 countries that emerged from the Soviet empire in 1989–1991 constituted three more or less stable clusters roughly corresponding to east-central Europe (the most advanced in terms of movement towards democracy, the market, the rule of law, and civil society); central Asia, parts of the Caucasus, and Belarus (the least advanced); and the largely eastern Slavic middle (situated somewhere in between).[34] That these three clusters were not randomly aggregated suggests that their origins lay largely in the institutional frameworks—specifically, in the degree, or extent, of totalitarian control and Soviet imperial rule—that these countries inherited from the past, with a secondary role being played by pre-Soviet local traditions.[35] Those countries that were least totalitarian and least imperial by and large joined the first category. Those that were most totalitarian and most imperial joined the third, and those that scored in the middle on the totalitarian and imperial scales joined the second.[36]

Thus, the first group consists of entities that emerged from the USSR's informal empire in east-central Europe (the Baltic states may, for a variety of historical reasons peculiar to them, also be partially assigned to this category). They were least totalitarian and least imperial and, upon attaining real independence in 1989–1991, were best equipped to act as genuinely independent states. As formally independent states (unlike the Soviet republics), they had possessed more or less complete state apparatuses, bureaucracies, elites, armies, police forces, and courts, and relatively coherent economies, as well as a variety of less autonomous social institutions, if not quite full-fledged civil societies.[37] Also crucial was the fact that they were only subjected to communist rule after 1945. Not only, therefore, was their experience of communism almost 30 years shorter than that of the Soviet republics, but they did not have to suffer the effects of the Leninist revolution after 1917; and though they suffered terribly from Stalinism from 1947 to 1953 (the Baltic states in 1940–1941 and again after 1944), this experience was also a great deal shorter than that endured by Soviet society. It is therefore not surprising that the most advanced countries constitute all the first-wave candidates for EU membership.

The second and third sets consist of the successor polities of the formal empire—some of the institutionally more totalitarian east-central European states, the majority of non-Russian republics, and Russia itself. Although all these entities possessed their own communist parties, bureaucratic apparatuses, and the accoutrements of symbolic sovereignty, these states emerged from the Soviet collapse with stronger and longer totalitarian and imperial traditions that resulted in their bureaucracies being shapeless, their ministries being either undermanned or nonexistent, and their policy-making and policy-implementing cadres, trained to receive orders from Moscow, being anything but effective elites. What differentiated the countries in the third category from those in the second was, in general, the extent of imperial rule—with the former having experienced more direct imperial rule than the former. A few of the second-wave candidates for EU membership are in these two categories, but the vast majority of these countries are, like Ukraine, on no EU list.

Because the gap between the east-central European front-runners and the rest is largely systemic in origin, it cannot, almost be definition, be overcome easily or quickly. Unless revolutionary breakthroughs are attempted—and, for better or worse, they rarely succeed in bringing about their intended outcomes—the structural and institutional features of these systems can change only with the passage of time.[38] Under conditions such as these, the developmental gap between western Europe and its eastern neighbors can but grow while the institutional barriers between them rise and thicken to form a Schengen curtain.[39]

The Russian Problem

Exclusion from Europe matters—for Ukraine no less than for Poland, Hungary, Estonia, and the Czech Republic—as much because of the intrinsic attractiveness of the European Union as because of the fear that exclusion means deliverance to Russia. Although it is impolitic for policy makers to say so, the reality is that all the east-central Europeans distrust Russia to varying degrees. Some hate Russia and Russian culture with a passion bordering on racism; others fear that their similarities with Russia are so great as to require undue emphasis on otherness and difference; and all fear Russia—for its size, military strength, imperialist traditions, and potential for instability. Significantly, all three stances are represented among Ukrainian elites and publics.[40]

The last point—fear of Russia—is not, alas, wholly unfounded. Russia is, and is likely to remain, a brittle semiauthoritarian state and a regional superpower. Were it a democratic superpower, one might at least expect it to exert a benign hegemony over its neighbors and abjure the more ruthless kinds of meddling and expansionism. Were it a weak authoritarian state, it could not embark on imperialist projects, even if its elites wanted to do so. Unfortunately, the combination of authoritarianism at home and regional superpower status abroad means that Russia is, and is certainly perceived as, a potential threat to the stability and security of some of its neighbors. In the western part of the former Soviet Union, only supporters of Belarus's president, Alexander Lukashenko, appear to disagree with this assessment, but his desire to unify his country with Russia may, ironically, be interpreted as an attempt to forestall Russian expansion by anticipating it.

To be sure, as of 2001 the Russian state was weak, and it is likely to remain weak for some time to come. Its authority in the provinces is tenuous; its ability to tax, administer, and maintain law and order—the classic functions of the Weberian state—is questionable. Its military is badly equipped, badly paid, demoralized, and bogged down in a brutal and probably endless guerrilla war in Chechnya. Even within Moscow, the state apparatus is fragmented, with ministries and functional elites competing for scarce resources, criminal alliances, and influence while eluding the efforts of the executive to achieve greater intrastate coordination.

Yet the weakness of the Russian state has to be viewed comparatively. While the Polish, Hungarian, Czech, Slovak, and Baltic states are relatively stronger, Russia's state is much stronger than its counterparts in the "near abroad," for three reasons. First, the Russian state's resource base—at least as measured by Russia's vast mineral wealth—is enormous. Second, Russian elites are far more skilled in statecraft than those of the non-Russian republics; after all, it was Russians (or thoroughly russified Ukrainians and others) who by and large occupied the key positions within the Soviet state apparatus. And third, the Russian state's ministries have an institutional history—even if one somewhat deformed by the Soviet experience—while those of the non-Russian states by and large emerged ex nihilo in 1991–1992.

Although its authoritarian qualities are belied by many of the formal trappings of democracy—elections, presidents, legislatures, courts, parties, and so on—like many other countries round the world, Russia has been ruled in a semiauthoritarian manner since at least the fateful presidential elections of 1996, when Boris Yeltsin threw his lot with the oligarchs and blatantly rigged the electoral process. The second Yeltsin administration thereby acquired all the characteristics of a "soft" dictatorial regime, one attentive to public opinion at home and in the west, but basically committed to a nondemocratic, nontransparent, nonaccountable form of politics outside the rule of law.

Vladimir Putin has done little to change the essence of this form of rule. Some of the players are different, but the regime is either the same or, arguably, even more explicitly authoritarian as a result of Putin's efforts to centralize power in the executive, insinuate generals and secret police officers into positions of authority, play the nationalist, great-power card with respect to Chechnya and the world, and establish what he calls the "dictatorship of the law."[41]

There is no reason not to expect Russia's authoritarian system to survive in its present form for many years to come. Russia's increasingly close resemblance to such developing-world states as Egypt suggests as much.[42] Such systems have staying power for three reasons. First, the fragmentation of power among political and economic elites lodged at various institutional and regional levels means that mounting serious challenges to the central authorities is a virtually insurmountable coordination problem.

Second, parasitical elites in cahoots with economic oligarchs and organized criminal elements benefit greatly from the system and have little incentive to change it. Their power and welfare are firmly rooted in the personalized, nontransparent, relation-based structure of economic and political activity and interaction.

Third, despite widespread discontent, most of the population has little time or incentive to engage in political activity. Moreover, there are usually few if any organizational vehicles for channeling mass misery into political activism. Ironically, we may expect mass expressions of discontent in Russia *after* democratic substance, market practices, some level of material well-being, and a civil society take root.

Besides being a semiauthoritarian system, Russia is also a regional super-power with the capacity to exert at least limited hegemony over many of its neighbors. Although the countries of east-central Europe and the Baltic have shifted their trade away from Russia, most of the non-Russian republics—in particular, Ukraine—remain highly dependent on Russia, especially for energy. By the same token, although the conventional wisdom has it that Russia is hopelessly weak[43]—indeed, in comparison with the United States, Russia may be only a developing-world state with nuclear arms—Russia far outstrips its neighbors in traditional power categories.

Consider only the disparity between Russia and Ukraine, its closest competitor. Whereas Russia's share of the post-Soviet population is 50 percent, Ukraine's is 17. Russia's share of post-Soviet GDP is about 90 percent, while Ukraine's is about 4. Russia's share of armed forces is in the 60 percent range, while Ukraine's is about 18. Last, Russia's share of total post-Soviet defense budgets is 94 percent, while Ukraine's is a mere 1 percent.[44] Russia's share of "soft power" is also impressive, as Russian language and culture—films, television programs, books, magazines, and so on—continue to dominate most of the post-Soviet territory, particularly Ukraine.

No less important than the imbalance in power categories is the fact of Ukraine's many—perfectly "natural" and mutually beneficial—economic links to Russia. Ukraine imports much of its energy from Russia (and negotiations are under way on merging both countries' energy systems); 47 percent of Ukraine's exports go to Russia, and 26 percent of its imports come from Russia; informal cross-border trade is also significant, although non-quantifiable; and Ukrainian migrant workers in Russia (like those from Georgia, Armenia, and elsewhere) number in the hundreds of thousands, with their remittances playing a highly important part in the economies of certain Ukrainian regions.[45]

So overwhelming a strategic imbalance and economic dependence can but continue. For things to change significantly, Russia would have to go into free fall—politically, economically, socially, and culturally—while its non-Russian neighbors would have to experience almost miraculous upswings in each of these spheres. Neither of these extreme scenarios is likely.[46] Moreover, because Russia and its non-Russian neighbors share so many of the institutional legacies of the Soviet past, it is far more probable that they will develop more or less in tandem, thereby preserving the current power imbalance for many years.[47]

In sum, there is no reason to think that Russia will suddenly become either more democratic or substantially weaker than its immediate neighbors. Quite the contrary, it is likely to remain a semiauthoritarian, nationalist regional superpower for a long time to come. After the European Union expands, Ukraine will therefore be caught between a powerful, menacing, and possibly meddlesome east and a powerful, in principle benign, but indifferent west. Under conditions such as these, the best Ukrainian policy elites will be able to do is walk a fine line between exclusion and dependence, in the hope of minimizing both and maximizing Ukraine's space for independent maneuvering. Whether will they succeed in this endeavor depends on a variety of factors, which I will now discuss.

Ukraine's Tightrope Act

Avoiding the dangers of both Scylla and Charybdis has historically been a feature of the political choices faced by independence-minded elites in Ukraine. In the mid–seventeenth century, the Cossack leader Bohdan Khmelnytskyi sided with Muscovy against Poland. Some 60 years later, Hetman Ivan Mazepa forged an alliance with Sweden's Charles XII against Peter the Great.[48] Dmytro Dontsov, a leading Ukrainian nationalist, argued in 1913 for annexing the ethnically Ukrainian territories within the Russian empire to Hapsburg Austria.[49] Following the collapse of the tsarist empire, while some Ukrainian elites opted for ties with the Central powers, others placed their bets on the Russian Bolsheviks or Whites, and still others turned to Poland for support. In the interwar period, the Organization of Ukrainian Nationalists programmatically claimed that it would rely only on "its own strength," but, in reality, threw its lot with Germany against Poland and the Soviet Union.[50]

During and after World War II, the nationalist underground in Soviet Ukraine turned to the secret services of the United States and United Kingdom for support. The dissident movement of the 1960s, 1970s, and 1980s was by and large pro-western, inasmuch as the west embodied the democratic ideals it stood for. By the late 1980s, however, as the USSR was visibly falling apart, Ukrainian elites made the same choices faced by their counterparts in the aftermath of the revolution of 1917: Some hoped for the support of, and rapid integration into, the west; others retained their loyalty to Moscow. Even since independence in 1991, Ukrainian elites have faced the same choice of east versus west.[51]

One look at a historical map of eastern Europe shows why this choice is an endemic feature of politics in Ukraine. The country known as Ukraine emerged in the interstices of great-power conflicts. Although Ukraine (or *okraina*) means "borderland," Ukraine was not some one state's borderland, but the borderland of several states.

In essence, Ukraine is the "space between," a territory that, by virtue of its being placed where a number of empires—Muscovite, Polish, Ottoman, and Habsburg—met, remained beyond their full control and thus could establish a cultural and political identity of its own. For better or worse, Ukraine at the start of the twenty-first century is still the space between; now, between the European states grouped in the EU and NATO and Russia.

It is not surprising that independent Ukraine's policy elites have adapted to the reality of being in between by pursuing a "multi-vector" foreign policy aimed at establishing and/or maintaining good relations with both Russia and the west. Although the term "multi-vector" is of relatively recent vintage, the foreign policies of both presidents Leonid Kravchuk and Leonid Kuchma have been virtually identical in seeking to ingratiate Ukraine with both sides.[52] Such consistency is not surprising. Remaining on good terms with Russia was, and remains, a strategic imperative in light of Russia's power, size, and proximity—and Ukraine's all too complex historical and cultural relationship with its "elder brother."[53] Establishing good relations with the United States and the European Union—that is, the west—made, and continues to make, geopolitical sense, inasmuch as it permits Ukraine to balance against Russia. It also makes economic sense, inasmuch as it promises integration into the world's most dynamic economies. The result has been that, at least since 1992, Ukraine has succeeded in managing post-imperial tensions with Russia while expanding postcommunist relations with the capitalist west.

Ukraine's ability to successfully pursue a credible multi-vector foreign policy is overwhelmingly a function of four factors: Russia's relations with the west; Ukraine's relations with Russia and the west; domestic developments within Ukraine; and Ukraine's relations with east-central Europe. Because of a historical conjunction of these factors in the post–cold war period, Ukraine not only did not have to choose between Russia and the west but would have been foolhardy to have made such a choice.

The first factor—Russia's relations with the west—is the most important for Ukraine for the simple reason that it establishes the overall strategic framework within which Ukraine has to pursue its foreign policy. Needless to say, Russia still has some, not completely unjustified, claims to global great-power status and thus represents a genuine security concern for the west. Russia's weakness, the more or less pro-western leanings of the Yeltsin administration, the west's attempt to keep Russia engaged, and the relative absence of truly divisive issues—with the possible, though fleeting, exception of NATO enlargement and the Kosovo war—meant that Russia's relations with the west were, on the whole, satisfactory for most of the 1990s. As a result, as of 2001 Ukraine had not had to choose between two quasi-partners, nor would it have made much sense, either geopolitically or economically, to have done so.

Not siding with either Russia or the west made sense mostly because of Ukraine's own relations with them. For a variety of reasons involving geographic proximity, economic and energy dependence, and relative military weakness, Ukraine has no choice but to view Russia as its overriding geopolitical concern. By contrast, although the west is attractive as a source of investment and as a possible balance against Russia, Ukraine's parlous economy places strict limits on the extent of western investment. Meanwhile, the west's sense that Russia is its primary strategic interlocutor necessarily circumscribes the degree to which it, the west, would be willing to help Ukraine assert itself against Russia. After all, it takes two to tango, and it is hard to imagine that, other things being equal, the west would choose Ukraine over Russia—except in very specific circumstances (to be addressed below). Once again, therefore, Ukraine has little choice but to pursue good relations with both all-too-near Russia and the all-too-distant west.

Third, domestic developments within Ukraine have also argued for a multi-vector policy. Although Ukrainian elites have generally promoted a pro-western orientation, the population has been, and remains, divided. Roughly half—generally inhabiting the central and western oblasts and more or less supportive of Ukrainian language and culture—are broadly inclined towards a pro-western orientation. The other half—generally inhabiting the southern and eastern oblasts and more or less favoring Russian language and culture—support a pro-Russian orientation.[54] In the 1990s, Ukrainian elites—beset with a declining economy, questionable legitimacy, and a weak state—were in no position to alienate substantial segments of the population by opting for either Russia or the west.

The final condition facilitating a nonchoice is that, throughout the 1990s, Ukraine was able to enjoy good relations with east-central Europe in general and Poland in particular. Indeed, if there is any country that truly functions as Ukraine's strategic partner, it is Poland, which sees Ukraine's continued independence and possible prosperity as guarantees of its own interests vis-à-vis Russia.[55] Ukraine could pursue the east-central European option, however, only because east-central Europe, like Ukraine, occupied a position between Russia and the west. In particular, although Poland expressed its preference for integration into European security and economic structures soon after the fall of the Soviet Union, it was able to promote a partnership with Ukraine precisely because it had not yet been fully integrated into the west.

Which, if any, of these four factors are likely to remain in place after the European Union expands? Once Poland, like many of its east-central European neighbors, is anchored firmly in the west, Polish governments will be forced to subordinate Ukraine to the imperatives of adapting Poland's institutions to those of the EU. Polish elites may declare their unconditional support for the partnership with Ukraine, but it is hard to believe that they would jeopardize Poland's European connection for the sake of Ukraine. Ukraine's population, meanwhile, is likely to remain as basically fragmented as in the past.

The fundamental east–west divide will not be bridged any time soon, if at all. And even if Ukraine finally alights on the path of sustainable growth—and that, alas, is a big if—it is unlikely to become a vastly better place to live, as far as most ordinary Ukrainians are concerned. As a result, the legitimacy of the Ukrainian state is likely to remain limited, in the view of large sections of the population. This tendency will be exacerbated in the eastern and southern regions if Russia also grows and maintains its clear economic lead over Ukraine—thereby continuing to exert a pull on Ukraine's divided population.

Ukraine's relations with Russia and the west are also unlikely to change dramatically in the near term. Russia will inevitably remain a strategic priority for Ukraine. That will be true regardless of whether Ukraine's energy dependence on Russia grows or diminishes. For one thing, some substantial degree of energy dependence will remain even in the best of circumstances; for another, there are so many other, no less persuasive, reasons for Ukraine to worry about Russia. As for the west, Ukraine's chances of joining NATO or the EU any time soon are, as I have argued above, nil, while the west's interest in Ukraine can but remain secondary to its interest in Russia.

Thus far, the ledger argues for a continuation of Ukraine's multi-vector stance. However, the central factor promoting such a policy was, is, and will remain the west's relations with Russia. Should they remain more or less positive, or perhaps even improve, Ukraine will remain committed to a multi-vector policy. Should they worsen, Ukraine may have to choose. How it will choose would then be overwhelmingly a function of the second and third factors—the divided population and Ukraine's relations with Russia and the west. Should such conditions arise, then only if the west comes out strongly for a Ukrainian connection—and that would probably have to entail membership in either NATO or the EU or both—would Ukraine be able to resist the pull of Russia.

The west, in turn, will opt clearly and decisively for Ukraine if and only if its relations with Russia worsen dramatically, perhaps to the point of a return to something resembling the cold war. Such a scenario is not inconceivable. Continued NATO enlargement could, together with a turn to authoritarianism, nationalism, and anti-western sentiment within Russia, lead to a serious deterioration in the west's relations with Russia. Even so, it is not likely that relations will take such a rapid and radical turn for the worse, especially because such a pessimistic outcome would presuppose a willingness on the part of both Russian and western elites to permit such a denouement. This might in certain circumstances be true of a U.S. administration, but it is very much less likely in the case of Germany, France, or even the United Kingdom. It is more likely, therefore, that the future will see a continuation of the western–Russian relations of the 1990s—occasionally tense, frequently complicated, but ultimately reconcilable.

With the three most important facilitating conditions of Ukraine's balancing act in place for the foreseeable future, the conclusion seems inescapable: *Other things being equal*, Ukraine will continue its multi-vector policy. Neither quite with Russia nor quite with the west, Ukraine will maintain its balancing act as long as its population remains divided (as it surely will), Russia remains its primary strategic concern (as it surely will), the west does not embrace Ukraine (as it surely will not), and the west's relations with Russia remain reasonably amicable (as they probably will).

Intervening Variables

This relatively optimistic prognosis is premised on at least two factors being held constant—the level of democracy and rule of law in Ukraine and

Russia, and the global economic environment. Unfortunately, if we loosen this requirement, the outlook for Ukraine worsens markedly. If, as is all too possible, both countries move away from democracy and the rule of law and prove incapable of coping with globalization, their relations with each another will, almost inevitably, intensify and deepen. Although a continued multi-vector policy is not inconceivable in such circumstances, Ukrainian elites would find it vastly more difficult to avoid having to choose between either growing dependence on or conflict with Russia.

As I have noted above, the 27 post-communist states could be divided into three more or less stable groups for most of the 1990s. As of 2001, however, recent developments in east-central Europe and the former Soviet Union have suggested that a gradual realignment of these groupings may be taking place.[56] There is evidence of a fracturing of the middle group. Some of these countries—Croatia, Slovakia, and Bulgaria—have clearly moved towards the most advanced category, while some—Russia, Ukraine, Georgia, and Kyrgyzstan—have moved in the direction of the least advanced category.

Croatia and Slovakia were able to get "back on track" fairly quickly and easily once Franjo Tudjman and Vladimir Meciar left the scene; Bulgaria has, despite a number of serious crises, been able to proceed steadily in the right direction; and significantly, although still mired within the least advanced category, Yugoslavia may be poised to leapfrog the Slobodan Milosevic inter-regnum and adopt a course of democratic and market-oriented reform. In marked contrast to these countries, Russia, Ukraine, and Kyrgyzstan are moving towards more personalized forms of authoritarian rule by Putin, Kuchma, and Askar Akayev.

The main reason for this emerging bipolarity is institutional. Slovakia, Croatia, Bulgaria, and Yugoslavia experienced substantially lower degrees of totalitarian and imperial rule than did Russia, Ukraine, and Kyrgyzstan. It is therefore expected that the east-central European states (including, with time, Macedonia and Albania) will resolve the institutional contradictions of second-category countries in favor of democracy and the market, return to their institutionally "natural" trajectories, and thus rejoin the first category.

Those states with deeper totalitarian-imperial roots, such as Russia, Ukraine, and Kyrgyzstan, just as "naturally" tend toward despotism. Bur-dened with their institutional legacies, they cannot as easily resolve the con-tradiction between democratization and marketization on the one hand and bureaucratic authoritarianism and elite parasitism on the other in favor of the former. Other things being equal, Georgia, Armenia, and Moldova should at some point join them in their downward slide. Seen in this light, the February 2001 parliamentary elections in Moldova, in which the communists triumphed, may be a harbinger of things to come.[57]

Worse, the increasingly authoritarian systems found in Ukraine, Russia, and many other postcommunist states will not fare well in a rapidly globalizing world.[58] Although globalization may not be quite as inevitable or beneficial as its advocates suggest, there is little doubt that a rapid acceleration of cross-border forces involving the movement of ideas, capital, people, and goods is currently under way and that it can, albeit not unconditionally, improve economic performance and standards of living.[59] Unless they quickly experience virtually miraculous change for the better, however, Ukraine and Russia will be globalization's relative losers.

Several studies measuring the competitiveness of the post-Soviet economies, the level of their perceived corruption, and their openness provide a good sense of how far both countries are from meeting the challenges of the global economy. While the World Economic Forum's 1999 ratings give Singapore a score of 2.12 (the highest), the United States a 1.58, and the European Union a 0.57, Ukraine's is minus 1.94 and Russia's is minus 2.02. Similarly, Transparency International in 1999 assigned a score of 7.6 to the European Union, 7.5 to the United States, 2.6 to Ukraine, and 2.4 to Russia. Moreover, in 2000 the Tuck School of Business at Dartmouth University rated Singapore's degree of openness at 86 (out of 160), Estonia's at 78, Russia's at 52, and Ukraine's at 48.[60] Although excessive importance should not be ascribed to any one of these numbers, together they position Ukraine and Russia near the very bottom of the industrial world's economies and strongly suggest that they are likely to remain there for a long time.

The combination of growing political authoritarianism and economic isolation is, I suggest, likely to have three consequences. First, Ukraine and Russia—as well as most of their neighbors—will recede institutionally even further from the states grouped within the European Union. As Europe's institutions respond and adapt to globalization more or less successfully, those of the east will either stagnate, relatively, or experience indigenous forms of development different from and possibly even inimical to those in the EU.[61]

Second, the incapacity of Ukraine and Russia to compete in the global economy will reduce their chances of embarking on and adopting successful market-oriented economic reform. As a result, a tendency to seek "third ways" involving greater state intervention is likely to take hold. Authoritarian solutions are especially likely, if and when relative economic stagnation continues and "confining conditions" appear to require "revolutionary breakthroughs."[62]

Third, both of the other developments are likely to increase the isolation of Ukraine and Russia from more industrialized countries and their dependence on one another—and especially on Russia, the former imperial core and current military and economic power.[63] It is, alas, difficult to imagine that growing marginalization in the global economic system will counter the tendency towards parasitic authoritarianism internally. On the contrary, these developments are likely to be mutually reinforcing.

Under conditions such as these, Ukraine's relations with Russia will be framed by two possible outcomes—neither of which is especially palatable for Ukraine. On the one hand, an isolated and authoritarian Ukraine may find a commonality of interests with an equally isolated and authoritarian Russia. Joining forces in order to resist the hegemony of the west and to survive the impact of globalization could easily make growing sense to Ukrainian and Russian policy elites cognizant of the fact that the west had essentially relegated them to the developing world.

On the other hand, such insecure, brittle, and authoritarian states could also degenerate into squabbling and even conflict with each other. This possibility is increased by the fact that Ukrainian and Russian identities and relations rest on historical and cultural ambivalences that are as capable of promoting tensions as they are of leading to rapprochement. Whatever the outcome, Ukraine will inevitably be the junior partner or younger brother of Russia—a role to which it has long been inured by historical experience.

Alternative Futures?

Is there no way out of this cul de sac for Ukraine? Three developments could make a difference.[64] First, the prospect of Ukraine's growing isolation from a rapidly integrating world presupposes that globalization will proceed inexorably and smoothly. But this may not be the case. On the contrary, the exact forms that globalization will assume, its consequences, and the degree to which it will continue unabated are issues that were, as of 2001, intrinsically unknowable. Indeed, inasmuch as we know anything from history about untrammeled capitalism, we know that its capacity to do harm can be just as great, if not greater, than its capacity to do good. Even where there is rapid economic growth, this has often led not to political stability but rather to increased social and ethnic differentiation, and therefore to increased political and national tensions.

Unemployment, poverty, social instability, political decay, and economic decline are the flip side of globalization's coin for many people in many societies. Even if it is true that people and governments have no choice but to submit to globalization, we know from history that some angry and determined people and some governments will always refuse to accept what is called the "inevitable"—recall the dissidents in the Soviet Union—and rebel. They may be right to do so, or they may be wrong; all that matters is that they will, equally "inevitably," resist. Globalization will therefore, sooner or later, meet an immovable object that, for better or for worse, will change its trajectory and thus the nature of globalization itself. If and when globalization "stalls," countries such as Ukraine may win some time to develop their domestic institutions and put their house in order.

Second, although the European Union's enlargement would create the functional equivalent of an iron curtain between itself and the new developing world to its east, as of 2001 there was still some reason to think that Europe may not incorporate the east-central European states quite as rapidly as they might wish and as European bureaucrats publicly proclaim. The Nice Treaty wholly failed to accomplish many of the essential *internal* reforms that the EU needs to carry out as part of the enlargement process. It is possible therefore that Brussels, daunted by the complexity of the task involved in simultaneous broadening and deepening, may indeed decide to buck the discursive trend and avoid enlargement for much longer than the few years currently envisaged. This is all the more possible because, for its own geopolitical reasons, Germany insists that Poland must be in the first round of EU enlargement, even though Poland is clearly far more difficult to integrate into the EU than smaller and more economically successful states such as Estonia, Hungary, and Slovenia.

By the same token, it could happen that east-central European elites and publics decide that their hard-won sovereignty is too precious to abandon to the faceless institutions of the EU. My sense is that these eventualities are far less probable than enlargement in the near term, but even so, they are possible. Under conditions such as these, Ukraine would be spared some of the binary choices that this chapter has discussed. It could, at least for some longer period of time, share in the fate of its frustrated neighbors to the west.

With their help and that of some of the former Soviet republics (currently joined, rather ineffectively, in the GUUAM grouping—Georgia, Ukraine, Uzbekistan, Azerbaijan, and Moldova),[65] it could attempt to resist Russian hegemony. More important perhaps, with its economic relations with Poland, Hungary, and the Czech Republic not fully subservient to the EU's dictates, Ukraine would be in a better position to avoid economic marginalization and the ravages of globalization.

Third, history shows that even "stagnant" developing-world countries can grow economically and thus develop and modernize. The Asian "tigers" have exceptional records that may be beyond Ukraine's reach, but there is no reason why Ukraine should not be able to emulate, and possibly even replicate, India's recent economic experience. If quasi-socialist, monstrously bureaucratic, overpopulated, undereducated, and profoundly inefficient India can move towards growth, then so can Ukraine. Indeed, according to official statistics, Ukraine actually experienced substantial industrial growth in the period 1999–2001. And there is reason to think that this growth may not be quite ephemeral. Unlike Russia, Ukraine did not experience a severe drop in the value of its currency in the aftermath of the August 1999 financial crisis. Nor has Ukraine been able to benefit from the rise in world energy prices; quite the contrary, higher prices have burdened its balance of payments with Russia. This suggests that there may be solid domestic bases for Ukraine's growth.

With any or all of these three developments, Ukraine's future could be different—although probably only to a limited extent—from that outlined in this chapter. But I must emphasize that even if all three intervening circumstances transpire exactly as suggested above, they will have negative consequences for Ukraine as well. A slowing down of the world economy can ultimately be to no one's benefit, especially because globalization's deceleration will also mean even less foreign direct investment in Ukraine. A stalled European Union could easily become a zone of instability and would hardly increase Europe's political and economic interest in such impoverished countries as Ukraine.

Moreover, prolonged exclusion from the EU could promote nationalist backlashes in some of the east-central European countries and encourage them to turn away from European values. Instead they could seek "indigenous" nationalist values and solutions—with part of the justification for these probably being the perceived threat from Russia. Such a development, while ameliorating Ukraine's sense of isolation in the short term, would of course have a disastrous impact on the European project in general. And in the long run, Ukraine would also suffer particularly badly from a regional swing to retrograde ethnic nationalism. From the point of view of any sensible Ukrainian, a fractious, nationalist, and authoritarian eastern Europe is surely not preferable to EU expansion.

Finally, as was noted above, economic growth can easily have negative side effects. First, it is unlikely to be equitable, favoring all sectors of the population in the same way and to the same degree. Thus a booming Ukraine is likely to witness even greater income disparities than at present. Second, economic growth can easily produce a variety of social tensions and dislocations, ranging from strikes to land seizures to mass layoffs. Particularly ominous in the Ukrainian case is the fact that in many countries, growth has also led to increased tensions between favored and less favored regions. Third, rapid growth, in combination with growing social and regional tensions, has (in the past at least) encouraged leaders to abandon democracy and adopt authoritarianism. In sum, an economically booming Ukraine is likely to be far less stable, and possibly far less peaceful, than at present.

I must conclude therefore that in almost all circumstances, EU enlargement will only harm Ukraine's overall prospects. Even sadder is the fact that with or without EU enlargement, the future of independent Ukraine is relatively bleak. This is, however, not a reflection on Ukraine as such. The prospects for all the post-Soviet states, including Russia, are bleak.[66] At best, Ukraine will remain a miserable country surrounded by even more miserable countries, all of which remain isolated from developments taking place within Europe and the leading regions of the world. Worse, Ukraine is likely to become even more authoritarian and have to cope with a no less authoritarian, and possibly even nationalist, Russia—also in isolation from the rest of the world.

At worst, Ukraine, Russia, and many of their neighbors may become authoritarian states in national competition or even conflict with each other. Europe, whatever its official size, will then have to coexist for decades to come with a new developing world on its doorstep—a region featuring the instability and conflict of the old developing world.[67] If the former Soviet region does develop in this direction, it is likely to increase still further existing tendencies in the EU towards "fortress Europe." Already, domestic anti-immigrant pressures in Germany and elsewhere have contributed to barriers against the movement of people which are clearly harmful to the

EU's own economic growth, let alone the progress and European integration of the non-Schengen east European states. If this Schengen curtain develops even more ferrous characteristics in the future, it could contribute to a split in geographical Europe which will last not for decades but for an epoch, or for all foreseeable time.

Notes

1. European Union, *Agenda 2000: Eine stärkere und erweiterte Union* [A stronger and enlarged Union] (Brussels: European Commission, 1997).

2. "The European Union Decides It Might One Day Talk Turkey," *Economist*, December 18, 1999, pp. 42–43.

3. "The Nice Summit: So That's All Agreed, Then," *Economist*, December 16, 2000, pp. 25–28. The Gothenburg summit of June 2001 essentially recapitulated Nice.

4. "Jacques Delors und Vaclav Havel—der frühere EU-Kommissionschef und Tschechiens Präsident im Gespräch" [The former head of the EU Commission and the President of the Czech Republic in Conversation], *Die Zeit*, February 1, 2001, <www.zeit.de/2001/06/Politik/200106_havel_delors.html>.

5. See "Could Everything Now Go Horribly Wrong?" *Economist*, June 16, 2001, pp. 49–50.

6. See Neill Nugent, *The Government and Politics of the European Union* (Durham, N.C.: Duke University Press, 1999), for a detailed description of the discursive practices that define the EU's governance procedures.

7. See Michael Mandelbaum, *NATO Expansion: A Bridge to the Nineteenth Century* (Chevy Chase, Md.: Center for Political and Strategic Studies, 1997).

8. See Gideon Rachman, "Europe's Magnetic Attraction: A Survey of European Enlargement," *Economist*, May 19, 2001.

9. See Adrian Karatnycky, Alexander Motyl, and Aili Piano, eds., *Nations in Transit, 1999–2000* (New Brunswick, N.J.: Transaction, 2001).

10. See John Peet, "Europe's Mid-Life Crisis," *Economist*, May 31, 1997, pp. 14–15.

11. Ulrich Schäfer, "Magnet für Einwanderer" [A Magnet for Immigrants], *Der Spiegel*, February 19, 2001, p. 116.

12. "Vertrag von Nizza unterzeichnet" [Nice Treaty signed], *Frankfurter Allgemeine Zeitung*, February 27, 2001, p. 1.

13. See "Bann über Österreich?" [Boycott of Austria?], *Die Zeit*, February 10, 2000, p. 1.

14. For a discussion of the challenges posed by enlargement, see Andrew Moravcsik, "Europe's Integration at Century's End," in *Centralization or Fragmentation? Europe Facing the Challenges of Deepening, Diversity, and Democracy*, edited by Andrew Moravcsik (New York: Council on Foreign Relations, 1998), pp. 36–41.

15. See Karatnycky, Motyl, and Piano, *Nations in Transit*.

16. See Oleksandr Pavliuk, *The European Union and Ukraine: The Need for a New Vision* (New York: East–West Institute, 1999), pp. 13–15.

17. Fraser Cameron, "Relations between the European Union and Ukraine," in *Ukraine and Its Western Neighbors*, edited by James Clem and Nancy Popson (Washington, D.C.: Woodrow Wilson International Center for Scholars, 2000), p. 79.

18. Such exclusion is not just discursive. The EU's protectionist agricultural and industrial policies work to exclude competitive products—such as steel, textiles, and meat and dairy products—from Ukraine as well as many other former communist states.

19. Helmut Schmidt, "Wer nicht zu Europa gehört" [Who does not belong to Europe?], *Die Zeit*, October 11, 2000. See also "Edmund Stoiber trifft Helmut Schmidt: Ein Gespräch über die Zukunft der EU und deutsche Interessen" [Edmund Stoiber meets Helmut Schmidt: A dialogue about the future of the EU and German interests], *Die Zeit*, February 8, <www.zeit.de/2001/07/Politik/200107_stoiber.html>.

20. "Die Grenzen Europas," interview with Jacque Le Goff [in German], *Die Zeit*, December 11, 2000 <www.zeit.de/2000/50/Kultur/200050_legoff.html>.

21. Samuel P. Huntington, *The Clash of Civilizations and the Remaking of World Order* (New York: Simon & Schuster, 1996).

22. See Charles Tilly, *Coercion, Capital, and European States, AD 990–1990* (Oxford: Blackwell, 1990).

23. See F. Stephen Larrabee, "Ukraine's Place in European and Regional Security," in *Ukraine in the World*, edited by Lubomyr Hajda (Cambridge, Mass.: Ukrainian Research Institute, 1998), pp. 257–59.

24. Semyon I. Appatov, "Ukraine, NATO and EU: Problems of Cooperation and Security," paper presented at the 42d Annual Convention of the International Studies Association (Chicago, February 22–24, 2001), p. 6.

25. "Ten Years since the Wall Fell," *Economist*, November 6, 1999, p. 22.

26. See Madeleine Albright, "Enlarging NATO," *Economist*, February 15, 1997, pp. 21–23; James Sherr, *Ukraine's New Time of Troubles* (Camberley, U.K.: Conflict Studies Research Centre, 1998); Bruce Clark, "NATO," *Economist*, April 24, 1999, pp. 3–18.

27. "Ukraine on the Way to the European Union," Occasional Report 71 (Kiev: Center for Peace, Conversion, and Foreign Policy of Ukraine), October 15, 1998; Werner Weidenfeld, ed., *Central and Eastern Europe on the Way to the European Union* (Gütersloh, Germany: Bertelsmann Foundation, 1995); Robert Cottrell, "Europe Survey," *Economist*, October 23, 1999, pp. 14–15; Clark, "NATO."

28. See Rey Koslowski, "European Migration Regimes: Emerging, Enlarging, and Deteriorating." *Journal of Ethnic and Migration Studies*, October 1998, pp. 735–49.

29. David Hearst, "Poles to Police Europe's Lace Curtain." *Guardian*, December 2, 2000.

30. Pavliuk, *European Union and Ukraine*.

31. Natalia Tchourikova, "Ukraine: EU Entry Depends on Internal Developments," *RFE/RL Weekday Magazine*, October 21, 1998; "Kuchma Says European Union Slights Ukraine," Reuters, October 28, 1998.

32. *Foreign Policy of Ukraine Newsletter* (Kiev: Center for Peace, Conversion, and Foreign Policy of Ukraine), March 11–17, 2000, p. 10.

33. *Foreign Policy of Ukraine Newsletter* (Kiev: Center for Peace, Conversion, and Foreign Policy of Ukraine), January 8–14, 2000, p. 4.

34. *Most advanced*: Czech Republic, Estonia, Hungary, Latvia, Lithuania, Poland, and Slovenia. *Middle*: Albania, Armenia, Bulgaria, Croatia, Georgia, Kyrgyzstan, Macedonia, Moldova,

Romania, Russia, Slovakia, and Ukraine. *Least advanced*: Azerbaijan, Belarus, Kazakstan, Tajikistan, Turkmenistan, Uzbekistan, and Yugoslavia. I base these categories on the ratings contained in Freedom House's Nations in Transit reports. See Adrian Karatnycky, Alexander J. Motyl, and Boris Shor, eds., *Nations in Transit, 1997* (New Brunswick, N.J.: Transaction, 1997); Adrian Karatnycky, Alexander J. Motyl, and Charles Graybow, eds., *Nations in Transit, 1998* (New Brunswick, N.J.: Transaction, 1999); Karatnycky, Motyl, and Piano, eds., *Nations in Transit, 1999–2000*; and Adrian Karatnycky, Alexander J. Motyl, and Amanda Schnetzer, eds., *Nations in Transit, 2001* (forthcoming). This and the next paragraph are drawn from Alexander J. Motyl, "Ten Years after the Soviet Collapse: The Persistence of the Past and Prospects for the Future," in Karatnycky, Motyl, and Schnetzer, *Nations in Transit, 2001*.

35. See Leon Aron, "Structure and Context in the Study of Post-Soviet Russia," *Russian Outlook*, winter 2001.

36. Like any theoretical generalization, mine does not claim to be based on the discovery of a natural law, suggest that any category of countries was uniformly affected, or insist that all other factors have no explanatory relevance. As Anatol Lieven correctly points out, ethnic and cultural traditions have some—probably not insignificant—role to play in accounting for the systemic maladies of the countries of the Caucasus and Central Asia. Conversely, it is probably possible to subsume even these factors under my totalitarian and imperial umbrellas.

37. See Alexander J. Motyl, *Revolutions, Nations, Empires: Conceptual Limits and Theoretical Possibilities* (New York: Columbia University Press, 1999), pp. 55–57.

38. Motyl, *Revolutions*, pp. 58–60.

39. See the argument of Borys Tarasyuk, "Ukraine in the World," in Hajda, *Ukraine in the World*, pp. 14–15.

40. For a balanced discussion of these sensitive issues, see Anatol Lieven, *Ukraine and Russia: A Fraternal Rivalry* (Washington, D.C.: United States Institute of Peace, 2000).

41. See Thomas Graham, Alexander J. Motyl, and Blair Ruble, "The Challenge of Russian Reform at a Time of Uncertainty," *The Russia Initiative: Reports of the Four Task Forces* (New York: Carnegie Corporation of New York, 2001), pp. 37–63.

42. For a sustained comparison of the Soviet successor states and Africa, see Mark Beissinger and Crawford Young, eds., "The Quest for the Efficacious State in Africa and Eurasia," unpublished manuscript, University of Wisconsin, Madison.

43. See Jack F. Matlock, "Dealing with a Russia in Turmoil," *Foreign Affairs*, May–June 1996, pp. 38–51; Sherman Garnett, "Russia's Illusory Ambitions," *Foreign Affairs,* March–April 1997, pp. 61–76; Stephen M. Meyer, "The Military," in *After the Soviet Union: From Empire to Nations*, edited by Timothy J. Colton and Robert Legvold (New York: Norton, 1992), pp. 113–46.

44. International Institute for Strategic Studies, *The Military Balance, 1995–1996* (Oxford: Oxford University Press, 1995), pp. 75–167; *The Military Balance 1997–1998* (Oxford: Oxford University Press, 1997), pp. 73–163; *The Military Balance 1999–2000* (Oxford: Oxford University Press, 1999), pp. 79–170. All figures were rounded to the nearest whole number.

45. See Alexander J. Motyl, *Imperial Ends: The Decay, Collapse, and Revival of Empires* (New York: Columbia University Press, 2001), p. 100.

46. See Thomas Graham, "A World without Russia?" paper presented at a meeting of the Jamestown Foundation (Washington, D.C., June 9, 1999).

47. For a longer version of this argument, see Motyl, *Imperial Ends*, pp. 102–5.

48. See Orest Subtelny, *Ukraine: A History* (Toronto: University of Toronto Press, 1988).

49. See Mykhailo Sosnovs'kyi, *Dmytro Dontsov: Politychnyi portret* [Dmytro Dontsov: A political portrait] (New York: Trident International, 1974), pp. 98–107.

50. See Alexander J. Motyl, *The Turn to the Right: The Ideological Origins and Development of Ukrainian Nationalism, 1919–1929* (Boulder, Colo.: East European Monographs, 1980).

51. See Paul D'Anieri, Robert Kravchuk, and Taras Kuzio, *Politics and Society in Ukraine* (Boulder, Colo.: Westview, 1999).

52. See Alexander J. Motyl, "State, Nation, and Elites in Independent Ukraine," in *Contemporary Ukraine*, edited by Taras Kuzio, pp. 3–16 (Armonk, N.Y.: Sharpe, 1998).

53. For an excellent discussion of Ukraine's relationship with Russia, see Roman Solchanyk, *Ukraine and Russia: The Post-Soviet Transition* (Lanham, Md.: Rowman and Littlefield, 2001).

54. Roman Solchanyk, "Ukraine: 'Returning' to Europe?" *Ukrainian Weekly*, February 18, 2001, p. 2. See also Oleksij Haran', *Innenpolitische Faktoren der ukrainischen Aussenpolitik* [Domestic Political Factions in Ukraine's Foreign Policy] (Cologne: Bundesinstitut für ostwissenschaftliche und internationale Studien, 1999).

55. Stephen R. Burant, "Ukraine and East Central Europe," in Hajda, *Ukraine in the World*, pp. 51–59.

56. This and the following two paragraphs are drawn from Motyl, "Ten Years after the Soviet Collapse," in Karatnycky, Motyl, and Schnetzer, *Nations in Transit, 2001*.

57. Ironically, it is in these second-category countries with especially complex institutional legacies that individual policy makers came to play what appeared to be an unusually decisive roles. Although many were genuinely forceful personalities, their policy activism is best understood in terms of the institutionally contradictory setting within which they operated. By "balancing" one another, these institutions expanded the political space available to leaders and thus enabled them to exert exceptional influence on the policy process. Some leaders, such as Tudjman, Meciar, and Milosevic, deflected their countries from institutionally defined upward trajectories; others, such as Boris Yeltsin, Leonid Kravchuk, Kuchma, and Akayev, decelerated their countries' downward drift. Significantly, because such personalist interventions represented deviations from, and not culminations of, past processes of evolutionary change, their impact as "intervening variables" was perforce temporary—a claim with especially worrisome implications for Georgia after Eduard Shevardnadze.

58. See Stephen J. Flanagan, Ellen L. Frost, and Richard L. Kugler, *Challenges of the Global Century: Report of the Project on Globalization and National Security* (Washington, D.C.: Institute for National Strategic Studies, 2001).

59. For a compelling discussion of the downside of globalization, see Dani Rodrik, "Trading in Illusions," *Foreign Policy*, March–April 2001, pp. 55–62.

60. World Economic Forum, "Global Competitiveness Report," <www.weforum.org/publications/GCR/99rankings.asp>; Transparency International, "1999 Corruption Perceptions Index," <www.transparency.de/documents/cpi/index.html>; Tuck School of Business, "Emerging Markets Access Index," <www.dartmouth.edu/tuck/news/media/pr2000052_emai.html>.

61. Heinz Timmermann, "Russland: Strategischer Partner der Europäischen Union? Interessen, Impulse, Widersprüche ( ), *Osteuropa*, October 1999, p. 1003.

62. Otto Kirchheimer, "Confining Conditions and Revolutionary Breakthroughs," *American Political Science Review*, December 1965, pp. 964–74. Of course, it is also perfectly possible for revolutionaries to preach market reform. See Motyl, *Revolutions*, pp. 32–36.

63. Motyl, *Imperial Ends*, pp. 88–113.

64. This argument is drawn from Alexander J. Motyl, "Theorizing Ukraine: Transition and Development in a Post-Communist Context," in *Problems of Development of Ukraine*, edited by Wsevolod Isajiw (forthcoming).

65. Encouraged by the United States, this pact groups together Georgia, Ukraine, Uzbekistan, Azerbaijan, and Moldova. However, as of 2001, Moldova's membership became largely theoretical, while the ability of the other member states to help each other is very limited.

66. See National Intelligence Council, "Global Trends 2015: A Dialogue about the Future with Nongovernmental Experts" (Washington, D.C.: National Intelligence Council, December 2000), pp. 37, 68–69.

67. For a discussion of the consequences of such an outcome for Europe, see Reinhard Meier, "Die Ukraine beeinflusst Europas Zukunft," *Neue Zürcher Zeitung*, February 24–25, 2001, p. 1.

3

Does the EU Have an *Ostpolitik?*

William Wallace

In November 1970, when the six foreign ministers of the European Community (EC) met for the first time in the framework of European Political Cooperation (EPC), there were two substantive items on the agenda: the situation in the Middle East, and the question of how to respond to the Soviet proposal for a European Security Conference. It proved impossible to agree on the first of these. On the second, however, the German interest in providing a multilateral framework within which to pursue *Ostpolitik* and the French interest in developing European initiatives independently of the United States converged. European Economic Community foreign ministers began to negotiate with the USSR on the terms and conditions of a European security pact, while their American ally was preoccupied with southeast Asia. The Conference on Security and Cooperation in Europe (CSCE), as it became, represented a complex trade-off between the Soviet demand to guarantee the frontiers which had been redrawn across east-central and eastern Europe in 1945 and the western European desire to promote gradual political, social, and economic evolution within socialist regimes.

The lengthy negotiations which led up to the Helsinki Declaration of 1974 also provided the context within which EPC developed its characteristic procedures. Working groups of officials prepared for and followed up ministerial meetings, under the chairmanship of the member state holding the EC presidency; when economic issues were at stake, Commission representatives sat in on the discussions. The Danish president of the EC foreign ministers told the European Parliament, after the first two opening sessions of the CSCE in July and September 1973, that "the Nine" had made "a decisive contribution" to the development and tone of the conference as it got under way.[1]

The EU's Common Foreign and Security Policy (CFSP), erected on the well-established foundations of EPC in the Maastricht Treaty of European Union in 1991–1992, had thus been shaped from the outset by the challenges of managing relations with Russia (or with its predecessor state, the USSR). The relationship was, of course, transformed by the retreat of the Soviet Army from central Europe, the unification of Germany, the reorientation of the former socialist states of east-central Europe towards western Europe, and the disintegration of the Soviet Union. Territorial Russia thus became a distant country—at least until Finland joined the EU in 1995. It nevertheless remained important to EU member states, as a supplier of natural gas, as a minor but potentially major trade partner, as a source of transborder criminal activities, and as a necessary player in western efforts to extend stability, democracy, and prosperity to the lands "in between." The German government, more acutely than all its other twelve partners in the EU except the Danes, was conscious that a stable and prosperous Russia was an essential complement to successful enlargement to the EU's immediate eastern neighbors—and that an economically weak and corrupt Russia would threaten the security of the emerging democracies in its former European sphere of influence.

In 1995, enlargement of the EU to include Sweden and Finland again altered perspectives. The vigor which Finnish ministers and officials have demonstrated within the institutions and policy-making procedures of the EU has been remarkable; it has particularly been crucial in developing the "Northern Dimension" of CFSP into a complex pattern of relations with the central authorities of Russia and with the regional authorities closest to the Baltic Sea. Finland, Sweden, and Denmark have acted within the EU as "sponsors" of the aspirations of the Baltic states for membership. Estonia was accepted as a first-round candidate at the European Council in Luxembourg in December 1997, and Latvia and Lithuania were also invited to open negotiations at the Helsinki Council, at the conclusion of the first Finnish EU presidency, in December 1999.

After the intergovernmental review conference called in 1996–1997 to reexamine the development of CFSP had agreed to add the development of

"Common Strategies" to its multilateral procedures, it was—again—Russia which was the focus of the first to be drafted and published, a seventeen-page document reviewing the broad range of political and economic relations. The Russian government took this sufficiently seriously to respond with its own list of priorities in EU–Russian relations, as the basis for a more intensive bilateral dialogue. Prime ministers and chancellors, commissioners and the EU's newly appointed high representative, have traveled to Moscow more frequently than to any other capital outside the EU (and to Saint Petersburg, even to Kaliningrad), while Russian political leaders and officials have maintained an active—though not always easy—dialogue with Brussels and with western European governments. After the intensive exchanges with the applicant states, and the constant transatlantic dialogue with the United States, this has been the most active external relationship which the EU and its member governments have maintained; more visits by EU heads of government and commissioners have been made to Russia since the mid-1990s than to Turkey, a key NATO ally and an EU applicant, or to Poland, the most important of the states likely to join the EU within the next three to four years. For the Brussels institutions, for the German, British, and Nordic member governments, certainly, policy towards Russia was a high priority throughout the 1990s and remains a high priority today.

Strategy papers, however, particularly when written at such length and to be published, do not necessarily constitute the coherent framework for collective foreign policy which they claim to represent. The EU's foreign and security policy is not entirely "common"; German and Swedish assumptions about developments within Russia, and their significance, differ from those of policy makers in Madrid and Lisbon, where developments in the western Mediterranean and north Africa appear more urgent. The substance of the Northern Dimension has been about environmental pollution, border control, and crime rather more than about grand strategy or political diplomacy: a partnership between the EU and northwestern Russia, rather than an approach to Russia and the Commonwealth of Independent States (CIS) as a whole.

The agenda for negotiation between the EU and Russia in 2001 ranged from water treatment plants for Kaliningrad and Saint Petersburg, to training for military officers, to cooperation among law enforcement agencies: a practical *Ostpolitik* rather than a grand strategy. This raises the underlying question for western European policy makers twelve years after the cold war ended: Given the political and economic weakness of Russia, and the difficulties of developing a mutually confident political relationship with Russia's changing political leadership, what sort of *Ostpolitik* towards Russia should the EU attempt to pursue?

How "Common" a Common Foreign Policy?

After nearly 20 years of operating the intergovernmental procedures of European Political Cooperation, EC member governments in 1989 had developed an extensive network of communication among national foreign ministries, reinforced by regular working-group meetings among officials and frequent meetings by foreign ministers themselves. These procedures, however, were consultative rather than binding. Member governments frequently pursued independent initiatives without agreeing them in advance with their partners, sometimes even without consulting them: the French on the Middle East, the Greeks on relations with Turkey. Until the signature of the Single European Act (SEA) in 1985, the intergovernmental procedures of European Political Cooperation had been kept at arms length from the EC itself and the Commission as manager of EC external relations.

The SEA established a small European Political Cooperation Secretariat in Brussels, and formally linked these two arms of European external diplomacy through their joint subordination to the European Council. A small unit in the Commission Secretariat-General attempted to provide liaison, and to link the economic instruments of EC external relations to the political guidance of European Political Cooperation. Within most national foreign ministries, however, the political diplomacy of European Political Cooperation was managed by departments of the political directorate, with the political director himself playing a key role in the regular pattern of consultation, while the external relations of the EC fell within the economic directorate. There was therefore a wide gap between the ambitious rhetoric of European Political Cooperation and the extremely limited ability to deliver common policy through common instruments.[2]

Western European relations with the Soviet Union in the 1980s, as in the 1970s, were conducted primarily through bilateral channels and through the CSCE. Soviet refusal to recognize the EC as such, as an unacceptable symbol of capitalist integration, had left the Commission with only a handful of staff concerned with central and eastern Europe. Federal Germany and other European Economic Community member states had moved from the late 1970s towards substantial imports of natural gas from the USSR, against strong American opposition, in order to diversify away from dependence on Middle Eastern energy supplies. But the EC had not yet developed a common energy policy, leaving member governments arguing over energy security within NATO instead. The decision of the Group of Seven Summit in Paris, in July 1989, to nominate the European Commission as coordinating agency for economic assistance to countries emerging from state socialism therefore forced the Commission to improvise, transferring staff from managing aid to developing countries to initiating programs for eastern Europe. The Group of Seven decision appeared to some in Brussels a signal of confidence in the Commission; it was, however, driven in large part by the U.S. determination to transfer the financial responsibility for assisting economic transformation to its European allies.

Between 1989 and 1992, West European governments found themselves attempting both to come to terms with a rapidly changing set of demands from central and eastern European countries and to redesign their institutional framework for collective foreign policy. The Belgian proposal for an Intergovernmental Conference (IGC) on "Political Union," alongside the planned IGC on Economic and Monetary Union, swiftly followed in April 1990 by a joint Franco-German proposal along the same lines, was a response to the prospect of German unification. A united Germany of 80 million people, with direct frontiers with Poland and Czechoslovakia and an increasing interest and influence across central and eastern Europe, required a firm framework for concerted western European policy if future German governments were to avoid the temptation to act independently in pursuing their dominant interests. The French government was most actively concerned to bind Germany into a tighter foreign policy framework—though without accepting the German preference that such a framework should be contained in turn within a political union with federal characteristics.

Throughout 1991, officials and ministers from the twelve EC member states were thus engaged in complex negotiations over the definition of a "common foreign policy" and the instruments and procedures needed to realize the concept; while a parallel negotiation was under way within NATO over how far a stronger EC within a reuniting Europe might be allowed to develop security and defense policies autonomous from American leadership. While they negotiated, the national movements in the Soviet Baltic republics demanded full independence from Moscow, ethnic fighting broke out in parts of the Caucasus, Yugoslavia moved towards disintegration, and the process of reform within the USSR first slowed and was then blocked by an attempted coup. The Soviet Union formally ceased to exist days before the IGC endgame at Maastricht; and the treaty was agreed among governments in bitter dispute over the recognition of Croatia as an independent state.

Article J of the Maastricht Treaty on European Union declares that "A common foreign and security policy is hereby established," which "shall include all questions related to the security of the Union, including the eventual framing of a common defense policy, which might in time lead to a common defense." The shift from initial confidence to qualifying subclauses reflects carefully crafted compromises among member governments about the future relationship between NATO—as for the past 50 years the framework for cooperation on security and defense among western European states—and the EU, as well as about the degree to which the EU should move from its previously intergovernmental framework for foreign policy cooperation towards a federal model. The French government favored much greater autonomy from NATO, but within an intergovernmental framework. The British were skeptical about further moves towards closer cooperation in this field, particularly if they threatened to weaken NATO. The Germans wanted to move towards a more federal "political union," but were unprepared for such a union to pursue an active or autonomous defense policy and anxious to retain close ties with the United States. CFSP was thus much less of a radical departure from the loose procedures of European Political Cooperation than a first glance at the Maastricht Treaty suggested. It has taken a further ten years of mutual learning, with two further intergovernmental conferences, to give it substance.

The EU and Russia in the Early 1990s

Meanwhile, central and eastern Europe were changing, radically and continually, forcing western European governments to respond. The PHARE (Poland and Hungary, Aid for the Reconstruction of Economies) program of assistance for the "restructuring of economies" in Poland and Hungary, established in mid-1989 to assist the first two nonsocialist governments within the former socialist bloc, was extended to Czechoslovakia, and then to Romania and Bulgaria, as other regimes collapsed. A new financing instrument, the European Bank for Reconstruction and Development, was established in 1990 (under strong pressure from the French administration to create a new institution) to encourage and channel investment to these emerging market economies.

The disintegration of Yugoslavia presented the infant CFSP with its first major challenge, with the Luxembourg foreign minister (as president of the Council of Ministers for the first half of 1991) proclaiming that "this is the hour of Europe"; but the hour passed in confusion and disorder. Most member governments were reluctant to abandon the principle that existing state structures should be maintained within existing boundaries, even as fighting broke out between Croatian forces and the Yugoslav army; but the German foreign minister maintained both that the EU must move towards a more integrated approach and that Germany would if necessary recognize the independence of Croatia unilaterally.

Strong support for President Gorbachev within the USSR—and, within most western European foreign ministries, for the continued territorial integrity of the USSR—conflicted with concerns over disorders within several Soviet republics, and in particular with historical obligations to treat the Baltic republics as special cases. EU governments were unprepared for the Moscow coup of August 1991 (during which French president François Mitterand offered tentative recognition to the conservative coup leaders) and for the breakup of the Soviet Union which followed. In the course of 1991, western diplomats struggled to develop a degree of expertise on Georgia and Armenia, Uzbekistan and Tajikistan, Soviet republics which had not previously claimed any priority among western analysts.

The German government had the strongest incentives for pursuing close relations with the Soviet leadership during the transition from cold war confrontation. Successful unification of Germany required the withdrawal of 350,000 Soviet troops from East Germany, across Poland. A Soviet leadership which had confidence in the intentions of its German counterpart was more likely to press ahead with a speedy and peaceful withdrawal. German chancellor Helmut Kohl cultivated a close relationship with Soviet president Mikhail Gorbachev, through frequent meetings—though carefully balanced by close contacts with other heads of government within the EU and with the U.S. administration. German financial assistance was provided to build new homes for returning Soviet army personnel, as well as to underwrite other costs of economic and political transition. The bilateral German–Russian relationship was in many ways more important to the evolution of east–west relations within Europe in the early 1990s than the multilateral approach of the EU as an entity.

Nevertheless, the EU had moved collectively to accommodate the changes within the USSR itself, using the economic instruments of the EC more than the collective diplomacy of European Political Cooperation and CFSP. Most-favored-nation treatment for Soviet foreign trade was offered before the end of 1989; a Trade and Cooperation Agreement followed, which established a "Joint Committee" for multilateral consultations as well as offering limited economic concessions. The EU moved rapidly in the autumn of 1991 to recognize the independence of the three Baltic states, and to include them within its developing programs of assistance for central and eastern European states in transition. The breakup of the Soviet Union, which followed, led to the creation of a parallel program to PHARE, Technical Assistance for the CIS countries (TACIS): rapidly assembled by the Commission on the PHARE model, and chaotically run in its early years as staff assigned to this new activity learned both about their responsibilities and about the problems of operating within Russia and the newly independent states. In order to manage the TACIS program, and to develop economic relations with this previously closed region, the European Commission established representations in Moscow and across the rest of the CIS, moving more rapidly in this respect than most member states.[3]

The learning curve for the EU and for its member governments was steep. The 8 member states of the Warsaw Pact had now become 22 states in transition. Yugoslavia had disintegrated, as had Czechoslovakia; Albania had become much more open, and much more unstable. Pressures from Poland, Hungary, and the Czech Republic for early accession to the EU and NATO were countered by farming lobbies and by textile and steel interests opposed to offering them the trade concessions they most urgently needed. The rapid unification of Germany proved far more expensive, and painful, than Chancellor Kohl had anticipated; his promise to the German electorate that taxes would not have to be raised substantially to meet the costs of unification led to increased borrowing by the German government, which pushed the EU economy into a moderate recession. Negotiations on the new Europe Agreements with the governments of "the lands between" Germany and Russia proved contentious within the EU, once the management of negotiations passed from the rhetorical commitments of heads of government to the detailed defense of entrenched interests by officials from domestic ministries.

The approach which the EU collectively developed towards the applicant states set a pattern, however—of conditionality, economic concessions promised in return for meeting stated political, administrative and economic conditions—which was relatively easy to transfer to negotiations with Russia and the rest of the CIS. The "Copenhagen criteria," spelled out at the Copenhagen meeting of the European Council (of EU heads of government) in June 1993 promised eventual full membership to Poland and the other applicants when they had satisfied the EU that they had firmly established democratic political institutions (including full application of the rule of law and respect for civil liberties and minority rights), had properly functioning market economies, and had demonstrated their ability to adopt the Community *acquis* in full. The Essen European Council the following year converted this into a "preaccession strategy," with annual reports from the Commission to the European Council on the progress each applicant state was making in meeting those targets.[4]

Negotiations with Russia started on a different basis, without the prospect of eventual EU membership as an incentive. Political conditions in return for economic concessions had, however, become the familiar pattern of negotiations within the CSCE in the years before 1989. Russia emerged as an independent state already heavily indebted to public and private western institutions, striking a bargain with the other CIS states that it would shoulder most of the accumulated Soviet-era foreign debt in return for retaining most of the USSR's overseas assets. Substantial financial assistance, and limited foreign investment and private finance, increased the negotiating imbalance between Russia and EU governments after independence. Conversely, stability in Russia mattered to western European governments, and the argument that the EU should do all that it could to support Russian president Boris Yeltsin and the domestic reform process carried political weight.

Negotiations on a closer institutionalized relationship between the EU and newly independent Russia were opened in March 1992. These led to the signing of a Partnership and Cooperation Agreement (PCA) with Moscow in June 1994, under which the EU promised to remove most quotas on Russian exports, to support Russia's candidacy for membership in the General Agreement on Tariffs and Trade (later the World Trade Organization), and to move towards the establishment of a free-trade area, conditional on progress towards a functioning market economy within Russia. PCAs on a similar model were thereafter signed with Ukraine and other CIS states.

The PCA established a framework of consultations at different levels, from twice-yearly summits between the Russian president and the EU presidency "troika" (the rolling group of three prime ministers or foreign ministers consisting of the current president-in-office together with his predecessor and successor) to expert working groups and meetings between European parliamentarians and the Duma. The intention to build a political, as well as economic, partnership with a western-oriented Russia was, however, disrupted by the Russian army's intervention in Chechnya in December 1994, delaying the EU's ratification of the PCA until late 1997.

In managing the detail of conditional economic and financial relations, however, it was the Commission which led, in consultation with ministries of trade and agriculture from the member states as well as with foreign offices, using the EC's economic instruments rather than the (limited) political instruments of CFSP. Characteristically, EU negotiations moved from initial political declarations to detailed and technical negotiations, in which broader strategic considerations were buried. The detailed scrutiny of administrative capacities, legislative adaptation, and economic regulation which was put in place for the applicant states was harder to impose on Russia: The Commission would have needed a much larger staff to monitor developments across the country, and the Russian authorities were less prepared to cooperate. Western commitment to support the Yeltsin regime conflicted with the principle that financial assistance should be calibrated against domestic reform. There was therefore a wide gap between declared policy and practice, between the intermittent declarations of EU heads of government and the management of relations in between.

"The main problem with the EU's policies" towards the former socialist states in the early 1990s, Jan Zielonka has argued, was that they did not "fit into any concrete design for Europe" as a whole. David Allen put it more strongly in reviewing the EU's approach to the former Soviet Union, concluding that "the EU [did] not have a clear and coherent policy toward Russia and the other former Soviet states."[5] Writing in 1996, Gunther Burghardt, the senior Commission official concerned with liaison between the economic and political pillars of the EU during this period, was even blunter:

CFSP so far has neither improved visibility nor continuity of the Union's external action. Discontinuity of widely overburdened six-month rotating "presidencies" is, on the contrary, the main feature of the system. . . . While the U.S. superpower teaches us how to achieve maximum publicity with often little cash, the EU is the champion of maximum, notably financial, contributions and minimum political gains.[6]

National Interests

One major obstacle to a consistent and coherent approach to Russia was the overload of foreign policy problems experienced by EU member governments. The management of the deepening conflict within the former Yugoslavia preoccupied them from 1992 on. British and French troops went into Bosnia with the United Nations Protection Force (UNPROFOR), to be joined by Dutch, Spanish, and other contingents. Western European ships began to patrol the Adriatic; later, western European representatives also attempted to monitor traffic on the Danube. Poland mattered most among the applicant states to the major western European governments, but frequent changes of government in Poland complicated relations and interrupted the process of transition. Developments in Slovakia, Romania, and Bulgaria required careful attention and explanation. Efforts to assist the transition within Ukraine were frustrated by the weakness of the regime; while in Belarus the new government appeared to be increasingly anti-Western. Civil war in Georgia, and conflict between Armenia and Azerbaijan over Karabakh, added to the complexity. Ministers and officials were forced to learn about the complexities of political conflict and economic weakness in states previously unknown to them, within a region which until 1989 had been beyond any western influence, under Soviet control. Outside Europe, in addition, several EU states contributed sea and air forces to the war to recapture Kuwait from Iraq, while the United Kingdom and France both provided division-strength ground forces.

Policy towards Russia was therefore made within national capitals in competition for ministerial attention with a multitude of other concerns. The management of multilateral relations with Russia, outside the economic competencies of the Commission, was supported by a multinational unit of 20 staff members within the Secretariat to the Council of Ministers. Beyond that, the direction of multilateral EU foreign relations depended on the efforts of the most active member governments and the leadership provided (or not provided) by the government holding the six-monthly presidency of the Council: Luxembourg for the first six months of 1991, followed by the Netherlands; Portugal for the first half of 1992, followed by the United Kingdom, Denmark, and then Belgium in 1993; Greece and then Germany in 1994; and France and then Spain in 1995.

Germany, as has been noted, had by far the most active national engagement with Russia, with substantial economic as well as political interests at stake. The United Kingdom retained from its cold war pretensions to great-power status a significant cadre of experts on Russia within its diplomatic and intelligence services. Past successes in prime ministerial east–west diplomacy, from British prime minister Harold Macmillan's relations with Russian president Nikita Khrushchev to British prime minister Margaret Thatcher's early cultivation of Gorbachev, encouraged John Major as British prime minister to pay personal attention to western European (and western) relations with Yeltsin and those around him—even though British economic interests in Russia were minor. French presidents and prime ministers also saw active diplomacy towards Russia as a symbol of their claims to be a serious European power.

Beyond these three, most EU member governments had few direct interests at stake in relations with the former Soviet Union, and limited national expertise. Italian governments had successfully pursued trading relations, and supported Italian investment, in socialist eastern Europe before 1989; the strength and self-confidence of the Italian Communist Party (PCI) had also made for a sophisticated understanding of the Soviet legacy. But the cold war legacy also shaped Italian politics in the early 1990s, as both the Christian Democrats and the PCI disintegrated and successor parties emerged, leaving little energy for an imaginative foreign policy. Denmark, which held the EU presidency from January to June 1993, had an active policy towards the Baltic states, and therefore towards their Russian neighbor. The Danish and German governments had launched the Council of Baltic Sea States in 1992, with the specific aim of involving Russia in multilateral cooperation within the region. But this was an approach towards north-western Russia, not a broad strategy towards Russia as a whole.

It was not until Sweden, Finland, and Austria joined the EU, in January 1995, that the EU gained a significant group of states which placed common policy towards Russia among the highest priorities of their foreign policies. Southern EU member states, indeed, resisted the diversion of funds and attention from Europe's Mediterranean associates to the states of central and eastern Europe that were in transition. At the Corfu European Council, in

June 1994, the Greek presidency had succeeded in placing the question of the balance between eastern policy and Mediterranean policy on the EU agenda, in particular persuading its partners to agree that negotiations for EU membership with Cyprus and Malta would start within six months of the conclusion of the forthcoming intergovernmental conference. The sequence of French, Spanish, and Italian presidencies in 1995–1996 led to a concerted effort by these governments to redress this perceived imbalance between the attention—and the financial transfers—dedicated to eastern Europe and to Europe's dependent south. The Spanish presidency in November 1995 launched a new Barcelona Process for Mediterranean Partnership, with an ambitious budget and future program.[7]

Skillful Finnish diplomacy, supported by the Swedes, managed once inside the EU to transfer Nordic initiatives to build links with Russia around common environmental and security concerns onto the EU agenda, without waiting for Finland's first turn to occupy the EU presidency, due for the autumn and winter of 1999. Finland's long land border with Russia necessitated a far more direct concern with domestic developments and with their overspill into international politics than other EU member states. The Finnish prime minister launched a Northern Dimension initiative in November 1997, the basic aim of which he described as "to integrate Russia into Europe as a democracy and a market economy." This northern initiative was, among other factors, intended to counterbalance the pull by other member governments to the south—as well as defining a security relationship with Russia across northern Europe which did not place NATO at the center (to the potential embarrassment of these two Nordic neutral states). Finnish initiative, rather than collective reflection, thus redefined a significant part of the agenda for EU relations with Russia. Regional interests, cross-border travel, trade, and illegal activities, nuclear safety, air and water pollution—first- and third-pillar issues more than the second-pillar issues of CFSP—were at the core of this Russia–EU relationship.

Second-pillar issues, however, unavoidably brought in the importance of NATO, as the forum within which western strategy towards the Soviet bloc had been shaped over the previous 40 years. American policy makers had preferred to define east–west strategy, with their European allies consulted once the overall approach was set. European *Ostpolitik* had been successfully developed under discreet German leadership, through the Helsinki process, while Richard Nixon's administration was distracted by Vietnam. The Kissinger "Year of Europe" initiative, in April 1973, was intended to reassert

American leadership over western foreign policy; it provoked a bitter confrontation with France, in particular, not only about east–west relations but also about western policy towards the Middle East in the wake of the October 1973 Arab–Israeli conflict, before a compromise on the relative autonomy of European consultations on foreign policy was negotiated, within the NATO framework, in the summer of 1974.[8]

The administration of George H. W. Bush had taken the lead, in close partnership with the German government, in negotiating German unification without making any formal concessions about the future of NATO.[9] Policy on NATO enlargement, between 1990 and 1997, was set and reset in Washington, with Bill Clinton's administration declaring itself committed to enlargement before consulting any of its European allies. American policies towards Russia and towards the lands between followed different priorities from those which seemed important to Germany and to other EU governments. American initiatives, to support the rapid transformation of the Soviet and then Russian economy, to provide financial assistance to Russia, to train (or retrain) Russian and eastern European police to combat cross-border organized crime, as often competed with or cut across EU initiatives as were successfully coordinated with them. Washington, in sum, was happier for the EU collectively to play a secondary role in supporting the economic and political transition of the former socialist states than to attempt to pursue an autonomous political strategy. Russia, the former superpower equipped with a deteriorating nuclear deterrent, was a subject for NATO strategic concern, not for too great a degree of European autonomy. Russian leaders, in return, continued to regard NATO as defining east–west security relations, while seeing relations with the EU—and the prospect of EU enlargement—as unthreatening.

German governments, constantly aware of the need to be attentive to their American patron as well as to their EU partners, were therefore discreet in their bilateral conversations with Russian leaders. British governments accepted that western European efforts should be ancillary to those of the western alliance as a whole, under American leadership. The limitations of EU post–cold war *Ostpolitik* were not only the result of divergences between northern and southern member states, and of competing external problems crowding in on national governments. They were also a reflection of the constraints which had grown up over the previous 40 years within NATO, and of ingrained assumptions about American strategic leadership and European acquiescence in that leadership, which made the definition of an overall policy towards the former Soviet Union a topic EU governments were reluctant openly to address.

Was the "Common Strategy" Truly Common?

Article J.4 of the Treaty on European Union negotiated at Maastricht committed member governments to consider revision of the provisions agreed on Common Foreign and Security Policy "on the basis of a report to be presented in 1996 ... to the European Council." This registered the unresolved differences between the French government and others over how far CFSP should aim to become autonomous from NATO, including the development of an autonomous defense capability, and allowed the French to reopen the question in the light of some years of experience of operating CFSP procedures. Delays in ratifying the Maastricht Treaty meant that by the time the next IGC convened, in early 1996, the treaty had only been formally in effect for some two years. But enough experience had been painfully gained, under the acute pressures of the Bosnian conflict most of all, for most member governments to accept that the intergovernmental mechanisms of CFSP were incapable of providing effective collective policies.

Eighteen months of negotiations—in which the willingness of smaller member governments to accept qualified majority voting on foreign policy issues without binding commitment to participate in the actions agreed balanced the determination of larger member states to maintain their predominant influence over EU foreign policy—led to the Treaty of Amsterdam, finally agreed in June 1997. The French proposal to create a "M./Mme PESC" (the French acronym for the "common foreign and security policy") to provide continuing leadership for CFSP in relations with developing countries and countries in transition had been modified into agreement that the secretary-general to the Council should be additionally designated "High Representative for the common foreign and security policy," with a new deputy secretary-general to assist with his other functions. The revised article 13 of the Treaty of European Union (formerly article J.3) committed the European Council to "decide on common strategies to be implemented by the Union in areas where the Member States have important interests in common," which should set out "their objectives, duration and the means to be made available by the Union and the Member States." Common strategies must be adopted unanimously by the European Council, with "joint actions" to implement strategies subject to qualified majority voting.

It had been understood throughout the tortuous negotiations on the closer definition of a common foreign and security policy and the procedures and instruments through which it should be realized that the first priority in developing such common strategies should be the relationship with Russia. EU governments had in practice been edging slowly towards a consensus on political relations with Russia since the outbreak of the first Chechen war. The Commission had presented a "communication" on the political context within which assistance to Russia needed to be placed to the informal foreign ministers' meeting in Carcassonne, in March 1995. It provided an inventory of the various projects under way between the EU and Russia, with a survey of progress towards economic and political reform, and a section on the place of Russia in the developing security and institutional "architecture" of post–cold war Europe. Further discussions and papers led to the adoption of an "action plan" by the General Affairs Council in May 1996, intended to promote the rule of law, further democratic reforms, and increase attention to nuclear safety within Russia—though the instruments through which it would pursue these aims remained limited.[10]

It is hardly surprising that the German government took the lead in drafting a formal Common Strategy towards Russia, in the course of 1998, reacting to the collapse of the ruble and looking ahead to the German EU presidency in the first six months of 1999. To the irritation of its Austrian predecessor, German diplomats had begun work with an informal group drawn from the most active and interested member states—the United Kingdom, France, and Finland (due to succeed Germany in the six-monthly presidency in the summer of 1999). Drafts were negotiated through the early months of 1999, with southern member states predictably resisting the provision of additional resources for a strategic partnership with Russia, the Finns stressing the importance of the Northern Dimension to EU–Russia relations, and the British emphasizing the importance of nuclear safety. The document which was published as part of the "Conclusions" to the Cologne European Council, in June 1999, was long, moving from an opening statement of the EU's "vision ... for its partnership with Russia" to detailed paragraphs on the fight against organized crime, on the development of "twinning programs" with Russian ministries and government agencies (another idea transferred from experience with the central and eastern European applicants), and on "cross-border and regional cooperation."

Implementation of this common strategy was hampered by three draw-backs. First, the Russian government launched its second intervention into Chechnya within months of the strategy's publication, leading to agonized discussions within the Council of Ministers and between the Council and the Commission about the suspension of some aspects of the PCA or even the imposition of sanctions. Second, the administrative and financial instruments available to the EU collectively were limited, and only loosely coordinated with bilateral programs initiated by member states.

Third, member governments still maintained their autonomy in pursuing relations with Russia. Tony Blair, the British prime minister, visited Saint Petersburg to get to know Vladimir Putin in March 2000, while the General Affairs Council was discussing what sanctions might be imposed and while the presidential election campaign was still under way. Gerhard Schröder, the German chancellor, followed this up with an invitation to Putin to visit Berlin. Meanwhile, six-monthly Russia–EU summits continued, with Putin, as the newly appointed Russian prime minister, presenting a formal response, in the form of a paper on Russia's "Medium-Term EU Strategy," to the EU–Russia summit in Helsinki in October 1999. Programs under the PCA continued relatively unaffected by the wider declaratory framework of the common strategy. The TACIS program was reshaped in the winter of 1999–2000, with scarcely any specific reference to the common strategy, and with a different set of financial priorities.[11]

Other common strategies followed that on Russia, with the Finns launching a parallel document on Ukraine at the Helsinki European Council, and the Portuguese presidency in June 2000 reasserting the importance of the dependent south by repackaging the Barcelona process as a Mediterranean common strategy. By the end of 2000, there was considerable disillusionment in Brussels about the whole concept of published common strategies, with papers circulating both within the Commission and the Council Secretariat questioning their value. The substance of collective EU diplomacy towards Russia was focused rather more towards the agenda of the Northern Dimension, with the Swedish presidency in the first six months of 2001 promoting this aspect of EU–Russia relations through an intensified program of conferences and ministerial meetings. Wastewater treatment in Saint Petersburg and Kaliningrad, the future of Kaliningrad itself after further EU enlargement, cooperation in border management and against cross-border crime, nuclear installations in northern Russia, and transit for Russian trade through the EU-applicant Baltic states—all were as central to this agenda as

Russia's future role in European security or its future relationship with western institutions.

Javier Solana and Chris Patten, jointly responsible for EU collective diplomacy as, respectively, high representative and high commissioner for external relations, were traveling repeatedly around western Russia, Ukraine, and Moldova during this period. The Commission produced a paper for discussion with the Russians on the future of Kaliningrad in January 2001. The "alternative troika," the foreign minister of the presidency together with these two senior officials, jointly met Russian leaders at a major Russia–EU conference in March 2001, speaking one after another with the ambassadors of EU member governments in Moscow gathered behind them.[12]

The Common Strategy had not succeeded, within the first two years of its intended four-year term, in pulling together the different strands of national and collective western European policies towards Russia. It can, however, be seen as a further stage in the mutual learning process of EU member governments, negotiating their shared and separate foreign policy interests and slowly converging towards a common view. The painful process of setting out common positions, advancing from one European Council communiqué to another, has marked the emergence of a loose consensus. The commitment in the Common Strategy to carry out an "inventory" of member state bilateral programs towards Russia marked another careful step towards closer coordination; the results of a Council questionnaire on this were under discussion in Council working groups in the winter of 2000–2001. Parallel moves within the EU towards the creation of a military staff in Brussels, sparked by French and British experience in Bosnia and by the consequent convergence of their national approaches, offered the potential for a more security-oriented perspective to be added to these collective negotiations.

The EU, as skeptical commentators have noted, is moving towards a "common" foreign policy but not yet a "single" foreign policy, towards Russia as well as towards the rest of the former Soviet Union and towards the dependent countries of the south. The degree of coordination of national policies has risen since the early 1990s, and the linkage between collective diplomacy and assistance programs and bilateral initiatives has improved. Unavoidably, however, the outcome does not yet begin to compare with the foreign policy capabilities of a federation, let alone a single state.

Russian Politics and Relations with the EU

A coherent western European *Ostpolitik* would need to incorporate a view on the future institutional relationship among Russia, the EU, and NATO, together with a range of political and economic (and if necessary military) instruments calibrated to encourage the Russian government to cooperate in pursuing preferred objectives, and to discourage it from pursuing policies of which the EU disapproved. In retrospect, the *Ostpolitik* the EU collectively pursued in the 1970s and 1980s, through the CSCE, served these purposes extremely well. Western European governments, however, had the advantage during that period of negotiating with a Soviet leadership which was anxious to be accepted within a wider European political framework, and to gain access to western trade and technology, while operating within the stable security frameworks of NATO and the Warsaw Pact.

In the 1990s, the persistent weakness of the Russian regime and its uncertain relations with Belarus, Ukraine, the new states of the southern Caucasus, and the Russian republics of the northern Caucasus, have made such a conditional strategy far more difficult. The Russian government, from Yeltsin's first administration through to Putin's first presidential team, has itself failed to develop a coherent sense of its approach to western Europe. It is torn between insistence on being treated as a strategic partner, concern about exclusion from the enlarging European Single Market, resentment at perceived European interference in Russia's relations with its "near neighbors" in the CIS, and resistance to Europe's attempted interventions in Russian domestic affairs. The changes in personnel across the Russian government which accompanied the transition from Yeltsin to Putin brought into ministerial office and key advisory posts a new generation with which EU diplomats were unfamiliar, and who themselves were largely unfamiliar with the complexities of western European multilateral politics and with the EU. The six-monthly rotation of the EU presidency, and the pursuit of separate bilateral relationships by EU member governments, did not make mutual understanding easier.

American attempts to pursue a more strategic partnership with Russia throughout the 1990s did not meet with conspicuously greater success. Overcommitment to rapid market reform, which depended on close relations with the early free-market reformers within the Kremlin, gave way to a commitment to support for the Yeltsin regime. Inclusion of Russia within the Partnership for Peace program did not reconcile Russian policy makers to NATO enlargement, forcing the Clinton administration to offer the NATO–Russia Joint Council as a gesture towards associating Russia with political and military consultations among NATO member governments.

U.S. management of relations with Russia as the Kosovo crisis developed was at times clumsy, at times dismissive. Russian illusions about its political and military status within the emerging post–cold war European order made it difficult either to cooperate with Russian policy makers or to handle their frustrated response to noncooperation. The strategic American response to the attempt by a small Russian contingent to occupy Pristina airport, and on that basis to establish a Serb-friendly Russian zone in northern Kosovo as NATO troops entered from the south, was to persuade Romania and Bulgaria to deny Russian planes overflying rights, and to order British troops to preempt them by dashing forward to occupy the airport first. The tactical British response was to surround the airport, providing the undersupplied Russian contingent with the food and water they had failed to secure for themselves. In such a confused and uncertain situation, where the rationale for Russian actions was unclear and the coherence of direction from Moscow was doubtful, flexibility and cooperation on the ground may have been more valuable than broader strategy.

Day-to-day exchanges under TACIS and related programs, as well as through bilateral programs, may appear to fall far short of the broad political strategy which the EU collectively might now have developed to handle its relations with Russia.[13] Closer coordination between national and collective activities, and between western European activities and those undertaken by the United States and through such western international institutions as the International Monetary Fund, would provide the EU with far greater leverage. Rivalry among major EU governments for prestige in cultivating relations with Russian leaders, and the underlying tensions between northern and southern EU members over the competing priorities of eastern and southern external relations, have held back the evolution of common policies. Yet in the uncertain circumstances of Russian domestic politics, and of the Russian economy, throughout the 1990s and in particular after 1998, it was unclear whether any more carefully crafted and executed common strategy would have been capable of fulfillment. The most appropriate interim response may include cross-border links; technical programs to train a new generation of Russian officials; and openness to consultation at different levels, even under adverse political conditions.

The EU collectively is, in any event, not yet capable of managing more than that. The long and painful learning process which the past ten years of CFSP represents—in which relations with Russia have formed a central part of the painful learning—may nevertheless be building the framework for a more coherent collective response to a more stable Russian regime, when that emerges. Such a coherent *Ostpolitik* would, however, require a much greater willingness by member governments to accept effective institutional leadership through the EU, rather than pursuing their own bilateral relationships. It would, in addition, require more generosity from southern member states in recognizing that the pursuit of partnership with Russia and other CIS states is a necessary complement to a Mediterranean strategy, not a competitive threat. Furthermore, it would have to form part of a broader EU approach to the CIS, Russia's own "near abroad," in which the Northern Dimension of CFSP would be complemented by similarly energetic initiatives towards the Black Sea states and the Caucasus.

The EU has not yet addressed the delicate question of how to build mutually-acceptable partnerships with neighboring states which do not include the long-term promise of membership. The crisis in relations with Turkey which followed its exclusion from the list of accepted candidates in 1997, and which led to its inclusion on that list at the Helsinki European Council of December 1999, demonstrated how difficult it can be to satisfy dependent neighbors with anything less. Russia, like Turkey, has pretensions to international status as a "power," with consequent expectations of equal partnership, not of peripheral association. Both states also have elites with a strong sense of national dignity, and a high sensitivity to perceived exclusion. The future framework of European international politics, after the anticipated further enlargement of both the EU and NATO in the mid-2000s, will depend upon the extent to which these two institutional frameworks coincide, and on the success with which they design patterns of association with their immediate neighbors.

The EU does not yet have a coherent *Ostpolitik*. It still lacks sufficient coherence among member governments about foreign policy priorities and objectives. The machinery for foreign policy coordination in Brussels, though much stronger than ten years ago, remains far too weak to provide the leadership and continuity needed, or to pull the different instruments of common action and of national foreign policies together. There will, however, be another Intergovernmental Conference among EU member governments in 2004, at which—as in the Maastricht Treaty in 1992, the

Amsterdam Treaty in 1997, and the Nice Treaty of 2001—reluctant governments are likely to agree that hard experience of foreign policy weaknesses necessitates further strengthening of common capabilities. As from the outset of European Political Cooperation, relations with Russia will continue to be one of the most powerful factors pushing member governments forward.

Notes

1. Knut Andersen, "Political Cooperation," Statement before European Parliament, October 17, 1973; *Bulletin of the European Communities,* no. 10, 1973, p. 104. See also William Wallace and David Allen, "Political Cooperation: Procedure as a Substitute for Policy," in *Policy-Making in the European Communities*, edited by Helen Wallace, William Wallace, and Carole Webb (London: Wiley, 1977).

2. Christopher Hill, "The Capability-Expectations Gap, or Conceptualising Europe's International Role," *Journal of Common Market Studies*, September 1993, pp. 305–28.

3. I recall visiting Tbilisi in the spring of 1995, to find an active EC Representation with close relations with the Georgian government, paralleled by national embassies only from Germany, Britain, and Greece.

4. Ullrich Sedelmeier and Helen Wallace, "Eastern Enlargement: Strategy or Second Thoughts?" in *Policy-Making in the European Union*, 4th edition, edited by Helen Wallace and William Wallace (Oxford: Oxford University Press, 2000); Alan Mayhew, *Recreating Europe* (Cambridge: Cambridge University Press, 1998).

5. Jan Zielonka, "Policies without Strategy: the EU's record in Eastern Europe," in *Paradoxes of European Foreign Policy*, edited by Jan Zielonka (The Hague: Kluwer, 1998); David Allen, "EPC/CFSP, the Soviet Union, and the Former Soviet Republics," in *Foreign Policy of the European Union: from EPC to CFSP and Beyond*, edited by Elfriede Regelsberger, Philippe de Schoutheete de Tervarent and Wolfgang Wessels (Boulder, Colo.: Lynne Rienner, 1997).

6. Gunther Burghardt, "The Potential and Limits of CFSP: What Comes Next?" in *Foreign Policy of the European Union.*

7. Esther Barbé, "Balancing Europe's Eastern and Southern Dimensions," in *Paradoxes of European Foreign Policy.*

8. Timothy Garton Ash, *In Europe's Name: Germany and the Divided Continent* (London: Cape, 1993); David Allen and William Wallace, "European Political Cooperation: Procedure as Substitute for Policy?" in *Policy-Making in the European Communities.*

9. The question of whether informal assurances were given to the Russian leadership in the course of the negotiations on German unification that NATO would not expand further east remains disputed. See, e.g., the accounts given in Philip Zelikow and Condoleeza Rice, *Germany Unified and Europe Transformed: a Study in Statecraft* (Cambridge, Mass.: Harvard University Press, 1995); and Roland Dannreuther, "Escaping the Enlargement Trap in NATO–Russian Relations," *Survival,* winter 1999–2000.

10. Hiski Haukkala, "The Making of the European Union's Common Strategy on Russia," in *The EU Common Strategy on Russia*, edited by Hiski Haukkala and Sergei Medvedev (Helsinki: Finnish Institute of International Affairs, 2001).

11. Stephan de Spiegeleire, "The Implementation of the EU's Common Strategy on Russia," in *EU Common Strategy on Russia*.

12. Personal observation, at conference jointly organized by the Swedish Institute of International Affairs and the EU–Russia Forum.

13. The PHARE program, which operated within the Baltic states as well as with other applicant states, included a number of projects on border management and control. INTER-REG, a commission program for promoting cross-border cooperation, also sponsored a number of projects which linked Baltic states, Kaliningrad, and Russian border regions around Saint Petersburg.

4

Challenges of EU Enlargement

Heather Grabbe

The European Union was slow to respond to the end of the cold war, and its approach to eastward enlargement is symptomatic of that hesitancy. The fall of the Berlin wall and the collapse of communist regimes in central and eastern Europe raised a set of new challenges for which the EU was ill prepared. At the start of the 1990s, not only was foreign and security policy still entirely the responsibility of individual member states with no formal collective role for the EU at all, but the Union's aid budget was also very limited. Moreover, EU leaders had other priorities. While its eastern neighbors began to reconstruct their societies and economies, the EU itself was preoccupied with finishing the process of creating the Single Market through the establishment of a single currency and new areas of common policy such as justice and home affairs. Few politicians were in any mood for grand gestures or financial generosity. Reunifying Germany was the first priority, and the evident political risk and financial expense of that unification made many leaders even more reluctant to commit themselves to enlarging the EU as a whole.

Against this background, the EU hesitated before responding to the demands of its eastern neighbors when they announced their aspirations to be included as equal partners. It took the member states until 1993 to even agree to a formal commitment to enlarge eastwards and to set some conditions for new members (these were, incidentally, the first formal conditions ever set for new member states). It then took another five years for accession negotiations—with only half of the candidates—to actually begin. It now looks likely that the first accessions will occur sometime between 2004 and 2006, a decade and a half after the revolutions that ended the cold war. Although EU leaders often refer to the "historical opportunity" and even the "moral imperative" of enlarging the Union to "reunite" the European continent, few have been willing to move ahead with the rapid reforms of the Union's own institutions and policies that are necessary for the successful integration of so many different countries.

The EU has sometimes been called a "colonial power" in extending its influence eastwards, accused of seeking to dominate eastern Europe just as the Soviet Union once did. If so, the EU must be the most reluctant colonizer in history. It has been slow to respond to those aspiring for membership and indeed has been very reluctant to commit itself to extending its borders. The EU is acting less like an imperial power than like a landlord unwilling to build an extension onto his comfortable dwelling to house lots of poor tenants. Might the new residents be awkward, noisy, and demanding? Might the new extension be costly and threaten the stability of the whole edifice? It is far easier to contemplate renovation and refurbishment of the existing accommodation than to embark on such bold new plans.

On the central and eastern European side, a complex mixture of political, economic, cultural, psychological, and security motivations lies behind the desire to join the EU. Inclusion is seen as a way of reorienting the foreign policy of these states westwards and proving that they are forever out of Moscow's shadow. It is also seen as a way of cementing the integration of the economies of these states into pan-European markets. Newly elected leaders in eastern Europe rapidly signed up with every international organization in an effort to speed up their integration into the world economy and the "international community" (i.e., the west and its associates).

Moreover, as the Balkans descended into war, joining NATO and the EU became an increasingly urgent priority for most eastern European countries. Many saw the EU as a bulwark against both a return to communism and the nationalism that was driving ethnic conflict on their borders. The EU also offers an implicit security guarantee. Although the Union does not yet have military forces of its own, most of its member states are also members of NATO and it is a community of nations. If a non-NATO member of the EU were attacked, other member states would, without a doubt, feel bound to defend it.

There is a very important psychological dimension to EU membership as well. The cold war created the strong feeling that the countries of central Europe had "lost" their European identity and that they needed to "return to Europe" in order to regain that identity. Of course, they had never left Europe geographically, but nonetheless many central European intellectuals felt cut off from Europe by history. By the end of the twentieth century, "Europe" had become synonymous with the European Union, even though it only covered the western side of the continent. Joining the EU thus became the central way of satisfying this desire for inclusion.

Contrary to the widespread view within the EU, the hope for money from Brussels is not in fact a key motivation for membership in the applicant countries. Few central European politicians see the EU as a giant cash register, and many ordinary citizens expect that joining the EU will actually cost their country money.[1] In discussing EU funds after accession, the main concern on the central and eastern European side is equality of treatment with other member states, not the sum of receipts. The states of central Europe just want to be subject to the same rules and have the same rights as current member states; the actual amounts of money received are less important, despite the desperate need for investment in infrastructure. These countries have already lived through the first, difficult decade of transition, turning their economies around and rebuilding their political systems with relatively few subsidies. The one partial exception is agriculture. Here the EU is demanding radical changes which will drive many existing farmers off the land, while concomitantly finding it impossible to promise the massive subsidies hitherto received by EU farmers under the Common Agricultural Policy.

This chapter will investigate why the EU enlargement process is so complex and difficult, how it has worked up to 2002, and how the accession of new members may be managed. It starts with a discussion of the nature and scope of the challenges facing both the EU and the applicants. We then turn to the complexity of the conditions for accession, and the progress made so far towards meeting them. The third section considers the impact of EU enlargement on surrounding countries, owing to the export of the EU's internal security policies (including borders, migration, and asylum). The chapter concludes that the EU must now develop a strategy for enlargement that takes into account the effects on those new neighbors of the enlarged EU which will not for the foreseeable future be members themselves.

The Scale of the Challenge for Both Sides

Why is eastward enlargement so difficult? Many Americans find it frustrating that the EU has not expanded much more rapidly, and particularly that it has not taken in those countries—namely, the Baltic states—which were not invited to join NATO in 1997. But while it is certainly disappointing that the EU has not moved faster, it is not surprising. Many of the major projects in the EU's history have taken much longer than expected. For example, monetary union was discussed for several decades before concrete plans were established. The EU's fifteen current member countries are especially wary about taking steps that will change the Union forever, as is the case with integrating several much poorer countries with very different histories.

The implications of eastward enlargement for the current member states are profound, and many of them are still unknown. The EU has evolved over the decades into a highly complex body, and the most deeply integrated regional organization in the world. It is not just a free-trade area (like the North American Free Trade Agreement), a security alliance (like NATO), or a negotiating forum (like the World Trade Organization). EU membership means that countries make binding laws together, agree on policies together, and transfer considerable sums of money from richer parts of the Union to poorer ones. Membership means giving the citizens of other member states equal rights to live and work in every other country. Letting in poorer countries implies an ongoing obligation to assist in their development. The new members' destinies become intertwined with those of the existing member states. Any economic collapse or serious political unrest in eastern Europe would be a matter of great and immediate concern to the other member states, because deep integration causes any crisis to have direct effects on the rest of the EU.

Enlargement will also have an immediate impact on the EU's internal functioning. Its major institutions (the European Commission, the European Parliament, the Council of Ministers, and the European Court of Justice) were designed for a community of far fewer countries, and they have already been pushed to their limits with the enlargement to fifteen member states from the 1970s to the 1990s. Larger numbers and much greater diversity will have an exponential rather than arithmetical impact on the EU's institutions and policies.

In the long term, the whole nature of the EU could change. It might have to abandon existing hopes of becoming a much tighter, more effective political and security union and instead revert to a much looser, inchoate group of countries, more like a free-trade area. This is just what many proponents of closer European integration fear. Their fears are only encouraged by the fact that many British opponents of integration support rapid enlargement precisely in order to make such integration impossible. Other supporters of integration, however, believe that the EU's creaking institutional structures need a thorough overhaul anyway, and that enlargement will simply force politicians to embark on long-overdue reforms.

For the applicants from eastern Europe, accession requires a profound and often extremely painful transformation of their economies, laws, institutions, politics, and indeed cultures and societies. Joining the EU is much more difficult and complex than joining NATO, which essentially requires political commitment, a democratic form of government (not even that, during the cold war), and changes to the armed forces. It is also much more difficult to join the EU of the early twenty-first century than it was for applicants in the 1970s.

The EU itself was less complex before the creation of the Single Market and a common currency, and therefore preparing to join it required fewer adjustments. Moreover, in past enlargements, the EU allowed long transitional periods and provided much more aid than it has offered to the current applicants. It was indeed partly the experience of past accession by poor countries like Greece and Spain which has led to such tight conditions for subsequent applicants. Not only was the previous process expensive, but its insufficiently tough conditions have meant that to this day Greece has not fulfilled all the promises it made to the EU on accession.

Today, by contrast, EU membership requires changes to almost every area of public policy, and a reshaping of most of a country's political institutions. EU members have developed some form of coordination, harmonization, or common law in almost every area of policy—although the extent of harmonization varies across policy areas. The effort to achieve such deep integration with the Union has made the EU one of the most profound transformative influences in the transition of postcommunist Europe. Its effects range very widely, from the creation of market regulators to civil service reform, from border controls to hygiene standards in abattoirs. It is striking that these conditions for accession have extended the EU's influence in central and eastern Europe even beyond the Union's remit for its existing member states.[2]

The Conditions for Accession

EU conditionality is not limited to enlargement. The EU applies both positive and negative forms of conditionality to developing countries and countries in transition on benefits such as trade concessions, aid, cooperation agreements, and political contacts. Since the late 1980s, political conditions have increasingly been applied along with economic ones. Both practical and ideological motivations lie behind the development of political conditionality, while protectionist politics have also had an influence. In its dealing with developing countries and countries in transition, the EU has shown a preference for using carrots rather than sticks, and conditionality has not always been applied consistently.

The most detailed conditions for accession ever have been set for the central and eastern European applicants. Even before the collapse of communism, as early as 1988 the EU began to attach conditions to aid, trade, and political relations with the members of the then Soviet bloc.[3] In 1993, formal conditions for membership concerning democratic government and market economics were then imposed, mainly so as to overcome opposition from several member states to eastward enlargement. The conditions set out at the Copenhagen European Council (see box 4.1) were designed to minimize the risk of new entrants becoming politically unstable and economically burdensome to the existing EU, and to ensure that they were ready to meet all the EU rules, with only minimal and temporary exceptions. The conditions were thus formulated both to reassure reluctant member states that any potential disruption would be minimal and to guide new applicants. This dual motivation has continued to play an important role in the politics of enlargement within the EU.

All three main Copenhagen conditions are very broad and open to considerable interpretation; elaboration of what constitutes their satisfaction has progressively widened the detailed criteria for membership, making the EU a moving target for applicants. The conditions are not fixed and definite, with new conditions added and old ones redefined at the biannual summits of EU leaders. This has caused immense irritation among the applicant states. Even more politically damaging has been the fact that while the pain of economic transformation is felt throughout the process leading up to membership, the benefits of membership come only at the end. The EU is the arbiter of what constitutes meeting the conditions and when benefits will be granted, but it also can and does repeatedly change the rules of the game.

Box 4.1 The Copenhagen Conditions

1. Membership requires that the candidate country achieve stable institutions guaranteeing democracy, the rule of law, human rights, and respect for and protection of minorities.

2. Membership requires the existence of a functioning market economy as well as the capacity to cope with competitive pressure and market forces within the Union.

3. Membership presupposes the candidate's ability to take on the obligations of membership, including adherence to the aims of political, economic, and monetary union.

This problem of the moving target has serious implications for the process of negotiating the terms of accession. Because the EU is both referee and player in the accession negotiations, it can and does defend the interests of its existing members. From the point of view of the applicant countries, this makes the whole game look rigged.

The first two Copenhagen conditions require definitions of what constitutes a "democracy," a "market economy," and "the capacity to cope with competitive pressure and market forces," all of which are highly debatable and slippery concepts. The EU has never provided explicit definitions of them, although there are implicit assumptions about their content in the Commission's opinions on the candidates' readiness for membership (published in 1997) and annual reports on their progress. There is thus no formal published rationale for how various EU demands will bring applicants closer to western European political and economic norms.

The third condition is concerned with the *acquis communautaire*; that is, the whole body of EU rules, political principles and judicial decisions. The *acquis* is divided into 31 chapters for the purpose of negotiation. This dimension of the accession process is the most quantifiable, because countries can show how many chapters have been opened, provisionally closed, or "set aside" for later consideration. Candidate countries have focused much of their effort on getting chapters provisionally closed, and opening new ones, in order to demonstrate their progress—even though closing chapters does not guarantee an earlier date for accession, and provisionally closed chapters can be reopened later in negotiations. Because this is one of the few clearly measurable parts of the process, this aspect of negotiations has received much attention in central and eastern Europe. However, dates for accession and the character of the final package will depend largely on the deals made in the last few months of negotiations.

The Moving-Target Problem

The Copenhagen conditions are not a straightforward case of conditionality, and they differ fundamentally from the traditional conditionality for benefits used by international financial institutions such as the World Bank and the International Monetary Fund. In its simplest formulation, the conditionality of these institutions links perceived benefits to the fulfillment of certain conditions; conditionality is a means of ensuring the execution of a contract, a promise by one party to do something now in exchange for a promise by the other party to do something else in the future.

By contrast, EU demands on applicants are not just a set of conditions to receive defined benefits, but an evolving process that is highly politicized within the EU itself. The link between fulfilling particular tasks and receiving particular benefits is much more ambiguous than in the traditional conditionality of the international financial institutions because the tasks are complex, and many of them are not amenable to quantitative targets that show explicitly when they have been fulfilled.

The accession conditions are general and vague, leaving a lot of room for interpretation by the EU. The second condition (market economy and competitiveness) is particularly difficult to define. The thrust of the EU's economic agenda for central and eastern Europe is neo-liberal. It emphasizes privatization of the means of production, a reduction in state involvement in the economy (particularly industry), and further liberalization of the means of exchange.

Considering the variety of models of capitalism to be found among EU member states, the accession policy documents (particularly the Accession Partnerships discussed below) promote a remarkably uniform view of what a "market economy" should look like; and very curiously, the socioeconomic system they implicitly promote has a more "Anglo-Saxon" flavor than the "Rhenish" social market economies of France, the Low Countries, and Germany; the social democracy of Scandinavia; or the "Latin" economic systems found in the southern EU. [4]

The third condition, on the "obligations of membership" is also open to interpretation. In previous enlargements, these obligations were held to lie solely in the implementation of the *acquis communautaire*, which already amounts to 80,000 pages of legislative texts but which continues to grow as the EU develops new policies and issues new directives, declarations, and jurisprudence. As concerns this enlargement, the *acquis* has been defined more broadly as "all the real and potential rights and obligations of the EU system and its institutional framework."[5]

Such a formulation is itself open to minimalist and maximalist interpretations, which in turn affect the demands made on applicants. So far, the EU has presented quite a maximalist interpretation to the applicants. Central and eastern European countries do not have the possibility of negotiating opt-outs like those negotiated by some member states concerning Schengen and monetary union. The candidates also have to take on the EU's "soft law" of nonbinding resolutions and recommendations.

The EU's Twofold Role in Eastern Europe

The EU has been a tough and unyielding negotiating partner for previous applicants owing to its insistence on maintaining the integrity of the body of law contained in the *acquis*. A widespread view among EU officials is that former communist applicants have to join the EU club on the same principle as past applicants like Sweden or Finland—that of accepting and implementing all the rules of the *acquis* before joining. However, others have argued that this "club membership" view of eastward enlargement is an inadequate response to the unprecedented challenge of postcommunist transition and the obvious development needs of eastern Europe.

The EU's role in the process of postcommunist transformation is twofold. On the one hand, the EU acts as an aid donor imposing conditions on relations with developing countries and countries in transition intended for their benefit by supporting their transition to democracy and the free market. Yet on the other hand, the EU is guiding these countries towards membership, which requires creating incentives and judging progress in taking on specific EU models—not just overall development.

How compatible are these two goals? The assumption in much of the language used in official EU publications on enlargement is that accession and "transition" are part of the same process and that preparations to join the EU are coterminous with overall development objectives. There are reasons to be skeptical about this assumption: EU policies and regulatory models were created to fit economies and societies at a very different level of development.

Moreover, these models contain anomalies, because EU policies are the outcome of a complex bargaining process among different interests and traditions. EU policies were not designed for countries in transition, and they often require a complex institutional structure for implementation that is little developed in former communist states. EU models in at least some policy areas are suboptimal for the applicants. For example, EU agricultural policy is widely viewed as wholly inappropriate for the farming sector in central and eastern Europe. For its member states, the EU's primary role is regulation of the Single Market and coordination in most other areas. The Union lacks the wide experience in development issues that is needed for guiding the transition of the eastern European states.

The Process of EU Enlargement

Every year since the fall of the Berlin wall in 1989, EU enlargement has seemed to be five years away—and it still does. But by the autumn of 2001, it seemed as though the EU would indeed admit its first new postcommunist members sometime between 2004 and 2006. When each individual applicant will join remains unclear. The timing depends on each country's own progress in meeting the accession conditions, as well as on the EU's own readiness to accept new members. At the time of writing, the EU had finished a series of intergovernmental conferences to prepare its institutions, but still has to define how its budget will be reformed for enlargement. Also still to be decided are the critical questions of how agricultural policy and regional aid will be applied to the new member states.

Ten eastern European applicants are now in accession negotiations, but each will finish at a different time. The five that began negotiations in 1998 (Czech Republic, Estonia, Hungary, Poland, and Slovenia) are all progressing well, and the EU aims to conclude negotiations with them by the end of 2002.[6] A further five countries started negotiations in February 2000; Latvia, Lithuania, and Slovakia are catching up with the front-runners, but Bulgaria and Romania remain many years away from accession.

"Accession negotiations" is in many ways a misleading term, because most of the key negotiating is actually happening between present member states. The compromises they reach will then be presented to the applicants—and the latter will largely have to accept what the fifteen current EU member countries have agreed to, because the EU is so much stronger than they are. The applicants have relatively little bargaining power, not least because they are poor, but also because each candidate wants to join much more than the EU wants to enlarge. Only Poland is large and assertive enough to make a lot of demands for transitional periods, and even Poland started withdrawing some of these demands in 2001 in the hope of making faster progress.[7]

Moreover, a great many EU rules and regulations are nonnegotiable because they are vital to the functioning of the Single Market. For example, product and process standards have already been established, and changing them would jeopardize free competition. In the endgame of negotiations, in order to bring the process to a close, the EU is likely to agree to various transitional periods that it will not currently discuss and to limit the cost of meeting its own standards (e.g., in environmental policy). However, these negotiations will not see the kind of trade-offs and last-minute concessions that are common in the final leg of talks for the World Trade Organization and other international institutions.

When Will the New Applicants Be Ready to Join?

The conditions for joining the EU look deceptively straightforward. An aspiring member has to be a stable democracy with a competitive market economy, and demonstrate that it is willing and able to take on all EU policies, both present and future. These conditions seem self-evident, a set of "motherhood and apple pie" criteria to which no self-respecting European could object. They are also essential to reassure present EU states that the central and eastern European countries will—if they become members— look like familiar, western European countries and will not bring instability, authoritarianism, or economic collapse into the Union.

On closer inspection, however, membership conditions are more confusing, and "readiness to join" lies in the eye of the beholder. The conditions are very general; they do not, for example, define what constitutes a market economy or a stable democracy. Do new member states need a German economy, British civil service, Swedish welfare state, and French electoral system? Or how about a Greek economy, Belgian civil service, Austrian industrial relations, and Italian electoral system? The EU does not present a uniform model of democracy or capitalism; nor has it tried to define one. Diversity is a key feature of the Union, and the principle of integration while respecting difference remains important.

But how does the principle of unity in diversity apply to countries that are still transforming their economies and societies after a half-century of central planning and imposed communist ideology? What exactly are the minimum standards for political institutions, public administration, implementation of legislation, and economic performance that are essential for joining the EU? It is not self-evident what kind of economies and political systems would meet the Copenhagen criteria. It is even hard to say whether all the current member states are "ready to join," because they have never been judged on the Copenhagen conditions. For example, Belgium's public administration, France's industrial policy, and Germany's state aids would probably be unacceptable if they were applicants. Some Commission officials claim that no current member state fully implements more than 85 percent of EU regulations. So is it fair to demand 95 percent adherence from the east Europeans? The question of double standards remains open.

It is very difficult to pinpoint exactly when each of the criteria has been met. The conditions established by the EU at Copenhagen in 1993 do not provide a checklist of clear objectives; nor do they specify the means to achieve stated goals. They are not like the conditions set by the International Monetary Fund, which are quantitative targets for macroeconomic performance. Instead, they are general goals, and what applicants have to do to meet them involves a series of tasks that has been defined incrementally during the accession process. The conditions have become a moving target as the EU's agenda gets more detailed and more demanding. For example, the rules for border policies under the Schengen Agreement were published as late as July 1999, and EU migration and asylum regimes will continue to develop considerably before the first applicants join.

Readiness is a political question for the EU. In previous enlargements, "readiness to join" was something determined by negotiations, which decided when a country was ready and willing to accept the conditions being offered. When the poorer Mediterranean countries applied in the 1970s, the EU had only a relatively limited *acquis*. The eastern candidates have a much bigger set of rules and regulations to implement, including everything from a more complex Single Market to a single currency, the Schengen *acquis,* and an emerging external security policy. The applicants are starting from a lower position as well; average income per head is between one-third and two-thirds of the EU average.

The eastern European candidates are expected to conform absolutely in areas viewed as essential to the future functioning of the EU. Regulatory alignment with the Single Market is nonnegotiable; the applicants must remove all trade barriers and meet EU product and process standards. Similarly, the candidates cannot have opt-outs on monetary union, Schengen, or the emerging European security and defense identity. Would-be members have to sign up to everything, even if it remains unclear which conditions must be met in their entirety before accession, and which elements can be adopted gradually after accession, perhaps with more help from the EU budget.

There are double standards, and some of the rules are more equal than others. Thus there has to be free movement of goods, services, and capital in central and eastern Europe, but the EU is not going to allow free movement of people from east to west immediately (even though free movement of workers is one of the four freedoms of the Single Market). State aid has to be limited according to EU rules, without the laxity that has been allowed to German *Länder* or declining industries throughout the EU. National subsidies to agriculture must be reduced, but east European farmers are not guaranteed access to the major Common Agricultural Policy funds.

Ultimately, the applicants will be ready to join when member states can be convinced that the new members will behave like good citizens in the EU. There are also some pet concerns of particular member states that require reassurance: Germany and Austria on cross-border crime and migration, the Scandinavian countries and Austria on environmental protection and nuclear safety, and all the member states on corruption and the quality of public administration. It is clear that applicants have to show a certain style of operation that looks familiar to member states if they are to be acceptable. New members will have to move towards German-style border controls, a British-model civil service, and a Nordic concern for environmental standards. Even if central and eastern European countries do not have to conform to a particular model of capitalism, they have to demonstrate euro-zone fiscal discipline, European Central Bank–style central banks, and American-looking free markets. They also have to show capacity to implement legislation effectively—an increasingly important part of meeting the conditions.

Political Management of the First Accessions

Enlargement is a huge political challenge for the EU. If it is mismanaged, the first accessions could be postponed for a long time, or the applicants could be forced into a second-class status by being denied key benefits of membership. In the worst-case scenario, this could lead to a collapse of political will and desire to join in key applicant countries, with Poles voting against membership in a referendum out of fury with EU greed, hypocrisy, and bullying.

Political dangers, rather than economic factors per se, thus present the greatest obstacles and risks to the enlargement process. Within the existing EU, several things could increase opposition to enlargement in the coming years:

- unfounded fears of large-scale westward migration by eastern Europeans,
- budget lobbying by farmers and regional aid recipients (especially border regions), and
- groups trying to add conditions for accession.

Several major fears are raised by opponents of enlargement:

- potential labor market disruption and migration,
- increased competition in the Single Market and consequent restructuring, and
- the cost of the whole endeavor.

Nonetheless, the European Commission looks likely to be successful in completing negotiations with at least some of the front-runner candidates by the end of 2002. Each member state would then have to ratify every individual accession treaty, which could take eighteen months or more, so the earliest entry dates still lie in 2004–2005. Traditionally, accessions have taken place on January 1, but if the Council agrees to a midyear date, 2004 may be possible for the first accessions. Otherwise, the first new member would join on January 1, 2005—more than fifteen years after the 1989 revolutions.

The EU member states have made a series of commitments that imply a timetable for enlargement, although it could still slip. In December 2000, EU member states expressed the hope that new members would join in time to participate in the 2004 elections to the European Parliament. However, this was not a binding commitment to allowing the first central and eastern European members in by that year, because the Treaty on European Union allows for participation in elections before countries have actually joined as full members. The Gothenburg European Council in June 2001 removed this ambiguity, stating the EU's "objective" to be participation in the 2004 elections "as members." The Gothenburg conclusions also reaffirmed the goal of concluding negotiations with the best prepared candidates in 2002.

The Final Triathlon in Negotiations

The EU faces three stages to finish the negotiations on time. The first stage includes *negotiations on the financial package*. Commission officials argue that the EU's current budget can cope with ten new members, and that there is as yet no need to sort out a longer-term deal. But the Spanish, Portuguese, and Greek governments are seeking assurances that their regional aid receipts will not be largely diverted to poorer eastern European countries. At the same time, France and other countries that do well out of the EU's Common Agricultural Policy want to protect it from enlargement. Poland is seeking equal access to farming subsidies with the current member states, which would be expensive for the Union. Negotiations will be very tough, and may not be concluded on time, because a deal cannot be done until after the French and German elections in 2002. That makes for a very tight timetable of just a few months to decide this critical issue.

The second stage includes *finishing negotiations by the end of 2002*. The conclusion of negotiations could be delayed beyond the end of 2002 for several reasons:

- Poland could hold out for better deals in critical areas like agriculture.

- The EU could find itself unable to push through the institutional reforms necessary for enlargement beyond 20 member states. In particular, the Irish population might vote no again to ratification of the Nice Treaty in a second referendum (probably in autumn 2002). The Nice Treaty contains essential provisions for institutional reform prior to enlargement.

- The fifteen EU member states could find it impossible to agree between themselves on a financial package that allows enlargement to go ahead.

The third stage includes *ratification of the accession treaty*. Once negotiations are finished, all fifteen national parliaments and the European Parliament have to ratify the treaty. Any one of them could throw it out, which means sixteen potential vetoes. If that happened, it could take months or years to sort out the mess. Member states will be under great pressure to hurry through ratification, but parliamentary agreement depends on acceptable deals on agriculture, regional aid, borders, and other sensitive issues. We cannot assume that ratification will be a smooth process on either side. There are dangers of a populist backlash against enlargement, particularly in Austria, Spain, Greece, and certain German *Länder*. On the central and eastern European side, there are signs that popular support could decline further, especially in the Czech Republic. There seems to be an inverse correlation between closeness to membership and the enthusiasm of the public about joining.

A long delay after 2004 could still occur owing to some major political pitfalls too. Right-wing populists across both western and eastern Europe have made electoral gains in 2002 that showed the power of scaremongering about migration issues. Many of the central European populists have revived the difficult questions of the expulsions of ethnic populations that took place at the end of World War II. There are some specific issues too: Greece is threatening to veto eastward enlargement if Cyprus is not allowed to join in the first round of new accessions; France might block the enlargement by arguing that further institutional reform is necessary; and the Spanish regions might prevent the ratification of accession treaties. Likewise, the EU might find that it has to reopen the budget deal and cannot close it again. Or there could be an economic crisis in the euro zone.

A long postponement of enlargement would carry significant opportunity costs. Failure to get the EU ready in time would undermine its credibility in the eyes of the current applicants and also of the Balkan countries that are using membership prospects as a motivation for painful reforms. Further delay would suggest that the EU is reneging on its promises, hardly a good example to set for democratization and good governance in its surrounding region.

For the central and eastern Europeans, the incentive of reforming for accession would also wane. Expectations of joining the EU have been a critical motivator for painful and difficult reforms, of both economies and political institutions. The accession process has been a very important stimulus to liberalize rapidly. It has helped central and eastern European policy makers to overcome domestic opposition to liberalization and policy reforms that are essential to developing these economies and opening their markets to EU firms. The accession process has also ensured continuity of policies despite frequent changes of government and fragmentation in some countries' domestic party politics.

This stabilizing effect on new democracies would be lost if the accession goal seemed unattainably far off. Losing the EU as an anchor for reforms and a stimulus to good governance could knock some central and eastern European countries out of their current virtuous circles of reform and restructuring—encouraging the emergence of populist politicians, and increasing the scope for protectionism and corruption. The emergence of "banana republics"—with authoritarian governments and poorly regulated economies—in the central and eastern European region would not be good for the EU, or for Europe as a whole.

The Impact of Enlargement on Current Applicants' Neighbors

Given the preceding discussion, it is essential that the EU live up to its promises in eastern Europe. However, successful enlargement will also bring considerable problems, particularly for the countries that will remain outside the enlarged EU. The implications of enlargement in stages are that EU membership will draw circles of inclusion and exclusion throughout the region. Specifically, those on the inside will have to upgrade their border controls to EU standards, cutting many of the human and economic ties that currently bind populations on either side of external frontiers.

There is also likely to be a "chilling effect" on the excluded countries as they see their neighbors accepted into the western rich people's club while they are denied the benefits of trade access and increased investment. This does not mean that the EU should not enlarge; the net effect on eastern Europe is likely to be positive, not negative. But it does mean that the EU will have to actively engage the countries lying on its new frontiers in order to solve their problems. There is no longer a well-guarded iron curtain protecting the fifteen current EU members against would-be migrants and other consequences of poverty and political unrest in neighboring countries. Nor should the EU seek to isolate itself, given its growing foreign policy responsibilities.

Until the end of the cold war, the EU was largely an economic club, with little harmonization of its members' foreign policies. But since the early

1990s, the Union has been establishing a major foreign policy role for itself. The EU's size and weight as a regional player will grow larger after enlargement; it will be a weightier trade bloc with a bigger market, and thus a stronger economic power. Meanwhile, its foreign and security dimensions are growing—slowly but surely—and it is developing military capabilities that might eventually be used independently of NATO.[8]

What does this new security capability mean for the rest of the region? For countries in the Balkans, Moldova, and Ukraine, a bigger foreign policy dimension increases the attraction of the EU as a club to join. For Russia, it will increase wariness about the EU's security and military dimensions. It will also have concrete effects in causing greater isolation for Russia's border regions. Eastward enlargement will have some very negative unintended consequences because of the ripple effects of its border and visa policies in the Schengen area.

The EU has slowly developed a zone of free movement known as Schengen, after the town in Luxembourg where an agreement was signed among a few member states in 1985. It started as an intergovernmental agreement outside the EU, but it was incorporated into the Union's institutional framework after the 1997 Amsterdam Treaty. The Schengen area is beneficial in many ways. It allows goods, people, services, and capital to travel freely around the EU without obstacles like passport controls and border guards— and applicants will benefit from all these after they join (although there may be a delay of several years before border checks are abolished). Development of a common visa, migration, and asylum regime means that once foreigners have a Schengen visa and enter one member country, they can travel freely throughout all the rest—from the Arctic Sea in Finland to the Mediterranean shores of Spain.

The problem for the applicants is that Schengen is a trade-off: Joining this free movement zone means that borders on the inside of the zone become porous (as frontier controls are removed) but borders on the outside of the zone have to become much harder to penetrate, precisely because they are the only external barrier to unwanted people from developing countries and countries in transition. This is a difficult dilemma; the benefits of removing barriers on the western borders come only at the price of much higher fences with eastern neighbors. These higher barriers against the east hinder trade, investment, and friendly interaction with neighboring peoples. They also run directly against the eastern policy of countries like Poland, which seeks to build bridges with Ukraine and Russia—

because the new bridges will have armed guards standing on them demanding visas.

The main effects on the surrounding region will be felt through the asylum and immigration policies that the EU is now developing and is already starting to export to the applicants as conditions for accession. Securing the applicants' borders against illegal migrants and cross-border crime is an important part of the EU's accession strategy because of the political sensitivity of these issues among current member states. In the past few years, the EU has been actively exporting its border control technology and practices to eastern Europe, as well as its emerging common methods for handling asylum claims and refugees. The next item on the EU's agenda is the export of its visa policies, but these are much more controversial because they will inevitably break socioeconomic and political ties across borders between applicants and nonapplicants. Not only do EU border policies go to the heart of these countries' newfound sovereignty, but their foreign relations will be affected as well.

The applicants' negotiating power is very small because Schengen is now an integral part of the European Union, and the politics of fear are driving countries on the EU's current border (like Germany and Austria) to stress full compliance with visa policies and border controls before new members can join. There can be no opt-outs (exceptions) for new members, even though current members have such arrangements—the United Kingdom and Ireland have special arrangements so that they are partly outside the Schengen regime, while Norway and Iceland are partly inside it despite not being members of the EU.

Unfortunately, candidates for EU membership cannot negotiate such exceptions—they have to accept the rules set by the current members, and these current members are determined to protect themselves against threats from the east. Schengen is different from other portions of the EU; it is not only about technical standards or legal harmonization, it is also a matter of confidence. Member states like Germany and Austria need to convince their populations that a high fence on the borders of central Europe protects them—otherwise, their parliaments could block enlargement to central Europe altogether.

To an extent, these fears are irrational. The number of migrants after accession will be limited, and organized crime is fought much better through targeted, intelligence-led policing in the cities, and not through border controls and visas alone. Criminals usually have access to forged passports and visas, so new border controls will have a much bigger effect on Ukrainian traders and Belarusian peasants than on organized crime. But politics is often irrational—opportunistic politicians exploit potent fears of uncontrolled migration, even if these fears are unfounded. EU governments have to respond to these fears by showing they are tough about building a strong frontier on the east, so that bringing new members into the Schengen zone does not compromise their security.

The applicants have started adopting the Schengen area's common visa regime, including the introduction of visas for Russians and some of the citizens of neighboring countries. Eastern European political leaders have repeatedly expressed their concern that such measures not introduce new barriers between their populations, but the priority given to EU demands has caused acute dilemmas for domestic policy makers. These leaders often talk about "not putting up a new iron curtain," but behind such statements lies a complex set of compromises whereby each country has tried to navigate between EU pressures and other policy concerns, both domestic and external.

Extending the Schengen area eastwards is already having an impact on relations and communications between applicants and nonapplicants. It will continue to move eastwards, as Ukraine comes under pressure to control the flow of Russians and central Asians in return for fewer restrictions for its own citizens traveling westwards. This has implications for cross-border trade and investment and also for security if Schengen once again drives apart regions that only recently started becoming reintegrated at the end of the cold war.

A further underlying problem is that exporting asylum and immigration policies (including visas) conflicts with what is supposed to be a central thrust of the EU's external security policy. A principal aim of the EU's post-1989 eastern policy is the stabilization of central and eastern Europe by employing the same methods applied so successfully in western Europe over the past half-century. The EU has encouraged regional integration with the aim of reducing socioeconomic disparities and knitting populations together so that tensions are reduced. The second prong of this approach is to sponsor peaceful resolution of bilateral disputes and good neighborly relations, both through its conditions for accession and by providing financial and political support for intergovernmental cooperation and subnational initiatives.

These goals are still present in the EU's enlargement strategy, but other policies are also being developed that run counter to them. EU border policies are raising new barriers to the free movement of people and goods, inhibiting the trade and investment between applicants and with non-applicant countries that is essential to regional integration. There is a risk that the EU could end up giving central European and Baltic countries the benefits of westward integration with their richer neighbors at the cost of cutting off ties with their poorer neighbors to the east, thereby contributing to their further impoverishment and isolation. The EU could even become an exporter of instability, rather than stability, to the countries beyond its borders. This bargain is still acceptable overall to most political leaders in central Europe; however, acceptance of the EU's terms has been accompanied by a great deal of unease about its unintended consequences for intra-regional relations. This is not just a problem for applicant countries, because the overall security of Europe depends on preventing the isolation of politically unstable, poor countries on the edges of an enlarged Union.

Conclusions

Enlargement could be the EU's greatest contribution to security and stability in Europe in this century—but only if it is managed well. There remains the potential for the process to be stalled, given the complex bargains that will have to be struck within the EU to allow enlargement to go ahead. But the opportunity costs of delay would be great, both for the applicants and the Union itself. The EU would benefit if enlargement forces long-overdue reforms of its institutions and policies. But inept handling of enlargement would exacerbate the tensions created by the eastward extension of Schengen borders; EU leaders need to develop parallel policies to mitigate the impact of enlargement on Ukraine and other neighbors of the current candidates. The Union should connect its enlargement policy with a foreign policy for its periphery and beyond, and address the contradictions between its external and internal security policies.

Although the EU has an accession process, it still has no true enlargement strategy that takes account of the long-term implications of enlargement for the continent of Europe as a whole. The failings of the EU's accession policy are increasingly evident—it has been very slow, technocratic, and at times directionless. The European Commission deserves credit for having kept accession negotiations going, but the process is reaching the limits of what the EU institutions alone can achieve. Now political leadership is needed both to make enlargement happen and to moderate its negative effects for the excluded countries to the east. Accession policy remains focused on getting the applicants to converge with the EU, but that will not be enough to ensure the successful integration of many new and diverse member states. It certainly will not be enough to sell enlargement to increasingly skeptical west European populations.

At the time of writing, even enlargement itself could yet be taken for granted. Myriad objections will be raised within the existing EU, by every interest group that receives EU or national subsidies, feels threatened by wage competition, objects to immigration, or just fears change. Far-right groups are already mobilizing against enlargement, starting in Austria and Germany. It is an easy target for opportunist politicians seeking a popular anti-EU cause. Enlargement can be portrayed as expensive and likely to cause mass immigration. Many of the calls for referenda and extra conditions for accession are all the more potent for being based on thinly veiled xenophobia.

Even when the remaining major negotiating issues are resolved, the inadequate preparations for selling enlargement to the EU populations could snarl ratification procedures. Even once negotiations are finished, each accession treaty will have to be ratified by all fifteen national parliaments, any one of which could throw it out. The delicate compromises reached over years of negotiations will be no use if the results cannot be sold to the member states.

The only way the EU can overcome interest-group objections is to have a clear strategy with a firm commitment to a date for the first accessions. The history of European integration shows that important and difficult projects—like the Single Market and monetary union—can only be kept on the road if there is strategic map with a date clearly marked. Without the discipline of a deadline, member states may carry on fiddling with the institutions and arguing about the budget forever.

The political climate is growing more hostile in the applicant countries as well. Although none would be likely to reject accession if a were referendum held now, support is growing—especially in Poland—for opponents of the EU and what it stands for. By the time of accession, there could be growing disillusionment and Euroskepticism in central Europe, creating awkward partners within the EU. There is a strong danger that if they are kept in the waiting room for many more years, significant numbers of central Europeans will turn against integration.

The opportunity costs of not enlarging are getting larger with every passing year. Failure to get the EU ready now would undermine its credibility in the eyes of the current applicants and also of the Balkan countries that are using membership prospects as a motivation for painful reforms. Further delay would suggest that the EU is reneging on its promises, hardly a good example to set for democratization and good governance in its surrounding region. Enlargement is an important EU foreign policy, not just an internal matter. The EU now needs to look up from its internal reforms and start living up to its regional responsibilities.

Notes

1. See, e.g., Jacek Kucharczyk, *Club Class Europe? An Examination of Socio-Political Conditions for a Eurosceptic Backlash in Poland* (Warsaw: Institute for Public Affairs, 2001).

2. The extent of the EU's influence in central and eastern Europe is analyzed in Heather Grabbe, "A Partnership for Accession? The Implications of EU Conditionality for the Central and East European Applicants," EUI Working Paper RSC 99/12 (San Domenico di Fiesole, Italy: European University Institute, 1999).

3. See Karen E. Smith, "The Use of Political Conditionality in the EU's Relations with Third Countries: How Effective?" *European Foreign Affairs Review*, vol. 3 (1998), pp. 253–74.

4. This uses a characterization of capitalist systems in western Europe developed in Martin Rhodes and Bastiaan van Apeldoorn, "Capitalism Unbound? The Transformation of European Corporate Governance," *Journal of European Public Policy*, vol. 5, no. 3 (1998), pp. 406–27.

5. See Carlo Curti Gialdino, "Some Reflections on the *Acquis Communautaire*," *Common Market Law Review*, vol. 32 (1998), pp. 1089–1121.

6. Cyprus also began negotiations in 1998, and Malta in 2000. Turkey is an official candidate, but it is not in accession negotiations. Although this chapter does not consider the progress of these countries in detail because their applications raise different questions from those of the central and eastern European countries, they are subject to the same accession conditions.

7. "Poland Softens Stance in EU talks," *Financial Times,* April 12, 2001.

8. See Gilles Andréani, Christoph Bertram, and Charles Grant, *Europe's Military Revolution,* (London: Centre for European Reform, 2001).

5

Belarus: Give a Dog a Bad Name

Leonid Zaiko

In Soviet times, Belarus was considered an ideal socialist republic. Even after the break-up of the Soviet Union, it appeared that it still lived on—in Belarus. In September 2001, the neo-Soviet regime in Minsk extended its term for another few years. Yet even a society which finds itself in a deep freeze cannot wholly shield itself from developments around it. Of these, the enlargement of NATO and the European Union on its western and north-western borders and the domestic evolution of Russia to the east have been of utmost importance.

Retarded Transformation and the "Revolt of the Masses"

In Belarus, totalitarianism has been succeeded so far by authoritarianism. This has roots in history. In the twentieth century, the Belarusian nation had to absorb several powerful shocks. They included two world wars heavily fought on its territory; Joseph Stalin's rule of terror in the 1930s, resulting in the extermination of the Belarusian intellectual elite; and the Chernobyl nuclear disaster of 1986 in neighboring Ukraine, which sent most of its fallout towards Belarus. The most recent shock, linked to the unraveling of the command economy, led to a dramatic drop in living standards and wide-ranging popular disappointment. Rampant corruption gave democracy, which had never had a real chance in Belarus, a bad name. It must be remembered that Alexander Lukashenko, then a political outsider, was first elected president in 1994 on a clear anticorruption ticket.

The Belarusians, in contrast to the Poles and the people of the Baltic states, shied away from the challenge of economic and political freedom. Instead, a majority of them sought a safe haven in the principle of social equality guaranteed by authoritarian rule. They were also understandingly deterred by the experience of raw privatization and general misrule in post-Soviet Russia. Thus, most Belarusians came to tolerate near-total state control and high government expenditures coupled with limited consumption and very low real wages. Ordinary people were simply afraid of too brutal and too sudden dislocations and concerned about their own lives. If the Soviet Union declared itself to have built "real socialism," post-Soviet Belarus can be said to have replaced it with "real neo-socialism." Neither, however, represents a viable model.

In the late 1990s, especially after Russia's 1998 default, a number of experts and editorialists alike toyed with the idea of adapting the Belarusian model to Russia (and Ukraine). No doubt this view was actively supported by a range of political forces in Russia itself, including the Communist Party and its agrarian and other allies. Indeed, the Belarusians could pride themselves on escaping the more violent features of Russia's wild capitalism. The Russian experience throughout the 1990s strengthened the illiberal attitudes within Belarusian society. However, Belarusian neo-socialism itself held out no promise but that of continuing misery, while Russia in 2000 went ahead with a new economic reform agenda. All talk of it following the path of Belarus had ceased. This finally defined the Belarusian way. Rather than emulating their western neighbors, or acting as pioneers for the eastern and southern ones, Belarusians had to resign themselves to trailing Russia, while avoiding its "excesses."

This conservatism of the Belarusian collective consciousness is rooted in a peasant mentality of a significant portion of the population. As a matter of fact, the share of the agrarian sector in Belarus's gross domestic product is twice as high as in Russia. This has clear political implications. All post-1990 Belarusian legislatures had a high level of agrarian representation next to a strong communist bloc. This made the Belarusian ruling elite truly green–red. That is generally true at the beginning of the twenty-first century. One new addition to this coalition is the construction industry lobby. The

Table 5.1 Preference for economic models (percent)

Support for:	Nov. 1994	June 1995	June 1996	June 1997	Nov. 1997	Sept. 1998	March 1999	Nov. 1999	April 2000	Aug. 2000	Nov. 2000
Market economy	51	52.1	53.8	65.4	69	74.6	67.4	72.2	74.1	73	73.5
Planned economy	46.2	45.1	44.2	30.3	25.7	22.8	23.9	24.8	22.7	23.4	21.5

Source: IISEPS News, March 2001, p. 58.

agrarian president has appointed former building sector managers as prime minister and chairman of the national bank.

The majority of those who live or have been born in the countryside continue to believe in a special role for the state, and long for charismatic leadership. Having lost faith in one such leader, they would look for a similar charismatic alternative. Yet the experience of the peculiar brand of neo-socialism is also taking its toll. "Order and equality" slogans were still vote-getters for the authorities in the 2001 presidential poll, but their effectiveness was declining. The attractiveness of authoritarian rule was also decreasing. Society may appear to be still in hibernation. But beneath the veneer of passivity, important developments are under way, slowly eroding the illusions of the past. Some of the changes in popular attitudes can be seen in table 5.1.

The dynamic, as is clear from the table, is clearly in favor of a market economy. Whereas in 1994, soon after Lukashenko's arrival in power, the respondents split almost evenly between preferring a "planned" rather than "market" economy, by the end of the decade nearly three-quarters supported a market economy. It is interesting that this trend is common to all groups of the population, including pensioners, the staunchest supporters of a socially oriented state.

A similar change is reflected in attitudes towards the authoritarian rule of President Lukashenko. Table 5.2 shows a high level of elite dissatisfaction with the incumbent head of state.

It is interesting to note that the elites are more critical of Lukashenko than is the general public. The official results of the September 2001 election show 76 percent voting for the president and only 15 percent supporting Viktor Honcharik, the opposition candidate. These figures are widely discounted as rigged, but various independent public opinion polls in the fall

Table 5.2 Answers to the question "Are you satisfied with the way Alexander Lukashenka runs the country?" (percent)

Variant of the Answer	All Respondents	Government Officials	Nongovernment Sector
Mainly unsatisfied	84.1	74.1	90.5
Partly satisfied	13.0	18.5	9.5
Mainly satisfied	2.9	7.4	—

Source: IISEPS News, May 2001.

Table 5.3 Answers to the question "At what kind of enterprise would you like to work?" (percent)

Variant of the Answer	June 1997	March 1999	April 2000	Nov. 2000
State-owned	62.9	58.7	48.4	47.1
Privately owned (individual)	28.1	30.0	40.0	46.0

Source: IISEPS News, March 2001, p. 59.

Table 5.4. Answers to the question "Is Belarus, in your opinion, a democratic state?" (percent)

Variant of the Answer	
Yes	19.6
No	42.2
No opinion	38.2

Source: IISEPS News, June 2001, p. 24.

of 2001 still gave Lukashenko 48 to 55 percent support, as against 17 to 21 percent for the united candidate of the democratic forces.

One of the myths whose hold on Belarusian society has been slowly slackened is the belief in the efficiency of state-owned property. Table 5.3 shows the downward slide in public support for government ownership of economic assets.

The popular view of Belarusians is that of an apathetic people, disinterested in democratic participation. There is nothing genetically or psychologically unique about Belarusians, of course. Table 5.4 demonstrates that they are capable of a healthy and hard self-criticism.

Thus, one can assume that Belarusian society is undergoing a process of self-reidentification through slow transformation. There is a gradual change of values, priorities, and public consciousness. It will be a matter of time before these changes manifest themselves.

Outwardly, Belarus has been remarkably stable. Yet rather than being monolithic, this society is developing multiple cleavages. These run along several lines, including attitudes towards (1) social and economic reforms; (2) union with Russia and a possible loss of sovereignty; (3) evaluation of the 1996 referendum which abolished the constitution, sharply reduced the role of parliament, and vested maximum power in the presidency; and (4) relations with countries belonging to the European Union and with the United States. By the turn of the century, it became possible to speak about a polarization of views across the entire spectrum of issues. For instance, while supporters of reforms value national independence and advocate cooperation with Russia on an equal footing, Lukashenko sympathizers want Belarus to consider joining the Russian Federation.

Western and Eastern Dimensions of Belarus

The official list of Belarus's international priorities includes Russia, Ukraine, and the rest of the Commonwealth of Independent States; as well as Poland, the Baltic states, and the rest of central Europe.[1] This emphasizes the immediate neighborhood of the country. However, which of the competing dimension—eastern or western—is exerting the most influence on Belarus?

The answer depends to a large extent on the topic being considered. Thus, in the field of electronic media, Russian television stations reign supreme. ORT (Russian Public Television, the first channel) alone has an audience of some 70 percent. By contrast, the consumer goods market is dominated by western and Asian manufacturers. Investment flows from western sources and Russian companies such as Gazprom. The Russians also dominate the local energy market. With regard to the issues raised in presidential elections, it would be safe to assume that 30 percent are primarily Russia-influenced, 20 percent are Western-dominated, and the remaining 50 percent account for internal Belarusian factors.

Belarus's relations with Russia are also changing as a function of developments in the Russian economy. Thus, until 2001 Russia was content to receive Belarusian barter payments for its goods, including energy supply. When Moscow then demanded money in return, this led to stoppages at big Belarusian enterprises, such as tractor plants. Russian business tycoons are also demanding a stake in the yet-to-begin privatization of the more lucrative Belarusian assets. As a result, Lukashenko's relations with Russian elites have soured.

Official Minsk barely hides its resentment and even hostility towards the west. Belarusian propaganda routinely refers to NATO, the United States, and the European Union as the country's external enemies. At least in part, this is a function of the west's support for the democratic anti-Lukashenko opposition and its refusal to recognize the president's constitutional coup of 1996. Thus, the "enemy within" is directly linked to the "traditional" external enemies of the USSR. Lukashenko became especially worried as he watched the fate of Slobodan Milosevic—first an object of a NATO military campaign, then deposed as president as a result of elections and mass street demonstrations, and finally a defendant facing an international tribunal in The Hague. The president has been continuously reshuffling the top echelon of his administration, betraying a sense of insecurity and lack of confidence in his immediate entourage.

Since the terrorist attacks against the United States in September 2001, Belarusian society, however, does not necessarily buy into this. Genuine anti-western sentiments are rare. For its part, the government has somewhat modified its stance. Propaganda rhetoric has been toned down, and two high-ranking former KGB officers, regarded as pragmatists, have been appointed to senior administration posts. This definitely reflects the impact of Vladimir Putin's policies in Russia, in particular his attempt to build a quasi-alliance with the United States. Minsk was also worried by the new U.S. toughness towards Iraq and Iran, with which it has been maintaining close contacts.

The public generally supports international anti-terrorist cooperation. However, about a third of Belarusians have not emerged mentally from the Soviet Union's cold war with the west. A public opinion poll conducted in September and October 2001 produced the results shown in table 5.5.

These attitudes have domestic implications. In Belarus, democratic forces are identified with the west. For a third of the electorate, everything which has links to the west is perceived in a negative light.

Since the late 1990s, the Organization for Security and Cooperation in Europe (OSCE) has been maintaining a monitoring group in Belarus to help establish dialogue between the authorities and the opposition. In the runup to the 2001 elections, the government was becoming less and less tolerant of the group's activities, accusing it of interference in Belarusian internal

Table 5.5 Answers to the question "What's your attitude toward terrorist attacks against the United States?" (percent)

Variant of the Answer	
It is a terrible tragedy for the American people	63.6
The loss of life is a pity, but this is the result of U.S. interference in other countries' affairs	31.4
Indifference	2.7
No answer	2.3

Source: National public opinion poll, fall 2001, unpublished data.

affairs. Since the election, the official government attitude towards the OSCE has been cool but no longer hostile. This has been the result of the growing closeness between Russia and the European Union. It is interesting, however, that the Belarusian public views the OSCE more positively than its country's presidency. It was ranked sixth among the most trusted institutions, after the Orthodox Chruch (which topped the poll), the military, the independent research centers, the Constitutional Court, and the government-sponored research institutes. It outstripped the state-run media and Lukashenko himself.

The Baltic countries, aspiring NATO and EU members, hold a special place in Minsk's foreign policy. The Belarusian government pragmatically cultivates special relations with Lithuania and Latvia in such areas as trade, transportation, and cross-border exchanges. These northern neighbors provide land-locked Belarus access to their Baltic ports. The local Belarusian diasporas have been largely pro-Lukashenko. So far, these relations have been conducted on a strictly bilateral basis, without Moscow's or Brussels's interference. With the accession of the Baltic countries to NATO and the European Union, this will change.

The Belarusian case not only demonstrates the degree to which domestic transformation can depend on external factors. It also shows what happens when there are several external factors at work, and their vectors and dynamics differ widely. If anything, the Belarusian electorate clearly prefers Russian president Putin to their own Lukashenko. Should both run for presidency of a united Russo-Belarusian state, Putin would receive 40 percent support to Lukashenko's 24 percent. When asked to nominate an ideal head of state on the eve of their most recent presidential election, the Belarusian public rated various world leaders, including their own, as shown in table 5.6.

Table 5.6 Answers to the question "The ideal head of state is ..." (percent)

Nominee	
Vladimir Putin	59.8
Alexander Lukashenka	34.3
Gerhard Schröder	16.4
Fidel Castro	13
George W. Bush	11.4
Jacques Chirac	11
Tony Blair	7.8
Alexander Kwasniewski	5.8
Vaclav Havel	5.1
Saddam Hussein	3.9
Valdis Adamkus	3.6
Vojslav Kostunica	3.5
Leonid Kuchma	3

Source: IISEPS News, June 2001, p. 37.

The Belarusians are not pondering the question of whether their country is part of Europe. For them, a more relevant issue is that of a "new European identity."[2] From this perspective, the enlargement of western institutions all the way to the Belarusian border is a very powerful factor. The western Belarusian border towns of Grodno and Brest—which have long maintained close economic and social contacts with neighboring Poland and Lithuania—will be immediately affected. In a broader sense, this is likely to boost the "European component" within Belarusian urban culture, emphasizing such values as rationalism and individualism. By contrast, Belarus's eastern dimension contains a heavy baggage of totalitarian and authoritarian rule, with all their implications for social psychology. These implications include social inertia, lack of initiative, and emphasis on the collective at the expense of individual rights and freedoms.

At the turn of the twenty-first century, Belarus finds itself on Europe's new line of division, which separates the more or less successful societies in transition of central Europe and the Baltics from the laggardly societies of the new eastern Europe—Russia, Ukraine, and Belarus itself. Essentially, this is a fault line between the mainly Catholic and Protestant west and the predominantly Orthodox east. This fact raises the question about public attitudes towards the new division; these attitudes can be seen in figure 5.1.[3]

It is quite obvious that most Belarusians see themselves as good neighbors to all bordering countries—whether Catholic, Protestant, or Evangel-

Figure 5.1 Answers to the question "Do you think that western civilization is hostile to Orthodox peoples?" (percent)

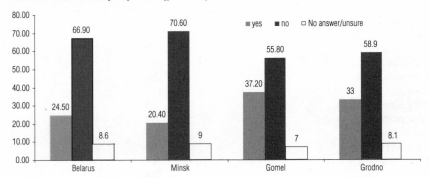

Source: Leonid Zaiko et al., "Strategy for Belarus" research project.

ical. It is also true that not all of regions in Belarus are equally tolerant towards Western civilization. There are considerable differences in the way Western values are perceived in different parts of Belarus. After all, western Belarus—about a quarter of the present territory—remained part of Poland through 1939, and it is the home to the country's Catholic minority, which accounts for 10 percent of the population.

Also, the opening of Belarus to outside influence has produced not only new affinities, but also new phobias. It is worth noting, for example, that the residents of the Gomel region show the least confidence in the peaceful intentions of the west. Nearly two-fifths of the poll respondents in that part of the country see the west as hostile. This looks surprising, because the Gomel residents have received the largest amount of humanitarian assistance from the west since the 1986 Chernobyl nuclear disaster and have sent the largest number of their children for recuperation to European countries. Does this view reveal the ungratefulness of the Belarusians or the stubbornness of their deeply held beliefs? This phenomenon begs for an in-depth study.

Paradoxically, Grodno was found to be the second least loyal region towards the west. Grodno is located in the immediate proximity of the Polish border, right near NATO territory. Its residents are highly critical of their closest neighbors. Why is that? Apparently, Poland's accession to NATO in 1999 has created a perception of a new barrier being created right at their doorstep. This has in turn strengthened their feeling of estrangement from Europe.

Underlying this is a centuries-old history of hostile relations within the Polish state between the dominant Catholics and the Uniates (Eastern rite Catholics), on the one hand, and the Orthodox minority, on the other. From the sixteenth century onward, the government in Warsaw pursued a policy of Catholicization of the Orthodox Christians in the territory of the Grand Duchy of Lithuania, which included present-day Belarus. Starting in the mid–eighteenth century, the ascending Russian empire assumed the role of protector of Orthodoxy in eastern Poland, interfering at will in the affairs of the decadent Polish state. This soon led to successive annexations of Belarusian lands by Russia. By the same token, the collapse of the Russian empire and the rebirth of Polish independence led to a Soviet–Polish war, which resulted in Polish rule again being extended to western Belarus in 1920.

During World War II, the "liberation" of western Belarus by Soviet forces in September 1939 in coordination with Hitler's attack on Poland, and the subsequent German occupation of the western Soviet Union, further exacerbated already complicated interconfessional relations in the region. Stalin's partial restoration of the Russian Orthodox Church at the end of the war led to the handover of former Catholic Church buildings to the Orthodox. Postwar Soviet propaganda routinely depicted Catholic priests as oppressors, intent on relentless expansion into the eastern Slav domain that was traditionally Orthodox.

Similar chords are being struck today. The Russian Orthodox Church, which considers Belarus, alongside with Ukraine and Moldova, to be part of its "canonical territory," loudly protests against "Catholic expansionism" in the area. Belarus in particular is singled out as an area where Catholics are engaged in "quiet missionary work" to reconvert the Orthodox who had lost their faith during the era of official Soviet atheism. In this context, the Lukashenko regime is being viewed by the Moscow patriarchate as a staunch defender of Orthodoxy where it counts the most—on the frontline. In 2001, as the pope was touring Ukraine, the patriarch pointedly visited Belarus. In 2002, President Lukashenko was awarded a high Orthodox decoration for his efforts.

All this helps to explain why Grodno, located as it is near the Polish border, is less positive towards the west than the more easterly Gomel or Mogilev. It also provides an insight into why Belarusian nationalism is not seen as truly patriotic by many Orthodox-descended Belarusians. The decision by some leading members of the Popular Front to adopt Uniatism as a

Table 5.7 Answers to the question "Do you think that the accession of the Baltic states, Bulgaria, and others to NATO represents a threat to Belarus?" (percent)

Variant of the Answer	
Yes	36.8
No	23.5
No answer	39.7

Source: National public opinion poll by IISEPS, April–May 2001.

form of Belarusian national religion was a dreadful mistake, now admitted as such by the more radical members of the anti-Lukashenko opposition.

Of course, Belarus has nothing to fear from the small armies of the Baltic states, but the combined military force of the alliance to which they will soon belong is formidable. The expansion of NATO's area of action under the 1999 Strategic Concept and the 2002 decision to include the territory of Belarus in the zone of responsibility of the U.S. European command has added to Minsk's worries. Lukashenko evidently fears an attempt to dislodge him with the help of external military pressure.[4] The view of NATO as a direct threat to their personal position is also shared by part of the old and new *nomenklatura*. By contrast, the nationally oriented groups have welcomed NATO's new proximity to Belarus, hoping that this will make the west pay more attention to internal developments in the country. As for the general public, its attitudes are revealed by table 5.7.

The answers given in the table show a calm but generally negative attitude towards NATO's enlargement. Only a fourth of the population sees no threat in NATO admitting new members. More than a third are convinced there is a threat, and two-fifths are undecided. There is a fear that Belarus may become a battlefield for a new cold war between the west and Russia.

In the past, Lukashenko used the NATO card in his dealings with Moscow, trying to "sell" his rabidly anti-western position in exchange for low prices charged by Russia for the energy it supplies to Belarus. In the post–September 11 situation, the Belarusian leader has toned down his criticism of his external "enemy number one," and he has indicated a willingness to engage in a dialogue with the business community at home. However, he has no plans to fundamentally change his foreign or domestic policies.

The enlargement of the European Union to include Poland and the Baltic states raises a number of practical problems for Belarusians, who became accustomed in the 1990s to traveling to neighboring countries on short shopping tours. The introduction of visa regimes and stricter border controls in anticipation of EU membership is affecting a large number shuttle traders and seasonal workers. There will also be consequences for customs duties and financial operations. What will be the wider implications of a division of Europe between the "new west" and the shrunken, but still vast east?

Possible Consequences of the New Divergence of Europe

Lukashenko's foreign policy has been officially described as a "multi-vector" one, but in reality relations with Russia are a clear priority. The official objective is the construction of the "union state." However, this supposed union is likely to remain a virtual one at the political level, while the degree of economic integration will probably grow. Customs and taxes are to be harmonized or unified. The Russian ruble is the designated new currency for Belarus, to be introduced in the mid to late 2000s. The big Russian investors are queuing up to take part in Belarusian privatization.

Belarusian democrats opposed a merger with Russia, which would finish off Belarusian independence. However, they were little encouraged by the attitude of Americans and western Europeans, for whom Belarus is a very peripheral country.[5] The European Union and the United States strongly criticized the rigged elections in Belarus, the government's suppression of free media, and human rights abuses.[6] The problem is, however, that Belarusians can hardly expect others do the job for them, and Belarusian society is very much split between westward- and eastward-leaning forces.

Expansion of the EU will be more, and more negatively, felt than the enlargement of NATO. Many western markets will be effectively closed to traditional Belarusian exports. The volume of two-way trade with Poland has already started to decline. It has to be borne in mind that the Baltic states are among Belarus's top trading partners. Belarus can hardly expect to continue selling its tractors to the Baltic nations when they become members of the EU and apply its prohibitively high (37 percent) tariffs to these goods. Belarus will also experience new problems in transporting its goods to the Baltic seaports of Klaipeda, Ventspils, and Kaliningrad. As many as 90 percent of Belarusian trucks may not meet EU standards. Thus, Belarus is in danger of losing many markets for its goods in central and eventually also eastern Europe.

There are social consequences resulting from the strengthening of border regimes. The year 2000 marked the end of essentially visa-free travel to Poland, the Czech Republic, Hungary, Bulgaria, and other countries in the region. The new visa fees are considered to be too high in comparison with average incomes in Belarus. The Belarusians fear a return to a Sovietlike situation, when they could not travel freely. This time, however, it is other countries, not their own government, that could restrict the free movement of people.

Politically, the expansion of the west could have five consequences for Belarus. The first would be a closer relationship with Russia, both within the Eurasian economic community and at the bilateral level. As of now, roughly 50 percent of Belarusian trade is with Russia and another 10 percent is with the rest of the Commonwealth of Independent States, as opposed to 40 percent with the west and the developing world. The west's share may further decrease. In particular, Belarus's trade with Poland and the Baltic states, worth between $600 and 800 million, can be reduced by 30 to 50 percent. Minsk may also be expected to play the role of Moscow's deniable proxy in the international arms trade, and to increase its ties with Iran, Iraq, and Libya, as well as China.

The second consequence would be a further consolidation of authoritarian rule inside Belarus. The third would be a direct attack against democratic forces, nongovernmental organizations, and the free press as an imaginary "fifth column" of NATO and the United States. (Already, presidential decree 8, "On Measures to Improve the Distribution and Use of Foreign Humanitarian Aid," effectively bans foreign donations to the nongovernmental organizations that are involved in any form of activity.)

The fourth consequence would be a further strengthening of censorship and control of the mass media under the new doctrine of information security. And the fifth would be a sharp reduction of social and personal contacts with Poland, Lithuania, and Latvia (Estonia already is barely present on Minsk's horizon).

Self-Identification and the Future: East or West—Home Is Best?

In the context of the geopolitical, geostrategic, and geoeconomic restructuring taking place between the Baltic and Black Seas, self-identification is key. It is thus interesting to analyze the opinions of Belarusians about the

Table 5.8. Answers to the question "Would you like to live as in ...?" (percent)

Country	June 1999	Nov. 1999	April 2000
Germany	36.4	39.23	36.8
United States	15.8	20.8	17.8
Lithuania	1.9	2.2	1.3
Latvia	1.3	1.2	1.2
Poland	6.2	6.4	6.4
Russia	0.6	0.7	1.2
Switzerland	2.5	1.6	1.9
China	2.5	3.0	0.8
Belarus	—	—	18.7
Sweden	1.1	2.3	5.7

Source: National public opinion poll by IISEPS, April–May 2001.

countries which might serve as models for their own (see table 5.8). It has to be stated that due to the lack of first-hand experience, most people base their opinions on second- or third-hand information.[7]

As the table shows, Germany and the United States are certainly the leaders among countries viewed by the Belarusian people as an ideal model of a better future for themselves. The way of life in Bremen or Cologne is the desired image of the society to which most residents of Belarus aspire. The United States is also listed among countries with high achievements in social and economic development.

One can expect that the extent to which Poles and the Baltic peoples will be successful in modernizing their countries will have a direct and powerful impact on Belarus. The neighbors' success will be perceived as the manifestation of the robustness of western values and ways of life. It is to be hoped that this will undercut the ideology of the Lukashenko regime. Yet, given both historical legacies and current realities, most Belarusians do not *really* compare themselves with Poles or Baltic peoples, but rather with Russians, Ukrainians, and even Moldovans.

Integration with Russia is generally viewed as a way to gain economic benefits and ensure continued close social and cultural contacts. Attitudes towards the possible advantages of Belarus's integration with Russia are seen in table 5.9.

However, the expectations of a real rise in living standards as a product of integration with Russia are absent from most people's minds. While the elite sees the union as a way of consolidating its hold on power, most people are concerned with maintaining a modicum of security and stability.

Table 5.9. Answers to a question on the advantages of Belarus's union with Russia (percent)

Variant of the Answer	
Economic advantages	50.3
Guarantees of security	32.4
Political advantages	23.4
Cultural advantages	22.4
Social advantages	16.2
The union does not provide any advantages	0.8
Other	15.7
Nothing heard about this union	1.3
I am at a loss to answer	13

Source: National public opinion poll by IISEPS, April–May 2001.

In economic terms, as Russian reforms go deeper, the Russian market cannot be taken for granted by Belarusian producers. This strengthens the case for reforms in Belarus. Actually, there is evidence of Russia's positive influence on Belarus in certain areas. For instance, what neither the International Monetary Fund nor the World Bank could do in five years— namely, to help improve Minsk's monetary policy—Russia's Central Bank did achieve by taking a very tough stance in its dealings with the Belarusian National Bank. Other examples are available in such areas as tax and customs regulation and agrarian-sector reform.

There is also a positive effect from Russia on the political side, from the availability of the Russian media throughout Belarus to Moscow's progressively warmer relations with the EU countries, especially Germany. Thus, the eastern factor is essentially pushing Belarus in the same direction as the western one, contributing to the process of self-identification of Belarusians. The current phase of this process can be seen in figure 5.2.

Thus, three-quarters of the people residing in newly independent Belarus have identified themselves as its citizens. This is a positive development, as only 15 to 20 years ago the talk was of a Soviet supernation. It is equally symptomatic that the progress of globalization is deemphasizing national differences, the focus being on unity.

One small example of this phenomenon is the percentage of poll respondents who have identified themselves as citizens of the world. The fact that 7 percent of Belarusians—740,000 people out of 10 million—share this perception of themselves does not just reflect a play of emotions or the high expectations of a small proportion of Belarusians. It is, rather, an important

Figure 5.2 Answers to the question "Of which country do you consider yourself to be a citizen?" (percent)

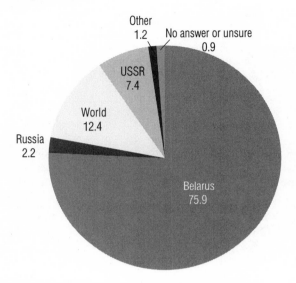

Source: Leonid Zaiko et al., "Strategy for Belarus" research project.

sign of the future. The country may not be well computerized, and the average monthly salary may barely be enough to purchase a visa to a neighboring state, but there are still 740,000 people who have surmounted these barriers of the present.

In Conclusion: Alternative and Synthetic Visions of the Future for Belarus

Traditionally, the question for Belarus has been whether to join with Russia against the west or become a western buffer on the Russian border. Until recently, this question was not for the Belarusians to decide. Moreover, Belarus was a battlefield of choice for Polish, Swedish, German, and French armies moving east, and for the Russian army moving west. Now, this situation of a permanent sufferer can be changing. Also, at the beginning of the twenty-first century, there is a third way: walking with Russia toward the west.

Table 5.10. Answers to the question "What is the preferred future for Belarus?" (percent)

Variant of the Answer	
Belarus should be in the union with Russia but remain a sovereign state	37.2
Belarus should enter the European Union	21.5
Belarus should be a part of Russia	16.1
Belarus should remain a nonaligned state	11.2
I am at a loss to answer, there is no answer	14

Source: National public opinion poll by IISEPS, April–May 2001.

The choice of strategic orientation will influence all facets of Belarusian society, stimulating and activating various public forces. At present, the bulk of the population remains ambiguous, as table 5.10 shows.

It is important to understand which categories of Belarusians adhere to which positions, and along what lines values and priorities are divided within the society. One could paint two portraits: one for the supporters of joining the EU (however fantastic the proposition), and the other for the supporters of a full merger with Russia:

- Adherents of the EU connection: young people, persons with a higher education, representatives of the nonstate sector, and residents of Minsk.

- Supporters of a full merger with Russia: persons over 60 years old, those with a primary to middle-school education, pensioners, residents of the Brest region, and peasants.

These two composite portraits are so typical and simple that no additional comment is required. If Belarus is to be guided by the past, it will choose Russia (or rather, the Russian *tradition*), but if it looks at the world through the eyes of its younger and better-educated people, it will choose "the way of Europe"—modernization. It will be interesting, however, to watch the impact of the problems created by EU accession in neighboring countries. Still, 37 percent of the people believe that it is both possible and desirable for Belarus to remain an independent state and at the same time enter into a union with Russia. If Russia continues its domestic transformation and integration with Europe, a close alignment between Minsk and Moscow may be positive for Belarus.

This, however, will not allow Belarus to escape the looming challenge of an eventual regime change. As the EU and NATO draw closer to Belarusian borders, and Russia continues its rapprochement with the west even as it struggles to transform itself, the domestic situation of Europe's last authoritarian ruler may grow progressively less secure. The ensuing showdown in Minsk would then be more than a local irritation. That is why ignoring Belarus, and simply writing it off as a failure, is a bad and dangerous policy.

Notes

1. "Substantive Features of the Program of Social and Economic Development of the Republic of Byelorussia for 2001–2005" (in Russian), *Soviet Byelorussia*, May, 16, 2001.

2. "By the way, there is a point of view, that democracy, as it was established by the Marshall Plan, arrived in full with the fall of the Berlin wall. Europeans have difficulty realizing that history turned a page that day"; Dimitri Machairidis, "Haider's Passage: Narrow Street or Big Avenues?" *Defensor Pacis*, April 2000, p. 11.

3. It gives the results of special public opinion poll conducted by experts of the group known as "The Strategy for Belarus" in March 2000. A member of this group is the author of the given article.

4. For this reason, in reply to military maneuvers of NATO, the Belarusian political leadership decided to carry out large maneuvers in the northern part of the country. The maneuvers will be on the eve of elections and will involve evacuating some of the inhabitants of a frontier zone. Such an approach should show the readiness of the opposition to NATO and to the Baltics. The authority wants to use this case for strengthening a negative attitude towards NATO.

5. Leonid F. Zaiko, "Belarus' na puti v tret'e tysyachelet'e" (Belarus on the path to the third millennium), Minsk, 2001, pp. 45–75.

6. "Update Report 11," September 2001, State Department noon briefing, September 10, 2001, distributed by the Office of International Information Programs, U.S. Department of State <http://usinfo.state.gov>.

7. These are the results of IISEPS public opinion polls during the period 1999–2000 that had 1,500 participants and a margin of error that did not exceed 0.03 percent.

6

The Dual Enlargements and Ukraine

James Sherr

The aspiration articulated in 1991 by U.S. president George H. W. Bush to create "a Europe whole and free" naturally kindled expectations in formerly communist Europe that newly resuscitated and newly established states would be welcomed into the institutions which had given integrity and definition to the "free" part of Europe since the cold war divided the continent. Ten years after this goal was proclaimed, NATO has admitted but three of the nineteen states which now make up this region, and the European Union has admitted none.[1] This fact has sobered expectations, but it has not always produced understanding, and it might still produce turbulence.

Great power does not always produce great policy. In western Europe and North America, the end of the cold war not only produced triumphalist declarations and "initiatives," but also contradictory expectations, competing priorities, timidity, confusion, and denial. Until 1994, there was reasoned speculation that NATO would simply disappear. The reasons that it did not disappear immediately were the timeless ones of habit, inertia, uncertainty, prudence, and corporate interest—sometimes but not always reinforced by a premonition that Soviet threats would sooner or later return in Russian national garb. Only in 1994–1995 did "partnership," enlargement, and conflict in the Balkans give NATO a new sense of purpose and an ambitious agenda of transformation.

More than two years before NATO committed itself to enlargement, the European Union agreed at its June 1993 Copenhagen European Council that it would consider former communist states as candidates for accession. Yet at the higher political level, quite a few political figures still harbored private ambivalence about the collapse of constraints which had kept not only Europe but Germany divided. At the working level, EU bodies remained fixated on a course of "deepening integration" which could only delay the widening of the Union. For all the thought given to strengthening the mechanisms of Common Foreign and Security Policy, little thought was given to the security implications which EU policy posed for nonmembers, let alone the need to develop a joint EU–NATO approach to security building in central and eastern Europe. It has taken two military conflicts in the Balkans to elevate the EU's security priority and refocus it.

Today, there is growing apprehension that what President George W. Bush defined as the "false lines" dividing Europe during the cold war will be replaced by real ones.[2] To Samuel Huntington and a still more deterministic school of post-Soviet Russian and Ukrainian geopoliticians, these new dividing lines are understood in "civilizational" terms. To participants in NATO and EU assistance programs and a vastly larger class of economic actors, great and small, these dividing lines are experienced daily in much more prosaic, but equally tenacious form: as differences of political, legal, administrative, and business culture. Ukraine's experience illustrates not only the irrelevance of cold war divisions, but the irrelevance of their dismantlement—for Ukraine has achieved not only a high degree of cooperation, but a small degree of integration with western military structures. Yet socially and economically, Ukraine's "vector of development" continues to diverge from its most dedicated "strategic partner," Poland, and even sympathetic observers believe that it is still failing in its "strategic challenge" of becoming a "full member of the European family of civilized nations."[3]

Were members of this "European family" to conclude that old dividing lines had simply moved further east, there might be cause for disappointment and depression, but not necessarily apprehension. Apprehension arises for three reasons, and Ukraine is central to all of them. The first of these is Russia. The perception that Ukraine cannot join the west despite the geopolitical ambitions of both parties risks reinforcing other arguments in Russia—for example, the "lessons" of the 1998 financial crisis—about the distinctiveness of "former Soviet space" and the harmfulness of western models to Russia itself. Moreover, the same perception can only strengthen those who believe that it is not only possible, but natural for Russia to emerge (q.v., Fedor Shelov-Kovedyayev) as the "leader of stability and military security" in this particular "space" and return to a bloc-to-bloc approach.[4]

Second, one should not assume that the deterioration of conditions in Ukraine—and with it, the proliferation of "shadow structures" and the progressive criminalization of the state—will simply affect Ukraine and other newly independent states, rather than prove (q.v., Anatoliy Grytsenko) "a source of additional threats to European countries in terms of drugs, weapons, illegal immigrants, prostitutes and ecological disasters [and, he might have added, money laundering]."[5]

Third, Ukraine is scarcely in a unique position. As Anton Bebler has noted, "the armed hostilities in the Balkans ... [have] caused a huge rise in the illicit traffic of arms, narcotics, falsified documents and forged currencies, and in the smuggling of persons, precious metals and stones, oil and essentials such as food, detergents and spare parts."[6] As Ukraine's minister of foreign affairs, Anatoliy Zlenko, noted in July 2001, conditions in parts of the Balkans, Transniestria, and the Caucasus (and, he might have added, Kaliningrad oblast) are already becoming "dangers for Europe as a whole." If Ukraine, with its population of 50 million and "unique geographical position" bordering several NATO and EU members (and the Black Sea) were added to this list, the dangers would surely be greater than they are at present. For all of these reasons, western leaders have described Ukraine's future as a "key factor" in the future security of Europe.

But Ukraine is only the most compelling example of a general proposition: what happens to the states who do not join the "greater Europe" will be felt by those who do. Many today fear that the Schengen border regime and other elements of EU's *acquis communautaire* could become an "iron curtain" dividing Europe. Yet bad as this case would be, it is not the worst case. In the worst case, Schengen would become the economic equivalent of a Maginot line, providing limited security or simply an artificial sense of it. Unless NATO and the EU develop an effective strategy for the excluded states—as well as a long-term strategy for including them—both entities might have to revise their assumptions about the costs of enlargement and the means required to maintain European security.

With this challenge as its backdrop, this chapter will examine two sets of questions:

1. In general terms, are NATO and EU enlargement policies broadly compatible or at cross-purposes? Are they diminishing the burdens placed upon states likely to be excluded or increasing them?

2. As a "pivotal" state, how has Ukraine responded to the stimuli and pressures of the twin enlargements, and how successfully have NATO and EU responded to Ukraine's needs and concerns?

The Two Enlargements: Genesis and Evolution

The European Union and NATO have brought different criteria and different methods to the enlargement process: methods which are having as profound an effect on states currently excluded from the process as on those brought into it. Therefore, the possibility exists that the two enlargements will proceed not only along separate paths, but at cross-purposes. The crosscurrents already in evidence are producing much disorientation in Ukraine, Russia, and several other countries, taxing the intellectual resources of those struggling to understand "objectively" what is taking place and, at the same time, struggling to define—and where necessary, redefine—their own national interests. Only in 1999 was there clear official recognition that divergences between NATO and the EU could prove damaging to both institutions and harmful to European security. Although this recognition is gradually producing innovations in structure and policy, these might not be sufficient to harmonize the dynamics of what are certain to remain two very different institutions.

Of the two institutions, NATO has been the more outward looking and the more positive towards enlargement. This is not merely on the grounds of self-perpetuation evident in the axiom (q.v., former secretary general Manfred Wörner) that "NATO has to go out of area or out of business." It is because NATO is a living rather than fossilized security organization and capable of seeing that "deterrence" and "defense" will offer very limited protection against post–cold war security challenges. It is also because the internal criteria which NATO aspirants must meet are easier to specify and vastly easier to satisfy than the necessarily complex, profound, and protracted internal transformations demanded of countries seeking to join the European Union.

For all this, the post–cold war NATO was for several years a reluctant enlarger (even after completing its Study on Enlargement in December 1995); and until the Madrid summit of July 1997, enlargement was largely a demand-driven process. Given the "Russia first" policy which prevailed in a number of member states well through 1994, it took some time for these demands to be understood. Although Poland, Hungary, and the Czech

Republic viewed Russia as a problematic factor in European security, by the time of Madrid, few viewed Russia as a military threat to themselves and no one of consequence believed that Russia was the prime factor making membership essential. The urgency was more fundamental and more transcendental. NATO membership was synonymous with being part of the west. Return to a "gray zone" was synonymous with insecurity—and not only international insecurity, given the need to guarantee the irreversibility of *internal* changes. These were a priori propositions, tenaciously held.

By 1997, these concerns were giving new emphasis to what had always been consistent, if second-order, justifications for NATO's existence. Lord Ismay's much quoted proposition—the purpose of NATO is "to keep the Americans in, the Russians out and the Germans down"—did not reveal a hidden agenda, but an open and avowed one: the prevention of conflict between NATO's members and the banishment of balance-of-power politics from the heart of Europe. The united Germany of Helmut Kohl was as sensitive to these concerns as the West Germany of Konrad Adenauer had been. Since 1949, the Federal Republic of Germany had predicated its foreign policy on the *illegitimacy* of the German national interest. Since 1989, as after 1949, Germans have been determined to confront security challenges as members of a European and Euro-Atlantic community and not as Germans. They were swift to grasp that the corollary of central Europe's exclusion from the collective structures and disciplines of NATO would be the renationalization of security policies in the region, including eventually their own. They were also swift to agree with Poles, Czechs, and Hungarians that nothing less than NATO membership would dispel the ghost of Germany in central Europe.

Moreover, well before Madrid, Bill Clinton's administration had concluded that NATO enlargement had become central to the continuing relevance of NATO and continued American support for it. This conclusion was vitally important to those, like Vaclav Klaus, who believed that a "European idea" which excluded the United States and Canada would have no attraction for his fellow citizens. It was equally important to western European governments convinced that the intertwining of security communities in NATO provided Europe with an indispensable means of ensuring that an isolationist or unilateralist spirit did not return to the United States. In sum, by the time of the Madrid summit, it had become obvious that NATO enlargement was essential not to protect the west from Russia, but in order to protect the west from itself.

Taken together, the effect of these concerns and imperatives has been to push classic military considerations into the background. To be sure, this shift in emphasis does not sit comfortably with a number of key institutional players. While two U.S. presidents, Bill Clinton and (to date) George W. Bush, have been enlargement enthusiasts, neither the U.S. Congress nor the U.S. armed services have always welcomed the proposition that the "defensibility" of new members should be secondary to supposedly more transcendental concerns. To date at least, they have. Thus far, enthusiasts and skeptics have been able to agree that enlargement should not *weaken* NATO's military potential, even if it does nothing to strengthen it. Whether this military minimalism continues to hold depends as much on internal politics in NATO countries as it does on the perceived absence or presence of military threats in East-Central Europe.

Partnership for Peace

At the Brussels meeting of the North Atlantic Council on January 10–11, 1994, the Alliance issued invitations to all non-NATO states belonging to the Organization for Security and Cooperation in Europe (OSCE) to join a newly established Partnership for Peace (PfP). It is ironic that this program, initially designed to deflect pressure for NATO enlargement (and much criticized by the candidate states of central Europe) instead evolved into an essential instrument of enlargement policy. Once NATO committed itself to enlarge, PfP acquired a twofold significance: as a means of preparing candidates for accession (reinforced in April 1999 by Membership Action Plans) and as a means of enabling states with no intention of acceding to draw closer to the NATO fold. As a series of 16+1 programs (now 19+1), PfP has been an exceptionally flexible instrument, allowing each of the 27 partners to determine the scale, depth, and intensity of its cooperation. Over the years, it has diminished the distinction between membership and partnership in four respects:

- limited but increasing institutional integration at NATO headquarters for partners so willing, including a progressive extension of partner participation in NATO planning and deliberations;
- participation in NATO exercises and NATO-led peace support and crisis-response operations;

- 19+1 programs of cooperation in areas relevant to interoperability of forces, national defense reform, and the establishment of civil-democratic control of national armed forces—programs strongly supplemented by a network of bilateral (e.g., UK–Ukraine, Poland–Ukraine) programs "in the spirit of PfP"; and

- an undertaking by NATO to "consult with any active participant in the Partnership if that Partner perceives a direct threat to its territorial integrity, political independence, or security"[7]—effectively, extending article 4 of the North Atlantic Treaty to partner countries. Assurances that PfP allows for joint operations with NATO in the event of such a threat have been given on at least one occasion.[8] At the height of NATO's military operations in Kosovo (Operation Allied Force), Romania received a temporary article 5 guarantee from the North Atlantic Council.

PfP has been "enhanced" on two occasions. At their spring 1997 Ministerial Meeting, Alliance foreign and defense ministers established an Enhanced PfP, upgrading the North Atlantic Cooperation Council to a more active and integrated Euro-Atlantic Partnership Council, establishing a Political Military Steering Committee on Partnership for Peace and, on the basis of Implementation Force/Stabilization Force (IFOR/SFOR) experience in the Balkans, strengthening the position of partner countries in the planning and conduct of NATO-led operations. At their April 23–25, 1999, Washington summit, the Allies established a Membership Action Plan for candidate members as well as an Enhanced and More Operational Partnership, including an expanded Planning and Review Process (PARP) for partner country armed forces, analogous to the Defense Planning Goals which NATO members agree every two years.

These innovations beg several questions. A prime objective of establishing liaison delegations and staff elements at NATO headquarters and the Partnership Coordination Cell in Mons is to expose partner representatives to a NATO working culture based on multinationality, decision by committee, delegation of authority, sharing of information, and "habits of cooperation." But exposure to a working culture and immersion in it are two different things. The balance of opinion at headquarters characterizes the quality and "spirit" of Ukraine's participation as falling well short of that of the Baltic states (who, unlike Ukraine, are candidates for membership) but as noticeably different in kind from that of the Russian Federation, whose participation, even in the relatively harmonious period between conclusion of the May 1997 Founding Act and NATO's military intervention in Kosovo, was largely focused on high-level forums and confined to areas directly impinging upon Russian interests.[9]

A second question is whether officers with NATO experience have influence in their military establishments. It is surprising that no systematic audit has been conducted of the career progression of partner officers with experience in NATO posts, NATO-led operations, and military academies of NATO member states. The fragmentary evidence available points to a positive trend, but also some surprising discontinuities. Even after Hungary's accession to NATO, mid-ranking officers complained that advance through the promotional ladder was slow; that they were often mistrusted by more senior, Warsaw Pact–trained officers; and that their experience was not always put to good use.[10] Where Ukraine is concerned, well-placed observers and specialists have until recently painted a picture similar to or even less favorable than this one. Within the past two years, however, the trend has become markedly more positive. At the middle and senior levels, NATO experience has been treated as a definite plus in filling a number of positions relevant to the country's defense reform: in the Ministry of Defense and General Staff, in training commands, the National Armed Forces Academy, the staff of Commander-in-Chief Ground Forces and in at least one of three Operational Commands.

The third question is whether "programs of cooperation" actually produce results in defense reform. All countries of the former Soviet Union and Warsaw Pact, not only Ukraine, have inherited armed forces—not to say security services, interior forces, and ordinary police—which are unsuited and in some ways threatening to their security. Such "force structures"— which in Ukraine as well as Russia have only proliferated since the Soviet collapse—were a staple part of a communist political culture founded upon hostility to civil society. Without transformation of these structures and the mentalities they continue to inculcate, there can be no meaningful correspondence between declaratory adherence to "democratic values" and political reality. Neither can there be meaningful integration with the states that now call themselves "Europe." But however laudable NATO's intentions, what is the actual result? As our subsequent discussion of Ukraine demonstrates, the determinant is the interest of the recipient country, not the number of programs which are implemented.

A fourth question—in fact two related questions—is what NATO's commitment to "consult" means in practice and what is meant by a "direct threat" to a partner's "territorial integrity, political independence, or security." "The Statement of the Ministry of Foreign Affairs of Georgia" of December 8, 2000, accusing Russia of "unilateral measures ... which actually means the violation of the territorial integrity of the state" has not produced, in the eyes of Georgians, a clear response from NATO.[11] Outside classified forums, to the author's knowledge, NATO has not formally deliberated upon its response if Ukraine were to become the object of a "direct threat."

What is known is that prior to the Kosovo conflict, Ukraine's 1998 State Program of Cooperation between Ukraine and NATO referred to NATO as "the most effective structure of collective security in Europe." It is also clear that elite opinion diverges from public opinion. According to a January–February 2000 poll conducted by Ukrainian Centre for Economic and Political Studies (UCEPS), only 10.5 percent believe in NATO's desire to defend Ukraine, and only 37.5 percent believe that NATO would honor an article 5 commitment if Ukraine actually joined NATO.[12] But the second half of the question is equally problematic. "Direct threat" is a perilously constraining term in a part of Europe characterized by fragmented states, powerful transnational structures, and multiple, opaque relationships among state bodies, "private" businesses, and criminal entities. In these postcommunist as well as post–cold war conditions, "direct threats" are the most difficult as well the least necessary ones to pose. As the authors of Ukraine's National Security Concept recognize, a defense and intelligence system organized to respond simply to such (largely dated) threats will find itself without the means to anticipate, forestall, or manage the types of crises which have a realistic chance of arising.

A fifth question, which NATO has forcefully articulated itself, is just how far the Alliance can assist states in the larger task of integration with Europe. As a security organization, NATO is limited in its ability to advance (viz. the National Security and Defense Council of Ukraine) a country's "strategic course" of becoming a "full member of the European family of civilized nations."[13] NATO cannot make Ukrainian goods competitive in European markets or decrease unemployment in Albania. Not even an intimate and comprehensive relationship with NATO will do more than a small amount to attract western capital to Bulgaria, Romania, or Ukraine, let alone enable them to become integrated with the rest of Europe in the ways that matter most—through business, trade, and investment. The Polish formula was economic transformation *and* security, with security being the dependent variable. Unless the less advanced countries of Europe can replicate the Polish formula and engage the *private* economies of western Europe and North America, most ordinary citizens will continue to ask the question they ask at present: "What does cooperation with NATO do for me?"

It would be easy to elaborate upon such questions and qualifications to the point where they appeared to negate all that NATO has done to transform defense priorities, defense cultures, and security in Central Europe. NATO's accomplishments should not be belittled. In new member states as well as candidate states, enlargement and its corollaries—PfP and Membership Action Plans—have been the prime, and in some cases the sole impetus for defense and security reform. Among candidate members, the animus to "renationalize" defense policy has stalled, and among new members it has virtually disappeared. Among new members and several candidates, "habits of cooperation" and integration of planning, procedures, and working arrangements are becoming a reality.

Despite divisions of opinion within populations and some arguable sins of omission by NATO itself, the vast majority of elites in candidate countries equate NATO membership with security, even if some are less inclined than they were before Kosovo to describe NATO as a "purely defensive alliance" and equate it with "the projection of stability in Europe." To be sure, these doubts are far more deeply entrenched in the countries that are not candidates. As a country subject to deep divisions of public and elite opinion, yet enjoying a unique intensity of cooperation with NATO for a noncandidate, Ukraine is a special and somewhat schizophrenic case.

Ukraine and the EU

Ukraine also has a measure of schizophrenia towards the EU. Like a number of other central and eastern European countries, Ukraine has gradually come to realize that the attitude of the European Union will have a deeper impact upon its future than the attitude of NATO. Significantly, EU membership is not only an official goal of Ukraine—which has no plans to join NATO "in the foreseeable future"—the goal is broadly supported by the population, 55.1 percent of whom believe that Ukraine should join the EU within the next five years![14] The schizophrenia lies in the failure of Ukraine to take significant practical steps to advance this aspiration. Schizophrenia is also accompanied by disappointment, a feeling shared by a number of other countries of the region. Until recently, the European Union has displayed an ambivalence towards Ukraine verging on coolness, and it could even be said to display an ambivalence towards its own undertakings to enlarge the Union, given at the Copenhagen European Council of June 1993 and reinforced by invitations to specific Group 1 and Group 2 countries at Luxembourg in December 1997.

There are three reasons for this ambivalence. First, until recently the internal culture of the European Union has not been focused upon security, but economics and integration. In practice, "ever closer union" has been a project designed to achieve further harmonization among member states whose legal systems, employment practices, welfare provisions, and economic policies are, by postcommunist standards, remarkably harmonized already. Therefore, the challenge for a nonmember state is not simply one of catching up, but catching up with a moving target. This contradiction—between the "deepening" of Europe (the further integration of those already inside it) and its widening—can be directly attributed to the European model itself. The refrain, common until quite recently, that "the EU is not seeking new members" not only illustrates the difference between EU priorities and NATO's; to many in central and eastern Europe, it also implies that the EU has limited interest in, and surely no responsibility for, developments which occur outside it.

Second, and in marked contrast to NATO, it has taken some time for the priorities of the EU to be materially affected by the ending of the cold war. As the quintessential cold war institution, NATO swiftly came under pressure to transform or dissolve—and was subject to this pressure first and foremost from the electorates of its member states. But as a nonmilitary institution, the European Union initially escaped these pressures. This largely explains why the EU continues to apply an old model—protectionist as well as *communautaire*—to the new task of enlargement. If a widening Europe does not reconsider the logic of "deepening," then EU enlargement could become the process of moving barriers east. Contrary to conventional wisdom, the EU, not NATO, has the greater potential to create "new dividing lines" in Europe—although Russia's perception is decidedly, and perhaps understandably, different from that of its neighbors.

To those with no immediate, let alone foreseeable prospect of accession to the EU, the Schengen Agreement on frontiers, signed in June 1985, meets the specifications of a new dividing line.[15] Ukraine, Romania, and the three Baltic states have used PfP not only to draw closer to NATO's web of institutions and relationships, but also to draw closer to the west as a whole. NATO enlargement has complemented and facilitated this process. Yet apart from the Baltic states (all of them now confidently on the path to EU accession), there is reasoned apprehension that EU enlargement could disrupt this process and reverse promising trends which are knitting regions together. These trends are at risk not only between Poland and Ukraine (where before 1999 some 1.7 million people per month crossed the border under a visa-free regime), but between Hungary and Romania, as well as Slovakia and the Czech Republic. The implications of Schengen for Moldova, the Kaliningrad Oblast, and other oblasts in Russia's northwest regions are also serious.

Still, it must be said that the implications for Ukraine are especially serious because its geographical location between the EU and Russia make it extremely difficult to implement measures which would enable it to harmonize its border regime with Schengen criteria, thereby maintaining a relatively open and friendly western frontier. Ukraine's fixed and consistent official position—that all of its borders must have the same legal status—is difficult for the EU to accept because the Ukraine–Russia border is the point of entry for two-thirds of contraband and 90 percent of illegal migrants. Ukraine's official position is also flatly unacceptable to Russia, which has consistently maintained that internal borders of the Commonwealth of Independent States (CIS) should be delimited (drawn on maps), but not demarcated.[16] Although it is Ukraine's view that "demarcation does not require the construction of walls or any obstacles,"[17] Russia continues to rebuff efforts to establish any kind of demarcation.

The third reason lies in the nature of the EU and the enlargement process. Enlargement is not a geopolitical project, but a process of integration. The social, economic, and political criteria for membership are uniform and, in principle, apolitical. But there are understandable reasons why this point is not as clear as the EU would wish it to be. First, there is the perception—not entirely unfounded—that the EU has several distinctly political concerns, notably the avoidance of steps which could be perceived as unfriendly to Russia. Ukraine, with arguable justification, has not perceived equivalent EU attentiveness to its own concerns and has interpreted the EU's delay in officially acknowledging its "European vocation" as a calculated snub. The point is further obscured by the trend explored in this chapter: the growing security-mindedness of the European Union, overtly expressed by its Common Foreign and Security Policy as well as its Common Security and Defense Policy.

Moreover, the EU has not sufficiently considered the implications of introducing its own radically apolitical values to a part of Europe which remains deeply politicized and profoundly geopolitical in its thinking. According to EU criteria, Ukraine and Russia "belong together" because of their common level of development—a view often expressed (albeit privately) by EU representatives and officials. To Ukraine's pro-western elites, these sentiments suggest that the EU regards a country's interests, sentiments, and aspirations as of no account. This is, indeed, a radical proposition, given the fact that common levels of development have not, until recently, produced harmony even in western Europe, where two great wars of the twentieth century were fought between economic equals.

The risk in present EU enlargement policy is therefore twofold: that it might encourage the tendencies (including fatalism and despair) which NATO has struggled to counter; and no less regrettably, that it might fail to realize the positive potential at the heart of enlargement itself. Is the European Union intended to be a magnet or a barrier? The case for barriers against illegal migration, organized crime, arms, and drugs is a priori and unanswerable. But must this necessarily translate into barriers against countries? And if it must, then for how long?

Today Ukraine and other states now understand that it is primarily the EU, not NATO, which will decide whether they become part of Europe or part of Europe's "gray zone." They are also just beginning to understand that in taking its decisions, the EU will not be guided by the foreign policies of these states, but their internal policies; indeed, they are at last beginning to grasp that their "European choice" entails Europe's growing involvement in their internal affairs.[18] The approach of the EU could therefore turn out to be the greatest single stimulant to the methodical and sustained reforms which "aid" and diplomacy have had such limited success in fostering. If these possibilities are to be realized, it would be in the interest of the EU to present the accession of Ukraine and other excluded states as a desirable and, in the long term, achievable objective.

Towards Convergence?

The commitment in the October 1997 Treaty of Amsterdam to frame a Common European Security and Defense Policy (ESDP)—reinforced by the Anglo-French initiative at Saint-Malo (December 1998) and the European

Councils at Cologne (June 1999), Helsinki (December 1999), Lisbon (March 2000), Feira (June 2000), and Nice (December 2000)—has sparked a vigorous and apprehensive debate within some NATO countries, not to say Russia, as to whether the EU could, by intention or misadventure, weaken the Alliance or divide it. The coming into force of the EU's Common Foreign and Security Policy (CFSP) in November 1999, the simultaneous appointment of Javier Solana as high representative for the CFSP and the establishment of a Political and Security Committee, a Military Committee, and a Military Staff have sharpened these debates, as has the Helsinki Council's establishment of a Headline Goal of dedicating 50,000–60,000 troops for EU led crisis response operations by 2003.

Those looking for anti-Atlanticist sentiments among the more visionary proponents of ESDP will have no trouble finding them. Nevertheless, the statements and actions of the majority of those responsible for developing ESDP point in a decidedly different direction. For one thing, ESDP framework documents are quite careful to state that there is no intention of conflicting with NATO or overlapping with it: ESDP limits itself to humanitarian intervention and regional crisis management, EU capabilities must be "separable but not separate" from NATO, Europe will only act "where NATO as a whole is not engaged," and NATO is to remain the sole guarantor of collective defense.[19] No less important, ESDP reflects an overdue recognition that enlargement is a profoundly complex security issue and that the EU must be as concerned with security in the future as it has been with economics in the past. In the words of NATO assistant secretary-general Klaus-Peter Klaiber, "The old formula, NATO does security and the EU does economics is no longer viable." What is more, there is increasingly emphatic recognition that "we must harmonize the [NATO and EU] enlargements."[20]

These statements beg many questions, not least for nonmember states, but there are logical as well as substantive reasons to doubt whether trends are leading to a transatlantic divorce, rather than the opposite: a more Europeanized NATO and a more Atlanticist EU. The first logical reason is that neither today nor in the foreseeable future is there a realistic chance that Europe will find the wherewithal to reproduce NATO's distinctive, specialized, and very costly defense capabilities. The EU, which has a gross domestic product equivalent to that of the United States, spends 60 percent as much as the latter on defense and for this expenditure acquires 30 to 40 percent of the capability. It will require formidable political will to alter this equation and a revolution in thinking and political priorities to equalize it.

Therefore, the logical conclusion is that any EU military operation will depend upon NATO assets, will require NATO consent, and hence will require the consultation, discussion, and debate which always have been the prelude to NATO consent. Indeed, it will also require the establishment of mechanisms of consultation between NATO and the EU which prior to ESDP did not exist. This is more likely to strengthen NATO's position in Europe than weaken it.

The second logical reason is that if ESDP develops at all, it will develop in the context of the consolidation of a broader western community and its further enlargement. The three newest NATO members and the majority of prospective EU members are decidedly Atlanticist. Poland, the Czech Republic, Hungary, and the three Baltic countries know in their bones that developments to their east will have a profound bearing on the character and security of Europe. They also fear that a Europe dominated by France and Germany—and from which the United States and Canada are absent—could become a Europe which, as of old, will be tempted to make bargains with Russia over their heads and at their expense. It is NATO's view that a more institutionalized EU–NATO relationship should reduce this fear. In Klaiber's words:

> There can be little doubt that a structured dialogue between [the EU and NATO] would make a coherent approach vis-à-vis Russia much more feasible. And it would eliminate any Russian temptation to play Europe and America against each other.[21]

Practice is confirming what logic would suggest. As early as 1993, NATO took steps to make its assets available for Combined Joint Task Forces in operations of the Western European Union (WEU), designed to fulfil the tasks set by the EU at its 1992 Petersberg (Holland) summit: humanitarian intervention, search and rescue, peacekeeping, crisis management, and peace making. NATO's Fiftieth Anniversary Summit in Washington in April 1999 unequivocally endorsed ESDP and the decision to build on existing NATO and WEU mechanisms.

Since then, a careful symmetry has been developing among ESDP planning, NATO's defense planning system, and its Planning and Review Process; the EU's Collective Capability Goals have been synchronized with NATO's Defense Capabilities Initiative, and a number of ad hoc NATO–EU working groups have been established. Despite discussions about questions of participation reminiscent of dialogues in *Alice in Wonderland*—eight members of NATO are not members of the EU and four members of the EU are not members of NATO—there can be little doubt that NATO hopes ESDP will evolve into the long-sought "European pillar" of the Alliance. President Bush's Warsaw speech suggested, in defiance of all stereotypes about his supposed isolationism, that this hope is shared by his new administration as well.[22]

More intriguing than this institutional convergence are steps relating to enlargement. Speaking in Latvia in spring 2000, EU President Romano Prodi declared that "any attack or aggression against an EU member would be an attack or aggression against the whole EU."[23] This declaration surely begs the question who is to *defend* "the whole EU," given universal agreement that the EU will not possess capabilities for collective defense. Nevertheless, Prodi's statement is further (and highly authoritative) indication that the EU is synchronizing its thinking with NATO's and at last becoming alert to the security implications of its enlargement policy.

Does this mean that the EU is becoming alert to the security implications for excluded states? The declaration by NATO secretary-general Lord George Robertson in Kiev (July 5, 2001)—"We will not leave a partner country alone in an emergency"—has not been echoed by the EU. At Feira and Nice, the EU discussed arrangements to make it possible for Ukraine and other nonmembers to contribute to joint operations. But it has not discussed how the EU might in turn contribute to *their* security. NATO's programs of cooperation (which reached the unprecedented total of 500 NATO–Ukraine events in 2000) have no analogue in the European Union. This has been lamented by Poland, which more than any other EU candidate state understands the acute "soft security" challenges which Ukraine and other countries face, as well as the assistance which the EU might be able to provide. This recognition is shared by the EU high commissioner for external relations, Chris Patten, who is rightly disturbed by the security gap in "civilian aspects of crisis management" and the EU's failure to better exploit its expertise in "police deployment and training, border control, institution building ... combating illicit trafficking, embargo enforcement and counter terrorism."[24]

The trend towards greater security-mindedness by the EU does not guarantee that the security interests of nonmembers will be adequately taken into account. But it makes it increasingly unlikely that the EU will be indifferent to them. By the same token, there is no inexorable linkage between greater attentiveness to the security needs of nonmembers and greater respect for their economic interests. Yet again, a Union concerned about the security implications of its actions is more likely to be alert to these connections than a Union which is not. Where Ukraine is concerned, at last there are signs that connections are being made.

Ukraine between the West, the East, and Itself

Since 1991, Ukraine's independence has been predicated on the "strategic course of entering Europe." It is in European, not Eurasian, terms that Ukraine has defined its statehood. The first *and only* governments of a modern, independent Ukraine have placed so much rhetorical emphasis on "integration with European and Euro-Atlantic structures" that setbacks along this road have been seen by many as setbacks for the state or worse, as challenges to its legitimacy. Yet, since the handing of the torch from President Leonid Kravchuk to President Leonid Kuchma in 1994, Ukraine has also pursued a "multi-vector policy." This policy reflects three realities.

The first reality is that for any independent Ukrainian state, Russia is bound to be a pervasive and problematic factor: pervasive because of a related (but far from common) history and an extensive (but far from unalterable) economic dependency; problematic not because Russia refuses to accept Ukraine's *nezavisimost'* (juridical independence), but because of its reluctance to accept Ukraine's nonaligned status;[25] and no less important, because of the widespread sentiments that *samostoyatel'noy Ukrainiy nikogda ne budet* ("Ukraine will never be able to stand by itself")—and that friendship and "drawing closer" are two sides of the same coin.[26] Even in the bolder and more creative period of his presidency (1994–1997), President Kuchma perceived that Ukraine would have no chance of remaining independent without a "strategic partnership" with Russia, that is, without Russian *consent*. Equally, he believed that there would be no chance of securing Russian consent unless Ukraine had strong ties with the west and the west displayed a strong stake in an independent Ukraine.

The second reality is that the west will not support Ukraine on an anti-Russian basis. President Kravchuk's efforts to persuade western governments to embrace Ukraine as a bulwark against a potentially resurgent Russia fell on stony ground. What western governments will accept is the proposition that progress in realizing Ukraine's "European choice"—and the essential corollary to this progress, internal transformation—can strengthen those forces in Russia who are democratically minded and who are determined to define the country's interest in post-imperial, rather than neo-imperial terms. This prospect is far more likely to be realized in conditions where Ukraine and the west enjoy mutually beneficial relations with Russia than in conditions where Russia feels estranged from either party.

The third reality is that inside Ukraine, as in Russia, there are deep divisions about the identity of the nation and state. In significant measure, these are regional divisions. Yet with two significant exceptions—the six oblasts of western Ukraine (which did not become part of a Russian dominated state until 1939–1940) and the Autonomous Republic of Crimea (which did not become administratively part of Ukraine until 1954)—they could not be fairly described as ethnic divisions. The celebrated 1994 poll of inhabitants of Donetsk region—in which 84 percent identified themselves as "Soviet people"—is indicative of a general pattern, inasmuch as the number of ethnic Ukrainians adopting this appellation was similar to the number of ethnic Russians who did so.[27]

Almost as important as these regional divisions is the divide between officials and experts on the one hand and the ordinary population on the other. It is in the nature of this divide that the difference between Ukrainian and Russian orientation to NATO emerges, for whereas the Ukrainian population is more polarized in its attitudes than the Russian public (and on the whole less negative), it is distinctly more skeptical towards NATO than the country's elite; whereas in Russia the elite is decidedly more critical of NATO than the population.[28] Although the polls reveal manifest divisions, they also reveal an important leavening characteristic: The majority of Ukrainians have a non-bloc orientation. Majorities of those expressing an opinion oppose membership in NATO as well as accession to the Tashkent Treaty.[29] In contrast, 52 percent favor membership in the EU within five years, very possibly because the EU is not perceived as a bloc; only 3 percent see EU membership as incompatible with "geopolitical closeness to Russia."

It is also noteworthy that whereas 86.9 percent describe Russia as a "priority strategic partner," respectively 65.5 and 62 percent describe the United States and Germany in these terms. Moreover, 65 percent believe that strategic partnerships are important primarily for economic reasons, while only 36 percent value them primarily on grounds of security.[30] In the minds of those who perceive the world in "either–or" terms, many of these polling results appear contradictory. Not unreasonably, the majority of Ukrainians do not see the world in this way. For this majority, there is no contradiction between being pro-Russian and wary of the Russian state—and no contradiction between being pro-western and wary of NATO.

Therefore, a Ukrainian president pursuing a multi-vector policy will not add to the country's divisions—at least on grounds of foreign policy. But what does the multi-vector policy mean in practice? Should it mean that Ukraine should synchronize its "advance towards Europe" with Russia (a view supported only by the Left)? Should it mean balancing movement towards Europe and NATO with strategic concessions towards Russia (the view of President Kuchma)? Or should it be a means of maneuver towards Europe designed, like the CIS à la Kravchuk, to continue the process of "civilized divorce" from Russia?

Viktor Yushchenko, Borys Tarasyuk, and most other supporters of the latter policy understand that without measures to increase Ukraine's *samostiynist'* (its "ability to stand"), their own policy will be unrealizable and the president's policy will cede control of Ukraine's economy and, progressively, its power of autonomous decision to its eastern neighbor. The measures designed to strengthen *samostiynist'* and strengthen the European course are identical. At the most basic level, they involve ending the negotiability of the legal order; putting in place property rights and contracts and mechanisms to enforce them; creating taxation regimes which stimulate entrepreneurship rather than stifle it; and establishing laws designed to restrain the powerful rather than enfeeble those who are already far too weak. They also involve establishing the minimal conditions of transparency: the ability to know *what* decisions are taken, *where* they are taken, and *by whom* they are taken. These measures are required not only in order to integrate Ukraine into Europe; they are required in order to integrate Ukraine.[31]

With the exception of Viktor Yushchenko's government (December 1999–April 2001), these issues have been addressed largely by declaration. The prime reason for this is obvious to any Ukrainian taxi driver: Beyond every "intractable" economic problem stands a powerful political force. The dual nature of Ukraine's anti-Soviet revolution—national as well as political—initially obscured the fact that in Ukraine, as in Russia, the revolution was a contained revolution and that power remained in the hands of local and national elites who swiftly learned how to transform bureaucratic into financial control. In this state of affairs—where, despite the collapse of central and local budgets, the size of bureaucracies has increased since Soviet times—licensing, regulation, and law enforcement have become rent-seeking activities (and instruments of political pressure), rather than ways of protecting the entrepreneur, the consumer, and the citizen.

A second, related reason is that the more formidable "oligarchic" interests in Ukraine—the fuel and energy complex, the financial and banking sector, and indeed the security and intelligence network—are transnational structures de facto; moreover not transnational European structures, but structures of the former Soviet Union, collusive, highly inbred, and wedded to a mode of business largely opaque to outsiders.[32] Western pieties of "transition"—and more recently "globalization"—have altogether ignored the real transition which has taken place from Soviet disintegration to the emergence of a "state of a new type" and a "new class" dedicated to preserving it.

In sum, the problem is not simply that civil society is too weak in Ukraine, but that other forces are too strong. Their strength was demonstrated all too clearly when Yushchenko was dismissed from power despite clearing the state's debt in pensions and wages and despite achieving the first real economic growth in Ukraine since independence. The "Yushchenko experiment" demonstrated that change is possible in Ukraine. But its outcome only reinforces the perception that "the principal security threat to Ukraine is Ukraine itself."[33]

Therefore, success along the internal vector is plainly prerequisite to success along the others. Yet not only is this point not conceded by all Ukrainian decision makers; it is not understood by all of them. One reason for this is that even many Ukrainians with a Euro-Atlantic slant preserve the belief that European integration is a matter of "high politics" rather than a process of instituting ordinary and practical changes in the way an economy works. To this day, many still speak of becoming integrated with European structures, as if this were synonymous with becoming integrated with Europe. A second reason for this misunderstanding, ironically, is Ukraine's past accomplishments. In the post-independence period, the dominant western image of Ukraine, reflected in a notoriously inaccurate 1994 U.S. Central Intelligence Agency report, was of a Yugoslavia in the making, threatened by separatism and ethnic conflict and (unlike Yugoslavia), threatening "nuclear anarchy."

Ukraine not only avoided these calamities, it carried through a program of unilateral nuclear disarmament and, without conflict or upheaval resubordinated and substantially dismantled armed forces of the former USSR on

Ukrainian territory. No less significantly, between 1994 and 1997, Ukraine's Ministry of Foreign Affairs ably compensated for internal weakness, securing for Ukraine a strong diplomatic identity, an active international presence, and a truly independent voice. The NATO–Ukraine relationship and the May 1997 accords with Russia were this policy's prime achievements. Nevertheless, these very achievements have done much to prolong the culture of declaration in Ukraine's political establishment and delay the emergence of a culture of implementation. For all the skills behind these achievements, they were also the fruit of favorable geopolitical conditions which have since deteriorated.

The geopolitical climate has deteriorated for three reasons. First, NATO's military intervention in Kosovo has had a traumatic and lasting effect. It has presented NATO in a provocative and even threatening light to a population which had largely viewed it in more benign, favorable, and even protective terms. (Today, 46 percent of the population view NATO as an "aggressive military bloc."[34]) It undermined the tenability of the multi-vector policy by rupturing good relations between Russia and the west. It sharply heightened concerns that Ukraine could be drawn involuntarily into disputes and conflicts outside its borders.[35] It also created precedents which could be used by others (e.g., Russia in Crimea) to override state sovereignty in the name of "human rights." Finally, it has persuaded pro-NATO Ukrainian elites that NATO has "demoted" Ukraine and that its Balkan commitments will divert NATO's attention for years to come.

Second, the combination of Kosovo, NATO enlargement, and the New Strategic Concept has had a strong effect on Russia, persuading much of the military and security establishment that the former Soviet Union could become a future venue for NATO's "coercive diplomacy." This perception of geopolitical pressure from NATO and U.S. "hegemonism" cannot be divorced from the determination to go for a final solution of the Chechen problem, transform the former Soviet Union into a "zone of special interest"[36] and adopt the "far tougher" policy towards neighbors which Ukraine has since had to suffer.[37] Ukrainian negotiators and decision makers perceive that Putin has disciplined, if not ended Russian *mnogogolisiye* ("multi-voicedness") and that he is using economic pressure as a tool to secure not only economic gains but geopolitical changes.[38] These pressures make it more difficult to oppose actions perceived as harmful to Ukraine's security (e.g., using Crimea as a base for training Russian naval infantry for combat operations in Chechnya).[39]

The third unfavorable factor, as already noted, is the impending enlargement of the European Union. Even unqualified reformers, like Viktor Yushchenko perceive that the rigors and pace of the accession process for Poland and Hungary do not present Ukraine with stimulants, but with tests which it is doomed to fail. Those who fear reform have simply concluded, along with President Kuchma, that "the West is closed for us now."

The perception that "the West is closed" certainly solidified after the revelations known as "Kuchmagate": the publication of tapes allegedly implicating President Kuchma in the murder of journalist Grigory Gongadze and in several other arguably more serious abuses of power. The scandal has not only weakened the legitimacy of Ukraine's political order, it has compromised what President Kuchma long ago identified as real independence, Ukraine's "freedom to choose." This is because the revelations have driven what appears to be an immovable wedge between the president and those most capable of advancing Ukraine's "strategic course of entering Europe," notably the supporters of former prime minister Yushchenko, dismissed on April 26, 2001. By the same token, the scandal has made him dependent on those whose commitment to this goal is merely declaratory as well as those who oppose it altogether. No less significantly, the scandal (which led not only to western recriminations, but also to moves to expel Ukraine from the Council of Europe) enabled Russia to assume the mantle of defender of Ukraine's sovereignty[40]—a role which most Ukrainians and westerners would have found implausible, if not unimaginable, even a short time ago.[41]

A Refocused Partnership with NATO

In view of the factors discussed above, it stands to reason that NATO–Ukraine cooperation would become more cosmetic and that defense reform would be exiled to the antechamber of pieties and hopes. In fact, since December 1999, NATO–Ukraine cooperation has entered an intense and highly practical phase, defense reform has finally acquired direction and substance, and both efforts have secured presidential support. Counterintuitive as these changes might appear, there are three compelling reasons for them. First, while conceding to Russia what he must, President Kuchma wishes to preserve as much of the multi-vector policy as he can and therefore has a clear incentive to reinforce the few channels of the western vector—the Polish–Ukraine relationship being another such channel—which produce benefits for Ukraine. Second, the worsened geopolitical climate (and a revised official threat assessment) argue strongly against further postponement. Third, the economic condition of the country has finally persuaded a critical mass of key players that a bloated and underfinanced defense establishment could become a social and, ultimately, a national security problem for the country.[42]

Today, as opposed to 1997, the prime goal of NATO–Ukraine cooperation is not advancing Ukraine's "European course" but, in the words of the minister of defense, army general Oleksandr Kuzmuk, "supporting defense reform in the country."[43] Now as well as then, no equation is made between cooperation with NATO and future membership. Indeed, the military leadership, like the political leadership, is as opposed to Ukraine joining NATO (on grounds of external security and internal concord) as it is supportive of closer ties with it. The conclusion innocently and widely drawn that those opposed to NATO membership are necessarily anti-NATO is therefore misconceived.

It is often forgotten that Ukraine did not inherit an army in 1991. What it inherited was a force grouping—without a Defense Ministry, a General Staff, and central organs of command-and-control. Moreover, this grouping, its formidable inventory of equipment and its highly trained officer corps were designed for one purpose: to wage combined arms, coalition, offensive (and nuclear) warfare against NATO on an external front and under somebody else's direction. In 1991, these formations were not equipped, deployed, or trained to provide national defense, or for that matter integrated military operations of any kind.[44] As they stood, they were bone and muscle without heart or brain.

In the post-independence period, therefore, Ukraine did not merely face the task of "reforming" an army, but creating one. Having accomplished this far from straightforward task, Ukraine's armed forces entered a period of stagnation whose ills only began to be addressed after President Kuchma established an interdepartmental commission on defense reform in December 1999, chaired by army general Kuzmuk (minister of defense) and Yevhen Marchuk (secretary of the National Security and Defense Council).[45] To understand what has and has not been achieved (as of August 2001), it is essential to analyze defense policy as well as its implementation.[46]

Unlike the operation of a market economy, national defense must be a planned activity. Failure to produce a tight correspondence among national security policy, military doctrine (the purpose and the priorities of armed forces), and military programs (detailed schemes for their development) will lead to waste, confusion, and in the worst case breakdown. Producing such a correspondence is not easy, particularly in the radically transformed circumstances confronting newly independent states, and in nearly all of these states it has not been achieved because old mentalities and strong interests continually intrude.[47] Programs therefore matter, because nothing sensible can be accomplished without them.

In contrast to the post-Soviet norm (which, according to President Putin, applied to Russia until 2000), Ukraine adopted a National Security Concept (approved by parliament in January 1997) which was a model statement of first principles. It assaulted the general war ethos (which has been inbred in the Soviet-trained officer corps of Ukraine) by stipulating that in conditions where both state and society were weak, the prime security challenge would be to forestall and resolve local crises, emergencies, and conflicts and prevent them being exploited by actors (internal and foreign) with ulterior political ends. Proceeding from this analysis, the Concept identified "the strengthening of civil society" as the first of nine security challenges for Ukraine. Ukraine's first State Program of Armed Forces Development (1997) had its merits, but was not consistent with these principles. A far more impressive consistency has been achieved in the current State Program of Armed Forces Development and Reform 2001–2005, which was submitted to President Kuchma in May 2000.[48]

The capabilities mandated by the program furnish obvious incentives to exploit NATO's post–cold war expertise in joint operations, complex emergencies, and "operations other than war."[49] Therefore, at the same time it was submitted to the president, the state program (minus a classified geopolitical assessment) was submitted to NATO for analysis and comment. In April 2001, NATO presented its recommendations at a meeting of the Joint Working Group on Defense Reform (a body established under the NATO–Ukraine Distinctive Partnership, which has no analogue between NATO and any other country). On the basis of NATO's assessment that stipulated force levels would still be grossly out of balance with resources, Ukraine has committed itself to a far deeper level and more intense schedule of reductions of roughly a third by 2005, which have begun to be put into effect.[50]

Cooperation with NATO has now moved beyond the formal exchange of ideas to a scheduled process of audit and consultation. In 2001, Ukraine became an active participant in NATO's Planning and Review Process

(PARP), a PfP program requiring each participating country at regular intervals to supply NATO with a detailed inventory of its military assets and, jointly with NATO, to identify real costs, as well as capabilities in short supply or surplus to needs.[51] Ukraine also was to draw up a detailed package of National Defense Reform Objectives for initial review by NATO in December 2001. A mechanism has also been devised to keep NATO advised on a regular basis of the program's implementation. These are significant steps for a military establishment schooled to regard transparency as a threat to departmental interests and national security.

These steps have also given more focus to the considerable volume of activities which take place between NATO and Ukraine each year. More than 500 bilateral activities were scheduled between NATO Allies and Ukraine in 2001, as well as 250 multilateral activities with NATO. These numbers in themselves, of course, say very little about the value of cooperation: For example, the establishment of the Polish-Ukrainian battalion (POLUKRBAT) has been worth several dozen such "activities." Although the volume of Ukraine–Russia military activities is comparatively modest (in stark contrast to cooperation in the military-industrial sector), this is not to say that Ukraine sees no value in such cooperation.[52] As a case in point, Russia's merger of Air Forces and Air Defense Forces is being closely studied. But few believe that the Russian armed forces are an attractive model for the conduct of joint operations and the regulation of civil conflicts. Additionally, as the issue of the joint naval force demonstrates, many question whether Russia's military cooperation goals are compatible with Ukraine's. As Leonid Polyakov, director of military programs at UCEPS, maintains:

> So far, Russian officials, unlike NATO's, have never voiced their concern about the weakness of Ukraine's defense or the slow pace of its military reform. One might infer that Ukraine's problems in building its Armed Forces are simply more acceptable to Moscow than Ukraine's success in that area.[53]

Eight months into the program, in early 2002, the catalogue of measures implemented was necessarily sparse. NATO representatives confirm that troop reductions have begun, that front-line organization is being overhauled, that reorganizations of the Air Force and Air Defense Forces are in train (possibly as a prelude to merger), and that preparations for the closure or merger of surplus facilities are proceeding. A major training command for peace support operations has been established, and a NATO bloc of courses is being established at the National Armed Forces Academy. Moreover, every new officer is now obliged to learn English, French, or German as part of his or her academic curriculum.

Yet there must be two areas of major concern. The first is resources. With a budget 75 percent larger than Ukraine's, Hungary is reducing the size of its armed forces to 45,000 and Ukraine to 200,000 service members.[54] This discrepancy is less indicative of the lack of realism of Ukraine's military establishment than the irresponsibility of its political establishment. Unlike Hungary, Ukraine is a nonaligned country bordering seven states (and the Black Sea) and lying in the vicinity of several conflict zones. Even as harsh a critic as Anatoly Grytsenko believes that the strength of Ministry of Defense armed forces should not fall below 150,000 and that the defense budget should not fall below 2.5 percent of gross domestic product.[55] But until Ukraine moves far closer to this position than it now is, the best one can hope for is progress in the priority areas of the program (downsizing, rationalization, and the training and provision of rapid reaction forces), modest advances in equipment repair and maintenance, token advances in professionalization,[56] and a halt to further deterioration in the research and development base and social sphere (housing, *dedovshchina*, and health).[57]

The second concern is that, with the limited exceptions of the Border Troops and Emergency Services, reform has not begun to touch non–Ministry of Defense force structures, which (excluding ordinary police and depending on the estimate accepted) employ just under or very much over 50 percent the number of personnel serving in the armed forces. Yet here reform is most vital, not only in the interests of combating emergencies and conducting "multi-component operations," but in the interests of democracy in the country.[58] Measured against a western template, progress in changing mind-sets and extending transparency throughout the Ministry of Defense military system is uneven, but by comparison with the Ministry of Internal Affairs and SBU (Security Service of Ukraine), it moves at lightning speed.

It is significant that the focus of the Joint Working Group will now be extended to include Border Services, the Ministry of Emergency Situations, and the Ministry of Interior (MVS). Where the latter body is concerned, this will be an uphill struggle. Reform programs for the MVS and SBU, promised in 1999, have not been published, even in an excerpted form. Here, as in Soviet times, the best information remains anecdotal. By no recognized standard could these forces be said to be under civil democratic control. At best, they are under control of an elected president, but the tape scandal has forced many to question even this. In this sphere, it might be no exaggeration to say (pace Grytsenko) that "military forces are developing on their own."

NATO–Ukraine cooperation is the one significant area of Ukraine's cooperation with the west which has fostered enthusiasm rather than mutual frustration. As refocused, its core objective, defense reform, proceeds unevenly but at last with deliberation. Defense reform, and NATO's approach to it, is also widening the circle of those who understand the connections between military and economic policy, between transparency and sound management, and among security, civil-democratic control, and democracy. Thanks to NATO's involvement in this process, the dozen or so nongovernmental organizations engaged in defense issues have gained in expertise and influence.[59]

The Evolution of Self-Interest

Since the end of the cold war, the creation of a "greater Europe"—"a Europe whole and free"—has not only been a dominant theme of diplomacy, it has been the principal piety of the post–cold war era. The piety has generated countless initiatives; it has created an entirely new class of experts, middlemen, and consultants; it has produced illusions and disillusionment in equal measure; and at a more mundane level, it has produced disappointment and waste. But it has also produced the enlargement of NATO, the reasoned expectation of its further enlargement and the all but certain enlargement of the European Union. Enlargement has been a major stimulant to change. But it has not always been a sufficient stimulant, and in some quarters it has stimulated resistance.

Like change, enlargement has limits. At one level, the limits are being defined by the character of the communities which others seek to join. The members of these communities have interests apart from enlargement, not least, the integrity of the communities themselves—integrity which can easily be lost if standards are compromised and membership diluted indiscriminately. Admitting new members has costs and risks for those who admit them. The costs and risks which the west assumed when it sought to create a Euro-Atlantic community at the start of the cold war are very different from those which it will assume now that "the cold war is over." The lesson of enlargement to date is that the west, like God, helps those who help themselves. On the self-help principle, the west has embraced Poland, the Czech Republic, and Hungary—and despite the Russian factor, it is embracing the Baltic states as well.

The second level, therefore, is being defined by the character of the candidate countries. In some of them, convictions, realism, and civil society have been strong enough to make external support the crucial variable. Elsewhere, external support has collided with real fault lines in political and economic culture, and it has also collided with the powers that maintain them. This is what has happened in Ukraine. Should we therefore conclude that there is no prospect of Ukraine joining the European Union in the long term or, in the midterm, drawing closer to it? Should we also treat these as foregone conclusions, immutable to our own efforts?

The adoption of these conclusions would have three serious implications. In the first place, they would signal to many that whatever Ukraine does to solve its problems, the "greater Europe" will be built without it. To many others, they would simply signal that meaningful change is not possible. These messages, fortified by feelings of betrayal, would shift the center ground of politics and the balance of power in every political institution. (The Putin phenomenon is evidence enough that the center ground of politics moves, that disillusionment is a potent force, and that not every democrat is a democrat for life.)

In the second place, these conclusions would make equidistance, not to say an independent course, between Russia and NATO untenable. It is a secondary issue whether this would lead to "integration"—which in the Soviet sense implies burdens and responsibilities as well as control—or simply a deeper and more extensive subordination to Russian interests. In either case, Ukraine's "freedom to choose"—which in 1996 Kuchma defined as the sine qua non of independence—would wither away.

Third, and therefore, these conclusions are likely to produce deterioration and turbulence. Ukraine is not Belarus. At least a quarter of its population is anti-Russian, and a much larger proportion is apprehensive about Russian state power and policy. Among the policy elite, where these proportions are higher, a considerable number understand what democratization and westernization mean in practice. Even if there were no connection between Russian influence, collusive and opaque norms of business and the "domination of authoritarian tendencies" in Ukraine,[60] the malignant characteristics present in the political system and dominant in the economy would surely grow if the west signaled that Ukraine had no prospects in Europe.

How damaging would these developments be to the west? The "west" is a product of the cold war. Throughout that period, the Euro-Atlantic community lived with dividing lines and prospered behind them. In defiance of all the incantations, security in the "new Europe" (i.e., *central* Europe) can be built without Ukraine, and it can be built without Russia. But it cannot be built on the basis of today's security policies and financial assumptions. The conviction that NATO enlargement should be driven by political rather than military considerations rested on the assumption of a relatively benign environment in the East. Given the present economic configuration of Europe, the emergence of an estranged or even hostile bloc of states in the former USSR would not force NATO to return to the defense policies of 1980. But it would force it to return from a world of "risks" to a world of threats.

NATO either would adjust its policies to suit such a world, or it would cease to serve a useful purpose. The pressures upon the EU would be no less severe. Today's concerns regarding the presence of zones of misery and conflict on the periphery of Europe—and corridors of migrants and crime through it—will grow by an order of magnitude if partnership is replaced by "zones of influence" and "information and intelligence struggle"—and if alliances between states, money launderers, arms smugglers, and assassins become a matter of course. The Schengen Agreement will not protect Europe from these developments.

The challenge for both NATO and the EU in Ukraine is to maintain the short-term conditions which make long-term battles worth fighting. This means extracting the maximum value from channels of influence which work (NATO–Ukraine cooperation and defense reform). It also means taking Ukraine's European aspirations seriously and hence *maintaining* the conditionalities, namely, the Goteborg European Council—"democratic development, human rights, the rule of law, and market-oriented economic reforms"—which remind Ukrainians to take them seriously. The Gongadze affair has been a sharp reminder that many who hold power do not.

Unfortunately, it is now an open question how—or even whether—the west will try to influence the shape of the post-Kuchma era. When the USSR collapsed, there were Russians and Ukrainians who declared that it would take a generation to overcome the Soviet legacy. Today, such declarations do not challenge the west, they deter it. This is a real change in the western climate, damaging to the west itself. If Ukrainians wish to avoid more serious damage, they will need to ponder Carlisle's question: "If I am not for myself, who will be for me?"

Notes

1. The 19 states are Albania, Belarus, Bosnia and Herzegovina, Bulgaria, Croatia, the Czech Republic, Estonia, Hungary, Latvia, Lithuania, Macedonia (former Yugoslav Republic of Macedonia), Moldova, Poland, Romania, the Russian Federation, Slovakia, Slovenia, Ukraine, and Yugoslavia. The number expands to 22 if the 3 states of the Transcaucasus—Armenia, Azerbaijan, and Georgia—are counted as part of Europe.

2. President George W. Bush, *Remarks in Address to Faculty and Students of Warsaw University,* June 15, 2001, <www.whitehouse.gov/news/releases/2001/06/20010615-1.html>.

3. Volodymyr Horbulin, secretary of the National Security and Defense Council of Ukraine, 1996–1999, "Ukraine's Place in Today's Europe," *Politics and the Times* (journal of the Foreign Ministry of Ukraine), October–December 1995, p. 15.

4. Fedor Shelov-Kovedyayev, *Strategie und Taktik der Aussenpolitik Russlands im neuen Ausland* [Strategy and tactics of Russian foreign policy in the new abroad], (Köln: Bundesinstitut für Ostwissenschaftliche und Internationale Studien, 1993). Shelov-Kovedyayev, a deputy foreign minister 1991–1992, was the first Russian Foreign Ministry official appointed with responsibility for relations with what is more commonly called the "near abroad."

5. Anatoliy Grytsenko, "Civil–Military Relations in Ukraine: A System Emerging from Chaos," Harmonie Paper 1 (Groningen, Netherlands: Centre for European Security Studies), 1997, p. 1.

6. Anton Bebler, "Corruption among Security Personnel in Central and Eastern Europe," *Army and State in Postcommunist Europe* (special issue), *Journal of Communist Studies and Transition Politics,* vol. 17, no. 1 (2001), p. 142.

7. Partnership for Peace Framework Document, Article 8.

8. Comments attributed to the chairman of NATO's Military Committee, Gerhard von Moltke, at the 1994 Istanbul meeting of the North Atlantic Cooperation Council, published in the official parliamentary newspaper of Ukraine, *Holos Ukrainy,* June 14, 1994.

9. Between the launch of Operation Allied Force (April 1999) and Lord Robertson's visit to Moscow in April 2000, all Russian cooperation with NATO was curtailed, and it has only partially been restored. The view of International Staff members maintaining direct liaison with the Russian delegation is that, both before this curtailment and after the partial restoration of cooperation, Russians at all levels of authority have been extremely reluctant to deviate from a "top-down" approach to NATO–Russia relations and have shown very little interest in participating in activities at the working level. In the view of one mid-level official, "the military and political leadership seem determined that cooperation not affect mind-sets." The headquarters view is that Ukraine's participation at the working level is considerable and that its interest in deepening this participation is genuine. Complaints are frequently expressed about

Soviet-style inhibitions about sharing information and—as in all other spheres governing relations with Ukraine—a gap between commitments and their fulfillment. In the latter respect, NATO's audit of Ukraine's Partnership Work Program in 2000 noted that implementation levels were considerable higher than they were in 1999.

10. James Sherr, *NATO's New Members: A Model for Ukraine? The Example of Hungary*, (Camberley, U.K.: Conflict Studies Research Centre, 2000).

11. A Georgian delegation to NATO headquarters in early 2001 was greatly dissatisfied with the reception they received when they sought to document Russian pressure. They were also taken aback by the confidence expressed by NATO officials that Russia would honor in full its base withdrawal commitments, given at the November 1999 Istanbul summit of the Organization for Security and Cooperation in Europe.

12. *National Security & Defence*, no. 8 (Kiev: Ukrainian Center for Economic and Political Studies), 2000, p. 15.

13. Horbulin, "Ukraine's Place."

14. *National Security and Defence*, no. 7 (Kiev: Ukrainian Center for Economic and Political Studies), 2000, p. 9.

15. Two states, Ireland and the United Kingdom, continue to "opt out" of the Schengen Agreement and subsequent Convention (and two non-EU states, Iceland and Norway, opted in). The 1997 Amsterdam Treaty abolished this opt-out for new members. Hence, Schengen automatically forms part of the *acquis communautaire* of Poland, Hungary, and other states on the path to accession.

16. The principle was once again formulated by the Russian Ministry of Foreign Affairs on August 16, 2001. It stated that "the Russian–Ukrainian border should be a border of peace, accord and interaction; it should unite not separate the people of our countries. . . . The formation of artificial barriers and obstacles would contradict these objectives and complicate contacts between people and cooperation between economic entities, especially in frontier areas"; *Interfax, BBC Summary of World Broadcasts*, August 16, 2001.

17. First deputy foreign minister Yuriy Sergeyev, head of the Ukrainian delegation to the joint border commission, "Borders of Ukraine: An Unfinished Area of a Decade of State Building," *Monitoring*, occasional report 27 (Kiev: Center for Peace, Conversion, and Foreign Policy of Ukraine, 2001), p. 5. See also "The Legal Status of the Russian-Ukrainian Border: Problems and Prospects," *Monitoring*, occasional report 18 (Kiev: Center for Peace, Conversion and Foreign Policy of Ukraine, 2001).

18. The term "involvement" is used advisedly, because it implies an activity that is more pervasive than "interference" but that takes place between equals.

19. At a symposium in Kiev, on July 4–6, 2001 ("The World in the Twenty-First Century: Cooperation, Partnership and Dialogue"), Brigadier Jean-Luc Lagadec, assistant chief of staff, EU Military Staff, affirmed that ESDP is designed to benefit NATO as much as the EU. A similar stance was taken by General Joachim Spiering, former NATO commander-in-chief north, who added that "the United States will remain the most important European power for years to come."

20. Spiering, Kiev symposium.

21. Spiering, Kiev symposium.

22. The relevant passages are: "All nations should understand that there is no conflict between membership in NATO and membership in the European Union. My nation welcomes

the consolidation of European unity, and the stability it brings. We welcome a greater role for the EU in European security, properly integrated with NATO. We welcome the incentive for reform that the hope of EU membership creates. We welcome a Europe that is truly united, truly democratic and truly diverse. . . . And all in Europe and America understand the central lesson of the century past. When Europe and America are divided, history tends to tragedy"; Bush, *Remarks*.

23. Bert Koenders (Netherlands), "NATO Enlargement: Draft Interim Report," NATO Parliamentary Assembly, Political Committee, Sub-Committee on Central and Eastern Europe, April 19, 2001.

24. Chris Patten, "The Future of the European Security and Defence Policy and the Role of the European Commission," paper presented at the Conference on the Development of a Common European Security and Defense Policy, "The Integration of the New Decade" (Berlin, December 16, 1999), pp. 1, 4.

25. Despite the May 28, 1997, Black Sea Fleet accords, Russia continues to propose the creation of a joint naval force (*soedineniye*) in the Black Sea. On May 14, 2001, deputy foreign minister Valeriy Loshchinin, appointed the previous month to supervise relations with the Commonwealth of Independent States, declared that the building of "allied and neighbourly relations with Ukraine is a strategic priority in Russia's foreign policy"; *Interfax, BBC Summary of World Broadcasts*, May 14, 2001.

26. The official aspiration of bringing Ukraine into the Russian–Belarus Union surfaced even in the wake of the May 31, 1997, "Big Treaty" between Russia and Ukraine, which was roundly presented by Kiev as de jure recognition of Ukraine's independent course. On June 10, one of the most arduous proponents of the accords, Ivan Rybkin (then secretary of the National Security Council) restated the view that "Russia, Belarus, and Ukraine" would benefit from being together (*Trud*, June 10, 1997), a view echoed by another supporter of the accords, Ivan Serov (then first deputy prime minister) on January 6, 1998. On June 17, a spokesman for the Russian Ministry of Foreign Affairs, Gennady Tarasov, warned against "attempts to interfere" in relations between Russia and the Commonwealth of Independent States and also linked Ukraine with Belarus as "priority countries" for Russia.

27. Hence, in a very different region, Kiev, a 1995 Democratic Initiatives poll revealed 62 percent of ethnic Ukrainians and 58 percent of ethnic Russians firmly in favor of independence; however, 16 percent of Ukrainians and only 10 percent of Russians pronounced themselves against it.

28. Whereas 32 percent of Ukrainians favor the country's eventual membership (23 percent within five years), 19 percent of Russian respondents regard NATO membership as a priority. Whereas 46.2 percent of Ukrainians regard NATO as an "aggressive military bloc," 56 percent of Russians do so. *National Security and Defence* (Ukrainian Center for Economic and Political Studies), no. 8 (2000), pp. 14–15.

29. Twenty-three percent favor NATO membership in 5–10 years, 9 percent in 10–15 years, 51 percent "never," and 17 percent "hard to say"; 27 percent favor acceding to the Tashkent Treaty in 5–10 years, 4 percent in 10–15 years, 42 percent "never," and 27 percent "hard to say."

30. *National Security and Defence* (Ukrainian Centre for Economic and Political Studies), no. 12 (2000), pp. 5–6. The poll shows eight countries as having "priority" importance, ranging

on a scale from 86.9 percent to 48.8 percent: Russia, the United States, Belarus, Germany, Kazakhstan, Poland, Canada, and Uzbekistan.

31. For a fuller discussion of Ukraine's economic and civic deficits and the imperative of establishing a "civic state," see James Sherr, *Ukraine's New Time of Troubles* (Camberley, U.K.: Conflict Studies Research Centre, 1998), pp. 7–15.

32. Indeed, they are transparent to very few insiders. Anatoliy Grytsenko's appraisal of Viktor Chernomyrdin's appointment as Russian ambassador is pertinent: "He is a man who knows exactly the economic value of everything that exists in Ukrainian–Russian relations. He knows not only the official reports of the state Committee for Statistics and the CIS Interstate Economic Committee, but also the shady schemes out of which both the Ukrainian and the Russian businessmen who now influence politics made their first capital. He knows exactly who owes how much to whom, which means that in this regard it will be both easy and difficult for the Ukrainian side to work with him"; <www.strana.ru>, May 11, 2001.

33. Oleksandr Goncharenko, presentation to conference on "The National Security of Ukraine in the Context of World Community Experience," Kiev, October 9, 2000.

34. Opinion poll presented in *National Security and Defence* (Ukrainian Center of Economic and Political Studies), no. 8 (2000), p. 19.

35. Russia's dispatch of a "humanitarian" convoy to Yugoslavia (halted on the Hungary–Ukraine border) in April 1999, its redeployment of the intelligence ship *Liman* (and initial preparation to redeploy other vessels) from Sevastopol to the Adriatic and its plans to transit Ukraine with Airborne Troop reinforcements after the "brilliant dash to Pristina" in June 1999 provoked anxiety and, in some quarters, alarm. For a more comprehensive discussion, see James Sherr and Steven Main, *Russian and Ukrainian Perceptions of Events in Yugoslavia*, paper F64 (Camberley, U.K.: Conflict Studies Research Centre, 1999), pp. 2, 17–24.

36. In late 2000, Andrey Fedorov, former first deputy foreign minister stated, "today we are speaking more or less openly now about our zones of interests. In one way or another we are confirming that the post-Soviet territory is such a zone. . . . In Yeltsin's time we were trying to wrap this in a nice paper. Now we are saying it more directly: this is our territory, our sphere of interest." Hence the declaration of deputy foreign minister Yevgeny Gusarov at the November 2000 meeting of the OSCE: "We have been warning our Western partners that we oppose the use of the OSCE for interference in the internal affairs of the countries situated to the east of Vienna. This time we are sending a clear signal: we won't allow this to happen." *Financial Times*, January 23, 2001.

37. These apprehension that the United States could use "human rights" as a flag of convenience to support separatist movements is present even in Central Asia. The March 30, 2000, communiqué of the Shanghai Forum (Russia, China, Kazakhstan, Kyrgyzstan, and Tajikistan) pledged the forum to "promoting multipolarity" and to "resolutely oppose any country's intervention in the internal affairs of other countries on the excuse of protecting national and religious interests and human rights."

38. A full discussion of Russian policy towards Ukraine under Putin is well outside the scope of this paper. The reader is invited to consult three of the author's papers on the Conflict Studies Research Centre website <www.csrc.ac.uk>: "A New Regime? A New Russia?" in *The Second Chechen War*, edited by Anne Aldis; "The Dismissal of Borys Tarasyuk," CSRC occasional brief 79; and "Viktor Chernomyrdin's Appointment as Ambassador to Ukraine," CSRC occasional brief 82.

39. Leonid Polyakov, "The Russian Factor in Ukraine's Relations with NATO: Possible Outcomes and Policy Implications for Ukraine and NATO," June 2001, p. 6, draft; quoted by permission.

40. For a Russian perspective which presents the Russian Federation not only as the prime beneficiary of the Gongadze affair, but comes close to implying a degree of Russian connivance in the scandal, see *Izvestiya*.

41. The apparent indifference of Russia's political authorities to the implications of "Kuchmagate" for the future of democracy in Ukraine would appear to substantiate the widespread perception of democratically minded Ukrainians of a linkage between Russian influence and "the dominance of authoritarian tendencies in the system of [Ukrainian] political power"; *Monitoring*, occasional report 3 (Kiev: Center for Peace, Conversion and Foreign Policy of Ukraine, 2001). The December 2000 Minsk and February 2001 Dnepropetrovsk accords, providing for extensive Russian participation in the privatization of Ukraine's energy infrastructure—sixteen documents which were presented *to Ukraine's government* in only excerpted form—substantiate a further concern: that Russian–Ukrainian relations in the energy sphere do not meet the minimal conditions of competitiveness and transparency.

42. On January 1, 2000, Ministry of Defense Armed Forces numbered 303,000 service members plus 90,000 civilian employees, all supposedly funded by a defense budget of some $450 million plus $80 million legally raised by the forces themselves. It is sometimes concluded that because this budget is disproportionately small in comparison with that of the Russian Federation ($7 billion for a military establishment of some 1 million personnel), Ukraine's forces are in even more parlous condition than Russia's. This, however, overlooks the costs of maintenance, testing, modernization, and command-and-control for a strategic nuclear force, along with three oceangoing fleets and other power projection capabilities absent in Ukraine. In both cases, these figures exclude substantial and heavily armed Interior forces and other non–Ministry of Defense formations.

43. Statement to the NATO–Ukraine Joint Working Group on Defense Reform, October 2000.

44. Unlike the Ministry of Internal Affairs and KGB, the Soviet Ministry of Defense and Soviet General Staff had no branches in the Union Republics. With one exception, the organization of the Soviet Armed Forces was functional and operational, not territorial. The one territorial component of defense organization, the USSR's fifteen Military Districts, grouped together entities responsible for conscription, training, and mobilization. But these districts were not territorially coterminous with the Union Republics, and they did not possess the capabilities and command structures required to plan or conduct coordinated military operations. What Ukraine inherited in 1991 were limbs without brain or body: three Military Districts and the forces which happened to be stationed in them.

45. For a scathing and well-documented critique of "military reform" before 2000, see Anatoliy Grytsenko, "Military Reform in Ukraine: The Start, or Another False Start?" *National Security and Defence* (Ukrainian Center of Economic and Political Studies), no. 1 (2000), pp. 2–40.

46. For a fuller discussion, see James Sherr, "A Fresh Start to Ukrainian Defence Reform?" *Survival* (International Institute for Strategic Studies), vol. 43, no. 1 (2001).

47. This has also been true for nearly all countries of the former Warsaw Pact. Even after their accession to NATO, the Czech Republic and (to a lesser extent) Hungary still have not put these difficulties behind them.

48. Unlike the 1997 Program, the current program is truly a *state* program, drawn up in consultation with experts from the Ministry of Finance and in accordance with a *Long-Term Defense-Related Funds Allocation Forecast to 2015*, approved by the Cabinet of Ministers.

49. The NATO–Ukraine Joint Working Group on Defense Reform has identified six areas for collaboration: rationalization of defense structure, professionalization, reform of border troops, reform of internal security forces, reduction of mobilization resources and stocks, and civilian democratic control.

50. In Ukraine, as in Russia, the deactivation of military units is an expensive business, as is the retirement of officers, given the legal stipulation that they be provided with housing.

51. In the former USSR, only the Baltic countries participate more intensively in PARP. Out of 27 Partners, 19 participate to some degree.

52. The number of Ukraine–Russia activities has gradually risen every year, from 28 in 1998 to 52 in 2000. In statistical terms, this puts it on a par with Poland and at about 60 percent of the Ukraine–United Kingdom level.

53. Polyakov, "Russian Factor," p. 15. Many also cannot understand the basis of Russia's proposals for a "joint naval force" in the Black Sea, given the fact that the two sides cannot even agree on their respective borders and exclusive economic zones in the Kerch Strait and Sea of Azov. The differences which exist over economic rights are surely no less than they are between Ukraine and Romania.

54. In a country whose illegal economy is at least as large as the legal economy, the Armed Forces benefit from a number of hidden subsidies, many of them perfectly legal. Much of the accumulated Armed Forces debt—an estimated 10–15 billion kopiyky since 1991—has been effectively written off. Military forces legally—and without charge to the state budget—provide services to regional authorities and farming cooperatives in exchange for provisions, food, and occasionally petrol. In addition to these activities, the Armed Forces needed to raise $165 million in 2001 from nonbudgetary sources.

55. *National Security and Defence*, Ukrainian Center of Economic and Political Studies, no. 1, 2000, pp. 32–33.

56. That there are such advances is shown by the fact that Ukraine now has two academies for noncommissioned officers.

57. *Dedovshchina*, systematic brutality against younger recruits by those more senior, is generally believed to be a less serious problem in Ukraine than in Russia—which is unsurprising, given the fact that Ukraine's armed forces are not employed in combat operations. Nevertheless, the problem is a very serious one. (It is estimated that between 60 and 70 soldiers committed suicide in 1999 (50 percent of all deaths for that year). In Ukraine, as in Russia, there is an active "Organization of Soldiers' Mothers," headed by Valentina Artamonova. There is also an ombudsman in the *Verkhovna Rada*, Nina Karpachova, whom soldiers have the right to address even in wartime.

58. According to a Ukrainian Center of Economic and Political Studies poll in late 2000, the largest percentage of citizens express trust in the Armed Forces (30.2 percent). The level of confidence in the militia (civil police, subordinate to the MVS) is 11.8 percent, just 0.1 per-

cent below the courts and 0.1 percent above the Office of Public Prosecutor. *National Security and Defence*, Ukrainian Center of Economic and Political Studies, no. 11, 2000, p. 10.

59. The Armed Forces have overcome some, but far from all of their former inhibitions about collaboration with nongovernmental organizations. Moreover, a key state research institution, the National Institute of Strategic Studies (which before its re-subordination to the presidential administration in autumn 2000 was a component of the National Security and Defense Council of Ukraine [NSDC]) contains about 60 analysts, some of whom now write with fresh and original perspectives.

60. *Monitoring*, occasional report 3.

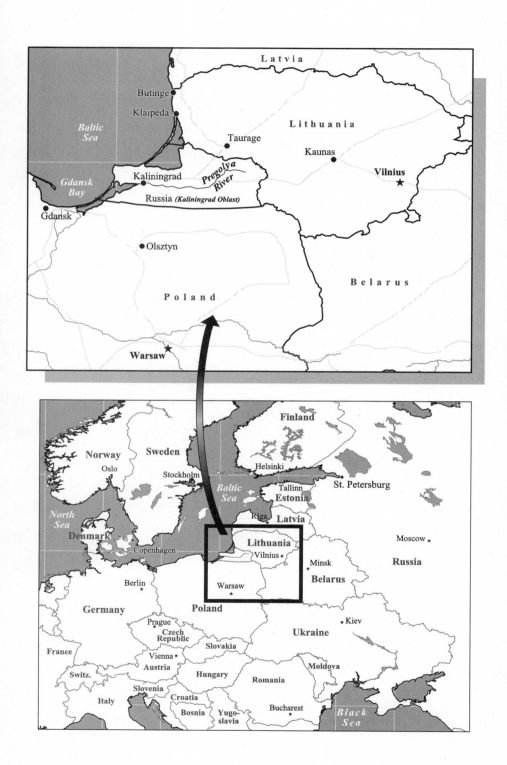

7

Kaliningrad

Alexander Sergounin

The question of the Russian region of Kaliningrad has become the single most difficult issue in relations between Russia and the European Union, with implications which stretch far beyond the borders of this tiny territory and the immediate question of Russian access to it (see map on facing page). Kaliningrad challenges both Russia and the EU to think seriously about their entire way of thinking and future course.

Because of Kaliningrad, the governing elites in Moscow have to decide whether they are really interested in deep cooperation with the EU, or whether they will stick to an old "realist" model of international competition. Kaliningrad also raises in acute form the question of how much real autonomy Moscow is prepared to grant to Russia's regions.

But the challenge to the EU is no less great. As of 2002, EU leaders and bureaucrats had for years preached the rhetoric of uniting Europe, overcoming old barriers and tensions, and encouraging a "postmodern" world in which frontiers would become permeable and old-style states less important. In fact, this has been a central part of the European belief in the supposed superiority of Europe to the harshly "realist" and geopolitically minded George W. Bush administration in the United States.

The author acknowledges the support for the research on which this chapter is based from the John D. and Catherine T. MacArthur Foundation, the Copenhagen Peace Research Institute, the Finnish Institute of International Affairs, and the East–West Institute.

Yet in crucial areas, EU policy has made a mockery of these European claims, and has moved instead to create something much more like "Fortress Europe," walled off from its European neighbors to the east. One such area is the imposition of the requirements of the Schengen Treaty on travel by non-EU citizens on those countries wishing to join the EU. As far as Kaliningrad is concerned, as of 2002 this was raising the imminent threat of, to a considerable extent, cutting its residents off from travel to and from Russia. Moreover, EU approaches to trade with the former Soviet Union remain highly protectionist, and fall well short of the more generous and visionary U.S. strategy towards Mexico reflected in the North American Free Trade Agreement.

The importance of Kaliningrad lies not in its size or economic resources, but in its unique history and location as a small Russian "exclave" on the Baltic Sea. After being taken by Joseph Stalin as a trophy of World War II, Kaliningrad became the Soviet Union's military outpost on the Baltic during the cold war. However, with the breakdown of the Soviet Union, Kaliningrad found itself sandwiched between Poland to the south and Lithuania to the east. The region has had to deal with numerous problems, ranging from the provision of basic supplies and transport (both civilian and military) to visa and customs regimes. Moreover, the enlargements of NATO and the European Union have created a new set of problems that are far from being solved.

These developments have attracted a great deal of attention from the world research community. One group of researchers has examined the socioeconomic development of the region in the postcommunist period.[1] Other scholars have studied its military and strategic aspects.[2] A third group has analyzed the implications of NATO and EU enlargements for Kaliningrad.[3] Finally, some experts have discussed the future of the region and made recommendations and suggested options.[4]

This chapter seeks to broaden understanding of Kaliningrad's place in the EU–Russia relationship by considering these fundamental questions:

- What sort of federal policies towards Kaliningrad should Russia have?
- How can the problems stemming from EU enlargement be solved?
- What is the future of the region? Will it remain an isolated "island" surrounded by EU "waters," or could it become a "gateway" or

"pilot" region that would be an attractive model for other Russian border areas?

There are also a number of more theoretical questions:

- Is national sovereignty over territories still important in the post-modern age?

- Do national borders matter in the world today? Do they divide or unite the peoples of Europe?

- How can the Kaliningrad issue help to shift the focus of European politics from the "hard" to "soft" security agenda?

- Is it possible to make a subregional or regional security system more stable through intensive cross-border and trans-border cooperation?

- Is Kaliningrad a place for intercivilizational contact and cooperation, a border between cosmos (the west) and chaos (the east),[5] or a manifestation of a Huntingtonian "clash of civilizations"?[6]

These questions are of great practical importance for Russia, the EU, Lithuania, Poland, and other regional players.

Historical Background

Kaliningrad is the former Königsberg, the capital of East Prussia. Königsberg was founded by German crusaders in 1255 and was subsequently a subject of dispute among Germans, Lithuanians, Poles, Swedes, and Russians. In 1701, the Kurfürst of Brandenburg crowned himself king of Prussia in Königsberg.

Russia briefly occupied East Prussia during the Seven Years' War of the mid–eighteenth century and at the start of World War I. In April 1945, Soviet troops again conquered Königsberg. At the Potsdam Peace Conference (July–August 1945), Stalin demanded Königsberg and the surrounding area on the grounds that the Soviet Union needed compensation for its war losses, wanted an ice-free port on the Baltic Sea, and claimed the area as originally Slavic. He also promised the southern two-thirds of East Prussia to Poland. The western allies agreed to Stalin's claim. The Memel (Klaipeda) region of East Prussia was handed over to the Soviet republic of Lithuania. Thus the German province of East Prussia was divided into three different parts.

In 1946, the Kaliningrad Region (or "Oblast") was formed as a part of the Russian Soviet Federal Socialist Republic. Ethnic Germans were deported from this territory, and the region was populated mainly by Russians, Belarusians, and Ukrainians.

During the cold war, the region was an important Soviet military outpost in the confrontation with NATO and became one of the most highly militarized areas of Europe. The headquarters of the Baltic Sea Fleet was (and is) located there. The Eleventh Guards' Army was also deployed in the Kaliningrad Oblast. A total of around 100,000 military service members (every tenth Kaliningrader) were stationed there. The region was totally sealed off from Poland and the west, and even Soviet citizens had limited access.

However, with the end of the cold war and the dissolution of the Soviet Union, Kaliningrad found itself in a completely new situation, for three reasons. First, it was separated from "big" Russia by the newly independent states of Lithuania and Belarus. The new geopolitical situation led to numerous problems—such as how to supply the region with basic provisions, energy, raw materials, and equipment; transport; communications; military transit; and travel. A new customs, border-crossing, and consular infrastructure had to be created in the region. As a result, an increasing feeling of isolation from "mainland Russia" has spread in Kaliningrad. For this reason, many experts prefer to call Kaliningrad a Russian "exclave" rather than an enclave.

Second, the military significance of Kaliningrad declined dramatically in the 1990s. In late 1997, the Kaliningrad Special Defense District was abolished (including the Eleventh Guards' Army). The residual land units were subordinated to the commander of the Baltic Sea Fleet, which also radically reduced the number of service members in the region to around 25,000 to 30,000. The configuration of the region's military structure became purely defensive. Third, in contrast to the Soviet era, Kaliningrad now is open to international cooperation and has one of the most liberal economic, customs, border, and visa regimes in the Russian Federation. The region established a free economic zone (FEZ), and then a special economic zone (SEZ), to attract foreign investment. German and South Korean automobile giants—BMW and Kia—have opened small plants in Kaliningrad, and Norwegian ships are repaired there. Unlike other Russian citizens, Kaliningraders in the 1990s enjoyed visa-free borders with Lithuania and Poland, though in 2002 it appeared that these would soon be abolished as a condition of these countries joining the EU.

Assuming that EU enlargement occurs, it will pose serious challenges for the region and Europe as a whole. First, Kaliningrad will become a piece of foreign territory surrounded by EU territory. This in turn could ultimately call into question Russian sovereignty over Kaliningrad, whose economy, trade, transportation, and mentality are likely to become increasingly oriented towards the west. At the same time, if Poland and Lithuania join the EU and the economic gap between them and Kaliningrad widens still further, Kaliningrad could become a source of socioeconomic destabilization for the whole of northern Europe. It is doubtful that quick and simple solutions to these problems can be easily found by Russian and EU leaders. But the problems are on the agenda, and the future of Europe depends on whether a cooperative or confrontational model of decision making will prevail among the regional players.

Kaliningrad in the Context of Russian Domestic Politics

Despite the importance of external factors, Kaliningrad is first of all a Russian problem, and responsibility for the oblast lies with Moscow and the region itself. In spite of a huge amount of paperwork, the central government has lacked any sound and coherent strategy towards the oblast.

In contrast to some other members of the Russian Federation, which during the 1990s regulated their relations with the capital through bilateral treaties and agreements, the status of the Kaliningrad Oblast has been defined mainly by the Russian president and government. Given the unique location and strategic significance of Kaliningrad, Moscow has preferred to keep its direct control over the region. In 1991–1998, the federal center adopted more than fifteen decrees concerning the Kaliningrad Oblast. No other Russian region can boast of such attention from Moscow.

The regional economy has been the most important problem, both for the center and the oblast itself. In November 1991, Russian president Boris Yeltsin issued a decree granting the City of Kaliningrad the status of an FEZ. A number of subsequent presidential decrees specified the rights of the Kaliningrad Oblast in the fields of foreign trade, customs, and hard currency. This legislation provided the oblast with a privileged status in the field of foreign economic relations. The region became a tax-free zone. Joint ventures received substantial exemptions from federal and local taxation. The Russian Ministry of Finance provided the oblast with a credit on privileged terms. And the oblast administration was allowed to use regional export quotas to increase local currency reserves.

The original justification for granting Kaliningrad an FEZ and other was that it was perceived as one way to compensate Kaliningrad for the expected inflationary effect of the cumulative costs of crossing three borders while in transit to the rest of Russia. Moreover, the FEZ was the first substantial concrete measure consistent with the "pilot region" idea that Kaliningrad has unique attributes requiring unique policies. The liberals who dominated Yeltsin's early governments hoped that the area could become a west–east trade bridge, Russia's Hong Kong.[7] Several hundred joint ventures were indeed registered as a result, but the great majority have been small service operations.[8]

Moscow favored the opening up of the oblast at that time and helped Kaliningrad to establish special relations with Poland and Lithuania. A Russian–Polish Council on Cooperation of Regions of North-Western Poland with the Kaliningrad Oblast and the Special Protocol to the Interim Russian–Lithuanian Agreement on Mutual Trips of Citizens entered into force in 1995. The latter was born out of the initiative of the Kaliningrad regional government. In cooperation with the local authorities, Moscow worked on the improvement of the border and transport infrastructure: Agreements were signed by Russia with Warsaw and Vilnius to open international border crossings in the oblast. In 1992–1995, the Russian central government invested more than $100 million in developing the border-crossing infrastructure. An international section was opened at Kaliningrad airport, a European-gauge railway from the Polish border to the city was restored, and the Russian part of the Kaliningrad–Elblag motorway was reconstructed.[9]

Differences between the Region and Moscow

However, differences of opinion grew up between Moscow and the Kaliningrad local authorities about the region's status and its prospects for economic cooperation with foreign countries. The regional government proposed transforming the free economic zone into a special economic zone with even more autonomy and privileges. But central officials, including then–deputy prime minister Sergei Shakhrai, complained that foreign investors there received significant tax and other concessions while investing insignificant amounts of money. As of September 1, 1994, while a total of 885 enterprises with foreign investments were registered in the Kaliningrad Region, foreign investors accounted for less than $2 million in investments. According to Shakhrai, the region was already being turned into a channel for the export of raw materials, including strategic resources, and for the creeping expansion of foreign influence in the economic and ethnic spheres, with the prospect of the creation of a "fourth independent Baltic state." As a compromise, Shakhrai proposed—instead of making the whole region an FEZ—creating limited zones of free-trade activity near ports and main roads in the region, stressing that "we have again to declare clearly the priority of Russia's military–strategic interests in the Kaliningrad Oblast."[10]

In October 1994, then–governor Yuri Matochkin succeeded in persuading the Russian Security Council to adopt a special document entitled "A Concept of the Federal Policy with Regard to the Kaliningrad Region of the Russian Federation" that was based on the draft originally proposed by the oblast authorities. The document emphasized the need for international cooperation (including the EU programs) to achieve the successful development of the region. The governor of the oblast was granted a right to deal directly with the Polish and Lithuanian governments on issues of subregional cooperation, including participation in the Euroregions. A special "curator" of Kaliningrad was appointed in the Russian Ministry of Foreign Affairs, and a representative office of the ministry was established in the region. Polish and Lithuanian consulates and honorary consulates from Denmark, Iceland, and Sweden were opened in Kaliningrad. The Kaliningrad Oblast opened trade missions in Vilnius and Gdansk, and special regional legislation to define their status and budget was adopted. The Kaliningrad City administration also opened representations, first in Bremerhaven and later in Brussels, though these have since closed.

However, under the pressure of the "centralists," the federal authorities tried to tighten their control over the Kaliningrad Region. In May 1995, Yeltsin suddenly abolished the customs exemptions, and this led to the annulment of a large number of contracts.

The regional leadership was able, however, to persuade Yeltsin to continue with the FEZ. On May 18, 1995, he issued a decree on the social and economic development of the Kaliningrad region which provided the FEZ with broad powers in foreign economic policy, granting it tax privileges and state support in protecting the region's producers, creating a ferry line between Kaliningrad and Vyborg, and establishing a unified maritime administration for the Port of Kaliningrad.[11]

In 1996, however, the power struggle between the center and the region continued. On January 22, 1996, Yeltsin signed the federal Law on the Special Economic Zone in the Kaliningrad Region,[12] with an official purpose to provide more favorable conditions for promoting the socioeconomic development of the region by expanding trade, through economic, scientific, and technological cooperation with foreign countries, and by attracting foreign investment, know-how, and expertise. According to the SEZ law, the following categories of goods are free of customs duties:

1. Goods produced in the SEZ and exported to other countries. The goods will be considered produced locally if the added value is not less than 30 percent, and for some electronics and modern technologies 15 percent.

2. Goods imported from other countries to the SEZ and then re-exported to other foreign countries (with processing or without it). There are no quantity limitations on these goods.

3. Goods produced in the SEZ and exported to "big" Russia, as well as to the territory of the Customs Union (four Commonwealth of Independent States, or CIS, countries, including Russia).

The new SEZ law had contradictory implications. On the one hand, the oblast got back some customs and tax privileges; on the other hand, the regional authorities lost part of their foreign policy powers. The center took control over the defense industry, mineral resources, energy production, transport, and mass media. Foreigners are not allowed to purchase land, but it can be leased for periods yet to be determined.[13]

Moscow Reformulates Its Strategy

In late 1997, Moscow tried to reformulate its strategy towards the Kaliningrad oblast. According to governmental regulation 1259 (September 29, 1997), the federal program of developing the Kaliningrad SEZ for 1998–2005 included four major strategic objectives:

- improving of the infrastructure (transport, energy, agro-industrial, and communications sectors);

- reorienting Russian goods traffic from the Baltic countries' ports to Kaliningrad;

- structurally reforming the regional economy, including federal support for export-oriented sectors; and

- improving the living standards of the local population.[14]

In 1998, the Russian federal government issued regulation 281 (March 5, 1998) and regulation 830 (July 24, 1998), which introduced import quotas with an official aim of supporting local producers. This, however, collided with the world's experience of free economic zones and, given the Russian financial meltdown of 1998, did not really stimulate local manufacturers.

The region failed to attract any significant foreign investment. In 1994–1998, foreign investment amounted to $66 million[15] while, for example, the Novgorod Oblast, a region with 737,000-strong population (200,000 less than that of the Kaliningrad Oblast), managed to attract $600 million in 1994–1999.[16] In 1998, 1,365 Kaliningrad joint ventures employed only 2 percent of the local workforce, while in the Novgorod Region 200 joint venture enterprises provided 20,000 with jobs (5.1 percent) and accounted for 62 percent of the region's industrial output, 32 percent of the local pension fund, and half the taxes paid to the region.[17] According to some assessments, the SEZ led to a tax loss of $2.5 billion for the period 1996–1998.[18]

In 2000, disappointment with the inefficiency of the Kaliningrad SEZ led to further attempts to abolish it. As a result of these concerns, in April 2000 the Kaliningrad Oblast Duma called on the State Duma to secure the status quo in the region.[19]

In January 2001, the State Customs Committee of the Russian Federation introduced the so-called Part II of the new Russian Tax Code that in fact deprived the Kaliningrad Region of SEZ privileges.[20] In turn, this resulted in a social and economic crisis in the oblast: Prices rose by 20–30 percent, and a series of protests took place.[21] Under pressure from the regional authorities, the office of the procurator general (with the obvious support of Russian president Vladimir Putin) abolished the customs decision. But at the time of writing the future of the SEZ still remains unclear.[22]

Unfortunately, Russia lacks a proper legal basis for managing center–periphery relations in the foreign policy domain. The Russian Constitution of 1993 is rather vague in defining the foreign policy prerogatives of the center and regions. The constitutional area of joint federal–regional authority includes coordination of international and foreign economic relations of members of the Federation, as well as implementation of international treaties (article 72).[23] However, it remains unclear exactly what the term "coordination" means. Should the regions inform Moscow about their plans in advance or post factum? Do they have the right to conclude international treaties or not? Could they establish diplomatic, consular, and trade missions abroad or not?

Improving the Legal Basis for International Activities

To improve their legal basis, Moscow has passed a number of federal laws regulating the international activities of the regions. The Law on International Treaties of the Russian Federation (July 15, 1995) stipulates that members of the Federation should participate in negotiating and drafting international treaties that concern regions' interests and competencies. The members of the Federation may also make recommendations to the center to conclude, suspend, or abrogate treaties. This law, however, does not clarify the status of international agreements signed by the regions.

The Law on State Regulation of Foreign Trade (October 13, 1995) included in the sphere of joint authority (1) coordination of regions' foreign trade, (2) adoption and execution of regional and interregional foreign trade programs, (3) receiving foreign loans under the regions' guarantees, (4) regulation of FEZs and cross-border trade, and (5) providing regions with information.[24] The law was received positively by members of the Federation because it provided the regions with both a proper legal basis and broader powers.

Presidential decree 370 (March 12, 1996) stipulated that the treaties between Moscow and the regions and accompanying agreements are not to violate the Russian Constitution and must respect its supremacy. They also cannot change the status of a member of the Federation and add to or change what is enumerated in articles 71 and 72 of the Constitution, which assign federal and joint authority respectively. The same day, President Yeltsin signed decree 375, On the Coordinating Role of the Ministry of Foreign Affairs in Conducting a Single Foreign Policy Course. The decree instructed the regions to inform the Russian Foreign Ministry about their foreign policy activities, including foreign trips and statements by regional leaders.

The federal Law on Coordinating International and Foreign Economic Relations of the Members of the Russian Federation (December 2, 1998) elaborated on article 72 of the constitution. The law limits international activities of the Russian regions to trade, scientific, ecological, humanitarian, and cultural cooperation with foreign partners. They are allowed to cooperate only with regional and local governments of foreign states. They can deal with central authorities of foreign countries only via Moscow. The law prevents regions from providing their missions abroad with diplomatic status. According to this legislation, regions' agreements with foreign partners do not enjoy the status of international treaties.[25]

In accordance with this legislation, the Kaliningrad Region concluded agreements on cross-border cooperation with Polish and Lithuanian districts. The development of the border infrastructure (including the Mamonovo–Gronovo and Gusev–Goldup crossings, the Kaliningrad–Elblag highway, etc.) were important priorities for such a cooperation.[26]

To sum up, by 2002, there was a fragile balance between the federal center and regions as regards foreign policy powers. Two contradictory tendencies can be identified. On the one hand, Moscow tried to specify constitutional principles regarding foreign policy prerogatives of the center and the subjects of the Federation and to tighten its control over the regions' external relations. On the other hand, Moscow was unable to restore the Soviet-like centralized model of federalism. The outcome of this tug-of-war between Moscow and the regions remains to be seen.

Putin's Administrative Reforms

When he assumed the Russian presidency after the spring 2000 election, Vladimir Putin started a process of administrative reform, particularly by introducing seven federal districts led by presidential envoys and reforming the upper house of the Russian parliament, the Council of the Federation. Both initiatives aimed to undermine gubernatorial powers, because governors now were subordinated to presidential envoys and lost their seats in the parliament upon completion of their gubernatorial term. It still remains unclear what powers the presidential envoys received in the foreign policy area, but some of their prerogatives will definitely affect the regions' foreign relations. For example, President Putin entrusted the envoys with monitoring local legislation and with coordinating the regional activities of federal bodies such as the representative offices of the Foreign Ministry and Ministry of Commerce and Economic Development, and the military, customs, border guards, procurators, police, and security services. The Kaliningrad

Region became a part of the so-called North-Western Federal District (NWFD), with its "capital" in Saint Petersburg.

There have been different opinions among Russian experts and politicians regarding the nature and implications of Putin's administrative reform. Some analysts believe that this reform will lead to recentralization of the domestic and foreign policies of the Russian Federation. Thus, border regions (including Kaliningrad) will have less opportunities for cross- and trans-border cooperation with foreign partners. Any cooperative schemes (like the EU's programs—Northern Dimension; Technical Assistance to the Southern Republics of the CIS and Georgia, or TACIS; Interreg; etc.) will become unrealistic. There has also been much criticism regarding the subordination of Kaliningrad to Saint Petersburg. The latter was and is Kaliningrad's natural rival on the Baltic. Many Kaliningraders would prefer to keep the status quo or become the eighth federal district.[27]

However, other specialists argue that Putin's reform does not aim at undermining the regions' authority and powers. Rather, it simply aims to harmonize federal and local legislation—to make the Federation more coherent and manageable and to fight corruption, bureaucracy, and organized crime. These changes do not prevent Kaliningrad from effectively cooperating with foreign countries and taking part in various collaborative projects. On the contrary, Moscow again and again emphasized the need for cooperation with the EU on Kaliningrad and promised its help to the regional authorities. According to this school of thought, the purpose of the inclusion of Kaliningrad in the NWFD is to develop the oblast's relations with adjacent Russian regions and stop its growing isolation from "big" Russia.[28]

Some specialists are accordingly inclined to see presidential representatives as not only Moscow's eyes and ears but also as lobbyists for regional interests in the central government. According to some accounts, in January 2001 the presidential envoy to the NWFD, Victor Cherkesov, supported the Kaliningrad authorities in their campaign against the State Customs Committee's decision to abolish Kaliningrad's tax privileges. Cherkesov also protected the oblast's interests in the federal government during the work on the new governmental strategy for the region.[29]

The victory of Admiral Vladimir Yegorov in the gubernatorial election (November 2000) led to an improvement of the region's relations with both Moscow and foreign countries. Yegorov was seen as a positive alternative to the corrupt and anti-reformist regime of Leonid Gorbenko.[30] Many experts believed that Yegorov would be able to fight corruption and crime, restore order and justice in the region, and start real reforms. He was supported not only by Moscow but also by some members of the team of ex-governor Matochkin. The mayor of Kaliningrad, Yuri Savenko, was also happy about the election's result.[31]

Yegorov tried to demonstrate his liberal views on economic policy and the role of international cooperation. His team was positive about developing various subregional schemes of cooperation. He called the Kaliningrad Oblast "a laboratory for the working out of new forms of cooperation between Russia and the European Union."[32] At the same time, he was regarded as a pragmatist and defender of Russian national interests, including resistance to further NATO enlargement and prevention of the negative implications of EU enlargement. His administration was active in formulating Kaliningrad's and Russia's position on the implications of EU enlargement for the oblast.

Towards Cooperation with the EU?

In early March 2001, a Russian governmental delegation led by the famous liberal-minded reformer German Gref (minister of economic development and commerce) visited Kaliningrad[33] to examine the implications of EU enlargement for the region. At the subsequent March 22, 2001, meeting of the Russian Cabinet, a new Concept of Federal Social-Economic Policy towards the Kaliningrad Oblast was discussed. The Concept was worked out by the Kaliningrad team of experts under the aegis of Gref.[34] Following the hopes of the liberal reformers of the early 1990s, the Concept emphasizes that the oblast should become the main Russian region of cooperation with the EU in the twenty-first century, a kind of a bridge between Russia and a united Europe. The document lists measures to increase the region's economic potential, to make it more attractive for foreign investment, and to improve its transport infrastructure.

Particularly, the document recommends that the procedures for expediting projects and issuing licenses for newly established enterprises should be simplified; a number of inspections made by government bodies should be reduced; the access of potential investors to privatization auctions should be improved; and a regional commission on the elimination of administrative barriers to entrepreneurship should be created.[35] However, in contrast to other Russian regions that are successful in attracting investment (Moscow,

Saint Petersburg, Novgorod, Kazan, and Samara), the document does not offer any additional guarantees or specific tax privileges to investors, and this casts doubt on the practical value of its recommendations.

The Concept suggests some measures to develop the SEZ, including providing the zone with long-term guarantees; inventorying local and federal SEZ regulations, with the aim to streamline them and eliminate conflicts between them; and simplifying customs formalities. The document also calls for concluding a special agreement between Russia and the EU. According to the Concept, the strategic aim of the Russian government is to transform the zone from a commercial to industrial one and to make it more competitive on both Russian and international markets.

The Concept identifies the transport system as an important priority for developing both the oblast and subregional infrastructure. The document sets up before the Russian diplomacy the task of negotiating lower transit tariffs with neighboring countries (including Lithuania and Belarus) to make local trade more profitable. Moscow also plans to negotiate transit tariffs with the EU when Lithuania joins the Union. The paper calls for the modernization of the Kaliningrad seaport and airport and for the development of the European transport corridors that cross the territory of the Baltic states and the Kaliningrad Region (first of all Via Hanseatica). To ensure Kaliningrad's energy security, the document recommends building a new electric power plant by 2003 and a second gas pipeline from mainland Russia to the oblast. The document acknowledges the severe ecological problems of the oblast and suggests an impressive environmental protection program, including building new sewage systems and water purification stations, reducing water and air pollution, introducing "clean" technologies, creating a single environmental monitoring system, and joining in ecological projects with the EU. The Concept outlines some prospects for developing the most promising sectors of the local economy, such as fisheries, the amber industry, tourism, and the agro-industrial complex.

There is a special section on visa issues. The Concept calls for concluding a special agreement between Russia and the EU on Kaliningrad in the Partnership and Cooperation Agreement (PCA)[36] framework, including:

- retaining a visa-free regime for Kaliningraders seeking to enter Poland and Lithuania (as an exception from the EU's Schengen rules);
- retaining a visa-free regime for Russian transit travelers; and

- simplifying the visa regime for Polish and Lithuanian citizens (and for all EU member states when Poland and Lithuania join the Union) seeking to visit the oblast.[37]

As of 2002, however, the EU was still rejecting any moves in this direction.

On December 7, 2001, the Russian government adopted a Federal Task Program on Development of the Kaliningrad Region for the Period Up to 2010. The program is based on Gref's concept and was drafted by a team of experts from the Kaliningrad regional administration and the Institute on the Transitional Economy led by Russian ex-premier Yegor Gaidar.

According to the document, the program's main objective is to "create conditions for sustainable socioeconomic development of the Kaliningrad Region, which should be comparable to the development level of neighboring countries, as well as for an attractive investment climate in the region to facilitate the Russia–European Community rapprochement."[38]

It is interesting that, among the geostrategic elements of the program, the following priorities are mentioned:

- making Kaliningrad a key transport junction in northwestern Russia (fourteen projects),

- providing sustainable energy supply to the oblast (nineteen projects), and

- protecting the environment (nine projects).

It seems from this that "soft" rather than "hard" security thinking now dominates the Russian government's approach to the case of Kaliningrad.

The program's planned implementation has two phases. The period 2002–2005 should see basic reforms, mainly directed at further developing of the SEZ. The period 2006–2010 should see continuation of previous projects with the aim of securing positive achievements.

The estimated cost of the program is 93 billion rubles ($3.1 billion). The sources of funding are the federal budget (8.41 percent); the Kaliningrad regional budget (3.08 percent); Kaliningrad enterprises (22.20 percent); commercial bank loans (7.24 percent); foreign loans (14.15 percent); and other sources, such as Gazprom, municipalities, and the like (44.92 percent). The document states that upon the completion of the program, the gross regional product will increase by 240 percent and 15,000 new jobs will be created.

Although the program is a positive contribution to solving numerous problems in Kaliningrad, several critical comments can be made. One comment is that the program is of a "technical/technocratic" rather than conceptual nature. The document enlists projects but does not explain why they are needed and what sort of Kaliningrad Russia wants—both domestically and internationally.

Another comment is that the paper calls for an export-oriented economy in the region, but some specialists doubt that other European countries (both EU member states and candidate countries) are interested in this. On the contrary, they do not like any new competitor and will hardly be helpful in developing Kaliningrad's export potential. These Russian voices instead suggest using the opportunities that the SEZ offers for attracting domestic and foreign investments in order to develop industries which are mostly oriented towards Russian domestic markets.[39] As far as financial sources are concerned, it is unclear whether commercial banks, foreign donors, Gazprom, and others have already confirmed their financial support or it is only planned.

Finally, it is also unclear whether the Russian federal and Kaliningrad regional governments will be able to keep their commitments and finance the program in full. It is well known from experience that other federal programs have often failed because of a lack of funding.

For these reasons, the new federal program on Kaliningrad can only be seen as a first and rather modest step forward. A national strategy on Kaliningrad remains to be developed.

The Russian Security Debate on Kaliningrad

Russian political "Realists" and geopoliticians view Kaliningrad (and the Baltic Sea area) as a manifestation of an eternal geopolitical rivalry between Russia and the west. In contrast to the past, the west prefers economic rather than military instruments for putting pressure on Russia. According to these paradigms, the aim of EU policies is to turn Russia into the west's "younger partner" and source of cheap natural resources and labor.[40] They believe that the Kaliningrad SEZ is detrimental to Russia's economic security and serves only as a camouflage for smugglers and corrupted officials. According to this school, the west is not interested in reviving the local economy and plans to make Kaliningrad a mere transit point in communications between the Baltic states and the "mainland" part of the EU. This means that foreign investment will only help in developing a transport infrastructure rather than in modernizing local industry and agriculture.

Some so-called Realists believe that the EU is only a vehicle for German geopolitical ambitions: In their view, Berlin dreams about returning the former East Prussia into the "German empire." As the first step of this geopolitical plan, a sort of a German economic protectorate over the Kaliningrad Oblast could be established.[41] These fears were widespread in the region in early 2001, when some rumors that Germany could forgive a part of Russian debts in exchange for securities of Russian companies (including Kaliningrad-based firms) arose. There was a series of rallies in Kaliningrad at which local residents appealed to the president to confirm or to deny these rumors.[42]

Other radical Russian fears are that the final goal of the west is to dismantle Russia and separate Kaliningrad from the country (the "fourth Baltic republic" concept).[43] Realists think that Kaliningrad should retain its strategic importance and criticize the government for prematurely dismantling the region's formidable military infrastructure. They recommend tightening the government's control over the oblast to prevent the region's potential drift towards the west. They believe that, in case of "western encroachments" on Kaliningrad, Moscow should make the region an "unsinkable carrier," including deploying nuclear weapons.[44] They also favor military cooperation with Belarus to counterbalance NATO's eastward extension and even make the Baltic states an "exclave" in a strategic sense.[45] They suggest providing Russia with the freedom of civilian and military transport via Lithuania, similar to what Germany had in East Prussia after World War I. If Vilnius disagrees, they suggest questioning the territorial integrity of Lithuania, which gained some Polish, Belarusian, and German territories as a result of the Molotov–Ribbenthrop Pact and World War II.[46]

Since the Realists and geopoliticians are influential schools in the Russian security establishment, their views have to be taken into account by the current Russian leadership (at least at the level of public rhetoric). During his July 2000 visit to Kaliningrad, President Putin stated that Russia must increase the size of its navy if it is to remain a major world power. "The navy is an important element in national defense, and we give particular attention to the development of the military fleet," said Putin, speaking from the decks of an anti-torpedo boat in the Baltic seaport of Baltiysk, where he was overseeing the navy's annual parade. "Russia cannot carry on without a navy if it wants to play a role in the new world order," he asserted.[47]

However, despite the *Kursk* submarine tragedy, which emphasized the need for the state's care of the navy, the above stance should be taken with a grain of salt, because the Russian leadership understands that the country simply has no resources for any ambitious programs, in Kaliningrad or elsewhere.

The liberal institutionalist school, in contrast, points out that the military significance of Kaliningrad decreased in the post–cold war period and the region is unable to play the role of the Russian military outpost. This change was proved at the doctrinal level. According to the previous Russian military doctrine (1993), the use of nuclear weapons had been limited to circumstances that constituted a "threat to the very existence of the Russian Federation as an independent sovereign state." According to the new doctrine (2000), the use of nuclear weapons is justified "if all other means of resolving the crisis situation have been exhausted or proved ineffective." Such a situation had been simulated in a maneuver carried out in the summer of 1999, which assumed a NATO attack on Kaliningrad. According to the scenario upon which the maneuver was based, Russian conventional strike forces were only able to hold out for three days.[48]

The liberals believe that due to its unique geoeconomic location, Kaliningrad has a chance to be a "pioneer" Russian region which is included in regional and subregional cooperation. They think that a priority should be given to the issues that unite rather than divide regional players—trade, cross-border cooperation, transport, the environment, health care, people-to-people contacts, and so on. They view the EU Northern Dimension project as a helpful framework for such cooperation.[49] They are sure that if mutual trust develops, technical problems such as visa regimes and border controls could be easily solved.

According to Igor Leshukov, research director at Saint Petersburg's Center for Integration Research, the EU poses challenges to both Russia's economic and security interests. He says Kaliningrad will pose a special problem. If the EU expands to the Baltic, the Kaliningrad Region will be wholly within the Union. He adds that Moscow, the Baltic states, Poland, and the EU should start working out a special status for Kaliningrad, because that will prove very difficult. "Integration will not be possible if Russia keeps full sovereignty over Kaliningrad. A concrete dialogue about the Kaliningrad issue between Russia and its EU partners is necessary. There's a mutual interest in this because the expansion of the European Union to Poland and the Baltic region without a resolution of the problem of Kaliningrad's status is not possible. Kaliningrad would then remain an abscess that hampers normal development."[50]

A third school is the "globalists." They go further than the liberals in terms of the possible participation of Kaliningrad in international cooperation. They believe that globalization and regionalization are worldwide processes and that Russia cannot avoid them. According to this school, Kaliningrad is a place where these two tendencies are intertwined.[51] On the one hand, Kaliningrad is a subject of a dialogue between the two global players—the EU and Russia. On the other hand, there is a clear tendency to create a new international region—the Baltic Sea area—where Kaliningrad could find a mission of its own.

The globalists think that Moscow should not push sovereignty-related issued onto the regional agenda and should provide the oblast with additional powers for external relations. They call for the EU to implement a "two-track" approach to cooperation with Russian regions. In their view, along with some other pioneer regions, Kaliningrad can be put on the fast track for further cooperation with the EU. Particularly, they hope that such Russian regions could join the European Free Trade Area or even become associate partners of the European Union (before the mainland part of Russia receives the same status). They insist on the feasibility of this model by referring to northern European countries such as Finland and Denmark where some territories have special status with regard to relations with the EU (the Åland Islands, and Greenland and the Faeroe Islands, respectively). Similar to liberals, the globalists welcome any cooperative initiatives, including the EU's Northern Dimension.

Some radical globalist subschools believe that we are living in a world where state borders are increasingly obsolete. International borders are becoming so porous that they no longer fulfill their historical role as barriers to the movements of goods, people, and ideas.[52] This can be seen as very close to some western European approaches that look for social integration, transfer of sovereignty, and cross-border cooperation, whereas new states (or newly reborn states like Russia) naturally focus on borders, security, exclusion, sovereignty, and national economies.

However, as was noted at the beginning of this chapter, the EU itself falls well short of a truly globalist approach when it comes to Kaliningrad and the whole issue of travel and immigration to the EU. A debate on this subject has begun within the EU, though it is hindered by the strongly anti-immigrant sentiments of the conservative parties and large parts of the populations of several key EU states. Thus a European University Institute study of 1999 says that the EU's external border cannot be treated simply as a physical line on the ground to be defended solely by the apparatus of repression. The attempt to make it impermeable is doomed to failure and can increase instability by disrupting economic and cultural ties between neighbors. The conclusion is that border management—a broader, more encompassing concept than narrowly defined control at the physical border—implies deepening cooperation with the candidate countries and the new eastern neighbors in a wide range of areas: policing and judicial affairs, the economy, trade, cross-border cooperation, education, training, and culture.[53]

On the Russian side, despite the dominance of the Realist geopolitical school, there are some signs that alternative paradigms also have some say in policy making.[54] For example, Moscow indicated its interest in the Northern Dimension initiative and presented its suggestions to be included to the Action Plan. Moreover, Russia's medium-term strategy for the development of its relations with the EU (2000–2010) underlines the possibilities regarding Kaliningrad as a pilot region for the EU–Russia relationship and as a test case for this relationship in connection with EU enlargement.[55] It mentions the option of a special arrangement for Kaliningrad in view of enlargement, and it is hinted that cooperation could in the future cover—if Kaliningrad turns out to be a successful test case—northwestern Russia at large.

In the past, Kaliningraders sometimes complained that Moscow did not fully understand their situation. It has been reported that this situation has changed. Moscow has become more involved, for the following reasons. The forthcoming abrogation of bilateral agreements has caught Moscow's attention. Regional administration initiatives, according to an official of the administration, have also been a factor, as have the Northern Dimension and the Copenhagen conference (May 2000), which have recognized Kaliningrad's unique situation.[56]

Europe and Kaliningrad: Past Collaborative Experience

In institutional terms, there are several venues for cooperation between the European multilateral organizations and Kaliningrad: the EU, Council of Europe, Council of the Baltic Sea States (CBSS), Nordic Council, Nordic Council of Ministers, European and Nordic financial institutions, and so on. But the EU is by far the most important institution among them.

TACIS is one of the most helpful instruments for intensifying cross-border contacts. According to some reports, it was rather difficult for the Kaliningrad government to get funding from this program at the initial stage. The support of E. Mueller-Hermann (advisor to the then–Kaliningrad governor Yuri Matochkin) and Ottokar Hahn and Sigrid Selz (EU officials in Brussels) was crucial in this sense.[57]

There is an annual TACIS cross-border cooperation program which began in 1996 with a budget of 30 million ECUs for projects along the borders of Russia and its neighbors, including Finland. In the period 1992–1996, TACIS contributed more than 35 million ECUs to different projects in northwestern Russia. In the 1990s, TACIS implemented eighteen projects in Kaliningrad, ranging from municipal infrastructure to educational efforts.[58] According to the EU data, TACIS has spent €40 million for various projects in the oblast.[59]

In 1998, the EU Commission's document "A Northern Dimension for the Policies of the Union" recommended "further programs of technical assistance and investment within TACIS and PHARE [Poland and Hungary, Aid for the Reconstruction of Economies] ... for projects spanning the Russia–Baltic and Russia–Poland borders." Also, the suggestion was made that programs of technical assistance devoted to promoting customs cooperation, future administration, training, and cooperation in the fight against organized crime should be considered through cross-border cooperation programs for border areas; that is, for the Kaliningrad region of the Russian Federation.

Several areas of concern have received TACIS's support in Kaliningrad.[60] These include *regional economic development*, with support in excess of €10 million given to the development of the FEZ and SEZ; *enterprise restructuring*, and the energy sector; and *cross-border cooperation and trade and transit facilitation*. A number of programs are being implemented which aim at facilitating trade and the movement of goods and persons through the development of infrastructure, modernization of border procedures, improvement of the port, and training enforcement agencies' staffs to detect unlawful activities and increase their capacity to collect tax revenue.

At present, there are 23 crossing points between Kaliningrad, Poland, and Lithuania. In order to ensure the efficient flow of goods across the EU's future external border, investment is needed in physical infrastructure and in processing, including in upgrading information systems. Under the TACIS Cross Border Cooperation Programs, two border crossings in

Kaliningrad received priority funding: Chernyshevskoe–Kybartai–Nesterov (road and rail) and Bagrationovsk–Bezledy (road), on the borders, respectively, with Lithuania and Poland. These crossings, identified after a detailed feasibility study, are the major ones located on the Pan European Transport Network. Works on the Bagrationovsk–Bezledy project (€3 million) will start once expropriation issues are resolved by Russia.

The fears of EU citizens concerning Kaliningrad are focused above all on the supposed threat of the spread of crime and disease (especially AIDS) from the oblast, above all through illegal immigration and "people smuggling." The Task Force on Organized Crime in the Baltic Sea Region is making a valuable contribution to tackling these problems. On the local level, cooperation is needed to deal with problems such as car theft. Cooperation could also be directed at improving the independence of the local judiciary, in particular via training and twinning programs. TACIS has provided €1 million in funding to assist in fighting organized crime. Concerning health, TACIS has a €2 million northwestern health replication project for the Kaliningrad, Murmansk, and Archangel regions. The project aims to reduce health and social disparities across the border by supporting the reform of the local health system.[61]

In the field of environmental protection, several activities are currently being undertaken. These include a water environmental monitoring and management project (€2 million) dealing with water quality on the borders with Lithuania and Poland, and a waste management project in Kaliningrad's coastal zone (€3 million) designed to alleviate the impact of waste generation on both public health and the environment.[62]

Kaliningrad is specifically identified as a priority in the 2002–2003 TACIS Indicative Program for Russia and in the Cross Border Cooperation Program. A specific focus under the Russia TACIS National Program (2002–2003) will be on improving the capacity of municipal authorities to deliver essential public services, such as water, heating, and housing, and also waste and wastewater treatment[63]

The Euroregion concept is another opportunity for subregional cooperation. As mentioned, Kaliningrad belongs to the Baltic Euroregion, which came into being in 1998. It was established as an international lobbying group of local governments from Poland, Sweden, Denmark, Lithuania, Latvia, and Russia. The president of the Baltic Euroregions has said that the most important task for cooperation between communes from various countries is subregional economic planning and construction of transport routes.[64] Since 1999, a new Euroregion named Saule is under consideration, involving the Kaliningrad towns of Slavsk, Sovetsk, and Neman, along with participants from Lithuania, Latvia, and Sweden. Kaliningrad also can participate in the Neman Euroregion, which is designed to link Kaliningrad, Lithuania, and Belarus. However, Moscow believes that the current charter of the Neman Euroregion does not reflect Russian national interests and has blocked the signing of the documents.[65] Nor is it by any means clear just how committed the EU really is to this idea, or how it can be compatible with the visa requirements now being demanded by the EU.

Kaliningrad and the Northern Dimension

The Northern Dimension was a Finnish initiative, launched originally at the international conference on the future of the Barents–Euro-Arctic region in Rovaniemi (September 1997). A Foreign Ministers Conference on the Northern Dimension subsequently was convened in Helsinki on November 11 and 12, 1999. It was organized by the Finnish presidency in partnership with the European Commission. The conference created a common political platform between the EU member states and seven invited partner countries—Estonia, Iceland, Latvia, Lithuania, Poland, and the Russian Federation—with the aim of discussing the concept and developing concrete ideas to advance it.[66]

At the EU–Russia summit in Helsinki in October 1999, Putin (at that time prime minister) presented a "Medium Term Strategy for Development of Relations between the Russian Federation and the EU." The Russian government believes that the Kaliningrad Oblast could become "a pilot region of the Russian Federation in terms of Russia–EU cooperation in the twenty-first century."[67]

However, in August 1999, Moscow also delivered to Brussels a list of fifteen Russian concerns regarding EU enlargement. According to the document, the freedom of travel and transit between Kaliningrad and mainland Russia is among the most important priorities of Russian policies.[68] In the spring of 2002, with EU membership for Poland and Lithuania fast approaching (at least according to the official EU schedule), this issue flared up into the biggest point of contention between the EU and Russia. Moscow also stressed that Kaliningrad should receive additional EU aid in order to avoid the emergence of a "socioeconomic gap" between the enclave and its neighbors.[69]

The Russian official documents note ongoing cooperation in the Council of Baltic Sea States and Barents–Euro-Arctic Council and a history of neutrality and collective security traditions in the area. In the Russian view, these form a basis for further cooperation within the Organization for Security and Cooperation in Europe. Russia notes the potential for cooperation in the economy, social, and environmental sectors. "Russia sees in the Northern Dimension not as a set of isolated resource export-oriented projects but, first and foremost, as an additional instrument for all-round development of her North-West, including the Kaliningrad Region as a part of the Russian Federation's territory and of its internal market. . . . Byelorussia should also become a participant, especially in the light of her traditional economic ties with North European countries, its important geographical position from the point of view of infrastructure and the existence of its economic and customs union with Russia."[70]

Western hostility to the Belarusian administration of Alexander Lukashenko, however, makes such an approach highly unlikely, and Russia's arguments only bring out the gaps between Russian and EU thinking on the future of this part of Europe. Basically, Russia wants to reduce and eventually eliminate the barriers between EU members and Russia, while EU policy is to strengthen those barriers while trying to diminish problems on the other side by means of financial aid and limited cooperation.

It seems, however, that by 2002 the Putin administration was trying at least to understand EU security thinking and to adapt its Kaliningrad policy to it. Russia acknowledged the legitimacy of European concerns about "soft" security risks emanating from the CIS countries. But Moscow tried to explain to Brussels that this sort of challenge could be better met by intensive subregional cooperation (on trade, investment, developing infrastructure, improving the environment, and strengthening the health care system) rather than by erecting new barriers such as Schengen requirements.

Moscow is therefore willing to maintain a dialogue both with Brussels and with Lithuania on the Kaliningrad issue. And the Lithuanian government has also shown more of a desire for compromise with Russia than has been present (as of 2002) in Brussels. In particular, Finland and other Scandinavian countries have taken the lead in pressing the EU to apply the full force of Schengen to Russians traveling to Kaliningrad. Thus on February 10, 2000, Russia and Lithuania together presented to the European Commission a list of joint projects to be included in the Northern Dimension Action Plan (the so-called Nida initiative), including proposals for the development of transport and energy links, as well as education, health, and environmental programs.

At one stage of the preparations for the EU Feira summit (2000), there was an annex to the draft Action Plan in which the above-mentioned projects were listed. The annex was, however, eventually removed on Finland's initiative because, as Ari Heikkinen of the Finnish Foreign Ministry argued in a speech at King's College, London, on November 11, 2000, without proper project preparations in the EU, it was not possible to signal any EU financial commitment through TACIS, PHARE, or any other program. Russian diplomats and the local authorities in Kaliningrad expressed their "deep disappointment" in this regard.[71]

In January 2001 (with the beginning of the Swedish presidency in the EU), the EU Commission published *Communication on Kaliningrad*, with the aim of encouraging the search for possible solutions to the most pressing problems in EU–Russia relations.[72] The *Communication* envisages that long-term, multiple-entry visas could be issued for transit between Kaliningrad and the Russian mainland for Kaliningrad residents traveling by specific routes. Transit visas could be granted free of charge or at a low cost, and ideally would be issued at the border. EU technical and financial assistance could be provided to raise the standard of local residence permits to a level where they could be considered adequate proof of identity to allow transit between Kaliningrad and Russia (with tightly policed issuance of documents to Kaliningrad residents). Russia could, in addition, introduce sufficiently fake-proof travel documents across the board. Both new and current EU member states could consider opening consulates (or sharing facilities to reduce costs) in Kaliningrad, to facilitate visa issuance and manage migration flows efficiently. It was also suggested that Kaliningrad be discussed at the EU–Russia Summit on May 17, 2001.

These EU proposals met with vehement rejection from the Russian government and Russian politicians, to a degree which surprised and shocked some EU officials. It was suspected in Brussels that Russia's harsh tone was partly a result of the warmer relations between Moscow and Washington, in the context of the war against terrorism, which seemed to put Russia in a stronger position vis a vis the EU. However, Sir Christopher Patten, the EU high commissioner for external affairs, emphasized in a speech on March 6, 2002, that

we cannot override our basic rules here, including the Schengen *acquis,* nor undermine the enlargement negotiations themselves.

Efforts will be necessary on all sides: for example, I hope that Russia will soon be able take steps to issue the Kaliningraders with valid international passports.

At the same time, he called on his Russian counterparts to be more responsive to the EU initiatives: "Let us move on from sterile argument about things like the format of meetings and start real cooperation on substance." The deadlock, however, could not be broken at the subsequent EU–Russia summit in Moscow in May 2002, and at the time of writing remains unresolved.

During his April 2002 visit to Brussels, Russian prime minister Mikhail Kasianov handed over to EU president Romano Prodi a memorandum on the transit of Russian citizens across Lithuanian and Polish territories. The document suggested a visa-free regime for transit passengers. Two transit corridors for crossing the Lithuanian territory by car or bus were proposed: (1) Kibartai (or Panemune)–Kaunas–Vilnius–Medininkai (260 kilometers), and (2) Kibartai–Mariampol–Ladziyai–Druzkininkai–Raigardas (130 kilometers). For train passengers, the so-called closed-door regime has been suggested. The memorandum called on Lithuanian and Polish law enforcement agencies to cooperate with their Russian counterparts to maintain these transit corridors. Moscow also suggested a simplified visa-issuing procedure for Kaliningraders after Poland's and Lithuania's accession to the Schengen Agreement.[73]

Russia has also pushed the Kaliningrad issue onto the bilateral Russian–Polish and Russian–Lithuanian agendas. During the March 2001 visit of Lithuanian president Valdas Adamkus to Russia, Vilnius and Moscow pledged to carry out the Nida initiative and to resolve problems related to military and civilian transit and the visa regime.[74] However, the two presidents were unable to persuade the Russian legislature to ratify the Russian–Lithuanian Border Treaty. Lithuania ratified the treaty in 2000, but the Russian State Duma has postponed ratification until the interests of the Kaliningrad Oblast are protected. Vilnius argues that it is impossible to satisfy all Russian demands in the short run (especially military transit and the visa regime) because Lithuania has to coordinate its policies with the EU.[75]

Nonetheless, there has been obvious progress in Russian–Lithuanian bilateral relations. President Putin promised to visit Vilnius in 2001. He ordered the Russian Ministry of Justice to negotiate and sign a treaty with Lithuania on the extradition of criminals.[76] The heads of the Kaliningrad and Russian border guard services met the chief of the Lithuanian border police in Moscow to discuss the problem of illegal migration. They shared the idea that the ratification of the Russian–Lithuanian Border Treaty could facilitate cooperation between the two border guard services. They also stressed the need to harmonize national legislation on illegal migration. For example, in Lithuania the organizers of illegal migration can be sentenced to fifteen years in prison, while in Russia they are subject only to administrative amenability.[77]

In contrast to the EU and EU-candidate countries, the United States is not very active in the case of Kaliningrad, although Washington is aware of the magnitude of the problem. Initially, the United States tried to compete with the EU with regard to northern European cooperation. A Northern European Initiative (NEI) with U.S. participation was launched in September 1997, in Bergen, Norway. The NEI has six priorities: support of entrepreneurship; fighting organized crime; building civil society; energy security (including nuclear safety); environmental protection; and health care.[78] The NEI basically encompasses the old Hanseatic League, including the Nordic nations of Norway, Sweden, Denmark, and Finland; the Baltic nations of Latvia, Lithuania, and Estonia; and Poland and northern Germany.

The initiative includes some of Russia's most advanced and most distressed cities, its most cosmopolitan and its most remote. Among them are fairly westernized places such as Saint Petersburg, Kaliningrad, and Novgorod, and such far northern ports and mining outposts as Murmansk and Nikel. The NEI aims to create an economically and socially unified region, with strong ties across borders. The initiative seeks to steer western investment to Russian regions and to get the oblasts to cooperate in dealing with problems that affect their neighbors to the west, such as Finland, Poland, and the Baltic states.

"We're not trying to break up Russia," a U.S. State Department official said. "But Moscow doesn't have the resources to deal with some of the issues [addressed by this policy]." The official said western governments are keeping the Russian government informed as the policy goes develops. "Where appropriate, we want Russia involved," he said. "We want the Russians not to think that this is (aimed) at them. This is not anti-Russian."[79]

But the Russian government is keeping a wary eye on the project. "Moscow is not enamored," noted Stephen Larrabee of the RAND corporation. "It fears this will decrease the center's hold over the regions." The main problem with the NEI is that it covers not only "soft" but also "hard" security issues. One of the NEI's strategic aims is to include the Baltic states in the western security institutions, including NATO—something which still makes many Russians deeply unhappy, although by 2002 the Putin administration had stressed again and again that it would not oppose Baltic membership. Moscow prefers initiatives like the EU's Northern Dimension that clearly aim at the nonmilitary sphere and do not pose any potential security threat to Russia.

Because the U.S. role in this region has been above all through NATO, and because of continuing fears of U.S. geopolitical ambitions and hostility to Russia, Moscow is not happy about the idea of involving the United States in the Kaliningrad discussions. Nor indeed is Brussels enthusiastic about American involvement, because it perceives Kaliningrad as an EU–Russian bilateral issue rather than a global one. Moreover, Washington did not pledge any concrete economic and financial commitments in the case of the NEI. The U.S. government is ready to provide only limited funds and hopes that the main financial contribution will be made by the regional governments and the private sector. This has made the United States—in view of both Russia and the EU—a less valuable partner.

The Future of Kaliningrad: What Should Be Done?

Previous attempts to solve the Kaliningrad problem have all failed because they addressed particular issues (such as trade, transit, and the visa regime) rather than offering a complex, long-term strategy. To solve such a complicated problem, the regional players should first of all decide what sort of Kaliningrad they want in the foreseeable future.

The Russian and world research communities have suggested several options for the future of Kaliningrad. The first option is "muddling through": Russia takes a wait-and-see position and shifts responsibility for the future of the oblast to the EU. Since this inevitably would make Russian transit via Lithuania more complicated and impede the movement of people and goods in the subregion, the socioeconomic situation in Kaliningrad would significantly deteriorate.

A second, even more pessimistic scenario—though one which seems much less likely given the improvement in US-Russian relations since September 11, 2002—is a rearmament of the oblast as a result of NATO expansion to the Baltic states and a new cold war. This would make impossible any cooperation between the EU and Russia on Kaliningrad.

Under a third option, the oblast would become an autonomous repub-lic within the Russian Federation. Other options include partition; the estab-lishment of a condominium by the two neighboring states, Lithuania and Poland; independence; or reunification with Germany. For the foreseeable future, however, these outcomes are extremely improbable. There is also a possibility for Kaliningrad to serve as an entity with special links to a Baltic Euroregion or a "Hanseatic region."[80]

The last option is both realistic and preferable for most of the regional actors. It also fits with the concept of Kaliningrad as a pilot region which is acceptable to Russia and the EU. However, this concept still lacks a road map, and a detailed plan should be worked out by Moscow and the EU.

To make Kaliningrad a region of European cooperation, a future strategy should be based on Moscow's federal policies with regard to Kaliningrad as a member of the Russian Federation, and a Russia–EU dialogue on Kalin-ingrad.

Many Russian specialists emphasize that before Moscow negotiates the problem with the EU, it should have a clear vision of the problem and design a proper strategy on Kaliningrad.[81] First of all, the Russian leadership should fully understand that a close involvement of the EU and neighbor-ing states in solving the Kaliningrad problem will inevitably qualify Russia's sovereignty over the oblast. For instance, reaching agreements with the EU on trade, tariffs, transit, energy, and a visa regime would mean for all par-ties involved giving up some national sovereignty for the sake of a higher level of governance. The EU itself is a manifestation of limited national sov-ereignties and global governance. This means that all countries which want to joint the Union or to get closer to it should give up a certain part of national sovereignty, albeit to a different degree for the candidate and part-ner states.

In practical terms, this implies granting the oblast a special status within the Russian Federation. Moscow can not treat the region like any inner or mainland territory. There is no need for Russia to completely give up its sov-ereignty over Kaliningrad. But if Moscow wants to make the oblast a Euro-region, Kaliningrad should be provided with broader powers in such fields as foreign economic activities, taxation, property rights, customs formalities, border controls, and consular services.

Such a special status should be provided with a proper legal framework. This is important both from the domestic and international points of view. Domestically, it can be an effective safeguard against either bureaucratic "encroachments" on the oblast's powers (e.g., repeated attempts of the Customs Committee to abolish the Special Economic Zone's privileges) or corrupted officials, criminals, and the "gray economy" in the region.

Internationally, such legislation could be helpful for the dialogue with the EU. For instance, the EU says all the time that it cannot treat Kaliningrad as a special case because, from the legal point of view, Kaliningrad is not different from other parts of Russia and giving the region a special status could be perceived by Moscow as an interference in Russia's internal affairs (unless Russia gives a clear message to the Union). For example, the EU discussion paper on Kaliningrad (January 2001) emphatically states: "Since Kaliningrad is an integral part of Russia it would be difficult to grant any special status, such as free trade or a customs union. This would raise a number of political and legal issues apart from the fact that Russia is unlikely to grant the necessary degree of autonomy to Kaliningrad."[82]

Some Russian experts (e.g., Alexander Songal, Head of the International Relations Department, Kaliningrad Oblast Duma) suggest that it is desirable to develop the concepts of federal policy towards the Kaliningrad Oblast (1994, 1997, and 2001) and the 1996 SEZ law into a special Russian Constitutional Law on the Kaliningrad oblast. Such legislation should provide for

- more involvement and responsibility of the federal center in regional matters;
- more discretion for local authorities in foreign economic and trade relations;
- moving representative offices of federal bodies (primarily of the Ministry of Foreign Affairs) dealing with external relations to the region;
- appointing a Russian government official dealing with EU-related issues in Kaliningrad;
- setting up a subsidiary of the European Communities Delegation in Russia in the region;
- participation of Kaliningrad representatives in PCA committees where appropriate;
- launching a joint program (TACIS–FARE–Russian) to estimate the impact upon the Kaliningrad Oblast of EU-related changes in Lithuania and Poland; and

- arrangements to ensure the free movement of people and goods into and out of Kaliningrad.[83]

As far as the Russian–EU dialogue is concerned, specialists believe that signing a Kaliningrad Protocol to the PCA could be helpful. Other experts suggest concluding a special agreement on Kaliningrad between Russia and the EU.[84] Such an agreement should be based on the PCA, the EU Common Strategy on Russia, the EU Action Plan on the Northern Dimension, and the Russian Strategy on Cooperation between the Russian Federation and the EU (2000–2010). An agreement should have a binding force for both parties and be very specific.

According to this school, such an agreement should acknowledge Russia's general sovereignty over the oblast (to calm down Moscow). At the same time, the document should envisage more active participation by the EU in solving region's problems. Priority should be given to the integration of Kaliningrad into the European economic space. The Russian Federation should retain the status of the SEZ for the oblast but, at the same time, should introduce local FEZs that must be applicable to non-EU countries. The SEZ must be managed by an administration appointed by the Russian Cabinet. The Russian government should invest in the SEZ not less than €100 million a year. EU standards should be established for Kaliningrad-produced goods. A joint EU–Russia standardization committee should be created. Foreigners should be allowed to purchase land in the region. A regional development corporation should be set up to promote the oblast's development. Such a corporation could be established not only by the Russian federal government (which should allocate not less than €30 million) but also by the local authorities and the EU (the latter should contribute not less than €3 million a year to TACIS). The EU should apply the PHARE program to the Kaliningrad oblast because PHARE is more beneficial for recipients than TACIS.[85]

Regarding the movement of goods in the accession period, Lithuania and Latvia should provide Russia with lower transit tariffs and special agreements should be concluded (in consultation with the EU). After enlargement, the EU–Russia PCA should provide for free transit across these countries, without customs duties or any other transit duties (other than charges for transport and administration).[86] With time, Brussels can conclude a free-trade agreement with the Kaliningrad region and help the oblast become a part of various Euroregion arrangements.

As far as border-related issues are concerned, many Russian experts suggest retaining a visa-free regime for Kaliningraders who visit an EU–Schengen space for fewer than 30 days.[87] A reciprocal rule should be secure for the residents of the EU countries aimed at visiting the Kaliningrad region. There should be an exchange of representative offices between Kaliningrad and Brussels at the level of diplomatic missions to cope with consular, economic, cultural, and information issues. A coordinating committee on fighting organized crime should be set up as soon as possible. The more innovative ideas include a reduction of the need for strict visa procedures by establishing extensive data banks combined with the checking of fingerprints at borders. Such systems could potentially allow the reduction of visas to a mere stamp in the passport of those crossing borders, although they do not offer any quick solution taking into account that the Schengen Information System (SIS) is currently being redesigned and only expected to be ready around 2003.[88]

The Kaliningrad City administration believes that it is impossible to avoid the introduction of the visa regime, but Kaliningraders should be provided with some privileges. The administration's officials suggest, for example, adding to the visa application form a question about the duration of residence in the Kaliningrad Oblast. Those who have been living in the region for more than five years should be given greater privileges. Kaliningrad residents could be offered multi-entry visas valid for a period of up to three years, but allowing a strictly limited period of stay in EU countries on the occasion of each visit. The cost of visas should be reasonable so Kaliningraders can afford them.[89]

It must be stressed, however, that it will be impossible to integrate the oblast into the European economy without liberalizing the visa regime, and that this is an issue which demands vision and generosity from the EU. Even the so-called smooth solution (providing Kaliningraders with cheap multiple visas) will impede trade, business trips, and tourism in the subregion because of higher transaction costs and numerous technical difficulties (e.g., the lack of EU consulates and consular staff in the numerous cities of the huge Russian Federation, imperfections in the Schegen Information System, and an additional burden on Russian authorities to issue national passports for Kaliningraders in a short period of time).

Probably, the best solution is to keep the status quo for the transitional period (until Poland and Lithuania join the Union), namely, a visa-free regime with these two countries and the use of internal identification documents by Kaliningrad residents. When Poland and Lithuania join the EU, the visa-free regime for Kaliningraders should be retained as well (e.g., for a stay of up to 30 days). However, the Russian authorities should take care Kaliningrad residents with national passports of sufficient quality. Despite the obvious threat of forgery, it should be easy in principle for Schengen border guards to distinguish Kaliningrad residents, because there is an indication of issuing authority (the code of the local police directorate) in Russian national passports. To strengthen the border control regime in the oblast and to fight organized crime, smuggling, and illegal migration, Russian and EU law enforcement agencies can work together to create a joint database on individuals who are ineligible to visit the Schengen space.

To convince the EU to liberalize its visa policies and to attract more tourists and businesspeople, in mid-May 2001 Russia introduced a new visa regime in Kaliningrad, Moscow, and Saint Petersburg. Now, foreign visitors can get a visa directly at the port of entry and stay there up to 72 hours. Moscow hopes that there will be reciprocal measures on the part of the Schengen countries.

The United States also can provide a useful input to the EU–Russia discussion on visa issues because it has experience dealing with mass migration from Mexico and other Latin American and Asian countries. Before September 11, 2001, Washington was less suspicious about Russian travelers: In April 2001, U.S. secretary of state Colin Powell even said that the United States does not exclude the possibility of introducing a visa-free regime with Russia (provided that Russian travelers have enough money to stay in America and a return ticket).[90] Why could not the EU do the same, at least for Kaliningraders?

To facilitate the movement of people and goods in the subregion, both the EU and Russia should provide additional funds to build new border crossings and to develop the existing crossings and transport infrastructure in the area.

Conclusion

As has been shown, there have been fundamental changes in both Russian security thinking and policies towards Kaliningrad since Vladimir Putin came to power. Although the Realist geopolitical paradigm still dominates the Russian discourse on security, the mainstream of Russian political thought does not perceive the oblast as Moscow's military outpost on the Baltic and favors opening up the region to international cooperation. The Federal Task Program of 2001 and a number of other documents laid down the foundation for developing a Russian national strategy on Kaliningrad and also suggested specific technical instruments. The PCA and Northern Dimension are seen by the Russian leadership and elites as appropriate frameworks for finding adequate solutions.

It should be noted that in contrast to the past, when Kaliningrad was perceived as only a Russian problem, there is a now growing feeling among the regional actors (including Brussels) that Kaliningrad is becoming a problem for both the EU and its candidate countries. This means that not only Russian but also EU policy towards Kaliningrad should be radically revised. This also calls for international rather than unilateral efforts and solutions.

Both Russia and the EU agree in principle that the EU's enlargement should not entail the rise of dividing lines in Europe and that the freedom of movement of people and goods in the region should be ensured. Both sides support various collaborative projects, including on the economy, trade, energy security, the social system, health care, the environment, and the improvement of the subregion's border and transport infrastructures. They also favor concluding a special agreement on Kaliningrad to define procedures for trade, transit, and border management and to facilitate the oblast's deeper integration into the European economic and legal space. There are, however, still numerous barriers to reaching such an agreement, stemming from the inflexibility of the EU and Russian bureaucracies and legislation as well as from differences in economic, political, and security interests.

More generally, one of the most important lessons that can be drawn from Kaliningrad is that subregional cooperation can become a more and more important security factor in Northern Europe. Subregionalism offers opportunities for developing Russian democracy and civil society. Subregionalism need not cause the further disintegration of the country. Instead, it can serve as a catalyst for successful reform and international integration. Subregional cooperation facilitates the rise of a mechanism of interdependence in northern Europe and promotes mutual trust and understanding among nations. By doing this, subregionalism helps to solve local security problems and to prevent the rise of new threats and challenges. If Russia and the EU are able to fully seize the opportunities of subregionalism, the Kaliningrad Region will become a contact zone and a bridge between civilizations, rather than the place for a Huntingtonian "clash of civilizations."

Notes

1. Council on Foreign and Defense Policy, *Baltiya—transevropeiskiy koridor v XXI vek* [Baltics are a trans-European corridor to the twenty-first century] (Moscow: Council on Foreign and Defense Policy, 2000); and Council on Foreign and Defense Policy, "Interesy Rossii na severe Evropy: v chem oni?" [Russian interests on the European north: what is it?] *Nezavisimaya Gazeta*, March 22, 2001, p. 11; Gennady Fyodorov, "The Social and Economic Development of Kaliningrad," in *Kaliningrad: The European Amber Region*, edited by Pertti Joenniemi and Jan Prawitz (Aldershot, U.K.: Ashgate, 1998), pp. 32–56; Andrei Klemeshev, Sergei Kozlov, and Gennady Fyodorov, "Kontseptsiya federalnoi sotsialno-ekonomicheskoi politiki v otnoshenii Kaliningradskoi Oblasti" [The concept of federal social-economic policy towards the Kaliningrad Oblast], *Kommersant*, April 2, 2001, p. 6; Natalya Natalya Smorodinskaya, *Kaliningradskiy eksklav: perspectivy transformatsii v pilotniy region* [The Kaliningrad exclave: prospects for transforming it into a pilot region] (Moscow: Institute of Economy, 2001); N. Smorodinskaya, A. Kapustin, and V. Malygin, "Kaliningradskaya Oblast kak svododnaya ekonomicheskya zona" [The Kaliningrad Region as a free economic zone], *Voprosy Ekonomiki* (Moscow), no. 9 (1999), pp. 90–107; Vitaly P. Zhdanov, "Napravleniya ekonomicheskogo i investitsionnogo vzaimodeistviya Kaliningradskoi Oblasti RF i Litovskoi Respubliki v kontekste stremitelnoi globalizatsii" [On the directions of economic and investment interaction between the Kaliningrad Region of the RF and the Lithuanian Republic in the context of impetuous globalization], in *Litva i Kaliningrad: perspectivy sotrudnichestva* [Lithuania and Kaliningrad: prospects for cooperation], edited by Raimundas Lopata, Solomon Ginsburg, Algimantas Jankauskas, and Kristina Vaiciunaite (Vilnius: Eugrimas Leidykla, 2000), pp. 66–70.

2. Richard Krickus, *The Kaliningrad Question* (Lanham, Md.: Rowman & Littlefield, 2000); Zdzislaw Lachowski, "Kaliningrad as a Security Issue: An Expert View from Poland," in *Kaliningrad: The European Amber Region*, edited by Pertti Joenniemi and Jan Prawitz (Aldershot, U.K.: Ashgate, 1998), pp. 130–48; Klaus Carsten Pedersen, "Kaliningrad: Armed Forces and Missions," in *Kaliningrad: European Amber Region*, pp. 107–16; Anatoly Trynkov, "The Region's Security: An Expert View from Moscow," in *Kaliningrad: European Amber Region*, pp. 117–29.

3. Yuri Deryabin, "*Severnoe izmerenie" politiki Evropeiskogo Soyuza i interesy Rossii* [The EU's Northern Dimension and Russia's interests] (Moscow: Exlibris Press, 2000); Lyndelle Fairlie, "Will the EU Use the Northern Dimension to Solve Its Kaliningrad Dilemma?" in *Northern Dimensions 2000: the Yearbook of Finnish Foreign Policy*, edited by Tuomas Forsberg (Helsinki: Finnish Institute of International Affairs, 2000), pp. 85–101; Solomon Ginsburg, "Problemy rashireniya Evrosoyuza v kontekste razvitiya Kaliningradskoi Oblasti" [The EU enlargement in the context of the development of the Kaliningrad Region], in *Litva i Kaliningrad*, pp. 50–51; Sylvia Gurova, "EU/Kaliningrad: Future Aspirations," in *The EU & Kaliningrad: Kaliningrad and the Impact of EU Enlargement*, edited by James Baxendale, Stephen Dewar, and David Gowan (London: Federal Trust, 2000), pp. 117–25; Pertti Joenniemi, Raimundas Lopata, Vladas Sirutavicius, and Ramunas Vilpisauskas, *Impact Assessment of Lithuania' Integration into the EU on Relations between Lithuania and Kaliningrad Oblast of the Russian Federation* (Vilnius: Institute of International Relations and Political Science, Vilnius University, 2000); Krickus, *Kaliningrad Question*; Igor Leshukov, "Rossiya i Evropeiskiy Soyuz: strategiya vzaimootnosheniy" [Russia and the European Union: a strategy of interaction], in *Rossiya i osnovnye instituty*

bezopasnosti v Evrope: vstupaya v XXI vek [Russia and the main European security institutions: approaching the twenty-first century], a Carnegie Moscow Center report, edited by Dmitri Trenin (Washington, D.C.: Carnegie Endowment for International Peace, 2000), pp. 23–48.

4. Lyndelle Fairlie, "Kaliningrad: Visions of the Future," in *Kaliningrad: European Amber Region*, 178–225; and Fairlie, "Will the EU Use the Northern Dimension?"; Ritva Grönick, Meri Kulmala, Laura Päiviö, *Kaliningrad: Isolation or Cooperation?* (Helsinki: Finnish Committee for European Security, 2001); Pertti Joenniemi, *Kaliningrad: A Region in Search of a Past and a Future*, background paper prepared for the International Colloquium on Kaliningrad. Future Prospects of the Region, Ostsee-Akademie (Travemunde, November 1996), pp. 3–5; Pertti Joenniemi, *Kaliningrad as a Discursive Battle-Field*, COPRI Working Paper 15 (Copenhagen: Copenhagen Peace Research Institute, 1999); Klemeshev et al., "Kontseptsiya federalnoi sotsialno-ekonomicheskoi"; Smorodinskaya, *Kaliningradskiy eksklav*; Alexander Songal, "Kaliningrad Oblast: Towards a European Dimension," in *EU & Kaliningrad*, pp. 99–115.

5. Ole Tunander, "Norway's Post-Cold War Security: The Nordic Region between Friend and Foe, or Between Cosmos and Chaos," in *Visions of European Security—Focal Point for Sweden and Northern Europe*, edited by Gunnar Lassinantti (Stockholm: Olof Palme International Center, 1996), pp. 48–62.

6. Samuel P. Huntington, "The Clash of Civilizations?" *Foreign Affairs*, vol. 72, no. 3 (1993), pp. 22–49.

7. According to Yuri Matochkin, the then–head of administration of the Kaliningrad Region, the FEZ was established to speed the socioeconomic growth of the region and raise the standard of living by expanding trade, economic, scientific, and technological cooperation with foreign countries; attracting foreign investments and technologies; etc.; Matochkin, "From Survival to Development," *International Affairs* (Moscow), vol. 41, no. 6 (1995), p. 9.

8. *Encyclopaedia of Conflicts, Disputes and Flashpoints in Eastern Europe, Russia, and the Successor States*, edited by B. Szajkowski (Harlow, U.K.: Longman Current Affairs, 1993); Matochkin, "From Survival to Development," p. 11.

9. Songal, "Kaliningrad Oblast," pp. 101–2.

10. *Baltic Independent*, November 4–10, 1994, pp. 1, 5.

11. Vladimir Shumeiko, "Kaliningrad Region: A Russian Outpost," *International Affairs* (Moscow), vol. 41, no. 6 (1995), p. 7.

12. See the English version of the law at the Kaliningrad Region administration's website: <www.klgd.ru>.

13. Joenniemi, *Kaliningrad: Region in Search of a Past and a Future*, p. 19.

14. Smorodinskaya et al., "Kaliningradskaya Oblast," p. 92.

15. Smorodinskaya et al., "Kaliningradskaya Oblast," p. 99.

16. Informatsia ob Investitsionnoy Deyatelnosti v Novgorodskoy Oblasti, 1999 [Information covering investment in Novgorod Region, 1999] (Publication of the Novgorod regional government, 2000).

17. Smorodinskaya et al., "Kaliningradskaya Oblast, p. 99; Viktor Troyanovsky, "Gubernator" [Governor], *Dom i Otechestvo*, August 1999 (special issue), p. 7; *Johnson's Russia List*, no. 1380, November 20, 1997; no. 3310, May 28, 1999.

18. Igor Leshukov, "The Regional–Center Divide: The Compatibility Conundrum," in *EU & Kaliningrad*, p. 133.

19. See <www.regions.ru/news/205091.html>.

20. *Rossiyskaya Gazeta*, February 13, 2001, p. 5.

21. *Parlamentskaya Gazeta*, February 14, 2001, p. 1.

22. *Nezavisimaya Gazeta*, February 27, 2001, p. 4.

23. *Konstitutsiya Rossiyskoi Federatsii* [The Constitution of the Russian Federation] (Moscow: Yuridicheskaya Literatura, 1993), pp. 27–28.

24. *Rossiyskaya Gazeta*, October 24, 1995, p. 4.

25. *Sobranie Zakonodatelstva Rossiyskoi Federatsii* [Compilation of Legislation of the Russian Federation] (Moscow: State Duma, 1999), vol. 2, p. 231.

26. See <www.gov.kaliningrad.ru/irelat.php3>.

27. Interview with Vladimir Nikitin, deputy chairman of the Committee on International Relations, Kaliningrad Oblast Duma, June 8, 2000; Anatoly P. Khlopetski, ed., *Strategiya razvitiya Kaliningrtadskoi Oblasti kak "pilotnogo regiona" sotrudnichestva Rossiyskoi Federatsii i Evropeskogo Soyuza: mezhdunarodnye aspekty regionalnoi strategii* [A strategy of development of the Kaliningrad Region as a "pilot region" in the context of cooperation between the Russian Federation and the European Union: international aspects of a regional strategy] (Kaliningrad: Kaliningrad Branch of the All-Russian Coordination Council of Russian Industrialists, 2000), p. 108.

28. Council on Foreign and Defense Policy, *Baltiya—transevropeiskiy koridor*, p. 36.

29. Besik Pipiya, "Victor Cherkesov reshaet vse" [Victor Cherkersov decides everything], *Nezavisimaya Gazeta*, April 11, 2001, p. 4.

30. Vadim Olshansky, "Seryoznye vybory v Kaliningrade" [Serious election in Kaliningrad] *Rossiyskaya Gazeta*, October 28, 2000, p. 4.

31. Nadezda Popova, "Novoye plavaniye Admirala Yegorova" [A new sailing of Admiral Yegorov], *Nezavisimaya Gazeta*, November 21, 2000, p. 4.

32. *Rossiyskaya Gazeta*, March 16, 2001, p. 6.

33. Alexander Ryabushev, "Delegatsiya Belogo doma posetila Kaliningrad" [The White House delegation visits Kaliningrad], *Nezavisimaya Gazeta*, March 12, 2001, p. 2.

34. Alexander Ryabushev, "Vladimir Yegorov: Kaliningrad byl, yest, i budet rossiyskim" [Vladimir Yegorov: Kaliningrad was, is, and will be Russian], *Nezavisimaya Gazeta*, March 20, 2001, p. 4.

35. Klemeshev et al., "Kontseptsiya federalnoi sotsialno-ekonomicheskoi," p. 6.

36. The PCA was signed in 1994 and came into force in 1997.

37. "Kontseptsiya federalnoi sotsialno-ekonomicheskoi politiki v otnoshenii Kaliningradskoi" [The concept of federal social-economic policy towards the Kaliningrad Oblast], *Kommersant*, April 2, 2001, p. 6.

38. Government of the Russian Federation, "Federalnaya Tselevaya Programma Razvitie Kaliningradskoi Oblasti na period do 2010 goda" [The Federal Task Program on Development of the Kaliningrad Region for the period to 2010], December 7, 2001, <www.gov.kaliningrad.ru/ofederal.php3>.

39. See, e.g., Andrei Klemeshev, Sergei Kozlov, and Gennady Fyodorov, *Ostrov Sotrudnichestva* [The Island of Cooperation] (Kaliningrad: Kaliningrad State University Press, 2002), pp. 136, 147–48.

40. Khlopetski, *Strategiya razvitiya Kaliningrtadskoi Oblasti*, p. 111.

41. Alexander Bubenets, "Eskadrenny subject 'Kaliningrad'" [Battleship subject "Kaliningrad"], *Nezavisimaya Gazeta*, February 24, 2001, p. 3; Alexander Velichenkov and Alexan-

der Chichkin, "Anshlus pod flagom MVF?" [Einschlus under the flag of the IMF?], *Rossiyskaya Gazeta*, January 27, 2001, p. 2.

42. Vladimir Nuyakshev, "A s platformy govoryat: eto gorod Kaliningrad" [There is an announcement on the platform: this is Kaliningrad], *Rossiyskaya Gazeta,* January 27, 2001, p. 7.

43. *Baltic Independent*, November 4–10, 1994, p. 5; Khlopetski, *Strategiya razvitiya Kaliningrtadskoi Oblasti*, p. 107; Victor Alksnis and Anastasiya Ivanova, "Baltiyskiy uzel" [The Baltic knot], *Nezavisimaya Gazeta,* March 28, 2001, p. 4.

44. Alksnis and Ivanova, "Baltiyskiy uzel," p. 4.

45. Bubenets, "Eskadrenny subject 'Kaliningrad,'" 3.

46. Alksnis and Ivanova, "Baltiyskiy uzel," p. 4.

47. *Johnson's Russia List*, no. 4432, July 31, 2000.

48. *Johnson's Russia List*, no. 4483, August 29, 2000.

49. Igor Leshukov, "Northern Dimension: Interests and Perceptions," in *The Northern Dimension: An Assessment and Future Development*, edited by Atis Lejins and Jorg-Dietrich Nackmayr (Riga: Latvian Institute of International Affairs, 2000), pp. 38–49; Leshukov, "Regional–Center Divide"; Leshukov, "Rossiya i Evropeiskiy Soyuz"; Stanislav Tkachenko, "Rashirenie ES i voprosy bezopasnosti Rossii" [EU enlargement and Russia's security concerns], in *Rossiya i osnovnye instituty bezopasnosti v Evrope: vstupaya v XXI vek* [Russia and the main European security institutions: approaching the twenty-first century], a Carnegie Moscow Center report, edited by Dmitri Trenin (Washington, D.C.: Carnegie Endowment for International Peace, 2000), pp. 49–75.

50. *Johnson's Russia List*, no. 4527, September 20, 2000.

51. Zhdanov, "Napravleniya ekonomicheskogo i investitsionnogo."

52. E. Berg, "'Border Crossing' in Manifest Perceptions and Actual Needs," in *Borders, Regions, and Peoples*, edited by M. Van der Velde and H. Van Houtum (London: Pion Ltd., 2000), pp. 154–65 (the citation is on p. 153); B. Burlak, "Humankind Needs a Program for Survival," *International Affairs* (Moscow), vol. 38, no. 1 (1992), pp. 16–24.

53. Judy Batt, *Final Report of the Reflection Group on the Long-Term Implications of EU Enlargement: The Nature of the New Border* (Florence: Robert Schuman Center for Advanced Studies, European University Institute with the Forward Studies Unit, European Commission, 1999), p. 61.

54. It is interesting that the Russian Council on Foreign and Defense Policy—a bulwark of Russian realism and geopolitics—devoted its 2000 report on the Baltics exclusively to economic issues. Kaliningrad is described as an important transport junction rather than as Russia's military outpost; Council on Foreign and Defense Policy, *Baltiya—transevropeiskiy koridor*, pp. 23–24, 32–33.

55. Rene Nyberg, "The Baltic as an Interface between the EU and Russia," paper delivered at the Third Round Table on Kaliningrad (Palanga, Lithuania, June 2–4, 2000), p. 8.

56. Interview with Victor Romanovsky, head of the International Office, Kaliningrad Oblast administration, June 7, 2000; Songal, "Kaliningrad Oblast," p. 103.

57. Songal, "Kaliningrad Oblast," p. 105.

58. Interview with Sylvia Gurova, head of the International Office, Kaliningrad City administration, June 8, 2000.

59. *Guardian*, April 7, 2001; Commission of the European Communities, "EU Support for Kaliningrad" <http://europa.eu.int/comm/external_relations/north_dim/kalin/index.htm>.

60. See, in detail, Commission of the European Communities, "EU Support."

61. Council of the European Union, *Draft Action Plan for the Northern Dimension in the External and Cross-Border Policies of the European Union 2000–2003*, Commission working document 28/2/2000 (Brussels: Council of the European Union, 2000), p. 32.

62. Commission of the European Communities, "EU Support"; "Speech of Mr. Jon Sigurdsson, President of the Nordic Investment Bank," in *Foreign Ministers' Conference on the Northern Dimension, Helsinki, 11–12 November 1999: A Compilation of Speeches*, edited by Marja Nissinen (Helsinki: Unit for the Northern Dimension in the Ministry for Foreign Affairs, 2000).

63. Commission of the European Communities, "EU Support."

64. Fairlie, "Will the EU Use the Northern Dimension?" p. 97.

65. Deryabin, *"Severnoe izmerenie" politiki*, p. 61.

66. *Foreign Ministers' Conference on the Northern Dimension*, p. 116.

67. Gurova, "EU/Kaliningrad: Future Aspirations," p. 120.

68. Deryabin, *"Severnoe izmerenie" politiki*, p. 46.

69. *Johnson's Russia List*, no. 4446, August 8, 2000.

70. Russian Federation, *The Northern Dimension in European Integration and European Cooperation: Russian Position* (unofficial translation).

71. Arthur Kuznetsov, speech at the International Conference on Developing Partnership Relations in the Baltic Sea Region in the Context of EU Enlargement (December 15–16, 2000).

72. Commission of the European Communities, *Communication on Kaliningrad, January 2000* (Brussels: Commission of the European Communities, 2001).

73. See <www.gov.kaliningrad.ru/news.php3?uid=607>.

74. Alexei Chichkin, "Vilnyus navodit mosty" [Vilnius builds bridges], *Rossiyskaya Gazeta* March 31, 2001, pp. 1–2; Victor Falkov, "Putin soglasilsya poekhat v Litvu" [Putin agreed to visit Lithuania], *Nezavisimaya Gazeta* March 31, 2001, p. 1; *Rossiyskaya Gazeta*, April 3, 2001, p. 7.

75. Galina Kurbanova, "Teply veter s Baltiki" [The warm wind from Baltics], *Parlamentskaya Gazeta*, March 29, 2001, p. 7.

76. Putin, "O podpisanii dogovora mezdy Rossiyskoi Federatsiyei i Litovskoi Respublikoi o peredache dlya otbyvaniya nakazaniya lits, osuzhdennykh k lisheniyu svobody" [On the signing of a treaty between the Russian Federation and the Lithuanian Republic on the extradition of convicted persons for serving of a sentence], *Rossiyskaya Gazeta*, April 7, 2001, p. 4.

77. *Parlamentskaya Gazeta*, April 4, 2001, p. 5.

78. Deryabin, *"Severnoe izmerenie" politiki*, p. 47.

79. R. C. Longworth, "Policy Could Weaken Moscow's Grip on Its Northwest," *Chicago Tribune*, April 1, 1999.

80. M. Hoff and H. Timmermann, "Kaliningrad: Russia's Future Gateway to Europe?" *RFE/RL Research Report*, vol. 2, no. 36 (1993), pp. 37–43.; P. A. Petersen and S. C. Petersen, "The Kaliningrad Garrison State," *Jane's Intelligence Review*, February 1993, pp. 59–62; Vladimir Baranovsky, "Conflict Developments on the Territory of the Former Soviet Union," in *SIPRI Yearbook 1994* (Oxford: Oxford University Press, 1994), pp. 169–204 (the citation is on p. 178); Alexander Sergounin, "The Russia dimension," in *Bordering Russia: Theory and Prospects for Europe's Baltic Rim*, edited by Hans Mouritzen (Aldershot, U.K.: Ashgate, 1998), pp. 15–71.

81. See, e.g., Council on Foreign and Defense Policy, "Interesy Rossii," p. 11.

82. Commission of the European Communities, *Communication on Kaliningrad*, p. 2.

83. Songal, "Kaliningrad Oblast," pp. 113–14.

84. Khlopetski, *Strategiya razvitiya Kaliningrtadskoi Oblasti*, pp. 124–28; Council on Foreign and Defense Policy, "Interesy Rossii," p. 11.

85. Khlopetski, *Strategiya razvitiya Kaliningrtadskoi Oblasti*, pp. 123–27; Klemeshev et al., *Ostrov Sotrudnichestva*.

86. The European Commission has already agreed to do that; Commission of the European Communities, *Communication on Kaliningrad*, p. 2.

87. Kuznetsov, speech at the International Conference on Developing Partnership Relations, <www.gov.kaliningrad.ru/news.php3?uid=607>.

88. Joenniemi et al., *Impact Assessment*; Khlopetski, *Strategiya razvitiya Kaliningrtadskoi Oblasti*, pp. 125–27.

89. Gurova, "EU/Kaliningrad: Future Aspirations," pp. 122–23.

90. *Nezavisimaya Gazeta*, April 28, 2001, p. 6.

8

The Dynamics of NATO Enlargement

Karl-Heinz Kamp

NATO's post–cold war evolution has been characterized by a *dual enlargement*: an enlargement of its scope of roles and missions as well as an enlargement of its membership. The year 2001 has brought crucial developments in both respects. With regard to NATO's role, the decision of the NATO Council to consider the terrorist attack on the United States of September 11 as a case of collective defense under article 5 of the Washington Treaty has in theory at least expanded the Alliance's geographical horizon from the classical "Eurocentric" view to an almost global perspective—though what practical consequences this may have is still very unclear. With regard to new members, by the end of 2001 it seemed likely that—barring some really radical development in the meantime—NATO's Prague summit in November 2002 would be the occasion for a positive decision on admitting new members to the Alliance.

Between Hype and Inattention

The revolutions of 1989–1991 created a fundamentally new security situation in Europe. One answer of the Atlantic Alliance to these developments was to open NATO for new members from the bygone Warsaw Pact. Careful political maneuvering and diplomatic skill transformed the enlargement issue from a single and highly controversial decision into a political process and helped make it in the end more or less acceptable to almost all parties involved. This process, however, has been characterized by a strange dichotomy. The first post–cold war enlargement of NATO was basically decided in January 1994 at the NATO Summit in Brussels and was completed with the formal accession of Poland, Hungary, and the Czech Republic on March 12, 1999. During the intervening five years, the international security policy debate was characterized by an "enlargement hype," leading to bitter controversies about the pros and cons of expanding NATO's membership, to fierce debates over the eligibility of particular candidates and to bitter disputes with Moscow over alleged violation of Russian interests and betrayal of promises made to Moscow during the process of German reunification.

In April 1999, the NATO heads of state and governments agreed at the Alliance's Fiftieth Anniversary Summit in Washington to take on the enlargement question at a future summit "no later than 2002."[1] Nine countries were more or less "officially" acknowledged as membership aspirants in the Washington Summit communiqué: Albania, Bulgaria, Estonia, Latvia, Lithuania, Macedonia, Romania, Slovenia, and Slovakia. Since early 2001, Croatia also tried to be included into this set of applicants. However, despite the fact that a new enlargement decision was clearly imminent, until the first half of 2001 few in NATO seemed to take note of this pressing issue—apart from the general assertion that NATO's door would remain open for new members and except for some declarations of individual politicians in favor of or against certain applicant countries.

The reasons for the general hesitation within the Alliance were obvious. Even before the disastrous terrorist attacks of September 11, 2001, the transatlantic security debate had been dominated by other divisive issues. NATO's war in Yugoslavia against the regime of Slobadan Milosevic and the subsequent conflict over a military engagement in Macedonia overshadowed the membership issue. Other transatlantic questions, such as the creation of a European Security and Defense Identity and the controversy over the U.S. intention to develop a missile defense system, grew in importance during this period.

Another reason for the lack of interest in the enlargement issue was the fact that up to 2001, no political "heavyweight" among the NATO partners had pushed the topic or had explicitly opted for a certain policy option—which was not surprising, given the delicacy of the issue. The question of new members inevitably raised the issue of membership for the Baltic states, and therefore threatened a serious clash with Moscow. Russia greatly dislikes NATO's eastward expansion in general; but expansion to the Baltic states was for a long time seen by Moscow as a hostile "quantum jump," involving the Alliance's expansion onto former Soviet territory, the potential isolation of the Russian enclave of Kaliningrad, a long NATO border with Russia, and the possible stationing of NATO forces within striking distance of Saint Petersburg.

NATO's lack of eagerness to take on these delicate questions displayed a kind of ambiguity, which has always characterized relations between NATO and the Baltic states and has led frequently to conceptual inconsistencies and rhetorical somersaults. When the Soviet empire started crumbling, western governments tended to regard the moves of the Baltic states towards independence with concern, as bringing the threat of Soviet collapse and consequent massive instability. Since then, such other core members of NATO as Germany and the United States have constantly declared themselves "advocates" of the Baltic states but have not always acted accordingly when it comes to the question of how to include these countries in NATO.

Instead, the sheer idea of Baltic NATO members always causes serious disagreements. Before 2001, Russia always drew a "red line" with regard to the admission of Estonia, Latvia, or Lithuania to NATO. The concern about the relationship with Russia, in turn, led some representatives of NATO governments to work against an invitation to the Baltic states.[2] For other leading politicians, however, especially in the United States, visceral hostility to Russia meant that it was precisely this Russian resistance which made them argue in favor of the idea of Baltic NATO membership—even when some of them are basically hostile to further U.S. military commitments.[3] It is worth noting, however, that the dividing lines on the Baltic question were not between various NATO countries or between governments and opposition parties, but instead went right across the entire political spectrum in NATO.

However, by the end of 2001 there were open signs that the new administration of George W. Bush was swinging towards the admission of not just the Baltic states but indeed of Romania and Bulgaria as well; and although the British, French, and German governments were deeply unenthusiastic about this, their officials stated in private that they would not oppose a clear U.S. move in this direction. A variety of factors contributed to this probable European acquiescence. The main one was general sympathy for the Baltic states and their historical sufferings. In the case of Germany, memories of the Molotov–Ribbentrop Pact of 1939, by which Hitler delivered the Baltic states to the Soviet Union, made it very difficult to take any stance which could be portrayed—however unfairly—as recalling that action. Conversely, it was also clear that if for whatever reasons the Bush administration backed away from a desire to expand NATO to the Baltic, then the leading western European NATO members would not themselves make a push for Baltic membership.

The Enlargement Debate in Germany

Principally, general interest in discussing a follow-up of NATO enlargement had been very limited in Germany—a fact that corresponded to NATO's delay. After the federal elections in September 1999, the new red–green coalition had to cope with the "teething troubles" of a new government and was confronted with the challenge of leading German forces in their first combat mission into Kosovo. Throughout 2000, the core issue in Germany's security debate was the restructuring of the Bundeswehr. Early in 2001, initial interministerial discussions on enlargement demonstrated that the Ministry of Defense in particular was reluctant to further enlargement steps, arguing that basic German security interests had already been satisfied by the first enlargement round.

In these talks, Defense Ministry representatives opted for a postponement of the membership question. They pointed to the wording of the Washington Summit Communiqué, which stipulated that NATO has only to *reconsider* enlargement at the forthcoming summit but not necessarily to *decide* on it. The Foreign Ministry was less hesitant to new members but agreed that it was much too early to debate the issue—let alone develop a German position on members and time frames. A consensus was reached to await the American position on enlargement, which was—due to the change of the administration in Washington—not expected until the spring of 2001 at the earliest.

Only a few German politicians publicly expressed their preferences with regard to NATO enlargement. The dividing lines between proponents and opponents were not drawn between parties but instead between individual representatives. Some, like Friedbert Pflueger, the chair of the European Committee of the German parliament and member of the Christian Democrats (CDU), opted enthusiastically for the inclusion of the Estonia, Latvia, and Lithuania.[4] He was supported by the Social Democrat Markus Meckel, who is one of the rapporteurs on NATO enlargement for the North Atlantic Assembly—the organization of the NATO parliamentarians.[5] Others, like the former defense minister Volker Ruehe (a CDU member) voted against the admission of the Baltic states and supported instead the inclusion of the southeastern European countries as a means of stabilizing the Balkans.[6]

Former foreign minister Klaus Kinkel (a member of the Liberal Party, or FDP) also rejected the idea of a Baltic membership. He referred to the legitimate security concerns of Russia, which had to be taken into account, and opted in favor of a postponement of the membership decision.[7] Behind closed doors, Baltic diplomats expressed their fury over the position of these German politicians, who had been regarded as the architects of the first enlargement round and who had always emphasized their sympathy for the Baltic states.

As a result of these divisions, until May 2001 neither the German government nor the various opposition parties could agree on a position on which countries were to be invited.[8] President George W. Bush's first visit to NATO headquarters combined with stopovers in other European capitals in June 2001, however, pushed forward the enlargement discussion. Notwithstanding the fact that the president was not too explicit with regard to enlargement, his various remarks and the subsequent comments of U.S. officials were interpreted as clearly favoring a vote to admit further countries into NATO. Thus, the idea of delaying the decision—frequently characterized as "zero option"—could no longer be regarded as a realistic outcome of the Prague Summit. In addition, the increasing signs of American support for Baltic membership, which emanated from political representatives in Washington throughout the summer,[9] strengthened the position of those German voices arguing for the inclusion of Estonia, Latvia, and Lithuania in the Alliance.

By the end of 2001, however, this had not led to an increased public exchange of views on enlargement—neither within the government nor in parliament. The government and the opposition were fully occupied first by disputes on Germany's participation in NATO's operation in Macedonia, and then, after September 11, by the issue of a German military contribution to the international efforts against terrorism and the question of whether the Bundeswehr would be capable to match such a challenge. In consequence, Germany subscribed to the more or less general consensus in NATO not to speculate publicly concerning candidates for accession before the annual progress report of the Membership Action Plan was presented to NATO in the spring of 2002. This document was expected to provide some evidence with respect to the "membership readiness" of the applicant states.[10]

Lessons of the 1999 Enlargement

The enlargement round of 1999 gave support to both advocates and critics—though the balance of the evidence was on the side of the advocates, since in the short term at least the more pessimistic predictions of the critics were not fulfilled. In particular, the west's relationship with Russia did not collapse—though before September 11 at least this was more because of Russia's weakness than because of any trust in NATO on the part of Russians, most of whom on the contrary remain deeply distrustful of the Alliance.

Other NATO concerns included a fear that because of NATO's principle of taking all political decisions within the North Atlantic Council by universal consent, more members would increase internal divisions and weaken the Alliance's capacity to act. As of 2001, this concern proved unfounded. Instead, NATO took the most difficult decision in its history, namely, to go to war in the Balkans on March 24, 1999, among nineteen members, some of which had joined NATO as full members only a couple of days previously. Hungary and the Czech Republic were highly unenthusiastic about this decision, but they did not oppose it. Of course, if NATO had had to launch a ground war, then internal divisions would have become extremely threatening—but these divisions would have been above all among long-standing members of NATO, not new ones.

Since 1999, NATO has agreed on a number of fundamental issues—for instance, on a new Strategic Concept—without particular problems with the number of "players" inside the decision-making structures. A separate issue is that voices in France in particular have expressed concern that the new members (especially Poland, and in future the Baltic states, if they become members) are too prone to agree with U.S. positions. According to press reports, some French observers have accused Poland of being the Trojan horse of the United States in NATO (see Christopher Bobinski's essay, the next chapter in this volume).[11]

However, a key deficiency of NATO's recent enlargement round was the lack of a coherent *strategic* rationale for expanding the Alliance.[12] Instead, one of the most prevalent justifications for taking in new members was the supposed national interest of existing members in "exporting stability" to the east. Otherwise, it was argued, NATO countries would have been at risk of "importing instability" from eastern Europe.

Despite its popularity, this argument contains some intellectual pitfalls. On the one hand, it displays an obvious contradiction between the justification for enlargement and the choice of the candidates. Had the idea of exporting stability been the key reason for enlargement, then neither Poland nor Hungary, or the Czech Republic, would have been justifiable as NATO's first choices, since all were in fact highly stable by 1999. Instead, such countries as Romania, Albania, or even Ukraine would have been more eligible with regard to potential instabilities in these regions. Inviting these countries, however, would hardly have been compatible with the ultimate need of keeping NATO functional.

Furthermore, the catchy idea of "stability export" assesses NATO enlargement first and foremost as an *instrument* for political change in areas outside of NATO—and in particular with regard to the Balkan region. This notion has gained significant support since the end of NATO operations in Kosovo. Unquestionably, there is a stabilizing effect as a by-product of NATO enlargement. However, the true and basic raison d'être of NATO— and the only one on which all of its members always agree—is preserving the security and stability of its existing member states.

This does not necessarily have to be limited to NATO territory. It might well include measures of crisis management or conflict prevention beyond the NATO area, so as to ward off developments (like a massive exodus of Albanians from Kosovo in 1999 or full scale civil war in Macedonia in 2001) which would sooner or later threaten the national interests of NATO members. However, as the bitter aftermath of the Kosovo war demonstrates, positing the stabilization of the Balkans as NATO's central goal vastly overestimates the ability of the Alliance—or any other outside force—to bring order to impoverished, unstable, violent, and hate-filled regions of the world. NATO has in fact acted with extreme caution in the Balkans, even in the face of attacks on Macedonia by Albanian forces based in territory supposedly under NATO's control. The same is likely to be true of any proposed operations beyond Europe's geographical boundaries in support of the U.S. "war on terrorism."

NATO never assumed that integrating even Poland, Hungary, and the Czech Republic into NATO military structures was going to be easy—but in fact, this has proved a good deal more difficult than most experts expected. What is more, there has been a tendency among all new members to reverse former pledges and original defense targets after the membership status has been achieved. In June 1999, for instance, Hungary scaled down its 1998 "Principles of Security and Defense Policy," pointing to scarce defense resources.[13]

This tendency has increased a determination, especially in the United States, to insist on the maximum possible military progress *before* a decision on membership, rather than relying on promises of further progress after it. The Alliance, after all, has no formal mechanism for expelling or disciplining inadequate or recalcitrant members. This issue may not greatly affect the Baltic states, whose tiny armed forces are of little real military significance and which will be barely noticed within NATO military structures. It is, however, of critical importance with respect to such larger states as Bulgaria or still more Romania. The Romanian military is still a long way behind the central Europeans when it comes to meeting NATO standards, and as of 2001 the rate of progress appeared to be slowing rather than increasing.

Criteria for NATO Membership

Notwithstanding NATO's discussions and all the lessons learned, NATO's Open Door Policy,—that is, the process of opening NATO to new members by a number of enlargement steps—will not necessarily be easier to be handle in the future. This is mostly due to the fact that none of the present nine candidates for membership or those countries which might join the group of applicants in the years to come has the political weight, the strategic importance, the military potential, or the broad support within NATO that the three previous new members enjoyed. Thus, the question of yardsticks for NATO's choice of which country to admit and the variables affecting the decision-making processes in NATO's capitals will be crucial for all future enlargement rounds.

One of the most frequent criticisms during the enlargement process of 1994–1999 was that NATO lacked a clearly defined set of criteria for membership applicants. Such an assertion is, however, erroneous for at least two reasons. First, whatever some of its public pronouncements may have suggested, NATO never actually intended to develop a well-defined checklist for enlargement candidates, since this would have limited its political room to maneuver. NATO members wanted to avoid a slippery slope to enlargement, whereby countries which were not deemed desirable for geopolitical or other reasons would be able to insist on admission because they could claim to fulfill all the formal conditions for entry.

Moreover, despite the lack of a formal checklist, a number of NATO documents, Alliance agreements, and national decisions can well be regarded as a framework of membership requirements. These include, first and foremost, the principle of self-determination supported by NATO—in essence that every country has the freedom to choose the organization to which it wants to belong. This credo finds its expression (with a geographical limitation) in article 10 of NATO's Washington Treaty of 1949, which states that NATO may "by unanimous agreement, invite any other European State in a position to further the principles of this Treaty and to contribute to the security of the North Atlantic area to accede to this Treaty."[14]

More precise criteria for admission can be found in NATO's Enlargement Study of 1995. Chapter 5 of this document states that there is no "fixed or rigid list of criteria" for membership applicants. Nevertheless, there are a number of expectations by NATO.[15] Countries that want to join the Alliance first have to accept the principles of the Washington Treaty and have to strengthen NATO's effectiveness and cohesion, which means preserving the Alliance's political and military capability to perform its core functions of common defense, peacekeeping, and other new missions. Furthermore, they need to acquire the entirety of NATO's achievements and principles— the "NATO *acquis*"—which implies basics like democratic control of the armed forces and certain well-established military and political procedures (repeatedly violated by Turkey, but observed in recent decades by all the other NATO members).

The criteria codified in the Enlargement Study were further detailed in the Membership Action Plan of 1999, which constitutes a feedback mechanism by NATO to support applicant countries on their way to membership. According to the plan, potential NATO members should—supplementary to the points of the Enlargement Study—have settled potential or actual ethnic conflicts or territorial disputes and should be committed to economic freedom, social justice, and ecological responsibility. In the military realm, NATO expects sufficient defense capabilities and a general determination to take on military responsibilities.[16]

In addition to this framework of NATO declarations and documents, certain declarations by individual NATO states also contribute to the overall set of membership conditions. Of these, the most important have obviously emanated from the United States. The U.S. Senate ratified the admission of Poland, Hungary, and the Czech Republic only on condition that in any future enlargement round strict preconditions—particularly in the military realm—have to be fulfilled by the candidate countries. The Senate resolution on NATO expansion obliges any U.S. president formally to affirm the military readiness of the applying state in great detail.[17] This is of great importance, since any further enlargement decision has to be ratified by two-thirds of the Senate, which adds up to 67 votes. Given the 19 senators who voted against the admission of three new members in the ratification process of 1998, only 15 additional skeptics in the Senate could cause an enlargement round to fail.

All these various criteria and conditions together can be condensed into a hierarchy of four fundamentals for decisions on further NATO enlargement. *First, the supreme guideline for NATO enlargement is the efficiency and viability of the Atlantic Alliance.*[18] Any applicant country has to be able to contribute to the security and the stability of the Atlantic area and to adhere to the requirements of the Washington Treaty. This holds true for the "classical" function of collective defense as well as for new tasks in the field of crisis management beyond NATO's borders.

Second, one of the most challenging security tasks for the foreseeable future will be the promotion of security and stability in eastern Europe, and especially of course the Balkans. NATO can contribute to meeting this challenge, and not only militarily. The variety of NATO's programs for partnership and cooperation, as well as the offer of possible future membership, create a major incentive for countries in the region to carry out political and military reforms. However, there is a tension between the demands of regional stabilization and of NATO efficiency; if NATO is overstretched by the integration of too many countries, this will neither benefit the new members, nor the regions which ought to be stabilized. This applies especially to the question of whether to admit Bulgaria and Romania.

Third, a significant political and strategic correlation exists between the two enlargement processes of NATO and the European Union. This is all the more true since NATO has always been a highly political alliance, whereas the EU is only belatedly and gradually taking on a military role. However, it is important to realize that each of these two enlargement processes has its own value and must therefore be assessed according to an individual and coherent reasoning. Thus, NATO membership must not be regarded as a "consolation price" for those not yet ready to be admitted into the EU.

Fourth, geostrategic arguments for the admission of certain applicants are still popular within NATO—for example, the often-requested "land bridge" to Hungary—but are nevertheless of decreasing value in the enlargement debate.[19] On the one hand, the geographic separation of NATO members is not a new aspect for NATO, for there has never been a "land bridge" to Norway, for instance. In addition, the military forces of almost all NATO allies are being upgraded and reorganized towards mobility, flexibility, and the creation of capabilities for power projection. Such restructured forces will be much less dependent on land bridges for their military efficiency. Furthermore, NATO's article 5 decision one day after the tragic events in New York and Washington may suggest future areas of military operations, where European land bridges would be irrelevant.

Variables in the Enlargement Debate and the Russian Question

Apart from the specified criteria and preconditions for membership, there are a number of variables and imponderables, which will also have an impact on any forthcoming enlargement debate. One of these will be discordant positions on enlargement among the individual NATO member states, which have not only been determined by differing national interests and assessments of the pros and cons of enlargement, but also by possible intersections with other national security issues.

Unquestionably, one of the core variables in the debate on the next enlargement round will be the position of Russia. As of the end of 2001, the future of Russia's attitude to NATO remained very unclear. On the one hand, the September 11 attacks encouraged a major public rapprochement between the Bush and Putin administrations, with the Russian government strongly supporting the war against terrorism, and greatly scaling down its public opposition to the enlargement of NATO and the abrogation of the Anti–Ballistic Missile Treaty. In return, the Bush administration greatly diminished its criticism of the Russian campaign in Chechnya.

However, in the following months the United States made a series of moves which increased Russian concerns that the history of the early 1990s was repeating itself, and they were being asked for endless concessions with no concrete gains in return. In particular, Russia was greatly alarmed by the threat of a new U.S. war against Iraq, and by the possibility of stronger U.S. pressure on Iran and on Russian ties with that country. Though the

Bush–Putin summit of May 2002 went off well, it led to few concrete gains for Russia. As a result, though Putin himself remains committed to a pro–United States path, these concerns remain among the Russian policy elite. They are somewhat balanced, however, by the growing closeness of Russia to both the United States and Israel in the war against terrorism, and the fact that western Europe is now a good deal more critical than the United States of Russian abuses in Chechnya.

The general tone of Russia's declarations concerning NATO has differed greatly over time. While on occasions the Russian government has said that as a "relic of the cold war," NATO, like the Warsaw Pact, should be dissolved, on other occasions the Kremlin's position on NATO has been much more relaxed. With regard to enlargement, however, Moscow's rejection has been remarkably consistent (with only very few exceptions) since 1994. Russia has been deeply concerned that the dominant (indeed, to a great extent, the only) security organization in Europe should be an alliance of which Russia is not a member, and which because of its cold war origins has certain built-in anti-Russian positions. The prospect that more and more NATO members from the former Warsaw Pact will have deep, historically derived anti-Russian prejudices is worrisome.

This fear was to some extent borne out by the role played by Poland and the Czech republic in December 2001 in persuading the United States initially to block a British initiative for a new institutional relationship between Russia and NATO. The subsequent lifting of U.S. objections, and the creation of a new NATO–Russian council with enhanced Russian rights of consultation, did a great deal to smooth the way for the U.S.–Russian summit, and for relaxed Russian attitudes towards the alliance.

Until September 11, 2001, at least, Russian worries were even stronger concerning the Baltic states, since Moscow saw their admission to NATO as constituting approval of past Latvian and Estonian moves to deny civil rights to wide categories of Russian speakers in these republics (an issue which in Latvia at least is still far from being solved)—though in fact the west did a good deal to moderate those policies. Moscow still remains anxious about NATO's advance to Russia's borders, the isolation of Kaliningrad, and the possibility that this will increase western moves against Russian influence in Belarus, Ukraine, and elsewhere.

Russia's past opposition to NATO expansion to the Baltic states created a major dilemma for NATO. On the one hand, a cooperative relationship with Russia was deemed of supreme importance for taking on various common security challenges. On the other hand, NATO cannot accept a Russian "veto" with respect to future member states, nor even a vague Russian *droit de regard* concerning future membership.

Despite the depth of past and possibly future Russian anger, and the bitterness of some Russian rhetoric, of course there were always powerful forces working in NATO's favor as far as Baltic membership is concerned. First of all, in the last resort, Russia since the end of the Soviet Union has simply been too weak to prevent it, and sensible Russians have known this. Given the decrepitude of the Russian armed forces, an invasion of the Baltic states was and is probably not even possible militarily, quite apart from the disaster for Russia's international position which would result. Even an attempt to impose some kind of naval blockade on the Baltic states would be doomed to failure and humiliation. This awareness of Russia's weakness in the end determined Russian behavior, even during the Kosovo war. This was the moment of greatest Russian anger with the Alliance; but rather than encouraging the Serbs to fight to the end, Russia—through its envoy Viktor Chernomyrdin— played a key part in bringing about a Yugoslav surrender.

Equally important, a really tough Russian response to NATO expansion would gravely worsen relations with Europe as well as with the United States. This would undermine or destroy a key element of Russian foreign policy under Putin, which has been to try to improve relations with the EU and western European countries in the hope of increasing divisions between the United States and Europe, or at least finding some more sympathetic ears in the west. While the controversy over U.S. missile defense plans gives Russia some promising avenues in this regard, this is much less true of NATO expansion.

In the end, whatever the doubts Europe has about the wisdom of NATO expansion, in any serious Russian–Baltic clash, fundamental western European sympathies will be on the side of the Baltic states, and Russian–EU relations will suffer accordingly. Recognizing these unwelcome truths, the Kremlin never in the end matched its anti-NATO rhetoric with concrete action. Even after NATO's war in the Balkans, which led to serious disturbances between NATO and Russia, Moscow finally returned to a pattern of dialogue with NATO, and of limited participation in NATO's peacekeeping missions in the Balkans.[20]

The events of September 11 obviously changed U.S.–Russian relations (and thereby NATO–Russian relations), leading to hopes that the common struggle against Islamist terrorism might become a new era of cooperation.

Notwithstanding the fact that it took the Russian president almost two weeks to demonstratively join the United States in its war against terror, Putin's support (expressed in a television address on September 24) has turned out to be very substantial. Russian intelligence information on the civil and military infrastructure in Afghanistan has been essential for the targeting of U.S. air strikes. Moscow has provided Washington with expertise on Islamic organizations in Chechnya which have helped to dry up financial flows to the al Qaeda network. Moreover, Russia has indicated that it is prepared to cooperate more closely in other areas as well—for instance, with regard to NATO enlargement. Other steps, like the announced closure of Russian military bases in Cuba and Vietnam, have helped to further improve the climate between Russia and the United States.

The path towards closer relations between NATO and Russia is nonetheless likely to be characterized by pitfalls and unpredictable factors. For example, despite the fact that the atmosphere between NATO and Russia had improved already before September 11, much of the political elite in Moscow was hardly prepared for President Putin's expressions of solidarity with the United States. Thus, to secure broader political consensus for his course, the Russian president will have to present the benefits of his policy—particularly to a skeptical Russian defense establishment.

However, Washington's decision to cancel the Anti–Ballistic Missile Treaty has already indicated that the Bush administration is not going to sacrifice perceived U.S. security interests—like missile defense or NATO enlargement—to a newly found consensus with Russia. What is more, other divisive issues like possible U.S. plans for an assault on Iraq, or the dispute over Russian exports of nuclear technology to Iran, are not going to simply disappear as a result of U.S.–Russian harmony. As of the start of 2002, the U.S. "honeymoon" with Russia seemed to be based overwhelmingly on common interests concerning combating international Islamist terrorism. The litmus test for the stability of the new relationship will come when the terrorist threat as such is no longer at the very top of the political agenda.

Russian Membership in NATO?

The question of whether Russia could itself become a full member of NATO has been one of the subliminal issues throughout the debate on enlargement. Some American voices—especially since September 11, 2001—

referred to the fact that article 10 of the Washington Treaty stipulates that NATO members may, by unanimous agreement, invite "any other European State" to join the Alliance. This could certainly include Russia as an at least partly European country. Conversely, critics of such an option have always regarded Russia's sheer size as an impediment to any kind of integration of Russia—be it in NATO or in the European Union.

In 2001, this debate flared up again when President Putin declared in a Kremlin press conference that Russia does not see NATO as a hostile organization and advanced the argument that the inclusion of Russia in NATO could create a "single defense and security space."[21] Another boost for the membership debate stemmed from the fact that after Putin's speech in the German Parliament on September 25, 2002, Chancellor Gerhard Schröder asserted his "openness" to the admission of Russia.[22] Throughout the year, op-ed essays in newspapers and political statements in Germany and in other NATO countries backed the idea of a Russian NATO membership, not only as a means of enlarging the Euro-Atlantic security space but also as a silver bullet to end existing disagreements with Moscow. With Russia in NATO, neither the Baltic membership nor the question of NATO's military engagement in the Balkans or Washington's project of a missile defense would be divisive issues any longer. Russia could become firmly anchored within the west, as was achieved for Germany after the end of World War II. And last, the point was raised that the attacks of September 11 had proven that Russia and the west were all in the same boat as targets of terrorism.[23]

As elegant and persuasive such a reasoning may seem at a first, for the time being it can hardly stand up to the litmus test of political practice. Notwithstanding the theoretical possibility of Russia joining NATO,[24] neither the Alliance nor Russia itself seems to be sufficiently prepared for such a step. This can be illustrated by examining four crucial questions. *First, can Moscow now and in the years to come really imagine membership in an alliance in which it would rank second at best—or, more likely, rank fourth or fifth according to its political weight, its military strength, or its economic performance?* Would Russian really be prepared to submit to NATO decisions where the consensus has been induced out of consideration for the interests of Denmark, Luxembourg, Belgium, or Portugal? Considering the unchanged self-esteem among Russia's political elite of its being a "great power"—at least in its own region—and given the still prevalent rhetoric of the "near abroad" with regard to neighboring countries, the answer to these questions is likely to remain "no" for the years to come.

Second, can it really be taken for granted that all NATO member states—particularly Poland, Hungary, and the Czech Republic—would be prepared to accept Russian membership? Is it likely that future NATO members like the Baltic countries would agree to the admission of Russia? How logical is the assumption that all parliaments of present and future NATO states would ratify such a step? To answer these questions, one might recall some of the underlying motives former Warsaw Pact countries had in applying for admission to NATO.

Third, does Russia already meet all the standards of a stable democracy? Are the principles for accession to NATO—like civilian control over military forces and the protection of minorities—sufficiently fulfilled? The case of Chechnya and other issues raise significant doubts in that respect. Of course, Turkey, if anything, meets even fewer of these standards than Russia—but Turkey was admitted to NATO in a very different era, and cannot now be expelled.

Fourth, can we imagine NATO as military alliance sharing a common border with China? Such geographical dimensions exceed the imagination of today's NATO military planners. What is more, those views of a truly enlarged, expanded NATO could contribute to turning popular predictions of a future China putting itself into the adversary's role of the bygone Soviet Union, into a self-fulfilling prophecy. This might also lead to great hesitation in Moscow should the question of NATO membership ever become a reality.

It is possible that in the more distant future the answer to all these questions will be "yes." This would be the time to take the option of a Russian membership seriously into consideration. However, it would require a fundamentally changed Russia and a completely different kind of NATO. To discuss such a far-fetched scenario already today tends to distract from the real and enduring challenge, which is to link Russia as a European power to the Euro-Atlantic security structures, but below the level of full membership in NATO and the EU.

Combating terrorism can certainly be one element of common activities and decisions, but it cannot be the sole foundation for close cooperation. Unfortunately, neither NATO as an institution nor NATO members have already developed a comprehensive "Russia Concept," which would turn the general interest in Russian stability and prosperity into an ample, coherent set of policy measures. How to develop such a concept, which goes beyond compensatory offers to overcome Russian criticism of NATO enlargement, will be one of the fundamental challenges for NATO in the years ahead.

NATO in the Years to Come

Gazing into a crystal ball to imagine how the future of NATO might look has always been a hazardous undertaking. After the horrible events of September 11, political and strategic forecasting seems to be even more difficult, since fundamental paradigms in international relations have become shaky. Popular catchwords of "nothing will be as it has been before" can hardly paper over the fact that the ranges and proportions of the tectonic shifts lying ahead are hardly yet being grasped.

Uncertain futures tend to lead political observers to base their assumption too much on present or past principles and guidelines—thus failing to imagine the dimensions of future change. Yet a very fluid-seeming future also tends to entice even sober voices in the field of foreign policy and security into pure speculation—leading in the case of NATO to some very bizarre suggestions concerning future tasks and members.[25] To avoid falling into these traps, my predictions will be limited to a description of some elements of a preferred future for the Alliance in the years to come:[26]

The number of NATO members will grow significantly in first decade of the twenty-first century. Whatever the outcome of the Prague Summit, further enlargement rounds are likely to follow. Every admission of new members will be accompanied by debates on the pros and cons of the respective enlargement step. NATO's final choices will not always be determined by a "strategic rational" or by military cost–benefit analyses, but instead by political decisions resulting from intense bargaining within the Alliance. A growth of the Alliance to 25 or more members will certainly strain NATO's decision-making processes, which will remain based on the principle of unanimous consensus.

However, two factors will contribute to soothing the problem of consensus building within the Alliance. First, the unique political and military role of the United States in Euro-Atlantic security will remain and will continue to help ensure a predisposition among the Allies to seek common solutions. Second, NATO's principle that it should decide *politically* on new members will do something to ensure that only those countries will be invited which are not regarded as detrimental to NATO's common decision making—though this does not exclude the possibility of major future upsets, especially if Balkan countries are admitted.

However, the growth of NATO will not be unlimited, but will be restricted by two constraints. On the one hand, the phrasing of article 10 of the Washington Treaty already confines the enlargement process to European states. Even if it is arguable in some cases (like Russia or Turkey) whether a potential applicant or even an existing member can be regarded as European, this legal condition provides at least a guideline. The other constraint is the necessity of an ongoing institutional rapprochement between NATO and the European Union. To render a Euro-Atlantic security architecture and European security and defense identity effective, a high level of compatibility between NATO and EU membership is inevitable—with the possible exceptions of Romania and Bulgaria. Hence Russia, but also Belarus and Ukraine, will remain outside NATO for years to come. In the case of Ukraine, the existing legal framework provides a useful setting for the future evolution of the relationship. It is worth noting, however, that Ukraine is still not able to match the expectations set by its own rhetoric of being a key player in European security.

The relationship between Russia and the United States has improved significantly and may well develop into a stable partnership—short of Russian membership in NATO. The newly found consensus against terrorism has contributed significantly to anchoring Russia as a western power. President Putin has convinced Russia's political and military elite that neither NATO nor the United States can any longer be regarded as an adversary. This will not exclude significant disagreement but it will provide fertile ground to take on upcoming differences pragmatically without falling back into ideological stereotypes of the past.

NATO's Partnership for Peace program and its Euro-Atlantic Partnership Council are likely to develop as the hub of a pan-European military cooperation and as a means of keeping particularly those countries unable (or unwilling) to join NATO closely associated with the Alliance. Both initiatives will cover the full range of military cooperation, including defense planning and defense reform—though whether such reforms will be successful in particular cases is of course another matter.[27] Other programs, like NATO's Mediterranean Dialogue, will transfer these principles to other areas.

This forecast of a benign scenario with NATO playing a vital role in Euro-Atlantic security and with Russia firmly established as a reliable partner might sound overoptimistic. However, it is based on three important observations:

- NATO still exists because its members *want* it to be vital and efficient. Hence, all members and applicants deem NATO to be an indispensable precondition for security and stability in the Euro-Atlantic area.

- Throughout the past decade, NATO has not only managed to adapt to the new political realities in Europe but also to evolve effectively to meet upcoming challenges.

- NATO's success is grounded in the basic approach of Alliance policy, which is to transform *problems* into *processes*.

NATO enlargement initially seemed an almost insurmountable problem, characterized by irreconcilable interests on all sides. By transforming this problem into a political process of intense discussion among all the parties involved, the problem has become manageable in a way that enables compromises to bridge disagreements. By 2002, the NATO process has evolved to the point where it gives significant hope for a positive future of Alliance enlargement and wider security cooperation for NATO, for Russia, and for the Baltic states.

Notes

1. See Washington Summit Communiqué at <www.nato.int/docu/pr/1999/p99-064e.htm>.

2. The German undersecretary of defense, Walter Kolbow, argued that way. See "Keine Aufnahme ohne Zustimmung Russlands" [No admission without Russian consent], *Frankfurter Allgemeine Zeitung*, June 20, 2000.

3. The conservative U.S. senator Jesse Helms, who had expressed some concerns on NATO enlargement in the last admission round, nowadays strongly supports the NATO membership of all three Baltic states. See Jesse Helms, "Address to the American Enterprise Institute," Washington D.C. January 11, 2001.

4. See Friedbert Pflueger, "An Atlantic Anchor for All of Europe," *International Herald Tribune*, December 5, 2000.

5. Markus Meckel, speech given at Friedrich Ebert Foundation, Washington D.C., June 12, 2001, <www.expandnato.org/meckelnato.htm>.

6. Volker Ruehe, "NATO Erweiterung ohne Balitikum" [NATO Enlargement without the Baltics], *Internationale Politik*, June 2001, pp. 19–24.

7. See Klaus Kinkel, "Rücksicht auf Russlands Vorbehalte nehmen" [Take Russia's reservations into account], *Focus*, no. 16, 2001.

8. For instance, in February 2001 the Foreign and Security Policy Committee of the conservative party CDU drafted a paper on enlargement arguing in favor of taking up at least one Baltic state. Due to harsh protest of some CDU parliamentarians, the draft was not approved.

9. A couple of well-respected senators have expressed their support for the Baltics (John McCain, Trend Lott, Richard Lugar, and Jesse Helms). In addition, in the late summer of 2001, the Bush administration had formally informed the German security advisor to the chancellor, Michael Steiner, that the United States would regard a Baltic membership as a serious option.

10. NATO launched the Membership Action Plan in April 1999 as a tool for supporting aspirant countries in their preparation for NATO membership. One element of the MAP is an

annual consolidated progress report on the performance of the nine applicant countries, which will be presented to NATO foreign and defense ministers at their regular spring meetings each year; see "Fact Sheet: NATO's Membership Action Plan," <www.nato.int/docu/facts/2000/natomap.htm>.

11. *The Times* (London), June 4, 2000.

12. See Hans Binnendijk, Richard Kugler, "NATO after the First Tranche—A Strategic Rational for Enlargement," *Strategic Forum*, (National Defense University), no. 149, October 1998.

13. See Jeffrey Simon, "Transforming the Armed Forces in Central and Eastern Europe," *Strategic Forum* (National Defense University), no. 172, June 2000.

14. See the North Atlantic Treaty, <www.nato.int/docu/basictxt/treaty.htm>.

15. See Study on NATO Enlargement, §70, <www.nato.int/docu/basictxt/enl-9502.htm>.

16. See Membership Action Plan, available at <www.nato.int/docu/pr/1999/p99-066e.htm>.

17. See Senate Resolution on NATO-Expansion, Section 3-E, *Arms Control Today*, April 1998, pp. 14–19.

18. This guideline has always be emphasized by U.S. representatives. Sandy Vershbow, U.S. ambassador to NATO, speech at the Netherlands Institute of International Relations (The Hague, March 23, 2001).

19. See Jeffrey Simon, "The Next Round of NATO Enlargement," *Strategic Forum* (National Defense University), no. 176, October 2000.

20. On his visit to NATO headquarters in Brussels early October 2001, Putin indicated that Russia was prepared to reconsider its opposition to NATO enlargement. See William Drozdiak, "Russian Tectonic Shift?" *International Herald Tribune*, October 4, 2001.

21. Excerpt from Press Conference with President Vladimir Putin, the Kremlin, July 18, 2001, NATO Information and Press Office, unpublished transcript.

22. Already in August 2001, Schröder had stated in an interview that the NATO–Russia Permanent Joint Council will certainly not remain the "last word" in the NATO–Russia Relationship and that he would take the suggestion of the U.S. national security advisor Condoleeza Rice of having Russia in NATO "very serious." See *Frankfurter Allgemeine Zeitung*, August 9, 2001.

23. See Alexander Rahr, "Schulterschluss gegen den Terror" [Shoulder to shoulder against terrorism], *Die Welt*, September 26, 2001.

24. Legally, however, one could argue whether only the European part of Russia—up to the Urals—would be covered by the Washington Treaty or whether the entire country would be dealt as a European state.

25. Reacting to the terrorist attacks against the United States, Israeli foreign minister Shimon Perez suggested that Russia, China, India, and Japan should become NATO members to strengthen the Alliance's capabilities to cope with the global terrorist threat. See Shimon Perez, "Terror als globale Bedrohung" [Terror as a global threat], *Frankfurter Allgemeine Zeitung*, October 13, 2001.

26. See Michael Ruehle, "Imaging NATO 2011," *NATO Review*, autumn 2001, pp. 18–21.

27. It is worth noting that in early October 2001 a NATO delegation headed by the assistant secretary-general for defense planning and operations visited Moscow to discuss with the Russian General Staff questions of Russia's defense reform.

9

The EU and the Baltic States

Žaneta Ozoliņa

In the decade following the collapse of the Soviet Union, the three Baltic states made tremendous progress towards joining the west, and they did so in an amazingly short period of time. For it must be remembered that unlike the Soviet satellites of central and eastern Europe, the Baltic states, as republics of the Soviet Union, did not possess even formal independence from their annexation in 1940 to their liberation in 1991. In consequence, not only did they need to radically transform both their internal and external policies and state structures, but they also had to build many of these structures literally from nothing.

Since the achievement of renewed independence, one of the main priorities of Estonia, Latvia, and Lithuania has been full membership in the European Union. This chapter begins by explaining why this has been the case, when the objective economic reasons for seeking this goal have not always been clear-cut. The second part of the chapter focuses on the strategies adopted by the Baltic states in their effort to achieve EU membership, and some of the side effects of this effort; the third examines the factors which have hindered the accession process; and the conclusion looks at the level of public support for EU enlargement, both in the Baltic states and the EU itself, and the challenges posed by the weakness of this support. For if the great majority of the political elites in the Baltic states (Russian-speaking as well as ethnic natives of the Baltics) have committed themselves to EU membership, the attitudes of members of the public in Estonia, Latvia, and Lithuania are far less clear on this subject.

Choosing EU Membership as an Urgent Priority

After the Baltic states regained their independence and won international recognition in 1991,[1] the three countries urgently needed to define foreign and security policy priorities. However, the underlying trends of Baltic policy had in fact in effect already been set out by the national movements and mass demonstrations from 1987 to 1991. The primary goal was to join the "community of western democratic countries" or the "Euro-Atlantic community."

However, until independence was achieved, and even for some times afterwards, fear of Moscow meant that the mainstream national movements declared that their aim was military and geopolitical neutrality. Even after independence, Soviet and then Russian troops remained based in the Baltic states for several years. In the first years of independence, the foreign policy of the Baltic states was therefore primarily aimed at determining potential friends and partners, because it was not possible to make policy freely during this period. This helps to explain why the Baltic states expressed the formal goal of joining the EU only in 1995, whereas the central European states had done so soon after the overthrow of communism in 1989.

Nonetheless, Baltic links with EU members and the European Commission were already developing rapidly during these years. The EU was one of the very first international bodies to recognize the renewed independence of the Baltic states—on August 27, 1991. On May 11, 1992, a Trade and Cooperation Agreement was concluded, which took effect in 1993. From 1992 on, EU financial assistance was given to the Baltic countries under the auspices of the PHARE (Poland and Hungary, Aid for the Reconstruction of Economies) program. A free-trade agreement was signed on July 18, 1994, and it came into effect in January of the next year. On June 12, 1995, a European Agreement was concluded with each country. This stage in the development of EU–Baltic relations was completed with the submission of applications for EU membership by Estonia, Latvia, and Lithuania in the autumn of 1995.

One central reason for the desire of the Baltic states to join the EU was always patriotic: the desire to complete their break with the former Soviet Union, and move decisively out of the subsequent Russian sphere of influence. For a long time after the Soviet collapse, this was still regarded by most people in the Baltic states as a very serious danger. This also helps to explain why the Baltic states were always so enthusiastic in responding to any offers of cooperation from the international arena and in joining any available international bodies.[2]

The Estonian foreign minister, Tomas Hendrik Ilves, set out this key aspect of Baltic motivation: "Speaking of European integration, we actually speak about the interests of Estonia and the Estonian people in a broader sense. For Estonia as a frontier state, joining the EU is a matter of cultural and economic space, a matter of stability and security."[3] Because the Baltic states had been forcibly incorporated into the Soviet Union, are on Russia's borders, and contain large Russian-speaking minorities, this feeling was even stronger there than in the central European countries.

Ethnic natives of the Baltic states believe that they have always been a part of western European culture, and there is a strong desire to anchor this in every way possible for the future. Since independence, the dominant public organizations, lifestyles, and publicly approved values of the majority societies in Estonia, Latvia, and Lithuania have identified themselves with western culture; and this has naturally had the effect of strengthening the desire to join western institutions.

Until recently, many of the Russian-speaking minorities, and a lesser number of ethnic natives of the Baltic states, continued to stress a line often heard during the independence struggles: that the Baltic states have historically been at a crossroads between western and eastern cultures and may well remain there in the future. However, the influence of this thinking has waned under the impact both of anti-Russian nationalism and—much more important—of the sheer economic, material, cultural, and political prestige of the west compared with that of Russia.

The economic motivation for the Baltic states to join the EU must not of course be underestimated. The withdrawal of the Baltic states from the former Soviet economic space, and the collapse of that space, meant that for some time after regaining independence, the Baltic economies were also in a state of near collapse. Because like other Soviet republics they had been completely integrated into the now-defunct Soviet economy, they had to develop new economic strategies from scratch. Only the Estonians had done any serious thinking about this before the achievement of independence.

Given the limited resources of Estonia, Latvia, and Lithuania and the fact that for 50 years they had been cut off from processes of economic cooperation in the western world, they had to find options that would help them to devise economic systems in a comparatively short period of time and with comparatively few resources which would enable them to follow international economic procedures and become competitive in the world. The tremendously successful economic example set by the western European countries (compared with the Soviet Union, and later with Russia and the other post-Soviet republics) helped to ensure that all three Baltic states chose EU-mandated economic reforms and the goal of EU membership as the most effective means for overcoming their economic crises and for establishing a "modern" economic life.

As elsewhere in the former Soviet bloc, westernizing reformers saw the EU accession process not only as the necessary path to membership, but also as the only way of forcing Baltic governments, politicians, and peoples to adopt necessary but often very painful economic and other reforms. They would have sought these reforms in any case, but they viewed the goal of membership, and the accession process, as providing a discipline without which it might have been politically impossible actually to push these reforms through.

Nonetheless, for the first few years after the restoration of independence, the Baltic states tried to pursue an economic strategy which sought a balance between a reorientation towards the stable market in the west and the continuing exploitation of the opportunities offered by Russia and the Commonwealth of Independent States (CIS)—a market which was well known and which had a potential for development. Initially, Russia and the CIS represented 95 percent of all Baltic foreign trade. In the years immediately after the Soviet collapse, some aspects of this trade greatly increased. Estonia, for example, became a major route for illegal metal exports from Russia.

This economic relationship continued to be very strong throughout the mid-1990s, despite various political tensions between the Baltic states and Russia. Trade with Russia and the CIS only declined precipitously following the Russian financial crisis of 1998, which laid bare all of the problems that occur when a country is excessively dependent on a single market. Many sectors in Latvia, and still more in Lithuania, suffered grave losses.

By then, however, the process of integration into the EU had proceeded so far that the shift of trade westwards was a great deal less painful than it would otherwise have been. Economic chaos to the east also served as another argument in favor of becoming part of a stable and secure economic environment. By 1999, EU member countries were by far the leading trade partners of all three Baltic states (see tables 9.1, 9.2, and 9.3).

Of course, political reform and institutional democratization are also central parts of the EU accession process. Like the central Europeans, the Baltic states adopted western democratic models and tried to learn from the western democratic experience—though in Latvia and Estonia, this process was considerably complicated by the presence of very large Russian-speaking minorities, most of whom were immigrants during the period of Soviet rule. As with economic reform, the discipline of the EU accession process was a major spur to the rapid development of democratic institutions.

An additional reason for the Baltic states to join the EU is common to all small countries. Unlike larger ones, the only way that such countries have of influencing international processes—including ones vital to themselves—is by joining larger groups or alliances of countries with roughly congruent goals. For both historical and contemporary reasons, an alliance with Russia was not nearly as attractive as membership in the EU and NATO; and as far as the EU is concerned, this has even been true of a great many Russian speakers in the Baltic states.

By becoming EU member states, Estonia, Latvia, and Lithuania will participate in taking decisions that are of decisive importance for the future of Europe instead of standing aside as observers of these processes—an exclusion that is of grave concern, for example, to politicians even in a highly industrialized western country like Norway.

Finally, the security dimension is of great importance. Until recently the main focus of the Baltic states and other EU applicant countries was on the "soft-security" dimension of EU membership: the way in which membership could indirectly deter any aggression. However, the adoption of the European Council's Declaration on Strengthening the Common European Security and Defense Policy (ESDP) in 1999 led to a situation in which membership in the EU is seen as playing an increasingly important role in hard security terms.

The response of the Baltic states to this new EU role—or intention—was twofold. On the one hand, politicians commended Europe's signal that it would undertake greater responsibility in crisis management. On the other hand, the Baltic states were in no great hurry to become too actively involved in adopting this process as a Baltic security policy, and most Baltic states retain considerably more faith in the United States and NATO in this regard.

Table 9.1 Trade with Estonia, 1999 (total value, in millions of euros)

Country or Group	Exports to Estonia	Imports from Estonia
EU fifteen member states	2,412	1,890
Commonwealth of Independent States	640	384
Denmark	95	117
Germany	309	207
Netherlands	89	169
Finland	1,201	560
Sweden	365	532
United Kingdom	79	136
Russia	515	256

Source: *Uniting Europe*, no. 115—October 2, 2000, p. 12; available at <www.stat.ee>.

Table 9.2 Trade with Latvia, 1999 (total value, in millions of euros)

Country or Group	Exports to Latvia	Imports from Latvia
EU fifteen member states	1,661	1,404
Commonwealth of Independent States	494	145
Denmark	113	120
Germany	479	314
Netherlands	131	219
Finland	258	37
Sweden	196	228
United Kingdom	102	318
Russia	336	71

Source: *Uniting Europe*, no. 115—October 2, 2000, p. 13; available at <www.csb.lv>.

Table 9.3 Trade with Lithuania, 1999 (total value, in millions of euros)

Country or Group	Exports to Lithuania	Imports from Lithuania
EU fifteen member states	2,095	1,616
Commonwealth of Independent States	534	1,164
Denmark	234	191
Germany	748	508
Italy	175	79
Finland	156	30
Sweden	160	142
United Kingdom	145	207
Russia	202	953

Source: *Uniting Europe*, no. 115—October 2, 2000, p. 14; available at <www.std.lt>.

Ordinary citizens of the Baltic states instinctively have more respect for U.S. military power, and Baltic elites are aware that more than 30 years of EU efforts to create a security and defense identity have been complicated and difficult, and have usually resulted in failure. It therefore seems to make more sense for the Baltic states to put their trust in an existing, viable, and powerful military alliance rather than to hitch themselves to one that is only just emerging and that may be weakened by internal dissent and an unclear relationship with the United States.

Nonetheless, as the EU continued to develop the ESDP, the interest of the Baltic states in this process increased. By 2002, the Baltic countries had affirmed their readiness to participate in the establishment of a European rapid reaction force. Baltic representatives each month participate in Common Foreign and Security Policy consultations, which, among other things, deal with the ongoing development of the ESDP. From the perspective of the Baltic states, it is also important that there is now an ongoing mechanism for consultations between the EU and NATO on the most important defense issues—such as military capacity, modalities of transferring means from NATO to the EU, and permanent joint arrangements.

The Baltic states saw it as highly important to have the EU and NATO draw closer together, because given that Russia has a significant interest in working with the EU and that Moscow does not object to its enlargement, it is possible to reduce its influence on and opposition to the expansion of NATO to the Baltic states. In 2000, Russia expressed its desire to participate in shaping the European security structure, and the EU affirmed that it will keep Russia informed about the ESDP.

Cooperation versus Competition

In comparison with other candidate countries, which are seen as fairly sharply differentiated, the three Baltic states are perceived by the international community as essentially a single region. And indeed, they have a common historical experience (at least for the past 200 years or so), comparable levels of development, the same general geopolitical location, and almost identical foreign and security policy goals, focused on admission to the EU and NATO.

However, in 1997 the European Commission recommended that negotiations be started with Estonia as the most industrialized of the Baltic states.

The consequences of Estonia's leap forward was a series of sometimes angry and emotional domestic and external discussions among the Baltic nations about the splitting up of the region, as well as about criteria that are used in evaluating various countries. A succinct explanation was given by EU commissioner Erki Likanene in Tallinn on July 17, 1997: that in terms of economic development and approximation of legislation, differences among the Baltic states were not all that large, but "Estonia was given preference over the other two on account of its functioning market economy and free trade."[4]

R. Davis and Paul G. Hare pointed out in the same year that "Estonia has adopted the most radical economic reform policies of the three Baltic states: (i) a currency board regime which eliminates most discretion on the part of the monetary authorities to stimulate the economy; (ii) a liberal foreign trade regime (including eschewing all tariffs); (iii) has refused to refund depositors of failed banks; and (iv) has modeled its privatization policies on the German Treuhandalstat."[5] These policies contrasted with the slower, more protectionist approach of Latvia and Lithuania. As a result, in 1996 foreign investment in Estonia reached $700 million, compared with $172 million in Lithuania, which has more than twice Estonia's population.[6]

The EU's favoring of Estonia was a serious shock to the Latvians and Lithuanians and led to considerable resentment and exacerbated competition between the three Baltic states—which do not at heart have a great deal of affection or respect for each other. The Lithuanian European affairs minister, Laima Andrikiene, said that even before the EU decided on early membership negotiations with Estonia, certain significant contradictions among the three Baltic states had already emerged. In an interview with the newspaper *Diena* before the EU announcement, she said that there is now "very serious competition, and during such processes, friendly neighboring countries become alienated."[7]

When the European Commission report was published a few weeks later, Latvian prime minister Andris Skele promptly declared that the Commission's views would serve to split Baltic unity.[8] Estonia promptly emphasized that it had no intention of stepping back from regional cooperation and that it was well aware of the serious responsibility which it had undertaken vis-à-vis the other two Baltic countries to create a favorable environment and atmosphere for Latvia's and Lithuania's movement towards the organization.[9]

This conciliatory tone has not, however, been true of all Estonian politicians, and some of their statements have caused bitter offence in the other two Baltic states. Thus Estonia's former foreign minister, Tomass Hendrik

Ilves, publicly recommended in 1998 that Estonia refrain from calling itself a Baltic country, because Latvia and Lithuania are destroying Estonia's authority. Ilves said that the "Baltic states" are not a reality but just an idea, and one that is unstable and peripheral in nature. He stated that "I saw that for years Estonia had suffered from the unsuccessfully planned policies of the other Baltic states. . . . Estonia is a post-Communist Nordic country, not a Baltic country."[10]

In 1998, however, Latvia began to catch up with Estonia in the EU's rating. A key factor was Latvia's passage of a new law on the naturalization of those non-Latvian Soviet citizens who had moved to Latvia under Soviet rule, and had therefore been denied citizenship in independent Latvia. The first naturalization law passed by the Latvian parliament was extremely restrictive, and was cited by the EU Commission as a severe barrier to Latvian accession. After a bitter political struggle, a referendum in 1998 confirmed the passage of a new, much more generous law. At the same time, Estonia suffered declined economic growth rates, and it postponed amendments to its own citizenship law urged by the EU.

It cannot be denied that competition among the Baltic states is expressed largely through external attempts to find more influential lobbyists on their behalf and to create the impression of a higher level of development. In terms of actual politics on the ground, however, cooperation among Estonia, Latvia, and Lithuania has proceeded normally—at least since the EU began negotiations with Latvia and Lithuania in 2000. Even Estonian president Lennart Meri, who has usually been the most skeptical about Baltic cooperation, said that "the decisions taken at Nice allow us to think that the Baltic states will become members of the European Union very soon, and we are deeply satisfied about this. Latvia, Lithuania, and Estonia have a common past and a common future, too."[11]

Cooperation also intensified at the practical level. On May 13 and 14, 2000, the first meeting of chief negotiators and senior officials from the EU candidate countries took place in Vilnius. At this meeting, the three Baltic states harmonized their policies and shared their negotiating experiences. A joint statement was released at the conclusion of the meeting, addressing the need not to slow down the EU enlargement process, to evaluate countries on the basis of their individual achievements, and to organize similar meetings in the future so as to promote an exchange of experiences.[12]

Baltic cooperation has been marred by a variety of trade "wars," including disputes over pigs, eggs, herring, and even oil as a result of measures taken by one or another county to protect its internal markets and national interests. Usually these conflicts have been resolved quite quickly. However, at the time of writing the dispute over the unratified Latvian–Lithuanian maritime border agreement has lasted for almost seven years and remains unresolved.

Despite these problems, Latvian president Vaira Vīķe-Freiberga was generally justified in saying in 2000 that

> the three Baltic countries can be considered a real example of success in the context of regional cooperation. We have successfully implemented a free trade agreement, and we are simplifying customs procedures among our countries. The Baltic region shows very clearly how small countries with small populations and limited resources can reach a comparatively high level of welfare and technological development in a relatively short time.[13]

Problems of EU Membership

It is of course a mistake to think that in trying to join the EU, the Baltic states and other applicant countries are aiming at a fixed target. In order to expand, the EU has also had to carry out very deep and painful internal reforms. These will continue long after the first set of applicant countries have joined. Indeed, thanks to important "derogations" on both sides from the standard conditions of the *acquis communautaire*, for a long time the new EU members from the former communist bloc will be in an unusual and in some ways inferior position within the Union. According to the newspaper *Latvijas Ārlietas*:

> Deeper political integration as well as a wider Union are needed in order to confront globalization and the advent of new global players. As with Alice, from *Alice In Wonderland*, not only Latvia but also Europe itself needs to be running faster just to stay in place. But running faster, completing the process of institutional reforms and taking in new members, should not mean "rushing." Quality and speed: both are very important.

The Baltic states and other applicant countries have also faced great difficulties in "closing the chapters" of the *acquis* necessary to achieve membership—and they will have to continue with serious reforms even after membership is gained. Once again, it is a mistake to think of EU membership, or the EU itself, as a static endpoint, or that once it is achieved, the Baltic states will also have gained complete stability and will no longer need to undertake important and painful changes. The areas at issue are so numerous and complex that it is impossible to deal with them adequately in a chapter of this length. I will therefore concentrate on a few key problems.

Minority Rights and National Integration

One area which has attracted much attention from the EU and other international bodies has been the question of the rights of ethnic minorities, and in particular the question of citizenship in Estonia and Latvia. Both Estonia and Latvia contained considerable Russian-speaking minorities under the Russian Empire, and in the independent states of 1919–1940. However, their numbers increased enormously as a result of immigration under Soviet rule—an immigration which was regarded by most ethnic Estonians and Latvians as illegal, and as posing a real threat to the future survival of their languages and national identities. Although in the 1980s the movement of people into these republics declined steeply, by 1989 only 52 percent of the population of Latvia was ethnic Latvians, and 61 percent of that of Estonia, ethnic Estonians. Lithuania, thanks to lower industrialization and adroit maneuvering by its communist leadership, received far fewer Russian-speaking migrants, and felt able on independence to grant citizenship to all its residents.

The new states of Estonia and Latvia restricted the automatic granting of citizenship to descendants of those who had lived in the republics before the annexation of 1940. The rest had to apply, and initially the conditions set were extremely restrictive, especially in Latvia. More gradually, measures were also introduced radically to reduce state education in the Russian language. This is regarded by most Baltic states both as a necessary corrective to russification under Soviet rule, and as essential if the Russian-speaking populations are to be integrated into the new Estonian and Latvian states.

However, they inevitably caused great anger both in Moscow and among Russian-speakers in those states, especially those who had supported independence on the promise of equal rights. It is important to note, however, that these differences remained almost entirely peaceful, and that there has never been any valid comparison between the ethnic situation in the Baltic states and that of the former Yugoslavia, let alone South Africa under apartheid.

It was soon made clear by the EU that modifications to the citizenship legislation were necessary if Estonia and Latvia were to be admitted to the Union. Western pressure on the Baltic states was orchestrated through the Organization for Security and Cooperation in Europe (OSCE). As a result, both Estonia and Latvia introduced major changes to their original legislation, and at the end of 2001 the OSCE felt able to close its offices in Tallinn and Riga, though it continued more distant forms of monitoring. The Council of Europe's Parliamentary Assembly had already discontinued monitoring in January 2002.

EU conditions in the fields of citizenship and minority rights issues were defined by the "Copenhagen criteria" adopted by the European Council in 1993. Before the European Agreement of 1995 with the Baltic states, the EU supported the main stances taken by the Council of Europe, the United Nations, and the OSCE. After 1995, when Estonia and Latvia gained the status of candidate countries, the EU became more closely involved in citizenship and minority-rights issues in the Baltic states.

The first assessment of the state of affairs was made in the European Commission's initial "Opinions" of 1997 on Estonia's and Latvia's applications for membership. Both countries were criticized for their reluctance to solve citizenship issues in a sound and effective manner. The Commission's main criticisms related to the slow pace of the naturalization process and lack of attention to the integration of society. There was also concern about wider issues of equality and the treatment of noncitizens and minorities.[14] However, Estonian laws were considered to be considerably better than those of Latvia, and this played a secondary part in the EU's initial decision to begin accession talks with Estonia and not Latvia.

The result was a bitter internal debate in Latvia. In the run-up to the EU's 1998 Vienna Summit, the imperative of opening the way for EU membership prevailed; for western European diplomats, backed by their U.S. colleagues, had made clear that if the law on citizenship was not changed, Latvia would continue to be excluded from the EU accession process. A new law on citizenship was passed, and subsequently confirmed in a referendum (in which, however, a majority of ethnic Latvians voted against the changes).

Under the new law, the so-called window system, which had greatly restricted naturalization for Russian-speakers, was abolished.

Although by 2002 a firm legal foundation had been established with respect to the relationship between residents and the state in the Baltic countries, the near-term prospect of EU membership requires stronger implementation of laws and programs—and this will remain the case long after membership has been achieved. The effectiveness of the naturalization process must be maintained, language training programs must be continued, and sufficient resources must be devoted to the integration of noncitizens into Baltic societies.

Here, results have been mixed. The pace of naturalization is a weak point. Some 15,000 people gained Latvian citizenship in 2000, but the number of applications in that year declined to 10,700, and this trend appears to be continuing. Encouraged by the EU, after 1998 the government took a number of measures to improve the work of the Naturalization Board and to make it easier for people to apply.[15] Surveys of opinion at the turn of the century showed widespread confidence in the board among citizens and noncitizens alike.[16]

The chief problem now lies not in the naturalization process itself, but rather in the creation of a motivation for Latvia's noncitizens to apply. By March 1, 2001, Latvia had provided naturalization to a total of 41,502 people, but according to Naturalization Board data, about 550,000 people, or 23 percent of the entire population, were still noncitizens at the end of 2000. Training in the Latvian language is proceeding well. In 1996, 23 percent of the Latvian population confessed to having no Latvian language knowledge at all, but by 2000 the proportion had declined to 9 percent. However, this question is linked to the extremely sensitive and as yet unresolved one of whether and/or how Latvia should move towards exclusively Latvian-language state education in secondary schools.

Of course, the legal structure for naturalization provides no guarantee that all members of society will become involved in the life of the state to an equal degree. Even as the level of institutional democratization increased in Estonia and Latvia, rapid economic change led to an increasing degree of social alienation in the two countries. This was more along social than ethnic lines—impoverished ethnic Latvian farmers in the countryside suffered as much as unemployed Russian-speaking proletarians in the cities. However, the concentration of urban unemployment among Russian speakers means that (as with immigrant groups in western Europe) there is a serious danger of social alienation taking on an ethnic cast. Sociologists have warned of the development of "skinhead" chauvinist groups. These are, of course, very common in western Europe, but the ethnic composition of the Baltic states makes such tendencies especially dangerous.

It has therefore been important to develop policies that will lead to a consolidated society. Both countries began public integration programs for this purpose. Estonia adopted the program in 2000, and Latvia followed suit in 2001 (although its draft program was written two years earlier). The two documents are similar in content, defining the main areas in which the integration strategy is to be developed—education, language, culture, citizenship and naturalization, information, nongovernmental organizations, regional aspects, science, and governmental structures.

The programs have been praised by experts, but there must also be the political will to deal seriously with these issues. As of 2001, these programs had many ambitious goals but little money to carry them out. Nor has the EU been generous in helping to fund them. As far as the public is concerned, neither Russian speakers nor ethnic Latvians have displayed much interest. Latvians often believe that there are no problems and that the only thing that needs to happen for integration to occur is that people need to learn Latvian. Non-Latvians feel that the integration program is far removed from them, because they did not participate in its elaboration. All this takes place against a background in which issues of integration and of minority rights are intensely politicized, with both Russian-speaking parties and Latvian nationalist ones seeking to exploit them for their own ends.

Agriculture

Citizenship aside, the two greatest areas of difficulty for the Baltic states, as for the other former communist EU applicants, have been the environment and agriculture. Meeting the environmental conditions of the *acquis* has been difficult both because of the dreadful environmental legacy of communist rule, and simply because of a lack of money to carry out the necessary changes. The Lithuanians have had great difficulty meeting the EU demands (driven above all by the Scandinavians) for the closure of the Ignalina nuclear power plant, which not only supplies much of Lithuania with electricity but also earns money from neighboring states. EU pressure over this, coupled with what is seen as EU parsimoniousness when it comes to compensation, has caused considerable resentment in Lithuania. In the

Table 9.4 Transformation of the economic sectors of the Baltic States, 1990–1999 (percentage of gross domestic product)

Sector	Estonia				Latvia				Lithuania			
	1990	1995	1997	1999	1990	1995	1997	1999	1990	1995	1997	1999
Service	20	63.1	65.8	69.0	32.0	56.0	62.0	68.4	29.0	55.1	55.4	60.1
Industry	40	23.1	21.5	19.9	36.4	28.1	27.4	20.0	32.8	26.1	25.1	23.3
Construction	n.a.	5.9	5.8	5.4	9.7	5.1	4.8	7.6	10.5	7.1	7.7	7.8
Agriculture	20	7.9	6.9	5.7	21.9	10.8	5.8	4.0	27.7	11.7	11.7	8.8

Note: n.a. means not available.
Sources: *The Baltic States: A Reference Book* (Tallinn, Riga, and Vilnius: Estonian, Latvian, and Lithuanian Encyclopedia Publishers, 1991); European Commission, regular reports from the Commission on Estonia's, Latvia's and Lithuania's progress towards accession, November 2000.

wider field of environmental provisions, at the time of writing it seems likely that the Baltic states (like Greece when it acceded) will be given extensive derogations for a number of years after accession, to give them time to catch up later.

Changing Baltic agriculture so as to allow the Baltic states to join the EU is even more difficult. This involves not only much new financing for the sector, but also radical changes in employment, lifestyles, and retraining, with a large proportion of the existing agricultural population leaving the land. However, the problems of the Baltic states are tiny in scale compared with those of far larger Poland, and—except in the case of Lithuania—are also not so socially and politically acute.

The agricultural sector has traditionally represented a larger share of the Baltic economies than is the case in industrial countries. Table 9.4 shows, however, that the share of agriculture in the national economies has declined very rapidly since 1991, while the presence of modern sectors such as services has increased. Over the course of ten years, Estonia has seen the share of its gross domestic product provided by the agricultural sector diminish fourfold. In Latvia it has been reduced fivefold, and in Lithuania threefold.

However, the number of people still employed in agriculture has not declined to nearly the same degree. In Estonia this figure has halved, but in Latvia and Lithuania the reduction has been very much less (in 1999, 20 percent of the Lithuanian population was still employed in agriculture; see table 9.5).

Another important problem here involves the broader matter of rural development. The situation is particularly complex in Latvia, where

Table 9.5 Percentage shares of employment in sectors, Baltic States, 1995–1999

Sector	Estonia			Latvia			Lithuania		
	1995	1997	1999	1995	1997	1999	1995	1997	1999
Service	55.3	57.1	59.4	54.6	52.6	58.7	51.4	50.9	52.9
Industry	28.7	26.2	25.3	23.1	21.4	20.1	20.9	21.5	20.7
Construction	5.5	7.3	6.5	5.0	5.4	5.9	6.7	6.9	6.2
Agriculture	10.5	9.4	8.8	17.4	20.6	15.3	21.0	20.7	20.2

Sources: *The Baltic States: A Reference Book* (Tallinn, Riga, and Vilnius: Estonian, Latvian, and Lithuanian Encyclopedia Publishers, 1991); European Commission, regular reports from the Commission on Estonia's, Latvia's and Lithuania's progress towards accession, November 2000.

development under the Russian Empire and the Soviet Union focused largely on Riga as the country's industrial center. As a result of this, Riga became home to one-third of the Latvian population. The concentration of the national economy in the capital city has left the regions underdeveloped. The number of employers in Riga and the Riga District has increased by about 15,000, while in Latvia, except for some other towns, the number of employers has declined by 10,000.

Although large proportions of the Baltic agricultural populations are aging and will sooner or later disappear, in the meantime they can exert a very strong electoral influence. This sector has been very hard-hit by the disappearance of the guaranteed Soviet market. Lacking the massive investment and subsidies available to western European farmers, Baltic farmers find it very difficult not only to compete in international markets but also to compete against EU imports into the Baltic states themselves.

In all three Baltic states, this sector is plagued by a lack of modernization, a shortage of competitive abilities, the preservation of old-time forms of farm management, a lack of clarity about the structure of the agricultural process, and low administrative capacity. In all three republics, a desire to escape from Soviet models and return to an idealized version of the pre-1940 societies led to the breaking up of Soviet collective farms, which were parceled out as small farms to the families which had owned them before 1940. Unfortunately, these farms are far too small to be economical in the Europe of the twenty-first century.

Baltic agriculture is bound to undergo wrenching changes, not only as a result of EU accession but also simply through adaptation to the modern world. However, without radical changes within the Baltic states and major assistance from the EU, the situation could become catastrophic.

The most important necessary change is to restructure traditional forms of farming. Rejection of the Soviet legacy led not only to the breaking up of the collective farms, but also to deep prejudices against agricultural cooperation in general—without which small Baltic farms cannot possibly survive. For even leaving aside EU health and environmental regulations, Baltic farmers cannot compete with western European goods unless they introduce modern technologies—and they cannot afford these unless they pool their resources. To survive in the EU market, they also need to change what they produce. If they fail to compete, there will be mass rural unemployment, with potentially serious political consequences.

In accordance with the European Agreement, the Baltic states have enjoyed privileged access to the EU market since the mid-1990s. However, as of 2001 this worked more to the advantage of the EU than the Baltic states. As of that year, and for the foreseeable future, the trade balance with agricultural products between the EU and the Baltic states strongly favored existing EU members. The only major exports to the EU from the Baltic states are dairy products, but the Baltic states import alcoholic beverages, coffee, tea and spices, fruits, meat, and a range of other products from the EU. The EU has promised to open its markets to more Baltic agricultural products, but this has met resistance from some members under the influence of their own powerful agricultural lobbies. Inadequate health and environmental safety provisions are a key factor in hindering Baltic exports to the EU. Thus, Latvia was not able to fulfill its EU export quotas for meat products because its slaughterhouses did not meet high EU requirements.

Similarly, Latvian farmers have not used opportunities to sell vegetables to EU countries, while the EU has fully exhausted quotas opened for exports of the same goods to Latvia. Although the Baltic states have had the greatest success with dairy products, while EU quotas allowed Latvian farmers to sell 4,000 tons of milk powder to EU countries from July 1, 2000, through June 30, 2001, they were able to sell only 1,708 tons. Similar figures applied to butter and cheese.[17]

With regard to the EU Common Agricultural Policy (CAP), the Baltic states, and eastern European applicants in general, are facing in an acute form the problem of the moving target. On the one hand, they are supposed to bring national legislation on agriculture into line with EU legislation. On the other hand, there have been repeated promises from the EU that the CAP would be radically reformed in the near future, in part to help the admission of new members—but this has led to extremely stiff resistance by western European agricultural lobbies, and intense wrangling between members.

At the time of writing, therefore, the most likely outcome seems to be that the Baltic states and other applicants will be admitted under special conditions. On the one hand, these conditions will exempt them for several years from full adherence to EU standards in a number of fields. But on the other hand, they will be denied access to most existing EU subsidies under the CAP. This is likely to lead to the perception that the new members are in fact second-class members compared with the western European ones, and this could be a cause of potent resentment in the future—especially, of course, in the countryside.

Some kind of derogation, however, is certainly necessary when it comes to EU standards, for the applicant countries cannot meet many of these in the short to medium terms. Thus in the case of Latvia, the European Commission *Regular Report 2000* stated:

> The process of bringing food processing establishments in line with EC requirements is far from being completed. Currently, 9 milk processing enterprises (total: 73 enterprises), 9 fish processing enterprises (total: 117 enterprises), and 4 refrigerator ships (total: 4 ships) have been approved for exporting to the EC.[18]

Lithuania faced similar problems, but it was also told:

> Much progress is still needed as regards both the adoption of the and the development of the administrative capacity. Particular attention should be paid to developing systems, procedures, control and audit measures in accordance with the EC rules. Also, additional staff resources and adequate training (for both administration staff and farmers) are necessary.[19]

In the end, however, the Baltic agricultural sectors are so small by international standards that it is difficult to see them becoming a crucial obstacle to EU membership or future integration. Indeed, it may well be that the most serious agricultural problem affecting Baltic integration will have nothing to do with the Baltic states themselves at all. This is the colossal obstacle to EU enlargement presented by Polish agriculture. Because of German determination that the first round of enlargement must include Poland, the difficulties of the Polish agricultural sector could hold up integration for all the other applicants as well.

Privatization and Corruption

Given the fact that all the eastern European EU applicants emerged between 1989 and 1991 from communist systems in which all major property was state owned or state controlled, privatization has naturally been a central part of their economic reforms and of the process of joining the EU. In the Baltic states, by 2001 privatization had been almost completed in Estonia, was approaching its final stage in Latvia (with two major exceptions), and was also proceeding in Lithuania (though somewhat more slowly). The Estonian position as front-runner is rooted in its radical approach to market reform in the early to mid-1990s, significantly ahead of the other two states and indeed of most of central Europe.

The Latvian Shipping Company (LASCO) is an example of the difficulties the Baltic states (like other former communist countries) have faced in privatization. It is a major company: the second largest enterprise in Latvia, the largest transnational corporation in central and eastern Europe, and the world's nineteenth largest shipping company in tonnage terms.

LASCO's privatization started at the end of 1996—which was already five years after independence. By 2001, there had been four attempts to sell the company, and all had failed because of several factors. Obviously, the Latvian Privatization Agency is charged with finding a balance between the highest price and the best investor. Deciding this is apt to be a complicated and controversial matter in the best of times, but in the case of LASCO it was made much worse by acute politicization. The politicians were unable to reach a consensus, and each privatization attempt was bedeviled by bitter accusations of corruption. Finally, there was widespread reluctance on national grounds to sell LASCO to a Russian company, which might have been in some ways the best purchaser.[20]

Latvia's other highly problematic major privatization has had a direct effect on the EU accession process. Lattelekom is Latvia' s only telecommunications company, in part because a decision by the Latvian government, before the European Agreement was signed, granted the company a monopoly until 2013—in contradiction of EU rules. Latvia was therefore faced with the simultaneous tasks of finding foreign buyers and of breaking up Lat-telekom's monopoly.

However, this process was gravely complicated by what appeared to be well-founded allegations of corruption.[21] Latvia has been identified by several international nongovernmental organizations as the most corrupt of the Baltic states, for a variety of reasons including Riga's status as a great port and money-laundering center. This has inevitably affected the privatization process, which has been widely viewed by the population as little better than robbery by the political elites, who used their position to buy state property at prices far below market rates.

The Latvian government has taken several anticorruption measures and adopted the relevant EU legislation. However, in the first half of 2000, only one person was sentenced for passive bribery out of a mere 25 registered cases and only four people were convicted of active bribery.[22] This is undoubtedly only the tip of the iceberg as far as Latvian corruption is concerned, and indicates that a huge gap exists between establishing laws and official programs and achieving real results.[23] It also reflects the enormous role of the "shadow" economy. In 1995, this was estimated to generate 45 percent of gross domestic product; by 2001, its share was estimated to have dropped, but only to about 40 percent. This has obvious negative results for everything from taxation to organized crime.

These problems are related to poor administrative capacity, a weakness throughout the former communist bloc and a barrier to EU membership.[24] In the rush to bring Latvian legislation in line with the *acquis communautaire*, the question of whether the Latvian bureaucracy and judicial institutions were actually capable of implementing these laws was somewhat neglected—and this later came back to haunt Latvia. Although formal criteria in this field are hard to establish (and certain existing EU members are notoriously poor in this area), western European states which wish to delay the enlargement process for whatever reason will undoubtedly exploit this issue to oppose early membership for the Baltic states and other former communist applicants.

EU Enlargement and Public Opinion

For the former communist states, EU membership involves all-encompassing economic, political, social, institutional, legal, and even cultural change, which touches or will touch the lives of almost every inhabitant of these countries. However, the movement towards the EU has not been one in which ordinary people have felt consulted or closely involved—and this creates dangers for the entire process. For not only will referenda on membership have to be held in several countries, but populations which feel uncommitted to the EU could in the future generate dangerous backlashes against it.

As several western European examples show, this type of reaction can occur even many years after accession. Indeed, one of the most worrying aspects of the enlargement process is the indifference or outright opposition of many ordinary western Europeans. According to Eurobarometer[25] research in 2001, the views of residents of EU member states concerning enlargement differed very greatly, ranging from outspoken support to opposition. Most did not think it of great importance—and this cannot but have an effect on their governments. The fight against unemployment was seen as a priority in 90 percent of survey responses, while the admission of new countries was a priority for only 28 percent of EU state residents, and 59 percent felt that it is not even an important part of EU policy.[26]

The most favorable attitudes towards EU enlargement were found in Greece, where 70 percent of respondents were in favor of admitting new countries. The respective positive responses in Italy and Spain were 59 and 58 percent—something of a surprise, because it was widely felt that concern about reduction of access to EU regional and other funds would incline the poorer southern European states against enlargement. Eurobarometer results in 2001, however, show that these countries had the largest percentage of enlargement supporters—higher in fact than the populations of the two traditional advocates for the Baltic states—Sweden, in which 56 percent of respondents (62 percent in 1999) supported enlargement, and Denmark, with 56 percent (60 percent in 1999). On average, only 44 percent of residents of all EU member states favored enlargement as of 2001. The most skeptical attitudes were found in the EU's largest countries—there were positive responses of 31 percent in the United Kingdom, 35 percent in France, and 36 percent in Germany. These are the countries which have the greatest influence on EU political decisions.[27]

Even more surprising is the fact that this skepticism is matched by the feeling of most ordinary citizens of the Baltic states themselves. Sociological data released in the context of various surveys in the beginning of 2001 showed that in Estonia, which is seen as the Baltic state that is the closest to EU membership, only 43 percent of residents would vote "yes" in a referendum on membership, while 57 percent would vote "no."[28] In Latvia, the figures among citizens are 44.5 and 32.4 percent respectively, and in Lithuania the numbers are similar—44.4 and 22.8 percent respectively.[29]

In these polls, Russian-speaking residents displayed strikingly more support for membership than ethnic Estonians and Latvians—partly because of the EU's role in defending their rights, and partly because among them nationalist commitment to full national independence obviously plays a much smaller role (concerning support for NATO membership, the ethnic percentages have been the reverse).

This skepticism concerning the EU is very widespread in all the applicant countries (and indeed, also in western Europe); but it is most surprising among ethnic natives of the Baltic states, whose desire to escape from "the east" and join "the west" is generally even stronger than elsewhere in eastern Europe. The reasons are rooted in various arguments and sentiments. Among them is the fact that national independence has been one of the most highly rated goals for ethnic natives of the Baltic states, and has been elevated by nationalist parties into a virtual cult. This leads to great unwillingness to surrender sovereignty to a new multinational union—a line which can also be heard in EU members like Denmark and the United Kingdom. The citizens of the Baltic states and other eastern Europeans were alarmed by the political boycott of Austria by the EU in 1999.

There is also a wider, more diffuse conservative and nationalist fear of the dilution, corruption, or even destruction of the distinctive Baltic cultures as a result of their submersion in the vastly larger and richer EU. This also is a line often heard elsewhere—and which, for example, has played a key part in the repeated refusals of Norway to join the EU. However, it is even stronger in the Baltic states because of their long and severe experience of near submersion in the Soviet cultural sea.

The lack of real public debate has also contributed to disenchantment. After independence was achieved, the new political elites committed themselves to NATO and EU membership, and they took the support of their populations for granted. It was assumed a priori that the best foreign policy route would be the one that would help the Baltic states pull away fastest from Russian influence. Little real attempt was made to inform the public of the admittedly highly complex issues of EU accession. The general approach was a technocratic and even elitist one.

Hostility among more radical nationalists in Latvia and Estonia was increased by the EU's role in condemning and changing legislation hostile to the Russian-speaking minorities, to which the nationalists had been strongly committed. Moreover, as has already been stressed, there is deep concern in the countryside about the impact of EU accession.

There is also widespread resentment of perceived EU and western European arrogance and meanness in a whole variety of fields. One important issue is the demands by EU member states (especially Germany) for severe restrictions on the movement of labor from the new eastern European members, lasting a decade or more after accession. These restrictions will almost certainly be incorporated into the final accession agreements, and are widely seen as personally humiliating and as condemning the Baltic states and others to second-class status within the EU.

Finally, Baltic politicians and officials have often been guilty of blaming EU pressure for painful changes which they would have sooner or later have had to implement anyway if the Baltic states are to join the modern world. This is true for issues ranging from agricultural reform to minority rights. In Latvia, the government even tried to blame an unpopular reduction in the number of administrative districts on the EU, though the EU had expressed no opinion on this matter.

As a result of all this, by 2001 increasing numbers of people in the Baltic states were calling themselves Eurorealists (rather than Euroskeptics or opponents of the EU). They admitted that in the long term the Baltic states had no choice but to join the EU, but they felt that this must not happen in the near future. First of all, they said, the Baltic states must strengthen their governing, economic, and financial systems and complete the integration of society. Only then, when the country can be a powerful partner of existing member states and can join the EU on equal terms, should there be accession to the Union.

These critics argued that if the Baltic states were to join the EU in the near term, they would be "swallowed up" by the large and powerful Union; and this would lead to the bankruptcy of local companies, increase unemployment among people who are not competitive in the EU labor market, and cause many able specialists to leave the three countries. People who argue this way often point to the example of non-EU members Norway and Switzerland—a rather weak argument, given the colossal differences between the economic and geopolitical situations of these countries and that of Latvia, for example. Although no major political party in any of the three Baltic states has come out openly and categorically against EU membership, several are trying to exploit these sentiments in a more discreet way.

In response to this gathering wave of criticism, the European Commission in May 2000 adopted the Enlargement Communications Strategy. Its goal is to engage in targeted and systematic work to keep people informed about the future of their countries in an enlarged EU. However, this strategy depends very largely on the applicant countries themselves—and given the budget constraints under which they are suffering, most cannot afford to make this a priority.

Conclusion

As of 2001, membership negotiations between the EU and all three Baltic states were proceeding apace, and many negotiating chapters had already been closed. The formal determination of all three states and governing elites to join the Union remained unshaken, as did the will of EU member states to carry out enlargement. Only just below the surface, however, numerous doubts and weaknesses remained.

As far as the Baltic states are concerned, one key problem—which will to a great extent remain the case even after accession—is that they are hostage to developments in other states over which they have no control and very little influence. Because the Baltic states are so small, they could be fully admitted not just to the EU but also to the CAP and the western European labor market without any significant or negative effect on existing EU members. But because Poland is so big, its problems are also likely to delay or at least heavily qualify membership for all the other applicant countries.

As has already been stated, the Baltic states and the other applicants are aiming at a moving target. They do not know what kind of EU they will actually be joining. They naturally therefore find it very hard to develop radically new policies so as to achieve harmony with an EU which is not only changing all the time but is itself deeply disharmonious. The Baltic states and other EU applicants are also confused, and increasingly worried, by the unclear and changing nature of relations among the EU, NATO, the United States, and Russia—relations which in the wake of the September 11, 2001, terrorist attacks could be facing truly radical change. What many citizens of the Baltic states have not yet realized, however, is that these dilemmas and challenges will not simply end at the moment when—God willing—the Baltic states become EU members. They may be reduced in importance, but in one form or another the Baltic states will have to face them for the foreseeable future.

Notes

1. The chronology of the restoration of the Baltic states' independence involves a number of points of reference. Original declarations of independence were adopted a year earlier—on February 11, 1990, in Lithuania; on March 30, 1990, in Estonia; and on May 4, 1990, in Latvia. The international recognition of the Baltic states and their return into international circulation, however, began only after the failed coup in the Soviet Union on August 19, 1991. The international society waited for the USSR to express its views towards the Baltic states.

2. Examples include cooperation between the Baltic and Black Sea states, joining the Visegrad Group, the establishment of a pan-Baltic alliance, and the Baltic Union.

3. Address by Toomas Hendrik Ilves, minister of foreign affairs, on behalf of the Government of Estonia to the Riigikogu (parliament), June 8, 2000.

4. Baltic News Service, July 18, 1997.

5. R. Davis Jr. and P. G. Hare, "The Baltic States: The Swings and Roundabouts of Transition to a Market Economy," vol. 13, no. 25 (1997), p. 287.

6. Davis and Hare, "Baltic States," p. 288.

7. *Diena*, June 26, 1997.

8. *Diena*, July 19, 1997.

9. *Baltic Times*, September 11–17, 1997.

10. See <www.bns.lv>, October 30, 1998.

11. Euronews, 21 December 2000.

12. See <www.urm.lt>.

13. *Latvijas Vēstnesis* , September 20, 2000.

14. See European Commission, "Commission's Opinion on Latvia's Application for Membership of the European Union" (Brussels, July 1997); European Commission, "Commission's Opinion on Estonia's Application for Membership of the European Union" (Brussels, July 1997).

15. In June 2001, the Latvian government adopted two regulatory decrees intended to facilitate the naturalization process. First, the general fee for an application was reduced by 33 percent. The number of categories of applicants eligible for a 50 percent reduction was enlarged to include university students and all groups of disabled people. Low-income applicants will be either exempted from paying the duty or will pay a reduced duty of 3 lats. Second, the language certificates received by students of non-Latvian-language secondary schools will hereafter be accepted as equivalent to the language certificate required for naturalization.

16. *NRA*, May 29, 2001.

17. *NRA*, June 15, 2001.

18. European Commission, *Commission Regular Report 2000: Latvia* (Brussels: European Commission, 2000), p. 54.

19. European Commission, *Commission Regular Report 2000: Lithuania* (Brussels: European Commission, 2000), p. 52.

20. Finnish researcher Kari Liuhto in his study "Born International: The Case of the Latvian Shipping Company," LUT, No. 124, 2001, has provided comprehensive analysis of LASCO and its privatization.

21. European Commission, *Commission Regular Report 2000: Latvia* (Brussels: European Commission, 2000), p. 18.

22. European Commission, *Commission Regular Report 2000: Latvia*, p. 18.

23. *Diena*, May 4, 2001.

24. As expressed in the last meeting of the EU and Latvian Association Committee on June 13, 2001, the biggest difficulty for Latvia during its integration process is mainly related to the country' s administrative capacity but not to other supplementary factors. Latvia was praised particularly in such spheres as in agriculture, competition policy, state support policy, and measures undertaken to implement social integration policy (Baltic News Service, June 13, 2001).

25. The various Eurobarometer surveys are conducted and produced by the Public Opinion Analysis sector of the European Commission.

26. Standard Eurobarometer 53, figure 3.12.

27. Standard Eurobarometer 54.

28. LETA, April 18, 2001.

29. There are great difficulties in comparing survey results on attitudes towards the EU in the Baltic states, because the studies have been run by different enterprises with different methodologies. Because the Eurobarometer study did not include questions about the candidate countries in recent years, however, we must make use of the studies that are at our disposal. At the same time, we must have a critical approach towards comparing these results. The most regular studies—four times a year—are conducted by the European Integration Bureau of Latvia. The latest data were extracted in February 2001. At that time, 41.4 percent of citizens would have voted in favor of EU membership, while 32.7 percent would have voted against. In February, Lithuanian residents reported that 46.6 percent of them would vote in favor, and 21.8 percent would vote against EU membership. For comparison, however, I have used data from the latter half of 2000, because 2001 data about Estonia are not yet available.

10

Polish Illusions and Reality

Christopher Bobinski

Poland's anticommunist opposition never lost sight of the dream of freedom, and of Poland's "western identity," during the entire period of communist rule. Those dreams seemed to become real for sixteen heady months after August 1980 when the Solidarity movement challenged the communist government and the Soviet Union. However, at that time, the Polish dream was of freedom of speech and organization, a democratization of economic decision making and autonomy for the country within the loosened confines of the Warsaw Pact. Mainstream opinion never publicly embraced membership in NATO or the EU as a goal.[1] This was seen by most Poles at that time as too far a dream—not only wholly unrealistic, but certain to provoke Soviet armed intervention—and was demanded only by certain intellectual groups and romantic nationalists.

The imposition of military-communist authoritarian rule in 1981 only temporarily crushed these aspirations. Within a few years, and long before Germans in the east or the west had any notion that the Berlin wall would be coming down, Poles in the leadership of both Solidarity and the ruling Polish United Workers Party (PZPR) realized that the stalemate which had started with martial law could not continue. Consequently, behind-the-scenes contacts between government and opposition led to a power-sharing deal in the late spring of 1989 which was dubbed the "Round Table Agreement."

These contacts took on additional urgency when such PZPR leaders as General Wojciech Jaruzelski and Mieczyslaw Rakowski realized that the Soviet Union under the leadership of Mikhail Gorbachev was no longer willing to defend its political and economic hegemony in central Europe by armed intervention or even the threat of it. Nevertheless, the results of the roundtable talks continued to reflect the caution of a generation of leaders who remembered Soviet interventions in Hungary in 1956 and in Czechoslovakia in 1968, and thus dared go no further than to demand partial democracy and social democratic economic options.

This situation changed radically with the partially free elections in the summer of 1989. These saw Solidarity win overwhelming support in the country and—somewhat to the opposition movement's own surprise—led to the formation of a coalition government with the Communists which ruled until the autumn of the following year. The new Solidarity-led government then quickly and almost as it were by accident abandoned Solidarity's social democratic economic plans. Instead, it embarked on a policy of "shock therapy" reforms crafted by Leszek Balcerowicz, the then–finance minister, which had been recommended by western advisors. At the time, these not only had the backing of a majority of the population but also the tacit support of the still strong Communist caucus in parliament.

Both the free-market and democratic reforms were highly audacious for their time. But for a while the new Polish government and elites still stopped short of openly challenging the Soviet Union's right to station its armed forces in Poland. Initially, talk of joining NATO was restricted to the right-wing, nationalist opposition to the government. There was also scant mention of membership in the EU.

It was only after the election of Lech Walesa as Poland's first noncommunist president in the autumn of 1990 that the first wholly noncommunist government under Jan Krzysztof Bielecki was appointed, and that talk of membership in both leading western organizations became more common. Under Bielecki, negotiations for an Association Agreement with the European Union accelerated, and talk of Polish membership in NATO became less of a taboo. It was only then that Polish accession to these organizations started to be portrayed publicly as a natural end to the reform process which had started in 1989 and as a natural outgrowth of Polish history and culture. Polish society was deeply conditioned to think of itself as part of the west, by reason of the Catholic faith, the Polish cultural tradition, and historical animosity towards the "eastern" Russia and Soviet Union. Most Poles wanted to join the "free world" and had demonstrated in 1989 that they were ready to ditch the Soviet-imposed system which had shaped the country for 45 years. Joining the EU and NATO therefore became widely seen as the most important sign that Poland was fulfilling its historical destiny and "coming home."

Nonetheless, support for these goals has always been far from universal. For some time, fear of the Soviet Union, and then of Russia, continued to have an influence. Enthusiasm for Polish membership in the EU was especially high in the early years, partly because it was seen as a nonmilitary and thus safer option than NATO. In June 1993, 74 percent of Poles were in favor of joining the European Union, and three years later the support rate reached 80 percent.[2]

Their attitude towards NATO was more cautious. After all, Soviet troops were still stationed on Polish soil till 1992. Thus in an opinion poll in May of that year, though about 35 percent of the population said they were in favor of NATO membership, 35 percent were against it. This changed as it became clearer that the Soviet Union was gone for good and Russia too weak to threaten Poland. The number of ayes in polls moved decidedly upwards, to reach 57 percent in June 1993; by January 1996, as many as 72 percent of Poles were saying they were in favor of membership in the Alliance.[3]

Those figures reflected a yearning for stability and security after more than two centuries of invasions, destructive wars, partition, and repeated losses of sovereignty. The high support figures also stemmed in part from the economic growth which had started in the summer of 1992. This strong growth rate, which continued through 1997, helped to bolster support for the government formed by the former Communist Left Democratic Alliance (SLD) and the Polish Peasant Party (PSL).

Because this economic growth reflected the success of westernizing reforms, it also increased support for membership in NATO and the EU. However, as in many other applicant countries, these positive feelings developed before the accession process to these organizations had begun, and therefore before most of society, or even the elites, had been able to consider the costs and duties of membership. It was therefore inevitable that there would be a certain degree of subsequent disillusionment.

NATO: The Discreet Accession

Once former Soviet troops had left Germany and Poland and memories of the Soviet Union faded, support for Polish membership in NATO soared. But there was much less willingness to make sacrifices in order to join. In

May 1996, the Centrum Badania Opinii Publicznej polling center looked at how Poles felt about the costs of joining NATO.[4] The great majority (83 percent) thought the financial burden would be high. When they were asked if the country should shoulder this burden "at the expense of other spheres of public expenditure," a mere 23 percent said yes. As many as 58 percent said that Poland should wait to join NATO until the country's economic situation allows for an increase in military spending.

However, these doubts on the part of the public were never translated into active opposition to NATO membership, because of the different nature of the NATO accession process. Unlike with EU accession, only limited areas of society and the economy had to be changed in order to join NATO, and the process could be conducted privately and even secretly by political, military, and bureaucratic elites out of the public domain. Thus the list of tasks to be set by NATO and implemented as a condition for Polish membership was never published and the cost of the program was never openly discussed. The tensions which the process of modernization and adaptation engendered within the armed forces never fully came out into the open.

By the same token, the criticism of the pace of implementation of these tasks by the Polish armed forces which was voiced in private by NATO was never articulated in public. Faulty procurement procedures for purchases of military equipment also aroused criticism in the United States and other western suppliers, but again these were rarely voiced openly. All this was in contrast to the EU accession negotiations, which were almost invariably conducted in an atmosphere of open dispute over the conditions of membership and thus had a direct effect on the way the public viewed EU membership (see below).

Thus when Poland, together with the Czech Republic and Hungary, finally joined NATO in March 1999, the general public was unaware of the inevitable tensions which had accompanied the accession process. Support admittedly had slipped to 60 percent, but opposition was at a low 11 percent, with the rest declaring that either they did not know or did not care.[5] Still, in the main, people saw NATO membership as a crowning achievement of Poland's democratization process, which had now been granted rock-solid security guarantees. It seemed then that the time had finally passed—which had lasted even as late as 1980 and 1981—of Poles fearing invasion. Thanks to NATO, Poland was supposedly set to enjoy the security which western European countries had had since 1945.

This feeling was not badly marred by the small shock caused by the Kosovo war. Just as Poland joined NATO, the alliance went to war for the first time in its history. The action admittedly failed to generate much enthusiasm and left public opinion divided on the issue of how far Poland should get involved. Opinion polls after three weeks of bombing showed that 61 percent of Poles thought that the Kosovo action could lead to a world war while 40 percent were against sending in ground troops if the bombing failed to achieve NATO's war aims. A smaller number—36 percent—thought that troops should be sent in. Even fewer—31 percent—thought that Polish troops should be involved, and the vast majority of that group thought that the soldiers should be volunteers.[6]

However, since the war was short and successful and Polish troops did not in fact have to fight, the long-term support rate for NATO was not affected. In February 2000, 60 percent declared themselves to be still in favor of continued NATO membership.[7] This was the same number as had supported membership in March 1999 on the date of entry. Support has remained remarkably stable since. In October 2001, after the United States had for the first time invoked NATO's article 5 and Polish officials in response had said publicly "we are now at war," support stayed the same as at the moment of entry—59 percent.[8]

Joining the EU: A Public Process

Comparing Polish attitudes towards NATO and EU membership is difficult in the sense that Poland has been a member of the military alliance since the spring of 1999, while at the time of writing, it seems that at best the country will join the European Union in 2004. Furthermore, while EU membership hardly impinges on the military sphere, it impinges on almost everything else—whereas NATO membership covers all things military but little else. And as has been stated, negotiations with NATO were conducted behind closed doors, whereas the EU negotiations are inevitably a very public process. However, attitudes to both are alike in that membership in both organizations is seen to represent different aspects of Poland coming home to the west and achieving full security.

In the early 1990s, Polish support for membership in the EU was high. As late as May 1996, support for EU membership in polls was at 80 percent while opposition reached a mere 8 percent. A year later, the support figure was at 70 percent and only began to dip (still to a high 66 percent) in mid-1998, when the membership negotiations started. A year later,[9] the support figure fell to 55 percent, and until 2002 it oscillated around 50 percent. Meanwhile, opposition climbed steadily to around 25 percent. (The balance was made up of the do-not-knows.)

This declining support for and rising opposition to EU membership reflects the fact that the public negotiation process has increasingly brought home to ordinary people the reality that EU membership would seriously change their present way of life—in many cases perhaps for the worse. This has been especially true of the countryside, where several factors are at work. These include a conservative nationalist and religious fear of the impact of "atheist" and "decadent" western culture (it is interesting that the countryside has also been less enthusiastic about NATO membership than the urban population, reflecting a deep insularity, conservatism, and suspicion of all things foreign on the part of the farmers).

Even more important, there is worry that joining the EU will not be in the interests of most living Polish farmers. They see the short-term negative impact of subsidized EU imports into Poland, and of EU demands for very costly improvements to Polish agricultural technology, especially in the fields of health and safety. Conversely, they think with good reason that under Poland's accession terms, the subsidies available to Polish farmers under the Common Agricultural Policy will be much smaller than those enjoyed by farmers in the existing member states. It is feared therefore that the ultimate effect will be to force most Polish small farmers off the land, while more and more of the agricultural sector is dominated by large agribusiness.

But even before the support rates began to fall to the point where the success of a referendum on EU accession could be in doubt, the answers to another poll question revealed a fairly high degree of nervousness about the process. When Poles were asked in December 1998 whether the country should enter the European Union "as soon as possible," 34 percent said yes. But 50 percent said that the country "should first modernize and then join."[10] This was contrary to government policy, which was to press ahead as fast as possible, but it showed a great deal of apprehension about local firms" and farmers' chances of survival in open competition with western European rivals in the Single Market.

These worries will inevitably have an effect on the result of the EU accession referendum. The referendum will also be decided on the basis of the general mood in the country; and this in turn will reflect the feeling of ordinary Poles about the whole process of westernizing democratic change and free-market reform which has occurred since 1989, of which EU membership is seen by many as the completion. For as Polish sociologist Lena Kolarska-Bobinska has noted, the only thing that is common to those who support EU membership is their support for the changes which came after 1989.[11] Conversely, those who are generally unhappy about developments since 1989 also tend to oppose membership in the EU.

Inevitably, therefore, the worse the economic situation, the less well people will judge the economic reforms which brought Poland a market economy, and this could translate into a rejection of the European Union. Indeed, the referendum will in this respect not be a vote for or against EU membership but rather a plebiscite on the post-1989 economic record.

As of 2001, there was, therefore, considerable anxiety among pro-EU forces about the likely outcome of the referendum. For as a result of the global economic downturn, in 2001 economic growth slowed and unemployment grew to record levels, even as inflation fell. At the time of writing, prospects for a recovery in 2002 or even in 2003 were slim. Thus the accession referendum slated for 2003 could well take place in a situation in which people are unhappier than ever before about the effects of the reform process.

Accession Negotiations and Polish Politics

The first phase of the negotiations, between March 1998 and September 2001, was handled by the center-right government headed by Jerzy Buzek, an academic and Solidarity advisor. His administration—which brought a cluster of right-wing parties around the Solidarity trade union into an uneasy coalition with the pro market Freedom Union—appointed Ryszard Czarnecki of the Catholic Christian Nationalist Union (ZChN) movement to head EU policy making. Czarnecki, whose ZChN party was never especially enthusiastic about the EU, adopted a combative pose towards Brussels and declared that under his direction Poland would "talk tough" with the European Commission. After a series of rows with Brussels, Czarnecki was asked by the prime minister to resign, and he did so. After that, relations with the EU improved.

However, the notion of "talking tough" and "extracting a good deal" from the accession negotiations entered the vocabulary of the political elite. This attitude may be good for assessing the success or failure of conventional talks between parties who have separate interests and who after the talks have ended will remain as separate entities. But accession negotiations with the EU are different, and all countries which participate in them soon realize that this is the case. For one thing, the body of community law, the *acquis communautaire* is nonnegotiable. The best that can be hoped for is to be able to negotiate exemptions, limited in time, from specific laws.

For another thing, the partner negotiating the accession agreement will be joining the EU as a result of the negotiations. Thus the negotiations are between the present and future members of the Union. In theory at least, this process is not antagonistic, but rather one in which both sides seek the best possible conditions of future cooperation within the EU. In practice, however, existing members often ruthlessly defend their national interests against those of applicants. This causes great resentment among applicants and naturally weakens their position still further.

Czarnecki set the tone for the nationalist right. The right is divided between those parties like the League of Polish Families (LPR), which won a foothold in parliament in the September 2001 elections and rejects Polish EU membership outright, and those parties like the ZChN or the newly formed Law and Justice movement (PiS), also now in parliament, which argue for EU membership—but on the "right terms." The right-terms issue is a pertinent one, because the September 2001 election was won by the SLD with a 43 percent share of the popular vote, which took them to just below an overall majority in the key lower chamber of the Polish parliament, the Sejm.

The SLD is a successor party to the PZPR, and while its democratic credentials are now impeccable (it has, after all, won two elections in the past eleven years within the framework of the present system), the nationalist right still views it as a party which in the past has betrayed Poland's independence and could do so again. This translates into a double threat for the accession process led by the SLD. For one thing, it is easy for the nationalist right to present the SLD as a party which is "genetically" unable to conceive of a truly independent Polish state.

The slogan employed by the nationalist right is "Moscow—yesterday, Brussels—today and tomorrow." By contrast, the center-right opposition is keen on EU membership for Poland and is ready, for want of a better alternative, even to see the SLD lead Poland into "Europe." But here again, there are growing suspicions that the SLD's undoubted commitment to EU membership is dictated not so much by the long-term interest of the country as a whole as by a party interest, which maintains that entry will be followed by an inflow of EU funds that will bolster the position of the ruling party and give it a run in power lasting another term or two.

All this tends to strengthen resistance to an EU entry drive led by the formerly communist SLD. Should the accession agreement fail to produce terms which could be presented to the Polish countryside and farmers as fair and generous, then the stage will be set for an anti-EU alliance among the rural population, the right-wing opposition, and small businesses afraid of competition. These forces could be cemented by a conservative and "Euroskeptic" Catholic parish clergy. And as certain western European examples show, the threat to the EU presented by such an alliance will not disappear even after Poland becomes an EU member.

As a result of these threats, *Unia & Polska*, an independent magazine devoted to EU affairs, invited the leaders of the six main political movements fighting the 2001 parliamentary campaign to sign a pact committing them to cooperate on EU issues after the election. The "Pact for European Integration" was signed a month before the election by Jerzy Buzek, the then–prime minister and head of the Solidarity Electoral Action (AWS). Bronislaw Geremek, the head of the Freedom Union; Leszek Miller, the head of the SLD; and Maciej Plazynski, the head of the Civic Platform, a free-market group. It committed the signatories to consult with each other on negotiating positions and to defend the negotiating policy against domestic critics once it had been agreed.[12]

But while the pact secured the support of four signatories, two other key elements failed to show up. These were Jaroslaw Kalinowski, the head of the PSL and Lech Kaczynski, the head of the right-wing PiS. Both failed to sign because they were afraid of criticism from the Euroskeptic wings of their respective movements. Indeed, Buzek also came in for a storm of criticism from his own AWS for signing the pact. After the election, the effectiveness of the pact was further weakened by the failure of either the Freedom Union or the AWS to win seats in parliament.

Meanwhile, the SLD won the election and established a government coalition with the Polish Peasant Party to secure a majority in parliament. But in an unexpected development, the strongly anti-EU LPR also entered parliament, as did Samoobrona ("Self Defense") a strongly populist and nationalist movement with a base in the countryside and small towns. These two groups proceeded to vociferously oppose Polish concessions which the

SLD had proposed to Brussels.[13] The fierce attack threw the SLD-led government, which had failed earlier to consult with the opposition on its new negotiating position, on the defensive.

Later efforts were made to revive the pact and repair relations with opposition parties such as the Civic Platform, with a view to once more presenting the drive for EU membership as a truly national effort and not just an SLD project. The whole EU accession process has therefore become completely intertwined with Polish domestic politics and political rivalries. By contrast, the negotiations with NATO—which were also conducted in the main by the SLD when in power—never had this problem, because NATO membership always enjoyed the support of a cross-party consensus.

The Future of Poland and the West

As of 2001, not only had no referendum on Polish membership taken place, but Polish–EU accession talks still had to close crucial and highly divisive chapters—agriculture, financial support for underdeveloped regions, and budget issues. However, one thing is already clear. Psychologically, Poland is joining the two organizations as they were in the past rather than as they will be in the future—and Poles are far from prepared for the changes that lie ahead. The widespread feeling that accession means achieving a position of unchanging, unchallenged stability is highly mistaken.

In the case of NATO, this has already become clear. Poles wanted NATO membership first and foremost as a guarantee of security against a possible resurgence of Russian territorial ambitions, from which they had suffered so terribly in the past. Polish support for an enlargement of NATO to the Baltic states and smaller countries to the south, such as Slovakia and Slovenia, is also aimed at increasing Polish security against a repeat of a Russian attempt to reach into central Europe; and many Poles hope that Ukraine and even Belarus might be turned into western buffer states against Russia.

This explains why article 5 of the NATO treaty is sacrosanct for Poles. That they interpret article 5 as an automatic commitment by all NATO members to go to the armed defense of any member which is attacked becomes clear. Core Polish security fears also lead Poles to a more unquestioning dependence on the United States than is the case among other NATO members; and this is strengthened by the belief that the Polish American lobby can influence U.S. policy in a pro-Polish direction.

This obsession with the supposed Russian threat also means that Polish governments will always instinctively accept United States–led operations like Kosovo or U.S. invocations of article 5 in the case of a terrorist attack—even though these do not belong within the traditional vision of NATO as it seen by the Poles. This also explains a certain Polish mistrust of EU plans for an EU rapid reaction force. This is seen as contributing little to the defense of central Europe against Russia while potentially weakening a United States–led NATO which can be relied on to react against Russian aggression.

This old-style, historically conditioned thinking among Poland's military and political establishment has remained largely untouched both by the colossal changes of the 1990s and by developments since the terrorist attacks of September 11, 2001—the event that led to the invocation of article 5 for the first time in NATO's history. The public discussion surrounding this, however, also brought out for the first time that the guarantees that article 5 appears to provide are not in fact automatic and that the clause stipulating that NATO members "shall undertake action which they shall deem essential" in response to an attack on one of them does not automatically secure action by all NATO members to defend Polish territory against all forms of attack.

More important has been the sudden improvement in relations between Russia and the United States, which found a common enemy in Islamic fundamentalist terrorism. This encouraged moves, strongly urged by the United Kingdom and some other western European governments, to create new NATO–Russian security institutions giving Moscow an equal say in some fields of NATO decision making. The improvement in U.S.–Russian relations may well prove short-lived. But if it continues, and Russia becomes a trusted partner of NATO, this will raise questions in Poland as to whether this is the NATO which Poland thought it was joining.

A key question is whether NATO will remain a military alliance or turn into a mainly political organization. Ironically enough, a transformation in this direction is also being encouraged by a process which Poland itself has strongly backed—namely, the expansion of NATO to include more and more disparate members. This question is all the more acute because although the United States invoked article 5 after September 11, it then conducted military operations—initially at least—almost alone, and insisted on unconditional control of them. This decision may have been understandable given the cumbersome nature of NATO's decision-making process, but it inevitably raised the question of what is the real purpose of NATO at the start of the twenty-first century.

At the start of the twenty-first century, this question was only beginning to be asked in Poland. When it was posed, the automatic answer from Poland's military tended to be that NATO is as it was and will always remain so—a manifestly inadequate response. There was a recognition among certain establishment figures—like former defense minister Janusz Onyszkiewicz or General Stanislaw Koziej—that article 5 needed to be reworded to take into account situations such as the one engendered by September 11. Indeed, Koziej noted after the September 11 attacks that article 5 may have been "invoked too hastily." He wondered aloud if the interpretation now given to article 5 "continues to look that optimistic from Poland's point of view."

Koziej also suggested that the very nature of the forces NATO has at its disposal should be changed. In his view, NATO should also be able to deploy police, anti-terrorist, and rescue units. "NATO should be able to operate in an integrated civilian and military capacity ... for if it remains as a purely military force then it will be fated to wither away." NATO forces must be reshaped in order to be able not only to defend their own territory but also conduct "expeditionary" operations.[14]

In the case of the EU, the process of internal reform remains quite inadequate—and this is likely to be cruelly revealed by the strains which will accompany enlargement to take in up to ten new members. In Poland, a debate on the subject of how the EU itself needed to change began at the turn of the century and was expected to run in parallel to the debate on Polish accession. Here again, though, the Polish desire was to join an EU which resembles the EU of the past as much as possible.

This meant an EU with a strong feeling of mutual solidarity between the member states, in which the European Commission defines the European interest and looks after the smaller and less developed states in the face of the bigger countries. It meant the continuation of a Common Agricultural Policy involving generous subsidies to new as well as old members. As in the past, defense and foreign affairs would be left to the member states and the central EU institutions would have no significant role in them. In a word, Poland is aiming to join the EU of the 1970s and 1980s—the body which helped Spain, Portugal, and Ireland to develop at a phenomenal pace but which in security and foreign policy followed the U.S. lead.

Unfortunately for Poland, it is very unlikely that the EU of the twenty-first century will be willing or able to subsidize its new eastern European members the way that it did previous generations of applicants. And although the future of the EU's Common Foreign and Security Policy is highly unclear, it is likely to include a considerable measure of friction with the increasingly unilateralist trend of U.S. policy.

Indeed, Poland and the other countries which have already joined or aspire to join NATO, and are candidates for the EU, risk falling into a trap of their own making. They are seeking to join organizations which they know from past experience to have been successful and which have brought benefits to their members. But the very act of their joining threatens to dilute those organizations and change them in such a way as to not permit them to deliver those same benefits in the future. Both NATO and the European Union could evolve into organizations with an inner core and an outer circle. Most of the "old" members would then become participants in an inner core, leaving the new members from the former communist bloc in the outer circle.

This scenario has already been posited by some observers in the EU, and such a development of NATO is suggested by the behavior of the United States in Kosovo and still more Afghanistan. NATO, as it stands, is an unwieldy instrument incapable of conducting far-off military operations. After still further enlargement in 2002, it will need an inner core of major states if it is to function effectively and justify its continued existence.

In either case, Poland and the other new NATO and EU members face the risk of being left out in the cold. Thanks to membership, they would receive a badge of approval supposedly signifying that they are full-fledged members of the "democratic free market community of nations." In reality, however, they would still remain outsiders and as such would be forced, by and large, to look after for their own economic and political development. Time will tell whether this is only a speculative illusion or whether it could become the reality for the new members of both NATO and an enlarged European Union.

Notes

1. In the late 1970s, the Polish Independence Caucus (PPN), a group of intellectuals headed by Zdzislaw Najder, working as an underground think tank, put out a policy paper postulating that Poland should join the European Union.

2. Centrum Badania Opinii Publicznej, BS 111, 1996 (Warsaw, May 1996).

3. Centrum Badania Opinii Publicznej, BS/33/33/96 (Warsaw, January 1996).

4. Centrum Badania Opinii Publicznej, BS/103/101/96 (Warsaw, July 1996).

5. Centrum Badania Opinii Spolecznej, BS/35/99 (Warsaw, March 1999).

6. Centrum Badania Opinii Spolecznej, BS/64/99 (Warsaw, April 1999).

7. Centrum Badania Opinii Spolecznej, BS/45/00 (Warsaw, March 2000).

8. Centrum Badania Opinii Spolecznej, BS /136/01 (Warsaw, October 2001).

9. Centrum Badania Opinii Spolecznej, BS/92/99 (Warsaw, May 1999).

10. Centrum Badania Opinii Publicznej BS/5/5/99 (Warsaw, January 1999).

11. Lena Kolarska-Bobinska, ed., *Polacy wobec wielkiej zmiany. Integracja z Unia Europejska* [The Poles face critical choices] (Warsaw: ISP, 2001), p. 9.

12. *Unia & Polska*, September 3, 2001.

13. The new government proposed two key concessions to Brussels in the autumn 2001. Both were designed to break the deadlock that the previous administration had left in the talks and to enable Poland to catch up with the other applicant countries. One concession saw Poland accepting a suspension of the right of citizens from the new member states to work in the present EU member states for between two and seven years. This went through without controversy at home. The other concession saw Poland lowering the period during which it would ban land sales to foreigners from eighteen to twelve years and agreeing to sell land to foreign farmers who were willing to cultivate it personally after leasing the land for three years. This provoked a fierce attack which saw LPR leaders accusing the SLD of "giving away our land."

The issue is an emotive one in Poland. This is because the struggle for land ownership marked a major part of the fight to maintain the nation's identity in the late nineteenth century in the face of efforts by the Prussian state to eliminate the Polish presence in western Poland. Currently land in Poland is cheap leading to fears that Germans will once more seek to purchase large tracts especially in the west of the country. Fears are also expressed that descendants of the German populations expelled from former German territories in 1944–1946 could return and gradually "re-Germanize" these areas.

14. Remarks by General Stanislaw Koziej at the conference on "NATO in the Twenty-First Century" organized by Poland's Euro-Atlantic Association, Warsaw, December 2001.

11

The Europe Question
in Romania and Moldova

Charles King

In 1919, on the occasion of a visit to Bucharest by a delegation of French academics, the preeminent Romanian historian Nicolae Iorga provided his guests with a *tour d'horizon* of Greater Romania, the enlarged state created in the territorial settlements at the end of the war:

> We, the fourteen million Romanians—living in ancient Dacia, between the Tisza, the Danube, and the Dnestr rivers, as well as beyond the Dnestr in the depths of Russia, and beyond the Danube ... in the gorges of the Pindus mountains and in the villages of Mount Olympus, the abode of our Thracian gods and of their brothers, the gods of the Hellenes ...—[we are] the most numerous people in Europe's southeast and the most capable of developing, with the support of our friends, a civilization superior to that of our neighbors. We are the scions of that oriental Rome, which we have piously preserved, far above any provincial distinctions, in the name of our language and our people: Romanian.[1]

Few ethnic Romanians today would disagree with Iorga's basic assessment. The boundaries of the state that emerged from World War I were somewhat diminished by the territorial changes following World War II, but

Romanian national mythology embodies a powerful image of the country as the inheritor of the language and traditions of Rome, a quintessentially European culture and civilization stranded on the periphery of the continent.

This image is a powerful and appealing one for Romanians, but it has always had a limited relation to reality. In recent years, it has sat very uneasily with the evolution of domestic politics and the vicissitudes of international relations across the Romanian lands, in Romania itself and in the former Soviet republic of Moldova. Romania's 1989 revolution, captured on television, seemed a legitimate popular uprising against communist tyranny.

But when the smoke cleared, it turned out that many of the senior officers of Nicolae Ceausescu's police state had simply replaced their former commander so that they could remain in power and redistribute state property to themselves and their business allies. President Ion Iliescu and the Party of Social Democracy (under several names) were based on the former Communist Party and secret service, the feared Securitate. They remained in office from 1990 to 1996; after a four-year hiatus, they were brought back to power in 2000, this time supported in a tacit parliamentary alliance by the chauvinist Greater Romania Party.

In the then–Soviet republic of Moldova, as the Soviet Union collapsed in the early 1990s, a separatist war by Russian-speaking Soviet loyalists erupted at the same time as a local pan-Romanian awakening. This left nearly a fifth of the country under the control of the unrecognized "Dnestr Moldova Republic" (Transnistria) and drew energy away from the tasks of political and economic reform. In 2001, the Communist Party was returned to power in Moldovan elections, on a platform of opposing radical economic reforms and seeking closer relations with Moscow. In both Romania and Moldova, the 1990s saw severe and continuing economic decline, which has still not been reversed. Social services and the living standards of the mass of the population in both countries in 2001 were well below their levels in the 1980s. More than a decade after the end of communism and the collapse of the Soviet Union, both Romania and Moldova may actually be farther away from western Europe in real terms than they were before.

This chapter assesses the nature of debates within Romania and Moldova about each country's relationship with European and Euro-Atlantic institutions, and the effects that future waves of enlargement of those institutions are likely to have on the two states. The first section provides a brief overview of political and economic developments in each country, highlighting their growing distance from the relatively successful developments in central Europe.

The second section describes the range of opinion in both countries about relations with the European Union and its members, and with each other. The third section turns to the institutional relations with the EU. The fourth examines several areas in which the next round of EU expansion will matter for Romanian and Moldovan affairs. The conclusion argues for rethinking the EU's relationship with these states and, more broadly, for developing a clear strategy towards countries that, for the foreseeable future, are likely to remain outside the new boundaries of the expanded Euro-Atlantic institutions.

The Interminable "Transition"

For average Romanians, the period of "transition" from communism to democracy and the free market has looked nearly endless, and there must be real concern about whether the country will in fact ever "arrive." The economy contracted significantly each year in the late 1990s, and experienced only modest growth in 2000. There are few major positive signs on the horizon; at best, miniscule growth in the coming years, with inflation above 30 percent in 2001 and perhaps, optimistically, about 25 percent by 2002. The economy is likely to remain, in the words of international rating agencies, "fragile."[2]

As of 2001, a third of Romanians live below the nationally defined poverty line.[3] The popular western media image of Romania—homeless street children, HIV-ravaged orphanages, packs of feral dogs loping around Bucharest—is not too different from the realities faced by average citizens. Emigration, legal or otherwise, has been the major outlet for their discontent. In 2000, the country's main intellectual journal, 22, sponsored an essay contest for teenagers on the theme "Why I would (or wouldn't) leave Romania." The first-place winner argued that, to her regret, she had to go:

> Today, neither the IMF nor the European Union can convince young people that there are reasons to stay in Romania. . . . Emigration has almost become a categorical imperative. . . . My motivations for leaving are to some degree the same as those of other young people: a desire for success, recognition of one's merit, security.[4]

Political developments have not been much more encouraging than economic ones. From 1990 to 1996, Romania was governed (under various labels) by the Party of Social Democracy (PSDR), with the party's effective leader, Ion Iliescu, as president. Over those six years, the country experienced interethnic violence—albeit fortunately limited—in Transylvania, several violent large-scale disturbances in downtown Bucharest, economic stagnation, and a growing distance between the country and its central European neighbors in terms of political reform and economic performance.

In 1996, western observers welcomed the electoral victory of the Democratic Convention (DCR), the main opposition coalition, and the advent of Emil Constantinescu, a former university rector, as president. But the former opposition proved as incapable as the PSDR of charting a clear reform course. Infighting within the governing coalition, and even within its core party, the National Christian Democratic Peasant Party, blocked serious progress.

In terms of corruption, government under the pro-reform parties turned out to be little cleaner than under Iliescu. Whereas the PSDR had overseen the sell-off of industrial assets to political supporters, the DCR government followed the same course in the banking sector. The failure of several important banks, because of nonperforming loans made on political rather than financial criteria, further weakened the economy. President Constantinescu was so dismayed by the performance of his own party's government that he announced in July 2000 that corruption and maladministration were so great that he would not seek a second term.

It was not surprising that Iliescu and the PSDR swept to victory in the 2000 elections.[5] But the most significant and worrying development was the strong showing by the Greater Romania Party (GRP) and its leader, Corneliu Vadim Tudor. The GRP—a strongly nationalist organization whose newspaper, *Romania Mare* (Greater Romania), regularly publishes diatribes against Jews, Hungarians, homosexuals, and other minorities—came in second place in the elections, with Tudor himself facing Iliescu in the second round of the presidential race.

The economic situation has been even worse in Moldova. In 1998, about 90 percent of the population lived on less than $2 a day, a figure that has probably not improved since then.[6] Corruption has become endemic, with Moldova now ranked as one of the most corrupt countries in the former Soviet Union—and one of the worst in the world.[7] Although political leaders still regularly speak of an economic "crisis," it is clear that Moldova is in fact chronically poor, a developing country where strategies of aid and assistance will be closer to those needed in central Africa than in central Europe. With government revenues at less than a quarter of GDP, the country does not have sufficient revenue to maintain even basic public services left by the Soviet Union.

Even if Moldova were to achieve the spectacular—and incredible—annual growth rate of 10 percent over the next decade, national income at the end of this period would still only be where it was before the Soviet Union disintegrated.[8] It should not be surprising, therefore, that the vast majority of Moldovans are strongly critical of their government. In a February 2000 survey, 88 percent said that "democracy" was not working out to their satisfaction—a figure roughly the same across all ethnic groups in the country.[9]

Individual solutions to these problems have been at times comic, but more often tragic. For a while, the Moldovan state telephone company sold its telephone switches for use by explicit phone-sex lines in the United States. The government even contemplated selling its international Internet identifier—".md"—to an association of American medical doctors. A highly disproportionate number of East European émigrés to western Europe, especially young women working as prostitutes, come from Romania and Moldova. Moldovan officials estimate that as many as 500,000 citizens—more than a tenth of the Soviet-era population—may now be working abroad in Europe, Turkey, and Israel, with hundreds of thousands more working in Russia.[10] In March 2001, the Moldovan representative at NATO headquarters joined them, disappearing without a trace after he faxed a letter of resignation to his embassy in Brussels.

By contrast, despite the parlous economy, Moldova's trend in democratization was rather good for much of the 1990s. Unlike many of its post-Soviet neighbors, the country has had a strong commitment to democracy; elections have been free and fair, and there has been no effort to create the effective single-party or quasi-dynastic systems characteristic farther east. But in 2001, Moldova's democracy produced the overwhelming victory of the Party of Communists and the subsequent election of its leader, Vladimir Voronin, as president.

Moldova thus topped a series of firsts: The first country in the Commonwealth of Independent States (CIS) to be admitted to the Council of Europe and the first to institute a constitutional system based on parliamentary democracy (in 2000), also became the first since 1991 to elect a government that still officially defined itself as "communist." One key reason for Moldova's failure to move towards western Europe was the unappealing example of neighboring Romania's economic decline. An economically successful Romania would have provided a westernizing magnet for Moldova, but this seems unlikely to be the case for the foreseeable future.

In both Romania and Moldova, behind the economic and political debacles of the past decade have run important debates about the strategic orientations of both states and, even deeper, about the place of Romania and Moldova in Europe as a whole. While these debates have sometimes been carried on in the rarefied air of intellectual publications and coffeehouse controversies, they do reflect the real complexity of the evolving relationship with NATO and the EU.

The Context of Debates about Europe

Like most of their southeast European neighbors, Romanians' conceptions of national identity have been fundamentally linked with western Europe. Indeed, far from being an atavistic reaction against modernity, Romanian nationalism was a product of it. From the late eighteenth century on, Romanian nationalism was strongest in the areas closest to central Europe, in the Transylvania region that was part of Austria-Hungary before World War I.

This was both the most economically developed of the Romanian lands, and the one where the Romanian identity was under the strongest threat of assimilation by the dominant Hungarians. It was Transylvanian Romanians who first worked to standardize written Romanian and to recreate its Latin roots and purge it of words loaned from Slavic and Magyar, and who provided the most articulate spokespeople for the Romanian national cause in Paris and London. Becoming "Romanian"—throwing off Iorga's "provincial distinctions"—has also been fundamentally about the aspiration to become "European."

There were, however, important countervailing trends. In the nineteenth century and early twentieth centuries, intellectuals less enthusiastic about Romania's modernization—often linked to the Orthodox Church, with its historic suspicion of the western churches—worried that the uniquely "Romanian" character of the state and culture would be lost in the shuffle to adopt western European values. The anti-cosmopolitan reaction, typical in many eastern European countries during the same period, took two major forms. One argued for a radical return to more "authentic" Romanian traditions, a kind of agrarian populism which saw the peasant as the embodiment of genuine Romanian identity and tradition. Another lambasted the false cosmopolitanism of Bucharest, which styled itself the "Little Paris" between the two world wars. As Titu Maiorescu, the most articulate spokesperson for this view, argued in the late nineteenth century, Romanians had created *forme fara fond*—forms without substance—in their drive to become fully European.

These debates played out very differently on the territory of present-day Moldova. Before 1918, much of the region had been the backwater province of Bessarabia within the Russian empire. Although the local majority population spoke Romanian, connections with the Romanian center to the west were slim. Bessarabia's inhabitants saw themselves as more "Russian"—in a broad cultural and above all religious, if not ethnic, sense—than Romanian. When a national movement did arise in the province in the early years of the twentieth century, it was originally no more "national" than that of many other outlying provinces, with its members arguing for the internal reform of the empire, not its destruction.

The turmoil of the end of World War I, however, squelched this nascent reform movement; with the assistance of local pro-Romanian sympathizers, Bessarabia was occupied by Romanian troops and absorbed into the newly created Greater Romania. It remained there, one of the poorest regions of the enlarged Romanian state, until it was taken by the Soviet Union in 1940 and transformed into the Moldovan Soviet Socialist Republic, with the addition of the Trandniestrian territory, transferred from Soviet Ukraine.

Both Romania and independent Moldova thus entered the postcommunist era with two different but related debates on the agenda of both policy makers and intellectuals: one about these newly sovereign or newly independent states' relationship with western Europe, the other about their relationship with each other.

Since 1989 in Romania, several questions about the past—about Romania's uniqueness, its supposed European heritage, its place within European history and culture—have inevitably once again come to the fore. Nationalism is rarely so self-confident that it can stand too much self-criticism. But because of the gap between aspirations and historical realities, Romanians have been particularly averse to reflective self-examination.

During the communist period, indigenous Romanian nationalism was fused with the ideology of Marx and the economic plan, creating a hybrid form of national communism whose basic tenets even survived the end of Soviet communism.

Indeed, two of the country's central cultural institutions—the National Museum and the National Military Museum—remained largely unchanged throughout the first postcommunist decade; the photos of Nicolae Ceausescu were removed, but the basic interpretation of national history remained essentially as it had been under the communists. By the late 1990s, works by Romanian and American historians began to appear which criticized many of these basic ideas.[11] But the spirited and even furious debates surrounding them illustrated the degree to which basic questions of nationhood remained serious issues.

One example of the problems of reassessing national identity concerns the legacy of three key twentieth-century Romanian intellectuals: Mircea Eliade, Emil Cioran, and Constantin Noica. During the communist period, few of their works were allowed to appear. Eliade and Cioran were seen by the communist establishment as bourgeois writers associated with the precommunist past. Eliade moved to the United States after World War II and began a celebrated career as a scholar of comparative religion. Cioran spent much of his writing life in Paris and died there in the early 1990s. Noica, a philosopher who remained in Romania until his death in 1987, was at the center of a small circle of waveringly dissident intellectuals, at times standing in opposition to the Ceausescu regime, at other times making their peace with it.

After 1989, Romanian publishing houses, especially the prestigious Editura Humanitas, began to reissue their works, which had either been banned or discouraged under communism. Eliade, Cioran, and Noica quickly took their place at the center of a new, postcommunist pantheon of Romanian thinkers—all three seen as Romanian originals who had contributed something to European thought in general.

Their legacies, however, have not been without their problems. Both Eliade and Cioran were sympathizers of the fascist Iron Guard movement between the two world wars and were clearly anti-Semitic for much of their early careers. Both were strongly influenced by Nae Ionescu, the philosopher and Bucharest university professor who provided much of the Iron Guard's ideological underpinning. Noica had also been a right-wing sympathizer in his youth, but retreated from public life after his release from prison as a dissident in the early 1960s.[12] In 1996, the Humanitas house published the journal of Mihail Sebastian, a young Romanian-Jewish writer who confirmed the vitriolic anti-Semitism of many leading Romanian intellectuals between the wars, including Eliade and Cioran.[13] When these issues were raised by Romanian writers in intellectual reviews and the popular press, however, they were roundly attacked in public as impugning the philosophical heritage of all three thinkers and, more broadly, questioning Romania's place in the western European intellectual tradition.

As much as they have captured the imagination of intellectuals in Romania, none of these issues has had the slightest resonance in Moldova. Indeed, since books and newspapers from Bucharest rarely find their way to the Moldovan capital Chisinau (or vice visa), debates about nationality and history in Moldova have been largely divorced from those in Romania. They have, however, been no less complex. One issue has lain at the heart of Moldovan domestic politics over the first decade of the country's existence: whether the primary cultural, economic, and strategic orientation should be towards Romania and the west, or towards Russia and the CIS. Pan-Romanianist voices seemed to be winning in the late 1980s and early 1990s, when Moldova adopted Romanian (although still called "Moldovan") as its official language, declared independence from the Soviet Union, and instituted a visa- and passport-free travel regime with Romania.

By the end of the decade, however, the pro-Russian orientation had experienced a resurgence, most notably with the success of the Party of Communists in the 2000 parliamentary elections. Pan-Romanianists retreated to the cultural institutions from which they had come during the late Soviet period—the writers' union newspaper *Literatura si Arta* (Literature and Art), the various institutes of the Academy of Sciences, the state university in Chisinau—and worked to instill a sense of Romanian cultural identity in a young population that still saw itself as Romanian in language but as Moldovan in national identity.

On the second broad set of issues—relations between Romania and Moldova—the debate has been even more complex. In the early 1990s, there was initially a great deal of support in both capitals for enhanced ties. Romania recognized Moldova's independence only a few hours after it was declared in August 1991. Within less than a week, accords were signed on the establishment of embassies and consulates. Some Moldovan Orthodox congregations shifted their allegiance to the Bucharest patriarchate. Early in 1992, both states formed special interministerial committees on bilateral relations, and the Romanian ministry of education set aside funding for scholarships for Moldovan students.

Throughout the 1990s, however, relations in fact oscillated between avowals of pan-Romanian solidarity and mutual recriminations between the two states. Immediately after independence, Moldovan public life was dominated by members and sympathizers of the Popular Front, a congeries of pan-Romanian intellectuals and politicians. But after 1994, when political forces less enthusiastic about the Romanian connection won in parliamentary elections, relations cooled severely. Moldovan voters, suffering from serious economic woes and with little affinity for a cultural heritage that they feel is more Moldovan than Romanian, are generally unenthusiastic about the idea of increased ties between the "two Romanian states."

Ethnic Moldovans, not to mention Slavic-speaking minorities in Moldova, are therefore far from unanimous in their enthusiasm for ties with Romania. Likewise, Romanian voters, preoccupied with their own declining economy and the distant prospect of salvation from Europe, do not see the Moldovan issue as one of their major concerns. Romania continues to assist Moldova: Periodic electricity deliveries have helped reduce Moldova's energy dependence on Russia, and many local journalists believe that Romanian money, perhaps coming from the intelligence services, lies behind the most popular Romanian-language newspaper in Moldova, *Flux*, whose editorial line is strongly critical of politicians the paper considers pro-Russian. But by and large, at the start of the twenty-first century, the ideal of a strong "special relationship" between the two countries has not been realized.

In Romania and Moldova, debates over the vagaries of national identity and "Europeanness" are usually tempests in teacups, carried out in weekly intellectual journals and literary reviews. Reading politics from them can be misleading—rather like trying to understand politics in the United States solely from the *New York Review of Books*. But in both countries, discussion of these issues has also reflected broader problems of party politics, reform, and security. The "Europe question" is, in fact, not just a matter for intellectuals, but a problem of everyday politics as well.

Euro-Atlantic Institutions

In the early 1990s, both Romania and Moldova were quick to distance themselves from the old Soviet and the new Russian orbit. Romania hastily signed a treaty with the Soviet Union in early 1991, but since the Union's demise, it has not negotiated a new interstate treaty with the Russian Federation. Moldova, although a member of the CIS, joined that body only after an effective Russian energy embargo and the threat of punitive trade sanctions; and for most of the 1990s, the country remained on the sidelines of the CIS, declining to participate in most of the Commonwealth's structures, such as the military cooperation agreement. Moldova was indeed a founding member in 1998 of a kind of counter-CIS, the United States–supported GUUAM group of former states (comprising Georgia, Ukraine, Uzbekistan, Azerbaijan, and Moldova).

By contrast, when it comes to western and pro-western institutions, few countries have been such eager team players. Both developed a clear strategy of joining nearly every organization that would have them. Romania was the first country to sign on for NATO's Partnership for Peace; Moldova joined soon after. Both were founding members of Black Sea Economic Cooperation in 1992, and Moldova lobbied hard to join Romania on the International Danubian Commission—even though the precise delimitation of its frontage on the river is still a matter of some dispute. Both joined the Council of Europe, with Moldova becoming the first country in the CIS to do so. Romania acceded to the Central European Free Trade Agreement and was a founding member of both the Southeast European Cooperative Initiative and the Balkan Stability Pact, both of which Moldova has also been keen to join. Because of the romance language spoken in both countries, they also, somewhat bizarrely, managed to gain membership in La Francophonie.

The real prizes, though, have been membership in NATO and the EU. On both fronts, Romania and Moldova have been in the laggard class. In the case of NATO, the needs of U.S. strategy in the Muslim world following September 11, 2001, may have greatly improved Romania's chances; but membership in the EU still looks like an extremely distant goal.

In the run-up to the 1997 Madrid summit, there was intense hope in Romania that the country might be included in the first wave of NATO entrants. It met most of the political criteria for procedural democracy (even if its economy remained weak), and given that it has the largest military in southeastern Europe and a strategic position on the Danube and the Black Sea, there was a clear geostrategic rationale for including it. Desire to join NATO has also meant that military reform has also been the most successful element of the Romanian reform process. But in the end, Romania lost out to the more economically advanced countries of central Europe. The consolation prize was a trip to Bucharest by U.S. president Bill Clinton and the signing of a "strategic partnership" with the United States.

Up to 2001, this was a mere phrase devoid of much real content—though in 1999 Romania helped with the NATO war over Kosovo by closing its airspace to Russian flights. However, the war in Afghanistan, and the prospect of a U.S. war against Iraq, meant that in the wake of September 11 the question of U.S. military access to southeastern European airspace and air bases gained a new importance for planners in Washington. This raised the possibility that despite its dismal record of economic and political reform, Romania (and Bulgaria) might be invited to join NATO in the near future.

In Moldova's case, a provision in the constitution commits the country to neutrality; the continued presence of Russian troops on Moldovan soil has also made relations with NATO difficult. The few eager Atlanticists in Chisinau, though, have pushed intermittently for the neutrality clause to be dropped.

The path to EU membership has been even more painful for both states. Romania officially became a candidate country at the 1999 Helsinki summit. Negotiations on Romanian adoption of the *acquis communautaire* have continued apace. But of all the countries with which Brussels has begun negotiations, Romania is clearly in last place. As of mid-2001, negotiations on only six chapters of the *acquis* had been closed. According to Günter Verheugen, the EU's commissioner for enlargement, the "political, social, and cultural heritage" of Romania make it the most difficult of all the accession countries to integrate into EU institutions.[14]

The EU's report on the progress of accession talks, issued in November 2000, is depressing reading. "Romania's democratic institutions are well established, but the process of decision making remains weak. . . . Little progress has been made in reducing the levels of corruption ... Romania cannot be regarded as a functioning market economy and is not able to cope with competitive pressure and market forces within the Union in the medium term."[15] In Moldova's case, EU membership is nothing more than a very long-term goal. Indeed it is probably no longer even on the table, given communist dominance in parliament and a barely functioning economy.

Despite the disappointments of the past decade, public support for western institutions remains remarkably high in Romania, higher even than in some countries of central Europe. However, this could be precisely because most Romanians understand less than most central Europeans about what the EU really consists of (the evidence of other applicants shows that opposition to membership tends to grow precisely as real negotiations over membership begin).

Polls in May 2000 and 2001 showed that three-quarters of Romanian citizens desired EU membership, and half of that group supported it "unconditionally."[16] The heads of all the major political parties are generally committed to NATO and the EU. One of the few things on which Romanian politicians have been able to agree over the last several years are the joint resolutions in which they have announced their unity on this question.[17] Even the Greater Romania Party has been strongly committed to joining NATO, if for no other reason than, in the words of Corneliu Vadim Tudor, to keep an eye on Hungary.[18]

Europeans, however, have not been nearly as enthusiastic about Romania as Romania has been about them. In March 2001, the EU visa regime for Bulgaria was lifted, making Romania the only one of the accession countries with visa restrictions for European travel still in place. At the public level, Eurobarometer surveys show that average Europeans place Romania last on the list of countries they would like to see join the Union; 45 percent are opposed to Romania's ever becoming a member.[19]

Moldovans have been more reserved concerning both the EU and NATO questions. In a poll in early 2001, just over 51 percent believed that Moldova should strive for integration into the EU; whereas 43 percent opted instead for closer ties with other CIS countries. Support tends to vary with age, but not astronomically so: A third of Moldovans between 18 and 29 years of age rejected the EU idea, compared with about half those over 60.[20] Most Moldovans report never even thinking of themselves as European. The ethnic breakdown, however, is not as one might expect; ethnic Russians tend to think of themselves as European more often than do ethnic Moldovans, and the former are also more likely to know more about the EU—where its headquarters is, for example—than the latter. The real ethnic difference is over NATO: At the turn of the century, 72 percent of ethnic Moldovans thought membership would be desirable, notwithstanding the political elite's commitment to neutrality, while only 31 percent of ethnic Russians felt the same way.[21]

Romania's drive to join the west has been politically consistent, if far from consistently successful, but beginning in early 2001, Moldova's political orientation underwent a significant shift. The emergence of the Party of

Communists, which won a huge majority in the parliament and elected the party leader, Voronin, as president, marked a serious transformation of Moldovan foreign policy. Voronin's first trip abroad, in April 2001, was to Moscow, where he backtracked on the idea of removing Russian troops from Moldova and reaffirmed Moldova's policy of holding aloof from the NATO accession process. Since then, he has also repeatedly stressed his desire that Moldova join the Russia–Belarus union and has said that the Chinese Communist Party could be a model for his own.[22] Moldova must now "resist Europe," he has said, "just as Cuba resists the U.S."[23]

The Impact of Euro-Atlantic Enlargement

Neither Romania nor Moldova will become members of the EU any time soon, and Moldova is also extremely unlikely to join NATO, except in circumstances of a complete overturn of the existing international system. The strong electoral showing by the Greater Romania Party darkened the chances of Romania even joining NATO—at least temporarily—even though the early performance of the PSDR-dominated government in the economic sphere was relatively encouraging.

Moldova, for its part, is now regularly labeled the poorest country in Europe. It is the first country in the world to bring Communists to power in free and fair elections; much of its territory is outside the central government's control; and it has a constitutional commitment to neutrality. For the foreseeable future, these two states will be the frontline of a wider southeastern European region on the periphery of NATO and an enlarged EU.

The process of European and Euro-Atlantic enlargement will nevertheless have an important impact on both countries. Domestic factors will continue to be the primary determinants of the behavior of Romanian and Moldovan politicians, but the shape and speed of EU and NATO enlargement can have an effect on the perceptions, incentives, and resources—especially rhetorical—of local actors.

The Primacy of Domestic Politics

Despite Romania's rejection by NATO in 1997, its possible rejection again in the second round of enlargement, and its last-place running in the race for EU enlargement, by the turn of the century there was very little back-lash in Romania against Euro-Atlantic institutions. Public support among the public and politicians for the EU–NATO path remained high, even if in practice politicians have been generally unwilling to make the hard reform choices that would make membership in the EU a real possibility.

Like his analogues elsewhere in eastern Europe, the rhetoric of the Greater Romania Party and its leader, Corneliu Vadim Tudor, can some-times be anti-European, especially when Tudor speaks of the need to pro-tect Romanian traditions and not sacrifice Romanian "dignity" for the sake of membership in the European club. However, electoral support for Tudor and his party in 2000 was far more the result of extreme dissatisfaction with the political alternatives—especially the disastrous Democratic Con-vention and its constituent parties—than with any fundamental agreement between Tudor and the masses on the more radical aspects of the Greater Romania program.

Indeed, Tudor has one of the highest consistently negative ratings of all Romanian politicians, his strong electoral showing notwithstanding.[24] His main base of support seems to be relatively poor, non-college-educated, middle-aged men who live in wealthier regions of the country, the Romanian equivalent of the "angry white males" of American politics.[25] (In the 2000 elections, however, age was not a predictor of support for Tudor.) His move-ment beyond this rather small base relies on there being a generally weak and divided slate of centrist candidates, precisely the situation that obtained in the last elections. Although Tudor is a talented rhetorician, and arguably the best campaigner in Romanian politics, the current government probably only needs to show a modicum of success—especially in the economy and the fight against corruption—to significantly diminish his showing.

But that, of course, is the rub. Successful economic reform has eluded every Romanian regime since 1989. Domestic discontent was the fuel for Tudor's campaign in 2000, especially for the many young Romanians out-side his core constituency who switched their votes to Tudor in the second round of the presidential race. But if there is a clear rejection of Romania by the west, Tudor's hand will be strengthened. Again, the reason has little to do with a Romanian "backlash" against Euro-Atlantic institutions. Eighty percent of Romanians believe the country was left out of the first round of enlargement because it failed to meet the criteria, and not because of anti-Romanian sentiment, a Hungarian conspiracy, or any of the other "expla-nations" proffered by Tudor's most recondite backers.[26] But the failure of the current PSDR government to show at least some success on the European front would nonetheless be a sign to Romanian voters, even the most pro-European ones, that they had little to lose by backing Tudor.

The Hungarian Question

By the turn of the century, Romania already bordered on a NATO country, Hungary, and seemed set to border the EU as well. NATO enlargement had had virtually no impact on Romanian reality; apart from a general sense of disappointment after the Madrid summit, life in Romania the day after the admission of Poland, Hungary, and the Czech Republic was no different from the day before. But by contrast, Hungary's accession to the EU had a shocking effect, and demanded that it be managed extremely carefully. One of the great regional achievements of the 1990s was the rapprochement between Hungary and Romania, and this was to a great extent a product of the EU and NATO enlargement processes. The 1996 treaty on interstate relations came about largely because both countries understood that good relations with neighbors were a prerequisite for moving closer towards Brussels. Although relations between the two states were sometimes tense—particularly over such issues as language and educational policy for Romania's nearly 2 million ethnic Hungarians—as of 2001 they had managed to weather both a right-wing government in Budapest and the rise of an extreme nationalist party in Bucharest.

But if anything can derail things, it is the "Europe question"—or more specifically, the impact of EU demands on its members. With Romania now an important source of illegal migration to western Europe—and an increasingly important transit point for migrants from the former Soviet Union and east Asia—the Hungarian government will come under increasing pressure to shore up its long border with Romania. At the same time, conservative voices in Hungary will continue to argue that Hungary should have a special relationship with ethnic Hungarian communities in Romania, perhaps even providing differential visas and work permits for Romanian citizens based on their ethnicity: looser for ethnic Hungarians, tougher for ethnic Romanians, Gypsies (Roma), and others.

There are many ways around this issue: taking Romania off the "visa blacklist" for the entire Schengen area; Hungarian assistance in creating a private Hungarian-language university in Romania; and Hungarian and

European development funds targeted towards Covasna and Harghita counties, the areas of central Transylvania with ethnic Hungarian majorities. But the key is to ensure that the process of European enlargement does not itself undermine the good-neighborly policies that were previously touted as its essential conditions.

The government of Hungarian prime minister Viktor Orban (elected 1998) was been strongly committed to codifying a special relationship with ethnic Hungarians, especially in Slovakia and Romania, in advance of Hungary's accession to the EU. Clearly, though, the issue is potentially explosive, since neither the Slovak nor Romanian governments will accept a policy under which Budapest creates special privileges for Slovak or Romanian citizens who happen to be Hungarian by ethnicity. As of 2001, there was generally good will in the governments concerned—in part because of strong behind-the-scenes pressure from the EU and NATO. Even Iliescu—who in the early 1990s repeatedly raised the Hungarian specter when he felt in political trouble—has now become one of the major spokespeople for multiculturalism and good-neighborly relations.[27] Still, since Hungarian–Romanian relations are wrapped up in the broader process of EU enlargement, they cannot be left merely to Budapest and Bucharest. The EU must itself develop a clear strategy for avoiding the unwanted consequences of enlargement.

The End of the Pan-Romanian Ideal?

As Romania—however slowly—moves closer to western Europe, it will move farther away from Moldova. The situation between the "two Romanian states" is very much unlike that between Hungary and Hungarian-speaking minorities abroad, for three reasons. First, there is considerable debate in Moldova over whether the country is even culturally Romanian at all, with the general consensus being that ethnic Moldovans speak the Romanian language but nevertheless form their own separate nationality.

Second, only a minority of the population and politicians of Moldova seriously desire a meaningful special relationship with Romania. And third, the Romanian government has not sought a real *droit de regard* over Romanian-speaking populations abroad, whether in Moldova or Ukraine (although interstate treaties, such as those with Hungary and Ukraine, routinely mention the special interest of Romania in the cultural life of Romanian-speaking minorities).

The 1990s saw the progressive weakening of the pan-Romanian ideal, both in Moldova and Romania. In the former, the Popular Front, the pro-Romanian movement that was at the center of political life in the late 1980s, had been reduced to its core constituency of committed pan-Romanianists, less than 10 percent of the voting public. With the ideal of pan-Romanian union on the wane, many nationalists, convinced that the cause was lost, simply emigrated. Some of Moldova's foremost poets and writers, who led the national movement of the late 1980s, now live in Bucharest.

Even Ilie Ilascu, Moldova's most celebrated political "martyr," who was held prisoner for nearly a decade by separatists in Transnistria, was elected in absentia to the Romanian parliament (on the Greater Romania Party slate) and moved to Bucharest upon his release in 2001. Even more than in neighboring Ukraine, a Moldovan nationalism that sees the country's past and future as fundamentally European is the province of a dwindling cultural and political elite.

Similarly, in Romania, outside the Greater Romania Party, Moldova elicits no great public response. If anything, as one Romanian essayist commented, there is a "growing Moldophobia" in Romania.[28] Given Romania's own economic problems and uncertain relationship with Europe, devoting serious energy to building bridges to a country farther east, less developed, and less Eurocentric than their own has not attracted the attention of many Romanian politicians. If anything, Romania has proved more than willing to sacrifice relations with Moldova to demonstrate its good faith to Brussels. Throughout the 1990s, Moldovans enjoyed easy, passport-free travel to Romania, but in July 2001 Romania imposed a passport requirement as part of the effort to control its eastern border, an important transit route for illegal immigration into Europe.

It has also been difficult even to conclude a basic treaty between the two countries. A draft was initialed in the spring of 2000, but the political changes in both Chisinau and Bucharest may mean that it will be some time before a final version is signed and even longer before it is ratified by both parliaments. In early 2000, 66 percent of ethnic Moldovans still favored stronger economic links with Romania, but that support was ambiguous; respectively, 59 and 70 percent desired the same with Belarus and Ukraine.[29] President Vladimir Voronin has welcomed the idea of Romanian assistance and investment in Moldova—both of which had been slim—but has repeatedly rejected the idea that Moldova should be defined as a culturally Romanian state. In May 2001, a visit to Moldova by the head of the parliamentary assembly of the Organization for Security and Cooperation in Europe—the former Romanian foreign minister, Adrian Severin—was cordial but produced no warm avowals of cultural brotherhood.

Moldova as a Quasi-State

The end of pan-Romanianism as a viable ideology (if it ever was one) is not surprising. There is no real reason why Romanians should care about the fate of Moldovans. Indeed, the ascendancy of the pan-Romanian ideal in the early 1990s was probably more the result of its mobilization by political elites in Chisinau and Bucharst than any real convictions about the destiny of the Romanian nation. In fact, although foreign observers usually worry about Romanian "nationalism," the Romanian government has been far less exercised about "its" minorities in neighboring states than have politicians in Hungary about theirs.

But at least the idea of a special relationship with Romania provided two things for Moldova: some degree of leverage in relations with Russia and a safety valve through which the passions of the more ardent pan-Romanianists could be channeled. Now, neither of those is available; and for the foreseeable future, Moldova as a state will remain mainly the figment of the international community's collective imagination. Without at least a modicum of support from Romania—the only country in the region that is likely to care at all about Moldova's future—Moldova risks becoming little more than an entity that might be labeled a "quasi-state": a country that does not collapse into fratricidal warfare and social anarchy, but nevertheless suffers from a prodigiously weak administrative structure, few social services, a minimal defense capability, and porous borders. In this sense, Moldova is closer in real terms to Transnistria than either Chisinau or the west have chosen to believe.

Moldova is likely to remain a fragile, perhaps eventually federal state, with a modestly reformist central government yoked to a retrograde regime in the separatist Transnistria region, a de facto country that continues to produce illegal immigrants and to serve as a transit point for moving weapons, drugs, and people into wider southeastern Europe. Indeed, the Moldovan case illustrates that international recognition of a country's statehood may have little real impact on the lives of average citizens: The difference between life in the unrecognized "Dnestr Moldovan Republic" and the areas under central Moldovan government control is now miniscule. In some ways, life in the separatist region—with its higher average income and energy-producing capability—may actually be rather better.

Of course, none of that is the result of EU or NATO expansion. But by creating further incentives for Romania to write off what happens to its east and build an effective wall along the Prut River, the process of expansion itself may ironically contribute to the very instability and poor interstate relations for which it was meant to be a remedy.

The Russian Connection

Despite the continuous 150-year-old public discourse about the Romanians' supposed Latin heritage and their antipathy to the Slavic world, one of the great unexplored dimensions of Romanian politics is the Russian one. Indeed, if one is looking for "Russia's traditional ally" in the Balkans, Romania probably has a better claim to that title than Serbia. It was during the period of Russian occupation of the Danubian principalities in the nineteenth century that Romania gained its first modern constitution.

During the Ceausescu years, Romania remained a generally loyal member of the Warsaw Pact, even though there was an effort to achieve distance from the Soviet Union in some foreign policy areas. After the end of communism, Romania was the only country in eastern Europe to sign an interstate treaty with the Soviet Union, only a few months before the anti-Gorbachev coup attempt. Today, Russia's Gazprom monopoly already controls sizable portion of Romania's gas distribution network, and investment by Russian companies, especially in the oil-refining sector, has been substantial.

This is not to suggest that Romania will seek stronger relations with Russia as a counterweight to the EU and NATO, should its bid for membership be rejected in the short term. That is not even a remote possibility, since all parties in Romania are convinced that Europe and NATO are the only options for the country's foreign policy. But the continued influence of Russian business and energy interests in Romania highlights the uncertainty of Romania's development outside the EU over the next decade or more. Especially in the vital energy sector, Russian interests may in fact be yet another block to the kind of thoroughgoing reform that would be necessary for Romania to move closer to the EU. Indeed, the rehabilitation of former intelligence officials under the PSDR government and the continuing influence of the domestic intelligence community in the Romanian economy have certain parallels to similar trends in Vladimir Putin's Russia.[30] It is not too much of a leap to speculate that there may even be some cooperation among both communities in the exploitation of their respective national economies.

All of that goes in spades for Moldova. The most pro-Romanian politicians on the Moldovan spectrum—whose numbers have progressively shrunk—openly speak of Russia as the country's foremost threat. But most Moldovan citizens, both the ethnic majority and the minorities, view relations with Russia as positive and nonconflictual. Only 10 percent of citizens (and 13 percent of ethnic Moldovans) think of relations with Russia as harmful; 59 percent (and 51 percent of ethnic Moldovans) consider that Russia presents no threat to the country.[31]

In some ways, the rise of the Moldovan Communists has reflected a broad public consensus that relations with Russia are beneficial and that the pan-Romanian ideals of the early 1990s pushed the country in the wrong direction. None of that is likely to change, regardless of what happens with the EU and NATO. As the Russian Duma member Georgii Tikhonov has commented, "Moldova was looking to Romania and Europe, while Transnistria was looking to Russia. Now they both look east, to Russia and Belarus."[32]

Western Europe's "Near Abroad"

Neither Romania nor Moldova figures prominently in debates about the future of Europe. The expansion of neither the EU nor NATO depends critically on what happens in either Bucharest or Chisinau; one can imagine several multiple rounds of enlargement without Romania's inclusion, and a future in which Moldova never becomes a member of either organization. Still, both countries do illustrate the need for policy makers to develop a more realistic strategy for the new borderlands of the Euro-Atlantic zone.

The EU's relations with its own east have been informed by a map and a metaphor. The map is one in which Europe is divided into an integrating west, a reforming center, and a troublesome east. The metaphor is one of a highway, in which all the countries of postcommunist Europe are headed for the same destination—liberal democracy and integration with the Euro-Atlantic world—but are simply moving at different speeds. This metaphor is intimately bound up with the idea, or ideology, of "transition." By the turn of the century, neither the map nor the metaphor was any longer really adequate.

Indeed, the entire idea of a "postcommunist" region has probably outlived its usefulness. There is nothing uniquely postcommunist about Romania's condition, and certainly not one that now makes a comparison with, say, Estonia enlightening or meaningful. The problems of Romania are problems affecting countries all over the "developing world": those of a state weak in its capacity to govern but strong in its capacity to capture assets and distribute them to a small elite. They are the problems of a powerfully etatist regime moving to a system that is more democratic in electoral terms but not necessarily more transparent in administrative terms. In that sense, the Romanian condition—and that of Bulgaria, Albania, and other countries in the southeast—looks far more like that of Turkey, a country that has also faced innumerable obstacles in its transition from a single-party, etatist (perhaps even quasi-Leninist) system towards a highly imperfect form of democracy. The countries of the wider southeast have far more in common than a now meaningless label such as "eastern Europe" might indicate.

Moreover, by 2001 it was very clear that the former communist states are not all on the same "path." Some have become consolidated democracies. Others have become equally consolidated autocracies, even quasi-dynastic ones. Even the idea of "transition" is now unhelpful, especially if it is applied to countries as diverse as, say, Estonia and Azerbaijan. In the former, transition is something closer to the experience of Poland, where the progressive reform of institutions and the fusion between local and pan-European norms are the defining characteristics. In the latter, transition is something closer to the experience of Syria—about managing the succession from one autocrat to another. One is about who governs and how; the other is about who rules and until when.

So far, however, European and Euro-Atlantic institutions have shown a remarkable ability to ignore both these realities. There is now a wider southeastern Europe—stretching from Albania to Azerbaijan—which includes postcommunist states, post-Soviet states, and Turkey. For at least the next decade, and perhaps for much longer, few of the countries across this zone (except Greece) will be members of the EU. None but Turkey and Greece will be members of NATO. But across the region, there is a congeries of weak recognized states—as well as surprisingly durable unrecognized ones, such as Transnistria, Abkhazia, and Nagorno-Karabakh—that will continue to present grave challenges to European security. How western Europe deals with its wider southeast as a distinct and problematic region has unfortunately not been a major focus of EU policy making. Developing a strategy for this zone, though, is crucial to dealing with a geographical space that is quickly becoming Europe's own "near abroad."

Notes

1. Nicolae Iorga, *Le rôle des roumains dans la latinité* [The role of the Romanians in Latin culture] (Bucharest: Cultura Neamului Romanesc, 1919), pp. 5–6.

2. *RFE/RL Newsline*, April 26, 2001.

3. *National Human Development Report: Romania, 1999* (Bucharest: United Nations Development Program, 1999), p. 42.

4. Andreea Plesea, "Balconul cu disperare sau banutul lui Caron" [Balcony of despair or Caron's toll fee], *22*, February 13, 2001, p. iii.

5. For an analysis, see Alina Mungiu Pippidi, "The Return of Populism: The 2000 Romanian Elections," *Government and Opposition*, vol. 36, no. 2 (spring 2001), pp. 230–252.

6. *Moldova: Poverty Assessment, November 1999* (Washington, D.C.: World Bank, 1999), p. xii.

7. See Transparency International's "Corruption Perceptions Index," <http://www.transparency.org>.

8. *Moldova: Poverty Assessment*, pp. 1–2.

9. Stephen White, *Public Opinion in Moldova*, Studies in Public Policy 342 (Glasgow: Centre for the Study of Public Policy, University of Strathclyde, 2000), p. 6.

10. Author's interviews in Chisinau, September 2000.

11. See, e.g., Horia-Roman Patapievici, *Politice* [Politics] (Bucharest: Humanitas, 1996); Alina-Mungiu Pippidi, *Transilvania subiectiva* [Subjective Transylvania] (Bucharest: Humanitas, 1999); Lucian Boia, *Istorie si mit in constiinta romaneasca* [History and myth in the Romanian consciousness] (Bucharest: Humanitas, 1997); Radu Ioanid, *Evrei sub regimul Antonescu* [The Jews under Antonescu] (Bucharest: Hasefer, 1998); and Irina Livezeanu, *Cultural Politics in Greater Romania* (Ithaca, N.Y.: Cornell University Press, 1995).

12. See Katherine Verdery, *National Ideology under Socialism: Identity and Cultural Political in Ceausescu's Romania* (Berkeley: University of California Press, 1991), especially chap. 7.

13. Sebastian's journal is available in English as Mihail Sebastian, *Journal, 1935–1944*, trans. Patrick Camiller (Chicago: Ivan Dee, 2000). For the debate surrounding its publication, see Norman Manea, "The Incompatibilities," *New Republic*, April 20, 1998, pp. 32–37.

14. *RFE/RL Newsline*, March 20, 2001.

15. European Commission, "2000 Regular Report from the Commission on Romania's Progress towards Accession," November 8, 2000, p. 87.

16. Institutul de Marketing si Sondaje, "Romania si NATO: Sondaj comandat de MApN" [Romania and NATO: Poll commissioned by MApN], May 13–21, 2000; *RFE/RL Newsline*,

May 4, 2001. The strongest support was where one might expect: young people, those living in the west of the country, and those with higher education.

17. See "Statement on the Adhesion [sic] of Romania to NATO," March 7, 2001, signed by the chairs of the Party of Social Democracy, the Greater Romania Party, the Democratic Party, the National Liberal Party, the Democratic Union of Hungarians, the Social Democratic Party, the Humanistic Party, and the parliamentary bloc of national minorities.

18. *RFE/RL Newsline*, March 5, 2001.

19. *RFE/RL Newsline*, May 4, 2001.

20. *RFE/RL Newsline*, February 15, 2001.

21. White, *Public Opinion in Moldova*, pp. 29, 33.

22. *RFE/RL Newsline*, May 18, 2001.

23. *RFE/RL Newsline*, April 23, 2001.

24. Institutul de Marketing si Sondaje, "Opinii si atitudini politice ale electoratului roman [Institute of Marketing and Opinion Polling, Opinions and public attitudes of the Romanian electoriate], Bucharest: March 2001.

25. Romanian Academic Society, *Political News and Forecast*, November 2000.

26. *RFE/RL Newsline*, February 27, 2001.

27. Razvan Mitroi, "Iliescu, spre Europa, via HarCov" [Iliescu, towards Europe, via HarCov], *Adevarul*, May 26, 2001.

28. Andreea Deciu, "Moldova de dincolo de Prut" [Moldova east of the Prut River], *Romania literara*, May 30, 2001.

29. White, *Public Opinion in Moldova*, pp. 27–28.

30. See *Oxford Analytica Daily Brief*, April 3, 2001.

31. White, *Public Opinion in Moldova*, pp. 26, 32.

32. *RFE/RL Newsline*, May 21, 2001.

12

Russian Views on NATO and the EU

Vladimir Baranovsky

This chapter considers the specificity of Russia's attitudes towards NATO and the European Union as the most prominent multilateral structures operating in Europe. The fundamentals of Russia's policy regarding NATO and the EU are also outlined. In both respects, the basic assumption is that Russia's views on NATO and the EU should be analyzed against a broader vision of Russia's European and international perspectives, as well as Russia's overall relations with the west.

Overall Framework

All uncertainties and zigzags of post-Soviet Russia's foreign policy notwithstanding, four fundamental factors promote the country's cooperative engagement in relations with the west. First of all, the classic cold war pattern has become a thing of the past in terms of its ideological substance, and the latter seems unlikely to reemerge. It is quite revealing that even numerous recent manifestations of negativism with respect to the west—both on the political level and, more important, on the level of mass public consciousness—look significantly different as compared with what was a predominant model of anti-westernism in the past.

During the Soviet period, even the rhetoric and the policy of "peaceful coexistence between two social systems" did not make irrelevant the assumption of basic antagonism between them. Nowadays, even the proponents of the ideology of "Russia's special way" would hardly proclaim total rejection of everything associated with the west. The policy of the latter may be a subject of severe (sometimes even hysterical) criticism, but ideas of a "fundamental alternative" seem overwhelmingly discredited and do not have chances to get any significant political support in the country, with traditionalist "old thinking" becoming only a marginal phenomenon.

Second, traditional military-related considerations, which were based on the assumption of a major east–west conflict, are no longer relevant. Even the most conservative, backward-oriented political forces in Russia could hardly consider "western aggression" a viable scenario, at least for the immediate and medium-term future. Their ideologically motivated hostility towards the west cannot be translated into politically acceptable and economically feasible recommendations for mobilizing the national resources to meet such developments. As for the opposite part of the domestic political spectrum, its representatives would argue that even in the worst-case scenario a model of a new rivalry between Russia and the west has no chances to evolve into anything similar to the "balance of terror" pattern that existed during the cold war. Last but not least, there is a widespread understanding that Russia simply cannot afford any significant increase of spending on defense, even if it wished to do so.

Third, Russia's interest in economic links with the west has considerably increased, because of both the imperatives of domestic reforms and a desire to obtain a better position in the world market. It is true that the vulnerability and poor competitiveness of the new business elites in terms of world market requirements strongly push them to lobby for highly protectionist policies. It is also true that the extent of criminal connections among Russian business firms do not make them enthusiastic about ideas of transparency, accountability, and so on. However, even those who "do not like the west" recognize the importance of dealing with it constructively rather than confrontationally.

Fourth, political interaction with major western countries is recognized as essential in order to ensure a respectable international status for Russia. Various domestic actors may have different, even mutually incompatible views on the would-be character of this interaction—depending on how they assess Russia's and world developments and their own interests therein.

Arguments vary along quite a broad spectrum, ranging from ideas of "getting involved in the community of civilized countries" to warnings of inevitable rivalry with them. However, there is a rather common understanding that their impact on almost all ongoing processes in the world (whether technology, finance, politics, security, or anything else) is essential, and disregarding this factor would be fraught with the risk of being pushed to the international periphery. In this sense, one might argue that "partnership"—submissive, cooperative, or competitive—is overwhelmingly assessed as essential to Russia's interests in the international arena.

However, relations with the west have turned out to be more complicated and less idyllic than was anticipated by many proponents of the democratic changes in Russia at the initial period of its post-Soviet developments. This has resulted in a certain reassessment of the earlier hopes and illusions stemming from the "end of history" model. At the same time, Russia is becoming concerned about the dramatic weakening of its international role and its new prospects as a "junior partner" of the west. This promotes "non-western" thought patterns with respect to Russia's would-be policy lines in the international arena. As a result, thinking about Russia's relationship with the west becomes colored with a certain confusion and ambiguity and ceases to be linear and "unidimensional."

In a parallel and somehow overlapping way, Russia's attitudes towards NATO and the EU are also deeply affected by reflections on the importance of Europe for Russia's international interests. In many respects, this region seems to be regarded as deserving very special attention on the part of Russia.

Indeed, it was in Europe that the overcoming of the cold war pattern had the most visible and impressive effects. It was in Europe that the elimination of east–west ideological, political, and military confrontation allowed reconsideration of Russia's security interests and concerns in the most radical way. It was in Europe that Russia might first of all see positive prospects for its constructive international involvement in the light of new circumstances in the world arena.

At the same time, during the past decade Europe has become an area of very profound change. The unification of Germany, the new activism of integration processes, the foreign policy reorientation of former socialist states, the dramatic conflict in the Balkans—all these elements of new European realities require the most serious attention on the part of Russia, objectively pushing it to reassess its interests and means of protecting them. In fact, Russia is facing a double challenge of enormous dimension: that of adapting itself to the emerging new European international landscape and that of affecting the process of its formation.

Three fundamental factors make this task even more difficult for Russia. These factors are connected both with deep transformations inside the country and with its dramatically changed position with respect to the outside world.

First, today's Russia represents a peculiar mixture of continuity and discontinuity with regard to the former Soviet Union and the pre-1917 tsarist empire. The country has certainly inherited much of their legacies, and its operation in the international arena has an undeniable solid historical background. At the same time, Russia has never before existed with its present territorial configuration and geopolitical environment, which creates considerable confusion with respect to its self-identification in the international arena, and thus unpredictability and uncertainty about its foreign and security policies.

Second, although the collapse of the old regime may have made Russia ideologically closer to Europe, it is not necessarily making the two more compatible. Ironically, even the contrary may prove true: It was sufficient for the former Soviet Union simply to proclaim its "Europeanism" to gain a sympathetic reaction from Europe, but this is no longer the case for post-Soviet Russia. Since it pretends to operate as a "normal" member of the international community, the quality of the factors certifying its participation in the family of civilized countries (democracy, human rights, a market economy, and so on) becomes a critical test. It is well known that the country is having serious difficulties in passing this test, which may lead to the paradoxical conclusion that Russia would have better chances of interacting with Europe as an outsider than as an insider.

Third, with the end of the bipolar division of Europe, Russia has unexpectedly found itself pushed to the periphery of European political development. What used to be the immediate neighborhood for the state which controlled half of Europe is now separated from Russia by two territorial belts comprising the former socialist countries and the former western republics of the USSR. Having suddenly become the most remote territory of Europe, Russia has lost some of the options that were available to the former Soviet Union, and its ability to affect developments in Europe has significantly decreased. In addition, almost all allies and clients have disappeared, whereas other international players are perceived as tending to

take advantage of Russia's poor domestic situation. This creates a certain bitterness, a temptation to regard itself as a victim of unfair treatment; if Russia
could not retain its position in Europe, it certainly did not deserve to be
forced out ruthlessly and treated as a defeated country.

These political and psychological complexes can be easily detected in the
ten-year record of post-Soviet Russia's foreign policy. The excessive eupho-
ria, enthusiasm, hopes, illusions, and misperceptions of the initial post–cold
war period have given way to calculations, statements, and actions aimed at
promoting Russia as an influential international actor. Sometimes, deliberations on Russia's "great power," "special responsibilities," and "sphere of
national interest" seem to become a new obsession evolving into arrogance,
assertiveness, and what can clearly be perceived as neo-imperial inclinations.
With respect to Russia's relations with Europe, this tendency has been most
clearly manifested in Russia's attitude towards the issue of the enlargement
of NATO membership and, to some extent, by its policy towards the Commonwealth of Independent States (CIS).

So, in some respects Europe and Moscow could become more difficult for
each other as partners. A constructive response to this would be to focus
upon problems in order to resolve them, whereas an evasive one would be
to turn aside with the hope of finding alternative solutions. Within the first
pattern, Russia must invest politically and even emotionally in the "European dimension" of its international course, notwithstanding all the incon-
veniences that might thus emerge. Within the second pattern, other
dimensions are presented as more promising and therefore deserving of
more serious attention, with the notion of "Eurasia" suggested as the key
word for identifying Russia's geopolitical interests and chances.

Although both elements are present in Russia's policy thinking and policy making, the pro-European arguments seem by and large more attractive
for the majority of those who are involved in the debate. In particular, this
is because Russia is believed to have better chances in Europe than elsewhere to be accepted as a prominent actor. Other states are expected to consider Russia's involvement in European affairs as absolutely legitimate, even
if not necessarily supporting it enthusiastically. In fact, it is first of all in
Europe that Russia could be recognized (and actually operate) as "regional
great power."

The centrality of Europe for Russia has only been reinforced by the failure to establish an entente cordiale with the United States. This brings in
one more important dimension of Russia's interaction with NATO and the

European Union—the transatlantic one. Indeed, it is remarkable to what extent the United States remains a visible or invisible factor in Russia's European policy (and in Europe's policy with respect to Russia as well).

Attitudes towards NATO

In Russia's perceptions, the role of NATO is the most acute problem of the emerging European international system, because of three basic factors. First, NATO is still very often perceived as a challenge to Russia's security interests, even if only a potential one. Second, Moscow wants to prevent the central security role in Europe from being played by a structure to which Russia will not have direct access. Third, Russia's overexcitement on the issue of NATO enlargement was (and still is) considerably promoted by purely domestic forces.

Even when analyzing the current state of affairs, it is worth recalling the expectations associated with NATO at the initial stage of the post–cold war era. In the early 1990s, there seemed little doubt that NATO, with the end of bipolar confrontation, would inevitably share the fate of the late Warsaw Treaty Organization, which had been dissolved in 1991. Indeed, NATO had been created to ensure the common defense of member states in case of war with the Soviet Union, and since such a scenario was no longer relevant, this meant the disappearance of its raison d'être.

This logic assumed that the system of maintaining security in Europe that had been based on military blocs was to be replaced by new pan-European mechanisms. They were to be created on a new basis and with the participation of all the countries that had gotten out of the bipolar confrontation.

Building a new system might also be possible with the use of "old elements," including NATO—but this would require changing its character (e.g., by making it more civilian and less militarily oriented). Even more important, it would be essential to make NATO open to all countries of the continent, including Russia. In this context, an option of Russia's joining NATO as a member was not considered as something absolutely unthinkable. It is true that this was not a practical issue—but if raised as such, it probably would not have been perceived as an excessively exotic one.

Thus, at that time there seemed to be two main scenarios concerning the future of NATO, and both looked basically acceptable to Russia. The first proceeded from the inevitable disappearance of the alliance that was a kind of memorial inherited from the previous epoch and could at best continue for a time, but only because of political and bureaucratic inertia. The second one described NATO as the core of the future pan-European security system, in which NATO would be radically transformed and that would include Russia as a sine qua non.

There were, however, doubts about the latter model—on whether it would be acceptable both for the west and for Russia itself. For NATO, Russia's participation might turn out to be a burden rather than an asset. For Russia, building something from the ground up might seem more attractive than joining what had been the enemy par excellence for several decades (which would require overcoming the deeply rooted heritage of hostility focused upon NATO). In this sense, joining was only the second best scenario for Russia, with building anew being undoubtedly the first one.

Increased Hostility

In reality, as is well known, neither of these two scenarios was implemented. The developments in and around NATO followed a "third way" and contained four components that were (and still are) perceived by Russia with considerable concern. First, this third scenario envisages the consolidation and growing role of NATO rather than its gradual erosion. Second, new military and political tasks are being ascribed to NATO in *addition* to the "old" ones rather than *instead* of them. Third, NATO, far from getting a lower profile, is carrying out a triple expansion—extending its functions, membership, and zone of responsibility. Fourth, instead of making the international law and the United Nations–based system the core elements of the postbipolar world, NATO disregards them both and pretends to have an exclusive *droit de regard* with respect to what is going on in the world.

None of these characteristics might make Russia very enthusiastic about the new dynamism of NATO. And when they are all considered together, this creates a critical mass of negative attitudes which make Russia feel particularly depressed. Such political, psychological, and even emotional frustrations represent the source of Russia's energetic (although not always coherent) opposition to this trend. It is noteworthy that this opposition—which combined the logic of rational arguments with an acute emotional reaction—endured throughout almost the entire 1990s.

The first wave of Russia's negativism towards NATO was provoked by the discussions on its eventual expansion onto east-central Europe—discussions that started in 1993. Russia's initial official reaction was ambivalent, when president Boris Yeltsin, during his visit to Warsaw in August 1993, expressed "understanding" with respect to Poland's desire to join NATO. Three weeks later, this benevolent indifference evaporated completely; in his letter addressed to leaders of some western states, Yeltsin strongly objected against the prospect of east-central European countries joining NATO. This "correction" reflected the predominant views within Russia's foreign policy establishment, which felt strongly motivated to engage in a massive campaign against the enlargement of NATO.

Indeed, the scale of this campaign was unprecedented in the whole of Russia's post-Soviet history. Soon it was argued that Russia was seeing the emergence of its first foreign policy consensus, bringing together representatives of all major political forces—from communists to democrats and from liberally oriented enthusiasts of market reform to proponents of "Russia's specific (i.e., not-like-the-others) identity." For Russia's fragmented political life, this phenomenon was rare indeed—although it should be mentioned that the "consensus" was built by those who had different (sometimes mutually exclusive) explanations of, and motives for their opposition to, NATO enlargement.

This, in turn, explained the internal weakness of Russia's opposition and the lack of coherence therein. Also, some arguments by no means looked convincing or in accordance with other elements of internationally oriented thinking. This was, for instance, the case with the "security argument" developed by many military and civilian strategists. Indeed, insisting that the enlargement of NATO would inevitably threaten Russia's security looked both artificial and to be reproducing cold war logic. Criticizing plans for NATO enlargement also did not look very appropriate in the light of the generally recognized right of states to join any international structures (or to refrain from doing so).

The practical results of Russia's "anti-enlargement" campaign also looked rather ambivalent. In east-central Europe, it was clearly perceived as a manifestation of Russia's "big brother" syndrome and brought about increasing domestic support with respect to the policy line of joining NATO. It is also possible that the voices of critics in the region would have been better heard if Russia had followed the above-mentioned "do-as-you-wish" formula that was actually used by Yeltsin in Warsaw.

To a certain extent, this hypothesis might be applied to the west as well. There, some opponents of NATO enlargement also found themselves in an ambivalent position: While objecting to this prospect in principle, they would be against providing Russia with a veto right in this regard.

At the same time, Moscow's vehement opposition increased the importance of the "Russian question" in western debates on NATO's future. These debates started to include a number of themes that soon became rituals: that the enlargement of NATO is not aimed at, and should not result in, the emergence of new dividing lines in Europe; that in parallel with extending its membership, NATO should offer a new partnership to Russia; that Russia should be actively involved in building a new European security architecture; and so on. For some time, the prominence of the "Russian theme" in NATO debates even made the candidate countries jealous for getting considerably less attention.

As far as Moscow was concerned, it felt somehow disoriented by such developments—which was clearly manifested by its attitude towards the Partnership for Peace (PfP) program. PfP was first perceived in Russia as an alternative to NATO enlargement plans (or at least as a means of slowing them down). But later, suspicions emerged that PfP was conceived mainly to involve Russia in cooperation on issues of secondary importance in order to divert its attention from, and to neutralize its opposition to, the enlargement plans. As a result, Russia's interest and involvement in PfP turned out from the very beginning to be limited and far from being considered Moscow's priority in international affairs.

In a paradoxical way, Russia's opposition to NATO enlargement was parallel to its attempts to build a relationship with NATO as a major pillar of the evolving European security architecture. This line proceeded from the idea of constructing a "special relationship" with NATO that would be deeper and more substantive than NATO's relations with any of its other partners. A maximalist interpretation of this logic, though never formulated as the official position of Russia, even required recognizing its right to enter into relations with NATO on behalf of other members of the CIS—a model that would most probably have been unacceptable to them.

In a nonmaximalist interpretation, the recognition by NATO of Russia's unique international role and responsibility would make possible an expanded dialogue between them going far beyond the PfP framework. It needs to be mentioned that such a dialogue did develop after the mid-1990s, although politically it turned out to be rather lightweight. In fact, both sides were cautious with respect to an option of increasing its salience, although for different reasons: NATO did not want to make relations with

Russia excessively "privileged," whereas Moscow was reluctant to be regarded as accepting NATO enlargement by the very fact of flirting with the Alliance.

The turning point for Russia came in December 1996, when the North Atlantic Council officially started the process of enlargement, thus making it inevitable. Russia had to recognize that its attempts to prevent NATO enlargement had failed, and considerable political efforts had been in vain. Under these circumstances, the Russian government was actually faced with the very real danger of becoming the hostage of its own anti-NATO rhetoric and wide anti-enlargement campaign.

Indeed, the enthusiasts of anti-enlargement were arguing in favor of reacting in the most energetic way, even at the expense of rational considerations of Russia's own security and political interests. For instance, among the proposed "countermeasures" were building a CIS-based military alliance, redeploying armed forces in the western areas of Russia, targeting east-central Europe with nuclear weapons, and developing a strategic partnership with anti-western regimes.

Following the logic of such a reaction would have been fraught with serious negative international implications; in particular, it would inevitably have nullified any prospect of building a cooperative security regime in Europe. The alternative line stressed the necessity of such a regime as the top priority, not to be undermined by differences over other issues, however important they might be. In this context, disagreement over NATO enlargement was not to be aggravated by other confrontational words and deeds; on the contrary, enlargement might make a breakthrough towards constructive interaction even more imperative and urgent.

The choice was made in favor of the latter approach, oriented towards developing a more cooperative and pragmatic relationship between Russia and NATO. This was confirmed by the decision to sign the NATO–Russia Founding Act in May 1997—a decision pushed through by then–foreign minister Yevgeny Primakov against considerable domestic opposition.

Symbolism matters; the fact that this document was signed before the official invitation to join NATO had been delivered to the three candidate states seemed rather instrumental in reducing Russian frustration. While the process was being finalized later on, Moscow looked considerably less nervous and more inclined to de-dramatize the issue as far as possible.

The Founding Act is controversial in Russia. Some analysts were (and still are) of a highly negative opinion in this respect: Moscow should have refrained from undermining the coherence of its opposition, legitimizing the enlargement of NATO, and providing this obsolete structure with new rationales for its continuation. Others believe that this did create preconditions for turning relations between Russia and NATO into one of the central elements of the European system, or even the central one. Furthermore, Moscow seemed to be open to further rapprochement with NATO (although this was conditional upon a number of factors, the first being nonexpansion onto formerly Soviet territory).

Testing this optimistic scenario turned out to be impossible. This option was seriously undermined—first, by the failure to provide the established Permanent Joint Council for Russia–NATO with a notable role; second (and most dramatically), by NATO's actions in Yugoslavia; and third, by the adoption of a new Strategic Concept of NATO at its fiftieth anniversary summit in Washington.

The military operation of NATO against Yugoslavia in the context of developments in and around Kosovo produced the most traumatic impact on Russia's official and unofficial attitudes towards the Alliance. Indeed, it was the Kosovo phenomenon that has contributed to the consolidation of Russia's anti-NATO stand more than the whole vociferous anti-enlargement campaign. The air strikes against Yugoslavia became the most convincing justification for Russia's negativism about the prospect of establishing a NATO-centered Europe.

Furthermore, if the thesis of Russia's opponents to NATO about its "aggressive character" had looked either like pure propaganda or something inherited from the cold war, the war against Yugoslavia became an impressive manifestation of its validity. Any possible arguments that NATO might play the role of a stability provider for Europe (e.g., with respect to the issue of Transylvania) seemed to have lost their relevance and become absolutely inappropriate.

The central issue was the question of Russia's further relations with NATO. Those who had been against signing the Founding Act in 1997 assessed the Kosovo situation as a convincing proof that their logic was correct and that cooperative relations with NATO are only an illusion legitimizing NATO's policy and restricting Russia's ability to oppose it. Accordingly, Moscow's negativism towards NATO's actions in Yugoslavia had to be expressed in breaking resolutely all relations with the Alliance.

However, many in Moscow apprehended the fact that such a break would lead to restoring a confrontational pattern in relations with the west. The political settlement of the situation around Kosovo also required interacting with NATO. The latter would remain an influential structure in the post-settlement context as well, and having no mechanisms of dealing with NATO would hardly be in Russia's interests. By and large, these interests seemed to amount to reducing the profile of relations with NATO considerably, without breaking them completely and irreversibly. This was the logic behind the decision to "freeze" Russia–NATO relations—a decision that represented a compromise achieved after a serious struggle between hawks and doves both inside and outside the Kremlin.

Some elements of Russia's attitude towards NATO in the context of the Kosovo crisis were striking in their apparent lack of coherence. Russia strongly condemned NATO military operations—but in June 1999 Moscow endorsed the NATO-promoted logic of resolving the crisis in Kosovo. Moscow helped impose the settlement designed by NATO on Belgrade—but it came very close to a serious conflict with NATO because of the famous "march" of 200 Russian peacekeepers from Bosnia to Pristina (on June 12, 1999). The policy of NATO with respect to Kosovo caused the "freezing" of Russia's relations with NATO—but for some time afterwards Kosovo was the only field of cooperative interaction of the two sides, with all other activities being effectively interrupted and chances of relaunching them looking close to zero.

Indeed, in 1999 the NATO military campaign in the Balkans and Russia's hostile reaction to it seemed to set a new long-term agenda for their future relations. There were serious grounds for being apprehensive about their worsening erosion, with the Kosovo factor becoming a constant irritant.

Contrary to such expectations, the post-Kosovo syndrome in Russia's negativism towards NATO has turned out to be surprisingly short-lived— much shorter than the scope of the campaign against NATO aggression and the overall indignation in both the Russian political class and public opinion would have led one to anticipate. To a considerable extent, this is due to domestic political changes in Russia and the possibility of a "new start" for Russia's new leadership. Indeed, the decision (supposedly, taken against considerable domestic resistance) to "defreeze" relations with NATO is especially impressive after all that was said about the Alliance in the aftermath of Kosovo.

Four facts deserve mentioning in this regard. First, the pace of positive changes looks extremely dynamic. In fact, by mid-2001 the NATO–Russia dialogue had practically resumed in full, and both sides had relaunched the program of developing a relationship that had been stopped in connection with Kosovo. Second, the tone of Russia's comments on NATO has almost completely changed; what was predominantly condemning and denouncing just two years ago is becoming more informative and unbiased; and even the most convinced anti-NATO activists prefer to remain noiseless rather than showing up. Third, the level of officials and representatives meeting on behalf of two sides has become considerably higher. Fourth, the prospect of further rapprochement is no longer excluded; although schemes favoring the development of a kind of "Russia–NATO alliance" are not officially endorsed, it is noteworthy that some analysts have started to raise the issue of possible Russian membership in NATO—which would have been absolutely inconceivable just a very short time ago.

Putin's Choice

What is behind such developments? Three main interpretations can be offered.

First of all, it is a manifestation of the pragmatism that has become a key stance of the new Russian administration under president Vladimir Putin. Russia would certainly prefer some alternatives to NATO, but if there are no political, financial, and military means for promoting them and downgrading NATO, it is better to get accommodated to this situation rather than reentering into an exhausting confrontation, with the chances of succeeding being close to nil. It is not a green light for anything NATO would like to do, but a deliberate decision not to get negatively overexcited with respect to what seems to happen anyway. At the same time, to the extent to which promoting bilateral relations with western countries and cooperative interaction with the west as a whole is considered to be in Russian interests, this line should not be damaged by maintaining a spirit of confrontation towards the organization of which most of these countries are members.

Second, there is a need to put Russia's attitude towards NATO into an appropriate context, without making it the central issue of the international agenda. Russia faces numerous challenges and must deal with them seriously—without being diverted all the time by the issue of NATO (and eventually even using it as leverage to promote Russia's interests in other areas). Some observers noted that during the formative period of the new U.S. administration, when its forthcoming policy towards Russia raised a lot of concerns in Moscow, that Moscow seemed to engage in considerably more intense dialogue with NATO officials than with those from Washington. Indeed, this could be viewed as a paradoxical pattern, when degrading and eroding relations with the United States were counterbalanced by Moscow via rapprochement with the structure that was traditionally considered as created, inspired, and controlled by Americans.

Third, the most serious test for future relations between Russia and NATO will be connected with the next phase of the Alliance's enlargement. One might expect that Russia's negativism about the eventual involvement of three Baltic states in NATO will be much stronger than in the case of east-central Europe. In contrast to the latter case, Russia's eventual arguments on the security implications of such a development could be considerably more coherent and substantive. Also, Moscow might expect that its reservations will have more chances to be taken into account—although Russia's right to draw a "red line" will by no means be recognized by other international actors. In addition, the issue might turn out to be extremely sensitive in relation to Russia's domestic situation. In a worst-case scenario, this all could develop into a very acute political situation that would be more dangerous than the previous wave of NATO enlargement.

One way of preventing such a crisis-prone development would be to change its context in a substantive, if not radical, way. Indeed, Russia's membership in NATO could be a fundamental solution, but it does not look practical for the time being. Another approach along the same line would be to ensure a very high level of relations between Russia and NATO. If achieved (or at least realistically designed) before the Baltic phase of enlargement, this would make any Russian concerns on the latter irrelevant. From this point of view, Russia's current rapprochement with NATO will broaden Moscow's future options if and when the issue of Baltic states' membership in the Alliance is put on the agenda.

It is also important to refrain from overdramatizing the issue in order to prevent a risk of becoming hostage to one's own propagandistic engagement. Interestingly enough, on the eve of NATO expansion into the Baltic region, Russia's mass media pay considerably less attention to this prospect than they did in the case of east-central Europe just a few years ago.

However, this is by no means a guarantee against destabilizing developments. Failure to ensure a qualitative breakthrough might easily bring about the erosion of relations and even a new crisis with the forthcoming incorporation of three Baltic states into NATO. Russia still oscillates between instinctive residual hostility towards NATO and pragmatic considerations that push it towards developing positive interactions with the Alliance. Building a reliable cooperative pattern in Russia–NATO relations remains a formidable and challenging task.

Attitudes towards the EU

During almost the whole of the 1990s, Russia's debate about the organization of the European international space was focused upon NATO. The European Union was regarded as being the most powerful economic entity on the continent, but its political impact was either underestimated or not properly assessed. Indeed, it was not clear to what extent the EU was able to translate its economic potential into political influence; to what extent it deserved attention as an integrated international actor rather than as a structure for defining a common denominator of national policies that otherwise operate individually; and to what extent the changing international landscape in Europe was affected by the EU rather than by other multilateral mechanisms—among which NATO has undoubtedly the most prominent place.

Seven factors have contributed to changing this indifference and lack of political attention towards the EU. First, the role of the EU as an economic power is viewed as becoming increasingly meaningful in terms of Russia's interests. This is certainly related to Russia's considerable dependence on the EU in trade, investments, credits, indebtedness, and so on. Indeed, the EU accounts for more than two-thirds of foreign investment in Russia and for approximately 40 percent of all its external trade. The very fact that the EU is by far Russia's most important economic partner makes Russia's cooperative interaction with the EU imperative. Ensuring the economic sustainability of Russia becomes a crucial political task for Moscow, and in this regard it is only natural that the EU has been promoted to the very top in the list of Russia's foreign policy priorities.

Second, there is a growing understanding that even such a strictly economic view of the EU should not be only related to Russia's immediate interests. The economic dimension of international relations is assessed as becoming increasingly important, with the emerging post-bipolar international system being strongly affected by trends in financial and technological developments rather than by traditional "high politics" issues. The need to "economicize" foreign policy is one of the most fashionable themes in the ongoing debates in Russia on its international activities. Within this dimension, the EU is undoubtedly one of the strongest international poles, and Russia's prospects will depend increasingly on how successful it is in relations with this economic superpower. Suffice it to mention that in deliberations on Russia's access to the World Trade Organization, the EU is often viewed as a much more important interlocutor than any other party.

Third, the EU's dynamics are regarded as an impressive manifestation of its viability and sustainability. The very fact of the EU's attractiveness to most of the European countries aspiring to membership in this organization is perceived as convincing proof of its promising international future. "Schengen," "Maastricht," and "euro" have become symbols of the vision of the future EU incorporating most of Europe's financial, industrial, technological, demographic, and political potential. In a sense, the prospects of the EU look more shiny and encouraging from outside (in this case, from Russia) than may be the case for internal observers and analysts. However, this perception seems to be prevailing in Russia's thinking about the EU.

Fourth, it has become clear during the past two to three years that the EU is expanding not only to new territories but also to new functional areas. A qualitative breakthrough in this respect is associated with post–Saint-Malo developments and the evolving "common European security and defense policy" (CESDP). Here again, Russian observers might both exaggerate and misinterpret the character of this new phenomenon in the framework of the EU. But what nevertheless seems obvious to them is the fact that the EU is entering the area that used to be prohibited to it and was the exclusive domain of either national policies or NATO. This is regarded as one more serious argument that the EU is becoming a "real" international actor, if not a superpower in the making.

Fifth, one more factor promoting the salience of the EU in Russia's international perceptions has emerged from Moscow's painful concentration upon various issues associated with NATO (enlargement, aggression in Kosovo, new Strategic Concept, and so on). Indeed, in the second half of the 1990s, Russia's negativism with respect to NATO became so powerful and overwhelming that any real or imaginable alternative started to seem attractive and deserving of support and encouragement. This, in particular, had implications for Russia's attitudes towards the EU—attitudes that were stoked by Russia's obsessive anti-NATO syndrome.

Sixth, Russia's positive and even supportive attitude towards the EU fits well in the vision of a multipolar world that is so dear to many Russian analysts, observers, and politicians and that was even politically upgraded to remain, for a while, a quasi-official foreign policy ideology of the country. This is closely related to the whole plethora of Russia's complexes with respect to the United States (the challenging unilateralism of "the only remaining superpower," its disregard for international law, its alleged pretensions to operate as demiurgic on the international scene, and so on). Strengthening the EU, according to this line of thinking, will make the international system more balanced and less United States–centric—which could only be in the interests of Russia. Moreover, it might be expected that the EU, in line with similar considerations, could find partnership with Russia attractive and as responding to its own long-term interests in the international arena.

Seventh (and not exactly in the realm of Russia's international priorities per se), the EU might represent for Moscow a fascinating model of how to organize relations between sovereign states in such a way that they become increasingly able to operate as an entity without losing their individual characteristics or by mutually accommodating them. In fact, it is a model of integration that looks particularly impressive against the background of the spectacular failures of the CIS, the post-Soviet structure that Russia would be interested in turning into a viable and sustainable organization.

Indeed, the differences between the EU and the CIS are so enormous and substantive that even comparing them might seem absolutely inappropriate. But some approaches, tools, organizational schemes, and policy archetypes that have been successfully tested in (and by) the EU could be eventually considered relevant to the CIS. In fact, the idea of "modeling upon the EU experience" might be applied even in a broader sense, both on the subnational level (e.g., by introducing the subsidiarity principle into the domestic political structure of the Russian Federation) and on the international one (e.g., to pacify and stabilize some of the areas of Russia's "near abroad," such as Transcaucasus). This approach, however, is derived from very broad thinking about integration in the EU rather than representing eventual elements of Russia's political agenda with regard to this organization.

There are certainly some reservations in Russia's perceptions of, and attitudes towards, the EU. In fact, these reservations could be formulated with respect to each of the above-mentioned "arguments" promoting Russia's increased attention to the EU. Thus, Russia's economic dependence on the EU has a unilateral character, and if the energy supply is put aside, Russia is a meaningless economic quantity for the EU, accounting for only 4 percent of its external trade. Or, however significant the EU's recent progress of common foreign, security, and defense policies might be, it remains predominantly a "civilian power," whereas Russia's international risks, challenges, and opportunities are widely associated with geopolitics—the area where the EU is not yet a significant player. Or else: Russia's calculations (or hopes) about the EU as the emerging "pole" in the international system with an increasing ability and predisposition to operate independently of Washington is more than mitigated by the close partnership between the EU and the United States—a partnership that in any circumstances would prevail over the EU's "Russian connection."

Therefore, drawing a picture of Russia's unrestrained enthusiasm about the EU would be certainly misleading. However, in recent years both sides have made important steps towards mutual rapprochement—a process that is being both developed on the political level and consolidated institutionally.

A Difficult Relationship

The Partnership and Cooperation Agreement (PCA) that was signed in 1994 and entered into force in 1997 created a solid legal basis for a relationship between the EU and Russia. The PCA is only a broad framework document that may be vulnerable to criticism of its practical importance as well as the readiness of both sides to implement its provisions. But the PCA did outline some new prospects for relations between the EU and Russia—for instance, an EU–Russia political dialogue was introduced by the PCA and has already become routine.

In 1999, the EU and Russia adopted new documents addressing their respective policies towards each other. For both sides, these documents represented a new kind of experience. The *Common Strategy of the European Union on Russia* was the first document of this type envisaged by the Amsterdam Treaty, and Russia could be pleased to have been chosen by the EU as the primary "target" of its new Common Foreign and Security Policy (CFSP) pattern. The *Medium-Term Strategy for the Development of Relations between the Russian Federation and the European Union 2000–2010* also represented a new genre for Moscow's foreign policy; it was considerably more elaborate than, for instance, the *Decree on Russia's Policy with Respect to the CIS States* of 1995. It should be added that the EU has a prominent place in the *Foreign Policy Concept of the Russian Federation* adopted in 2000.

Both "strategies" may be considered too vague and as lacking concrete and strategically significant actions. In addition, a close reading of the two documents reveals significant differences between them. In the case of Russia, for instance, special attention is paid to the notion of "equality"—which is in line with Moscow's emphasis on "national interest" as the foundation of its foreign policy but sounds very traditional and not very appropriate with respect to the EU as an unconventional international actor. However, the facts that the two documents were adopted almost simultaneously, are very cooperatively oriented, and both proclaim the goal of a "strategic partnership" between the EU and Russia seem telling and encouraging, even if only for considerations of political symbolism.

For Russia, the notion of a "strategic partnership" has clarified its long-term goals with respect to the EU. The idea of Russia's accession to the EU as a full-fledged member has more than once been mentioned in the past but seems to have been abandoned—at least at the official level. Three reasons might explain this "no accession to and no association with the EU" position of Russia.

First, the financial crash of August 1998 in Russia revealed the extreme vulnerability of its economy and the superficial character of its ongoing reforms. This in itself was a strong warning and raised serious question about Russia's ability to accommodate the realities of the EU.

Second, there is strong pressure for a more protectionist policy from the considerable part of the business community that fears external competition. At the same time, criminal and/or corrupted elements in all segments and on all levels of Russia's economy are by no means interested in making it more transparent and law-abiding.

Third, the prospect of accession would provide the EU with the most powerful political leverage vis-à-vis Russia, making it vulnerable to eventual pressures. Without this tool, rare attempts by the EU to exercise political pressure on Russia will most probably have no discernable impact on Moscow (as was proved in the case of the conflict in Chechnya).

In this sense, a "no-accession" policy means less responsibility and less accountability on the part of Russia (and probably less concern on the part of the EU). It is noteworthy that a new formula was suggested in 2001 by Russian diplomats (although only in a quasi-official way): "Russia would like its relations with the EU member states to be similar to those that these states have between themselves." If ordinary logic says that this means membership, in political parlance it might mean something very advanced but falling short of full membership (with its burdensome responsibilities).

A remarkable recent innovation in the relationship between the EU and Russia is the prominence of its political dimension. This, in particular, was underlined by the invitation of President Putin to take part in the session of the European Council in Stockholm in March 2001. In contrast to "ordinary" Russia–EU summits, this new pattern had both a symbolic character (since it involved Russia's head of state at what is considered to be the highest structural level of the EU political system) and raised the possibility of interaction with all the leaders of the EU states, not only with the one serving as chair of the Council. On the EU side, inviting leaders of states that are not members to its summits is an exceptional practice, and there had been only two earlier cases of a similar pattern of meetings (with Nelson Mandela and Yasser Arafat). It is not surprising that observers in Russia stressed the importance of this meeting and its qualitative specificity; it was regarded as reflecting the rising character of Russia's relations with the EU, as well as the deliberate intention of the latter to highlight Russia's role as its partner. Russian observers also pointed to the fact that the new U.S. president was to attend the next EU summit only three months later, in June 2001.

Besides political symbolism, the substance of deliberations between Russia and the EU also deserves attention. Putin's visit to Stockholm took place exactly at the moment of growing tensions with the administration of George W. Bush and coincided with the height of a scandal that led to the expulsion of Russian diplomats from the United States. Therefore the rapprochement with the EU seemed particularly impressive against the background of deteriorating Russian–American relations.

There are certainly other issues on which the EU and Russia could find common language when discussing some aspects of the U.S. policy: the nonratification of the Comprehensive Test Ban Treaty (CTBT) and the treaty banning landmines, the Bush administration's rejection of the 1997 Kyoto Protocol on reducing greenhouse gas emissions, and the U.S. government's hostility to the treaty creating an international tribunal on crimes against humanity. Another notorious example of how the EU and Russia might operate hand in hand (and partly in contradiction to the United States) concerns North Korea. While the Bush administration temporarily withdrew from active diplomacy on the Korean peninsula, the EU announced its plan to establish diplomatic relations with Pyongyang and sent a delegation there—which was objectively closer to the line advocated by Russia. Indeed,

President Putin was scheduled to meet with Kim Jong Il in April 2001 in an effort to persuade him to agree to reconciliation with South Korea and to abandon the ballistic missile program (which has been cited by Washington as a large part of its motivation for developing a missile defense). In this effort, Russia was actually joined by the European Union.

Thus, "high politics" seems to be present in Russia–EU interaction, even if not coherently and on a regular basis. Moscow is usually considered as supporting this line and as interested in making political issues more prominent in the Russia–EU agenda. However, there were cases when its "politicization" clearly damaged Russia—as happened when the Technical Assistance to the Southern Republics of the CIS and Georgia program and the ratification of the PCA were postponed due to the first war in Chechnya.

Russia and EU Enlargement

Nevertheless, political considerations seemed predominant in defining Russia's initial attitude towards the EU's enlargement plans. They were assessed first of all against the background of Russia's vehement opposition to NATO enlargement and as a preferable alternative to the latter. It is noteworthy that while the prospect of NATO expansion onto the post-Soviet territories generated almost mystical horror, the involvement of three Baltic states in the Western European Union "sphere of influence" as associate partners passed practically unnoticed. Paradoxically, for a time Moscow seemed to welcome the enlargement of the EU even more enthusiastically than did the EU's participants. In a sense, this "politicized" approach contributed to the overall positive image of the EU in Russia, while NATO was increasingly portrayed as the incarnation of evil.

However, some time later this approach started to give way to apprehension about the potentially negative consequences for Russia of EU enlargement. It is interesting that the "list of concerns" officially presented by Moscow as a subject for deliberations with the EU was predominantly focused on economic and technical issues, with the aim of preventing Russia's eventual losses in trade and cooperation with candidate countries when they become EU members. In addition, when the problem was analyzed more thoroughly, it became clear that in some respects Russia could even profit from access by these countries to the EU—for instance, due to the reduction of tariffs down to the considerably lower level existing in the EU.

Thus, the issue of the EU enlargement and its implications both for Russia and for Russia's relations with the EU need to be approached in a broader context. Three large themes require attention in this regard.

First, there are some elements of tension and conflict in Russia's relations with some of the candidate countries, especially Baltic states—such as unsettled borders or what is perceived as discrimination against ethnic Russians. If this conflictual potential is not reduced, it could be internalized in EU policy. An interesting question is to what extent this could complicate Russia's relations with the EU—or, on the contrary, there could be a positive effect when EU standards are applied to some of the issues that are of significant sensitivity for Russia. Some observers point to the fact that the latter has taken place even while countries have candidate status for EU membership—although this has passed almost unnoticed in Russia.

Second, there is the large theme of the Kaliningrad Region. It represents a problem for Russia in any case, but it will become a very peculiar one for its relations with the EU if and when the latter includes Poland and Lithuania—thus turning Kaliningrad into an enclave within the EU.

According to a pessimistic scenario, this might bring about a dramatic situation when the residents of Kaliningrad are forced to obtain a visa to reach "mainland" Russia, from which they are separated by two EU borders but which remains their own country. Trade will also be affected to the disadvantage of Kaliningrad, further undermining its links to both Russia and neighboring EU states. Finally, military transit to and from Kaliningrad, the Russian outpost on the Baltic Sea, might become one more complicating factor in Russia's relations with the EU.

An optimistic scenario proceeds from the assumption that a potential problem should be transformed into a strong incentive for positive interaction between the involved parties. On the basis of political will and close cooperation between the two sides, technical solutions could be found for the above-mentioned problems—for instance, by introducing some special provisions into the Schengen visa regulations. Furthermore, in promoting cooperation on (and in) the Kaliningrad Region, Russia and the EU would work out new forms, methods, and orientations for their constructive interaction in a broader sense. On the official level, this logic of turning Kaliningrad into a "pilot region" of cooperation between Russia and the EU has gained considerable prominence during the past two years and promoted the issue to the very top of their joint agenda.

While welcoming this approach, Russia may still have considerable concerns with respect to the future of this remote territory of Kaliningrad. Indeed, making it "more European" might undermine its Russian connection and trigger the process of alienation, with economic, communication, technological, and information factors sooner or later gaining the upper hand over ethnic and cultural affinities. In other words, if the "Europeanization" of Kaliningrad is promoted (which both sides intend to do) and Russia lags behind (which looks a very realistic proposition), the former could be lost by the latter forever. Thus, the optimistic scenario turns out to be colored with some pessimistic tones—although they have, so to say, an existential character and do not look likely to be translated into a policy line.

The third large theme associated with EU enlargement could also be considered existential in nature. Because it remains outside the EU, which is expanding its territorial space and functional scope, Russia may raise questions about its own role in Europe. Indeed, the further consolidation of the EU will sooner or later make it clear that the dividing line between members and nonmembers might become much more fundamental than in the case of NATO. In fact, this is the price to pay for a no-accession policy, as described above; the EU enlargement gives a more "concrete" character to concerns that might emerge in this respect and that have not been articulated so far in a very explicit way. There seems to be a growing awareness in Russia that this trend might damage its long-term interests and its prospects in Europe, unless mitigated by significantly stronger incentives for further rapprochement with the EU.

One possible approach energetically promoted by the EU consists in focusing upon the "Russian components" of the Northern Dimension—an initiative launched by the EU in 1997 that since has led to a number of high-level meetings, conceptual documents, and specific programs. Indeed, Russia has a prominent place in the Northern Dimension strategy; although this regional initiative still requires energetic implementation actions, it may be highly instrumental for strengthening Russia–EU relations through practical cooperation. Suffice it to mention the possibility of an energy partnership, joint efforts in the area of environmental protection, and enhanced transborder cooperation with the involvement of local administrative entities.

Russians offering comments seem to pay less attention to the EU Northern Dimension than it deserves. One explanation may be confusion with respect to its regional character. Indeed, "regionalizing" Russia–EU relations may seem inappropriate in the context of broader problems that both sides could be interested in addressing jointly. For instance, a partnership in the energy sector could go far beyond the regional scope—in both the scale of envisaged projects and their implications for each side.

At the same time, although the "neutral" political profile of the Northern Dimension has great advantages, it also reduces its chances of becoming a "big issue" in Russia's foreign policy agenda and mass media. In fact, this only reflects the traditional dilemma of "high politics" versus "low politics," and the problem here is basically with Russia's inclination to the former rather than with the Northern Dimension per se.

It is noteworthy, however, that the EU factor is presented as instrumental with respect to some concrete situations affecting Russia's interests. Such was the case with Poland's refusal to give a green light to the construction of a new gas pipeline circumventing Ukraine; this position of Warsaw, allegedly motivated by its solidarity with Kiev, was finally reported to be abandoned as the result of EU pressure. In a similar way, the "old" member states of the EU were reported to be more receptive to Russia's claims concerning free transit to and from Kaliningrad.

Russia's inclination to focus on the political aspects of EU developments may also explain the considerable attention Moscow pays to CESDP. Indeed, Russia might be attracted by its "pure" European characteristics, which decrease the United States–centrism and NATO–centrism of security arrangements in the western part of the continent. At the same time, this might provoke ungrounded (and erroneously oriented) hopes on Russia's part about the extent to which the EU is moving away from the United States—or, alternatively, concerns that security- and military-related dimensions of the EU's evolution might turn out to be dominated by NATO (and the United States). There is also a certain lack of understanding with respect to the emerging CESDP—in particular, that it is about crisis prevention and crisis management and not about collective defense.

In any case, Russia tends to consider the CESDP against the broader background of the possible, probable, or even inevitable evolution of the EU towards an entity performing traditional military functions. This touches upon issues of strategic character: the future of NATO, the role of the United States, the evolution of the international system, and so on. In striking parallelism with the attitude of the United States (although with an opposite vector), Russia's perceptions of "European defense" vary between sympathy and concern; the former is generated by the image of a certain counterweight to American primacy, while the latter is associated with the vision of a strong European pole alienating Russia.

In terms of practical policy, various possible approaches towards the CESDP discussed in Russia could be grouped into three categories. First, Russia should adopt a negative attitude towards the CESDP (since it will be attached to, and even controlled by, NATO and the United States; another variant of negativism is based on the thesis that an independent European military potential will be an existential challenge to Russia's interest). Second, the issue of the CESDP does not concern Russia (this approach fits into the logic of neo-isolationists, Eurasianists, or proponents of CIS-focused policy; some of them would warn that the CESDP might interfere in what they would define as Russia's exclusive zone of interest and influence). Third, Russia should develop an increasingly positive attitude, promoting cooperative interaction and involvement with the CESDP.

On the political level, this cooperative attitude was strongly promoted by the EU–Russia summit in Paris (October 2000), which adopted a special joint declaration on strengthening dialogue on political and security matters. However, there are concerns in Russia that the EU is not yet ready to go much beyond proclaiming formally cooperative intentions and that behind its supportive rhetoric there is deep reluctance to involve Moscow, which is suspected of being motivated by purely geopolitical calculations.

There may be reasons to argue along this line. For instance, the scenario of joint EU–Russia crisis-management involvement in Macedonia might be attractive to Moscow, both to help it move beyond its own reduced position in the Balkans and to promote an alternative to NATO's military role in the region.

However, there may be some other motives as well, ones with a functional rather than political character. According to a slightly simplified scheme, the CESDP could be instrumental in organizing a certain division of labor between the United States and the EU, with the former focusing upon major conflicts (like the Gulf War) and the latter on crisis management (as in Bosnia). Russia could find itself closer to the missions designated to the EU rather than to the United States—simply because it may be facing numerous challenges requiring crisis management (e.g., civilian riots, separatist violence, terrorist intrusion from outside Russia). If so, this means that Russia might have additional reasons for considering CESDP crisis management as deserving closer attention and as by no means incompatible with Russian armed forces' missions.

The EU is also expected to have a real interest in involving Russia. Russia might offer the EU a certain potential to assist in CESDP missions in such areas as transport aviation and satellite communication, observation, and navigation. The decision of the EU to promote a nonmilitary component of crisis management opens up one more area for cooperation with Russia, taking into account the ten years of experience of its Ministry for Emergency Situations specializing in rescue operations.

Thus, the area of crisis management opens the way for truly equal cooperation, and this might be politically and psychologically important for overcoming some of the residual instincts inherited from the cold war. Indeed, it is something relatively new; there is no burden of the past; and the agenda is less controversial than when addressing traditional defense issues. Furthermore, the fact that it is not yet finalized might be a positive element for mutual accommodation (which would be easier to accomplish than after the "rules of the game" have been already established).

If Moscow can overcome its inertia and the temptation to consider the problem exclusively or predominantly in the context of relations with NATO, and if the EU can overcome its instinctive reluctance to excessively "politicize" its agenda with Russia, both sides might have a good chance of finding new prospects for cooperative interaction. This effort would not provide miraculous solutions for "low politics" problems, but it could help create a favorable political atmosphere. Even more important, Russia–EU interaction could be the nucleus for a globally oriented mechanism of crisis management that functions well beyond Europe and that will be especially needed in the years to come.

13

Conclusions: The Pangs of Disappointed Love? A Divided West and Its Multiple Peripheries

Anatol Lieven

Europe and European integration were not directly affected by the terror-ist attacks of September 11, 2001; but the indirect effects will be immense, and immensely complicated. This applies in the first instance to the role of the United States, and of NATO, the principal vehicle employed by the United States for the projection of military dominance and geopolit-ical influence on the European continent. U.S. strategy has of course changed quite substantially as a result of the attacks, and NATO undoubt-edly will also change, mainly as a result of new U.S. attitudes, but also because of the new NATO–Russia relationship and other factors.

However, a paradox is at work here, which makes NATO's future hard to predict. For as a result of September 11, the United States is simultaneously both more and less engaged in European affairs. On the one hand, Europe's importance for U.S. military lines of communication has increased drasti-cally, compared with the post–cold war period, when this role diminished sharply. By the spring of 2002, U.S. troops had gone to war in Afghanistan and been deployed to Central Asia and the Caucasus. War was being con-templated with Iraq, smaller military operations in Somalia and elsewhere were under consideration, and the U.S. commitment to support Israel militarily was as strong as ever.

All of these tasks require the use of European refueling bases and staging posts, and access to European airspace. Without NATO as a frame, the United States would have to seek a number of unfavorable alternatives: agreements for bases with individual European countries like the United Kingdom, which as a result would be much more vulnerable to domestic protest against U.S. policies; reliance on Turkey or even Israel as a regional base, which as a result would mean still more deference to these countries' dangerous agendas; or a vastly increased and horribly expensive (and for the troops concerned, unpopular) permanent deployment at Diego Garcia or elsewhere.

Furthermore, the unsettled state of the Arab world, and the growth of anti-American sentiment there, has made the U.S. desire for guaranteed access to Caspian energy reserves stronger than ever, with implications not only for the Caucasus but for countries near that region. In consequence, as Charles King writes in chapter 11, Romania and Bulgaria have assumed a new strategic importance in U.S. eyes. When work on this book began, it seemed that for the foreseeable future Romania would have no serious chance of membership in either the European Union or NATO.

As King points out, Romania's relative lack of economic progress, and the depressing condition of its political scene, both previously made this highly unlikely. In particular, the elections of 2000, and the gains made by the extreme nationalist Greater Romania Party, caused considerable anxiety in the west. However, the shift in U.S. geopolitical priorities after September 11 radically transformed Romania's and Bulgaria's chances as far as NATO is concerned—without in itself improving the state of their economies or administrations. As of 2002, there were signs of economic growth in both countries, but at nothing like the level which would be required to allow them to become EU members in the foreseeable future.

Conversely, U.S. responses to September 11 also most probably mean *less* U.S. engagement in Europe, when it comes to direct U.S. military participation in wars or peacekeeping operations in the Balkans. Long before September 11, there was considerable unhappiness in the United States, and especially in Congress and large sections of the Republican Party, about the permanent deployment of large numbers of U.S. ground troops for tasks on the European continent which the western Europeans should be able to carry out on their own, given their wealth and the paper strength of their armed forces. This was reinforced by complaints from within the U.S. armed forces that these long-term "emergency" deployments were undermining other tasks and worsening morale. In consequence, even before September 11, the Bush administration had refused to send U.S. ground troops to participate in the NATO peacekeeping effort in the former Yugoslav republic of Macedonia, despite U.S. promises at the time of the Kosovo war to defend Macedonia against destabilization.

Of course, as a result of the U.S. response to the September 11 attacks, the demands on U.S. forces elsewhere in the world became vastly heavier, as did the U.S. feeling that the Europeans ought to take more responsibility for their own backyard. In March 2002, the U.S. administration announced that it would considerably scale down the U.S. contribution to the NATO-led military forces in Kosovo and Bosnia. It certainly seems extremely unlikely that the United States will be prepared to send ground troops to participate in any future NATO operation in the Balkans, in the event of a crisis or war in the region.

The U.S. contribution to such an operation through NATO would continue to be of great importance—notably for logistical support, and the threat of U.S. airpower. Nonetheless, such a diminished U.S. role would be bound to have an impact on the U.S.–European relationship, and on NATO. If the United States were to participate only to a limited degree in actual military operations on European soil, there would clearly be European resistance to allowing the United States the kind of political primacy and military command that it exercised during the Kosovo war—which would probably diminish still further any U.S. desire to participate.

There might also be increased western European resistance to serving as a U.S. military base and staging post for operations elsewhere—especially if most Europeans disapproved of those operations, and feared that they themselves would suffer attack as a result. Of course, European military forces and military structures suffer from glaring faults; European populations and political classes are deeply hesitant about taking on real responsibility for continental security (in part because of enduring and humiliating memories of the western European failures during the Yugoslav wars after 1991); and the EU as an organization is not at all fit for coherent strategic thought. Nonetheless, it is not difficult to imagine circumstances in which the EU might be forced willy-nilly into taking on an unprecedented military role; and despite deep U.S. suspicions of any autonomous European security structures, the United States would be forced to accept this.

NATO played only a tertiary role in the U.S. campaign in Afghanistan. Although the United States invoked article 5 (mandating collective defense if a member is attacked), in fact it made very little use of NATO structures. The reasons were twofold. Initially at least, the United States did not believe that it required any significant direct military help from its allies, whose military capacity it profoundly distrusts. Indeed, the United Kingdom was severely snubbed when it offered large numbers of troops. At first, the Pentagon was also largely uninterested in the role of the British and other Europeans in the International Security Assistance Force peacekeeping mission in Kabul, and actively opposed extending its geographical mandate.

By the spring of 2002, this U.S. reluctance to ask for help had diminished somewhat, as it became clear that in one form or another the fighting in Afghanistan was likely to continue for a long time. However, NATO as such remained excluded from Afghanistan, and the alliance's role was restricted to the long-term, less dramatic one of ensuring military compatibility and a capacity for joint operations among the forces of its various members. A key reason for this, which will doubtless continue to apply to all future U.S. operations of this kind, is that formally at least NATO is an alliance of sovereign states with a collective decision-making procedure; and the United States has no intention of allowing its military decisions or strategies to be controlled or even seriously influenced by any other states. It seems overwhelmingly probable that all future operations of this kind by the United States will be "coalitions of the willing," posses with the United States in the role of sheriff, and in unconditional command.

As a result of all this, it seems quite possible that as the first decade of the twenty-first century progresses, NATO will take a long stride away from its old function as a "hard" military alliance for mutual defense, and towards becoming a much "softer" kind of mainly political grouping. As Zaneta Ozolina and Christopher Bobinski write in chapters 9 and 10 respectively, this is not at all the kind of NATO that the eastern European applicants thought they were joining, or wanted to join. For eastern European confidence in western Europeans' ability or will to protect them remains minimal; and key motives for Polish and Baltic states' desires to join NATO remain fear of Russia (however exaggerated and even irrational) and a desire for U.S. military protection against Russia.

Indeed, as Bobinski indicates, from the late 1990s on there were indications that even after joining the EU, Poland and the Baltic states in particular would remain much more instinctively pro-American than the bulk of EU members;

and that if EU–American relations were to decline, Poland would remain in some sense a center of U.S. influence in Europe. In this, however, Warsaw would not be alone, since this determination to uphold a close alliance with the United States would most probably also be true of the United Kingdom (and even Italy, at least as long as the right remains in power there)—though there, fear of Russia would not be an important factor.

In the immediate aftermath of September 11, there was a tremendous surface warming in relations between the United States and Russia, and even renewed talk of "partnership." As Valdimir Baranovsky writes in chapter 12, this improvement did not come out of the blue. The desire to join the "west" reflects a strategy followed by Vladimir Putin since his accession to power. Equally important, it reflects an ambition of the Russian elites—and to some extent the Russian people—consciously formulated since the late 1980s, and with deep roots in precommunist Russian history. In the early twenty-first century, this is backed not only by intellectual and cultural sentiments, but also by the hard economic interests of the new Russian capitalist classes.

The new relationship with Russia after September 11 was used by some European governments, led by that of the United Kingdom, to urge strongly that NATO's further expansion eastwards should be accompanied by as deep as possible an integration of Russia into NATO structures and decision-making processes, though naturally short of full membership. Initially, this met considerable resistance from the United States, inspired in part precisely by the Polish American and Baltic American lobbies, but in May 2002, a new NATO–Russia council was created, with considerably enhanced Russian rights of consultation.

Despite this, as of 2002 and for the foreseeable future, the U.S.–Russian relationship remains in many ways a troubled one. Russian support in the overall war against terrorism is often taken for granted in Washington; while continued Russian links to Iran and Iraq cause American distrust and anger. The anger of many Russians with the United States is even greater, thanks to a series of U.S. snubs like the abrogation of the Anti–Ballistic Missile Treaty, and concern about the growing number of U.S. military deployments on former Soviet territory. In particular, the U.S. military mission to Georgia causes concern in Russia, given the various outstanding security issues between Georgia and Russia. Baranovsky recounts the incidents of the 1990s—notably the war with Yugoslavia over Kosovo—which contributed to deepening this Russian hostility to the United States. Until September 11,

European countries were more anxious in principle for good relations with Russia than was the United States, but their stance was complicated by the war in Chechnya, the atrocities committed by Russian troops there, and the demands of European human rights groups that those responsible be brought to justice.

Moreover, both because the EU and Russia share a continent, and because of the nature of the EU as a primarily economic body, EU–Russian relations cover an immense range of detailed and often extremely difficult practical issues, which do not affect the United States's relations with Russia to nearly the same extent. This, of course, also applies to the EU's relations with all the countries to its east, including Turkey. The problems that issues of human movement in particular cause in the EU's relationship with Russia are dramatically demonstrated by the case of Kaliningrad, described by Alexander Sergounin in chapter 7.

Ambiguities of EU Enlargement

In general, any direct effects of September 11 on the EU will probably be in the field of its internal functions—and especially its capacity for foreign, security, and military policy. It does not appear that the enlargement process as such will be much affected, for the simple reason that this process depends on immensely complex economic, social, political, and institutional developments both in the applicant countries and the EU itself. A major impact of September 11 on these would have been if the attacks had contributed to a really deep world economic depression; but as of the spring of 2002, at least this did not seem to be the case.

September 11 and its aftermath did not change the fact that the process of joining the EU—and still more of becoming fully integrated into western Europe—remains intensely difficult for the applicant countries, and also involves enormous and perhaps impossible internal changes for the EU itself. As Heather Grabbe describes the situation in chapter 4, the EU Commission is in a contradictory and even hypocritical position when it comes to negotiating EU enlargement. On the one hand, the EU has set enlargement as a central goal of the EU. This goal has been spoken of in the most grandiose terms as somehow fulfilling a mandate of European history and destiny by "reunifying" the continent. As several of the authors in this volume have written, this also strikes very deep chords in central and eastern

Europe, where people have been long conditioned to see themselves as "natural" western Europeans unjustly deprived of their natural destiny by Soviet domination and the iron curtain.

But on the other hand, as Grabbe explains, the EU Commission has to reflect the hard economic interests and wishes of its *existing* members; and these are by no means necessarily served by EU enlargement. Feelings of obligation, guilt, and shame towards the former oppressed countries of the Soviet bloc mean that it is difficult for western European politicians to express this opposition openly. As of 2002, the only open political rejection of the EU enlargement was the Irish referendum of 2001 rejecting the Nice Treaty, which was intended to pave the way for enlargement.

However, several EU member states have successfully put pressure on the Commission to drive the hardest possible bargain on a number of issues in the accession negotiations, and would certainly not be overly distressed if this led to the enlargement process being indefinitely delayed. And as several authors of this volume have pointed out, this has caused intense bitterness in the applicant countries—so much so that by the turn of the century, opinion polls in several applicant states were showing majorities against EU membership, and there seemed a real chance of majorities in referenda on membership voting against it. This tendency was increased by the fact that all the real candidates for early EU membership had been or were about to be admitted to NATO. This meant not only that (in their view) their key security concern had been taken care of, but that they had received a certificate of "western identity" from one of the two key western organizations. A good deal of the passion therefore went out of their desire to be embraced by the EU.

Their psychological position was therefore already a great deal happier than that of states which, while living in geographical Europe, see themselves as excluded for the foreseeable future—in several cases, probably forever—from "Europe" as it is usually defined in political, economic, media, and wider international discourse. For over the years, and particularly since the end of the cold war, the European Union has come to see itself as representing Europe. The EU and NATO together represent in their own eyes and propaganda the "Euro-Atlantic community."

Despite the fact that at the turn of the century well over half of the inhabitants of geographical Europe (if Turkey is included) did not live in EU countries, the tremendous relative wealth, cultural and technological prestige, and military strength of western countries means that a large majority of nonmembers have been prepared—willingly or unwillingly, consciously or unconsciously—also to see them as representing the true Europe. They are the core, and every other country occupies a bit of the periphery. They have in fact achieved a form of moral hegemony.

In consequence, nonmembers of the EU and NATO are generally seen, by themselves and others, as less than truly or fully European. Quite apart from the real advantages or disadvantages of EU and NATO membership, and the direct security consequences of EU and NATO expansion, this has helped produce a tremendous psychological drive for membership in these organizations; but it has also reawakened a whole set of deep historical anxieties and neuroses in those countries which look certain to be excluded from one or both of them. Certain negative consequences of NATO's expansion have been widely remarked upon, but so far little thought has been given to these ambiguities in the case of the EU enlargement process.

The countries which look certain to be excluded from the EU for the foreseeable future include the whole of the former Soviet Union (with the exception of the Baltic states, which under international law were never included in the USSR), and the whole of the Orthodox world, with the exception of Greece and perhaps, at some point, parts of the Balkans. As has been noted, Russia of course is explicitly excluded from NATO membership in the rhetoric of many advocates of NATO enlargement, who continue to see Moscow as the greatest threat to the region; but in some western and central European circles in recent years, there have also been attempts to portray both NATO and the EU as based on the traditional areas of Catholic and Protestant Christianity and the Enlightenment, thereby excluding the Orthodox world (a view which echoes wittingly or unwittingly in Samuel Huntington's schema).

The question of whether there is any merit to this very broad-brush historical-cultural approach lies beyond the scope of this book. What is unhappily true, however, is that (with the partial exception in the case of NATO for Romania and Bulgaria) existing economic, social, and political realities are tending to reinforce these supposed fault lines. As Alexander Motyl argues in chapter 2, far from closing the gap between themselves and the countries of central Europe, Ukraine and the other former communist states from the Baltic to the Black Sea (once again, with the exception of the Baltic states) are falling farther and farther behind in terms not only of economic reform but also of democracy. Quite apart from Russia and Belarus, which are special cases because of their partially anti-western geopolitical alignments, the difference between the geopolitical position of Poland, a NATO member, and Ukraine is already immense.

If (or probably when) the Baltic states and central Europeans join the European Union, the gulf between members and nonmembers in most fields of national life is likely to become immense, to the extent that in many cases it is difficult to see how it could be bridged for the foreseeable future. For as Motyl points out, the progressive adoption of the *acquis communautaire* is a truly revolutionary process, involving the most wrenching and profound transformations of the social, economic judicial, and political systems involved. No such transformation is taking place in the case of Ukraine and other states in the region; and indeed, the nature of the postcommunist ruling orders in these countries makes such a radical change almost impossible while the present elites and systems remain in power.

But as several authors in the volume have reminded us, even for the first-rank EU applicants, as of 2002 nothing about accession was certain. If a combination of a failure to reform, internal division, and an electoral backlash in various countries brought about the end or indefinite postponement of EU enlargement, this would be a disaster for the whole region, risking both economic and political progress for many years to come, and possibly leading to a regrowth of ethnic nationalism in certain areas—for example Latvia, where a more open policy towards the Russian-speaking minority has been explicitly linked by Latvian officials to hopes of joining the EU and to the "European project" as a whole.

However, successful EU enlargement to the first round of applicant countries will also bring with it some very considerable problems. Indeed, precisely because the EU affects societies and economies at a far deeper level than NATO, these problems could turn out to be far greater in the long run than those associated with NATO enlargement. They will affect the internal functioning of the EU. As Grabbe points out, the whole EU decision-making process will have to be radically reformed if it is not to grind to a halt under the stress of accommodating ten new members—but as of 2002, repeated attempts by EU summits had failed to introduce reforms on anything like the scale required. They will deeply affect the Common Agricultural Policy (CAP). Either this will have to be changed so as to accommodate the new members—with the subsidies to existing western European members radically reduced—or as seems likely, these new members will have to be permanently excluded from many of CAP provisions.

And as the example of the CAP indicates, it seems likely that for a very long time after accession, the new members of the EU from eastern Europe will in fact be second-class members, visibly inferior to western Europeans not only in wealth, but in formal status within certain EU institutions. If so, this will also inevitably mean that the resentments against the EU which have surfaced during the accession negotiations will not go away once accession is achieved. It would indeed be surprising if they do so, since as has been noted, anti-EU feelings are very common, even among some of the wealthiest western European and Scandinavian members.

Softer and Harder Frontiers

A different but even more acute set of problems stemming from the EU enlargement process are those which will affect (and are indeed already affecting) those eastern European states which for the foreseeable future will not become EU members. One key problem lies with the accession of the new EU members to the Schengen Agreement, which would dictate major new obstacles to travel to these countries from the nonmembers to the east.

As described by both Alexander Sergounin and Vladimir Baranovsky, this problem is especially acute for the Russian exclave of Kaliningrad, which risks finding itself isolated not merely militarily and geopolitically, but also from economic and human contacts. The question of when or how EU visa regimes can be modified in the case of Kaliningrad is becoming a major topic of discussion (especially in Scandinavia, Germany, Poland, and Lithuania), and will doubtless remain so up to the date of Polish and Lithuanian accession and beyond. Poland, for its part, worries that Schengen will undermine its links with Ukraine and Belarus, and its attempts to expand western influence in these countries.

The issue of the border between Hungary and Romania is even more acute, because of strong Romanian resentment at the restrictions on travel to the west, and because of the large Hungarian minority in Romania, which fears isolation from Hungary; conversely, any special travel rights for Romanian Hungarians risk increasing still further Romanian ethnic chauvinism. The Romanian elections of 2000 illustrated the risk that a country which is rejected again and again by western institutions may turn in reaction to resentful nationalism, stressing "native" values against those of the arrogant, decadent west.

Nationalist tendencies in eastern Europe could be still further strengthened in the future if the economic costs of EU enlargement, and increased immigration from eastern Europe, contribute to a rise in traditional nationalism in western Europe itself. This would increase the prestige of these ideologies across the continent. And it must unfortunately be recognized that in many cases, the ascendancy of liberal ideas in the former communist countries has not been chiefly due to a real understanding of them by the population, or a deep emotional adherence. Rather, they have been associated with the prestige of the west; and public allegiance to these principles has been explicitly demanded by western institutions as part of the price of membership.

The danger of a crumbling of the European liberal idea at its heart has been considerably increased as a result of September 11. For in several countries, nativist or indeed nationalist parties have increased both their political respectability and their vote by linking their opposition to (mainly Muslim) immigration to fears of Muslim terrorism. This is bad news not only for European political culture, and the European image, but for the EU itself; for these parties tend also to be strongly opposed to European integration.

Russia has also swung in a more nationalist direction as a result of real or perceived snubs and anti-Russian moves on the part of the west—most notably, of course, NATO enlargement. Assuming—barring some presently unimaginable shift in world politics and economics—that Russia will not become a member of either NATO or the EU, how will this affect Russia's sense of its own identity and its internal and external policies? Will most Russians go on, however, unwillingly, looking to the west for superior models of politics, economics, and culture? Or is there any serious possibility of the development of a Russian ideology derived from "Eurasian" and "Slavophile" roots?

At the level of policy and international relations, a key issue, as asked by Dmitri Trenin, is the future of the EU's Common Foreign and Security Policy (CFSP). At present, this is still embryonic in both its military and its foreign policy aspects, but it has already raised a host of questions and worries: If a distinctive policy and military identities do develop, what will they look like? Can the EU be a substitute for NATO as a security guarantee? Will CFSP lead to an increasing split with the United States? If so, how will it affect the U.S. commitment to NATO and to eastern Europe as a whole? What will be EU policy towards Russia? If the EU does develop its own military capacity, will Russia go on viewing EU expansion as vastly preferable to that of NATO? When Poland and other generally pro-American and anti-Russian societies join the EU, how will this affect EU policy?

Most important, what will be the long-term relationship between "Europe" (or the Euro-Atlantic part of the world) and the countries excluded from it? One possible parallel is the relationship between North America and Central America, where the richest and most dynamic country on earth lives next to poor ones. Such a comparison would tend to diminish concern; for no former communist country in Europe is as poor as Honduras or—with the exception of the Balkans—as racked with social and ethnic hatred as some of the Central American states. Moreover, because the populations of the former communist bloc countries are declining, there is nothing like the demographic pressure which fuels immigration across the Rio Grande or across the Mediterranean from North Africa (though any EU loosening of immigration from the west of the former USSR would have to be accompanied by measures to prevent this also being open to Central Asians).

This suggests, in principle, that the EU's relations with nonmembers could be managed successfully enough—at least if it were possible to move towards something like the North American Free Trade Agreement and U.S. policies on immigration. Due to their own steeply declining birthrate, the economies of western Europe are going to be in desperate need of new labor in the first decades of the twenty-first century; and in successive waves of emigration (notably after the World Wars I and II), migrants from Russia, Belarus, and Ukraine have proved that they can be quickly and successfully integrated into western societies—in sharp contrast to many of their Muslim equivalents from north Africa, south Asia, or Turkey.

Without greater freedom of movement from Russia, Belarus, and Ukraine to western Europe, it is difficult to see how EU rhetoric about the west's desire to "integrate" these areas can be anything other than empty: at best mere words, at worst a hypocritical cover for a deep unwillingness to think seriously about integration at all. And indeed, though EU officials speak as if membership is in principle open for Russia if it were to carry out successful reforms, when pressed, most admit that they cannot in fact conceive of circumstances in which Russia could be admitted.

The reasons are not just Russia's immense size, imperial self-image, and extremely complicated security situations on its eastern and southern borders. It is also that Russia continues to rule over many Muslims, including some nationalities which are highly restive, highly given to organized crime, and vulnerable to the lures of Islamist radicalism. It is as if France had tried to lead European integration while continuing to rule over a sizable portion of Algeria. Clearly therefore, if Russia is to be integrated into western Europe, then as with Turkey it can only be to a limited extent and well short of full membership.

However, as of 2002, anti-immigrant feeling in western Europe—and especially in Germany—was blocking serious thought of even limited moves in this direction. Feelings against immigrants in general have been fueled by hostility to Muslims in the wake of September 11; and right-wing parties with harshly anti-immigrant programs have gained a new legitimacy. Indeed, so hysterical was this feeling that it had even led to successful pressure in the accession negotiations for barriers to labor movement from applicant countries to be continued for several years *after* membership—a deeply insulting, stupid, and economically absurd measure, which as Bobinski points out, caused immense resentment in Poland and elsewhere.

In terms of any comparison of the EU and the former communist bloc with the United States, Central America, and the Caribbean, it must also of course be recognized that the lands to the south of the United States include no country resembling Russia, with its residual military strength, huge linguistic diaspora, massive superiority over its immediate neighbors, and traditional claims to dominate them. James Sherr writes in chapter 6 of the threats and dilemmas which this poses for Ukraine. If EU enlargement formalizes Ukraine's exclusion from "Europe," and in effect consigns it indefinitely to the economic world of the former Soviet region, will this also mean in the long run that Ukraine will follow Belarus in explicitly recognizing Russia's geopolitical hegemony? Or can the present situation continue indefinitely, whereby Ukraine is strongly tied to Russia economically but retains its freedom of action in foreign affairs? For that matter, as Leonid Zaiko asks in chapter 5, will Belarus itself remain indefinitely under Russia's wing, or will it too attempt its own path to the west? And if it does, will it succeed like the Baltic states or—as unfortunately seems very much more likely—will it follow the path of Ukraine, a stumbling one somewhere between the west and the developing world?

Conversely, is there a possibility of a middle way, whereby Ukraine reduces its explicitly anti-Russian positions—such as its participation in the United States–inspired GUUAM group (Georgia, Ukraine, Uzbekistan, Azerbaijan, and Moldova) of former Soviet states—but does not enter into any formal military alliance or political union with Russia? Here too, there might be a possibility of comparison with Central America. Thus Mexico is an independent state and a fully recognized member of the "international community." It is open to non-American investment and trade. For obvious historical reasons, Mexican nationalism contains a deep strain of anti-Americanism, just as Ukrainian nationalism does of anti-Russianism, and of course the cultural differences between Mexico and the United States are far deeper than those between Ukraine and Russia. Mexico has frequently taken foreign policy stances which are deeply irritating to the United States, for example, concerning relations with Cuba. At the same time, every responsible Mexican politician, and indeed just about every Mexican citizen, understands that given the depth of Mexican dependence on the United States, there are limits beyond which it must not go—and that a key one of these is the taboo against joining any alliance or combination of states actually or potentially hostile to the United States.

Whether a relationship of this kind develops between Ukraine and Russia will of course also depend on the nature of Russia's relations with the EU and NATO. As regards NATO, these relations seem likely to be problematical for a long time to come, at least as long as NATO remains in any way a serious military organization and remains dominated by the United States. For even after September 11, there are many points of contention and rivalry between the United States and Russia that could prevent the relationship between them from developing into a full and stable partnership; and these areas of tension are continually and assiduously stoked by groups on both sides which are implacably wedded to hostile positions. It has also proved extremely difficult for NATO as an organization to shed its cold war stance of hostility to Moscow, both in reality and still more in Russian eyes.

A Europe of Overlapping Circles

However, as has been suggested, if NATO's real importance for European security fades as a result of September 11, and if—which is by no means inevitable—the EU develops a serious security identity of its own, it might be easier for Brussels to create a new security partnership with Russia, and indeed with other excluded states. As William Wallace explains in chapter 3, the EU has had great difficulty over the years formulating and agreeing to clear positions on external policy (or any policy at all, for that matter). Nonetheless, when it comes to creating new security relationships with nonmembers or part-members of the existing west, the EU is in a somewhat easier position than NATO. The latter organization was created as a defensive military alliance against the Soviet Union. Not only for a long time after the cold war did that give NATO an enduring anti-Russian bias, and ensure Russian suspicion of it, but it meant that NATO—at least up to the events of September 2001 and their aftermath—was a clear-cut alliance, in which you were in, or out. The Partnership for Peace was not able to soften this harsh dividing line, and although in 2002 Russia gained a new position in NATO counsels, this only made the position of Ukraine and other states seem all the more marginal.

Moreover, on many international positions, including relations with Iran, the question of a U.S. war against Iraq, and the role of the United Nations, EU positions are actually closer to those of Russia than they are to those of the United States. Furthermore, should a new crisis erupt in the Balkans and the United States refuse to participate, then the EU would be virtually compelled to seek closer relations with Russia—and indeed with Turkey, for a truly frightening scenario for Europe would be a war in the Balkans in which Russia and Turkey lined up on opposite sides.

Yet when it comes to the "war against terrorism," the case of Chechnya makes the Vladimir Putin administration and the Russian military more sympathetic to the "tough" positions of the United States, Israel, and even Turkey—especially since all have suffered to one degree or another from what they at least think of as arrogant, hypocritical, and morally cowardly European criticism of their actions. By 2002, Russian–Turkish relations had greatly improved, and there was in fact beginning to be an interesting symmetry in their relationships to the EU.

In the cases of both Russia and Turkey, the realities of their economic and political systems, and of human rights abuses, all make full membership in the EU an impossibility for the foreseeable future. But when it comes to new relationships short of membership, especially in the security field, there are several possibilities. Some are suggested by a phenomenon touched on repeatedly in this volume: Rather than creating a relatively homogenous bloc of rich western European states, the process of EU enlargement is leading to an EU containing extremely diffuse regions and, in effect, different grades of membership.

We have spoken of this so far in terms of a Europe of concentric circles: a western European core of EU members; an outer circle of poorer EU members excluded from certain EU institutions; a further circle of EU nonmembers which are, however, members of NATO; and a periphery of geographically European states which are excluded from both organizations.

However, it might make more sense to look at the Europe of the future as consisting not only of concentric circles, as Dimitri Trenin suggests in the introduction, but also of overlapping ones. Indeed, as of 2002 there were already strong signs of this within the existing EU. Thus without doubt, at the start of the twenty-first century, the economic inner circle of the vEU was made up of the countries which had adopted the euro as their currency— a circle from which new members will be excluded for the foreseeable future, even after they join the EU.

But they may be in good company, since as of 2002 the United Kingdom was not in the euro zone, and seemed unlikely to join for a considerable time to come. Yet the British will have to be right at the center of the formulation of EU security strategies if such strategies are to exist at all; whereas a number of wealthy but small countries at the heart of the euro circle will be peripheral to the development and conduct of security policy. Then there are two countries—Switzerland and Norway—which are undoubtedly fully part of western Europe but are not members of the EU.

These already existing asymmetries might make it possible in principle for the EU to create yet another circle which would place Russia and Turkey at the heart of the European security community while continuing, inevitably, to exclude them from full membership in the economic community. One might envisage something like a European Security Council, in which the United States (another major power in Europe which is unlikely to join the EU in the foreseeable future) would also have a seat. Such a structure would in the short term be a means of assuaging the hurt feelings of some of the major excluded countries. In the long term, however, it might play a truly vital role in continental security if for whatever reason NATO's importance withers. Such a body could never of course constitute the core of a "hard" military bloc, such as NATO used to be; but it could still be a good deal tighter and more effective than the Organization for Security and Cooperation in Europe.

The desirability of such a body is increased both by the extreme difficulty of integrating Turkey and Russia into EU-dominated Europe, and by the danger of future trouble between Turkey and Russia over the Balkans and still more the Caucasus. The latter region in particular will for the foreseeable future remain extremely volatile, beset by extreme internal state weakness and by unsolved national and separatist conflicts. If the new U.S.

military presence in this region (notably the U.S. military mission to Georgia) is not accompanied by a successful move to solve these conflicts in partnership with Russia and Turkey, then the potential for renewed war will be high, as will be the possibility of Russia and Turkey lining up on opposite sides of any new clash.

However, the last years of the 1990s and the first years of the new century have seen a considerable improvement in Russian–Turkish bilateral relations, above all in the field of energy cooperation, but also more widely. One factor in the improvement has been greatly diminished Turkish support for the Chechen struggle against Russia in the war which began in 1999, compared with Turkish attitudes and policies during the war of 1994–1996. A key reason for this shift has been the greatly increased role of international, Arab-funded Muslim radicals in Chechnya since 1995. Because these years have also seen considerable growth in Islamist political mobilization within Turkey and in Turkey's strong alignment with the United States for the war against terrorism, the changed Turkish official attitude is very natural.

The improvement in relations is nonetheless remarkable given the history of warfare and hatred between the two nations, and gives hope that future cooperation to preserve stability in the Caucasus and the Balkans may be possible. Certainly, as of 2002 neither the Russian nor the Turkish administrations are in any way seeking renewed tension between their countries. This being so, a new European security body that included the United States might become a forum not just for the projection of western influences eastward, but also for fruitful engagement between some of the eastern states themselves.

Such a development would be highly desirable, given the dangers and challenges which the European continent may face as the twenty-first century progresses. For as several of the chapters of this volume indicate, the "enlargement of Europe" may well be a far slower and more problematical process than the optimistic propaganda surrounding it might suggest. In 2002, thirteen years after the fall of the Berlin wall, not one former communist country has yet been admitted to the European Union; while the impending "big bang" expansion of NATO eastwards comes at a time when NATO appears to be becoming less and less significant as a military alliance.

Meanwhile, in the wake of September 11, there are disquieting signs that pluralist democracy in western Europe may be less impregnable than had been assumed. If right-wing anti-immigrant parties grow in strength, this will be very bad news not only for the European model but also for the

EU as an institution, because most of these parties are also strongly hostile to the EU and to European integration and enlargement. In these disquieting circumstances, it is more important than ever for the leaders and elites of the EU countries to develop a continental vision and strategy, and for EU enlargement to be pushed forward by them sincerely and with all deliberate speed.

Figures and Tables

Index

Contributors

Christopher Bobinski was born in London and educated at Magdalen College, Oxford University. From 1976 to 2000, he worked for the *Financial Times*, notably as their correspondent in Warsaw. He is the publisher of *Unia & Polska*, a bimonthly magazine devoted to issues of the European Union and its enlargement.

Vladimir Baranovsky is deputy director of the Institute of the World Economy and International Relations in Moscow. He was previously a visiting professor at the Institut des Etudes Européennes in Brussels and a senior researcher at the Stockholm International Peace Research Institute. Among numerous other publications, he was editor and coauthor of *Russia and Europe: The Emerging Security Agenda* (Oxford University Press, 1997).

Heather Grabbe is research director at the Center for European Reform. She has been a visiting fellow at the European University Institute (Florence), the Western European Union Institute for Security Studies (Paris), and the Centre for International Relations (Warsaw), and she was an editor at the consultancy Oxford Analytica. She holds an M.A. from Oxford University and is currently completing a Ph.D. at Birmingham University.

Karl-Heinz Kamp is head of the International Planning Staff of the Konrad Adenauer Foundation (Bonn). From 1997 to 1998, he was on a temporary assignment with the planning staff of the German Ministry of Foreign Affairs. Since 1999, he has taught political science at the University of Cologne. He has published extensively on security policy issues, with articles in *Foreign Policy*, the *Financial Times*, *Survival*, *Frankfurter Allgemeine Zeitung*, the *Washington Quarterly*, and other periodicals. He holds a Ph.D. from the University of the German Armed Forces, Hamburg.

Charles King is assistant professor in the School of Foreign Service and the Department of Government at Georgetown University, where he also holds the Ion Ratiu Chair of Romanian Studies. His books include *Nations Abroad: Diaspora Politics and International Relations in the Former Soviet Union* (coeditor, with Neil J. Melvin; Westview, 1998) and *The Moldovans: Romania, Russia, and the Politics of Culture* (Hoover Institution Press, 2000).

Anatol Lieven is a senior associate in the Russian and Eurasian Program of the Carnegie Endowment for International Peace. He was previously editor of *Strategic Comments* at the International Institute for Strategic Studies. Among his publications are *Chechnya: Tombstone of Russian Power* (Yale University Press, 1998), *The Baltic Revolution: Estonia, Latvia, Lithuania, and the Path to Independence* (Yale University Press, 1998), and *Ukraine and Russia: A Fraternal Rivalry* (U.S. Institute of Peace, 1999), which are largely based on his work as a correspondent for the *Times* of London in the former Soviet Union from 1990 to 1996. Before that, he was a correspondent for the *Times* in Pakistan and covered the Afghan war from the side of the anti-Soviet Mujahedin.

Alexander J. Motyl is deputy director of the Center for Global Change and Governance at Rutgers University, where he is also associate professor of political science. His research interests include nationalism and post-Soviet politics. He is the editor-in-chief of *The Encyclopedia of Nationalism* (Academic Press, 2000) and author of *Imperial Ends: The Decay, Collapse, and Revival of Empires* (Columbia University Press, 2001), among many other volumes. He received his Ph.D. in political science from Columbia University in 1984.

Zaneta Ozolina is professor of international relations at the University of Latvia, and the author of several books on the Baltic region, security issues, and European cooperation. She previously worked as a project director at the Latvian Institute of International Relations, and for the delegation of the European Commission in Riga.

Alexander Sergounin is head of the Department of International Relations and Political Science at Nizhny Novgorod Linguistic University. From 1994 to 1998, he was professor of political science in the University of Nizhny Novgorod. He holds a Ph.D. (history) from Moscow State University (1985). His most recent publications include *Political Science* (Nizhny Novgorod Linguistic University Press, 1999), and *Theories and Approaches to International Relations* (with Kumar Vinay Malhotra; Anmol Publications, 1998).

James Sherr has been a fellow of the Conflict Studies Research Centre at the Royal Military Academy Sandhurst since 1995 and lecturer at Lincoln College, Oxford University, since 1986. He is a specialist adviser to the House of Commons Defence Committee, and a former director of services at the Royal United Services Institute.

Dmitri Trenin is deputy director of the Carnegie Moscow Center. He retired from the Russian Army in 1993 after a military career that included participation in the strategic arms control negotiations in Geneva and teaching at the Military Institute. He was the first Russian officer to be selected to attend the NATO Defense College, and he is a member of the International Institute of Strategic Studies. Dr. Trenin was a senior fellow at the Institute of Europe from 1993 to 1997, and holds a Ph.D. from the Institute of the U.S.A. and Canada. He is the author of numerous articles and books on Russian security issues, including *The End of Eurasia* (Carnegie Endowment, 2002).

William Wallace (Lord Wallace of Saltaire) is professor of international relations at the London School of Economics. He was previously director of studies at the Royal Institute of International Affairs in London, Walter F. Hallstein Fellow at Saint Antony's College, Oxford University, and professor of international studies at the Central European University. His most recent publications include *Policy-Making in the European Union* (with Helen Wallace and others; 4th edition, Oxford University Press, 2000), *Rethinking European Order: West European Responses, 1989–97* (with Robin Niblett and others; Palgrave, 2001), and *Non-State Actors in International Relations* (with

Daphne Josselin and others; Palgrave, 2001). In the House of Lords, he speaks for the Liberal Democrats on foreign affairs and defense.

Leonid Zaiko is president of Strategy, an independent Belarusian think tank. He was previously vice rector of the National Institute of Social Science in Minsk, and head of the research team for the United Nations Development Program report on Belarus in 2000. Dr. Zaiko is the author of numerous books and articles, including *The National and State Interests of Belarus* (Minsk: Analytical Centre "Strategy," 1999).

Carnegie Endowment for International Peace

The Carnegie Endowment is a private, nonprofit organization dedicated to advancing cooperation between nations and promoting active international engagement by the United States. Founded in 1910, its work is nonpartisan and dedicated to achieving practical results.

Through research, publishing, convening, and, on occasion, creating new institutions and international networks, Endowment associates shape fresh policy approaches. Their interests span geographic regions and the relations between governments, business, international organizations, and civil society, focusing on the economic, political, and technological forces driving global change. Through its Carnegie Moscow Center, the Endowment helps to develop a tradition of public policy analysis in the states of the former Soviet Union and to improve relations between Russia and the United States. The Endowment publishes *Foreign Policy*, one of the world's leading magazines of international politics and economics.